IN PERFORMANCE

Wayne Bailey

Arizona State University

NEW YORK   OXFORD
Oxford University Press

Oxford University Press is a department of the University of Oxford.
It furthers the University's objective of excellence in research,
scholarship, and education by publishing worldwide.

Oxford   New York
Auckland   Cape Town   Dar es Salaam   Hong Kong   Karachi
Kuala Lumpur   Madrid   Melbourne   Mexico City   Nairobi
New Delhi   Shanghai   Taipei   Toronto

With offices in
Argentina   Austria   Brazil   Chile   Czech Republic   France   Greece
Guatemala   Hungary   Italy   Japan   Poland   Portugal   Singapore
South Korea   Switzerland   Thailand   Turkey   Ukraine   Vietnam

For titles covered by Section 112 of the US Higher Education
Opportunity Act, please visit www.oup.com/us/he for the latest
information about pricing and alternate formats.

Published by Oxford University Press
198 Madison Avenue, New York, NY 10016
http://www.oup.com

Library of Congress Cataloging-in-Publication Data
Bailey, Wayne [date]
  In performance / Wayne Bailey.
    pages cm
  ISBN 978-0-19-938214-9
  1. Music appreciation. I. Title.
  MT90.B22 2015
  781.1'7—dc23
                                          2014044922

Printing number: 9 8 7 6 5 4 3 2 1

Manufactured in the United States by RR Donnelley
on acid-free paper

CONTENTS

PREFACE

Music is everywhere in Western culture—the Sunday newspapers in most cities list a dizzying array of classical musical offerings. We can attend the opera, a symphony concert, chamber music recitals, or jazz events just about any day of the week. We can also hear great music in our places of worship, and music has become a very important part of films. Obviously from this large number of offerings, hearing music live is still an important aspect of our lives. This text helps sort out all this music and aids the listener in finding what style(s) he enjoys.

Many textbooks lead students through the history of Western music. A few students are inspired to find and listen to more types of music. Sadly, some become mired in the historical facts of the development of music over a thousand years and never find classical works that inspire them to deepen their understanding of music's influence in their lives. In our daily lives we do not experience music in a historical fashion. Music becomes familiar to us by performer reputation or venue—it comes to us via the movie screen, the Internet, the concert hall, the elevator, the stage, the radio, the stadium, and many other places. Where music is performed often determines what *type* of music is performed. We are unlikely to stumble upon opera on the radio or Internet. Most often we have to go to a special place to hear opera. We usually hear a new style of music first in a place. Only then do we go to the Internet or music store to find more examples of the new style.

Teaching the history of music is not the aim of this text. Instead, the aim is to create life-long, active music listeners who understand the value of different types of music in various aspects of their lives. To do this, you will learn some music history, to be sure, but the focus is on listening to music and where to find great music—what to expect when you get there, and how music has been influential in our lives over the centuries. The listening guides focus on where and how music is performed and help you to understand why composers write different kinds of music and how it can enrich our lives.

Structure of the Text

The book is divided into five units organized by where music is performed. Within the units the chapters present material in a manner that follows the development of musical forms across time. This structure groups the material at the unit level by where the music is most often performed, then at the chapter level by what type of musician or ensemble performs it, and finally presents it within the chapter by historical development.

The Introduction outlines why and how music is created and includes material on commissions, creative inspiration, and compositional methods used in different circumstances. *How to Listen to Music* identifies ways of listening to music, each of which provides a differing level of musical awareness. *What to Expect at a Performance* guides the reader through the experience of attending an event from dealing with tickets and the box office to reading a program.

The fundamentals and instrument chapters of Unit 1 are intended to assist the student who is new to the study of art music. They provide important background information on music fundamentals, instruments, and historical eras. This course primer material is intended to even the playing field a bit for you and your classmates. Music appreciation classes are populated by everyone from students who have no experience with classical music to those who have had years of performing in ensembles and taking private music lessons. This unit also contains a chapter that provides an overview of periods of music history and the styles of music important in each.

The four primary units of the book all are structured around specific places where we hear music: the church, the concert hall, the recital hall, and the stage and screen. The text includes two online bonus chapters on jazz and popular music since 1950 for those instructors who include these musics in their courses. Students can access these via the Dashboard website.

Listening Guides

More than seventy-five important musical works are studied through listening guides and recordings. The listening guides lead the student through important pieces of literature that are regularly performed today in live settings. The listening guides and activities are the focus of this book. The guides direct students to musical signposts throughout the works, especially in the longer pieces. They also include information about why the work was created and how it was first used. Some guides (such as those for film music, ballet, and opera) include specific information about how the music interacts with the other art forms.

The works examined are available streamed through Dashboard, the book's website. (Links are given to a Spotify playlist for a few popular works discussed in the final chapters that are not available to license.) Musical notation within the guides helps those who read music to follow the progression of the music within the notation. Features at the end of the guides encourage students to listen further and to build their own playlists. It should be noted that in this feature the author has included some search key phrases for YouTube videos. In some cases the search phrases on YouTube contain typographical errors, and in order to maintain the search those errors have not been corrected in this text. To do so might jeopardize the success of the search.

Features of the Text

The chapters contain four feature items aimed at improving the student's understanding of how and where music has been performed over time. Within these features the students are often asked to complete activities or assignments that enhance the learning and listening experience for the chapter's topic. These features are intended to enhance the What, Where, Who, and How of the chapter. The four box features include:

WHERE IT'S PLAYING begins each chapter and points out places where the music studied in the chapter can be heard or accessed today. Recommendations are made on how to access live music.

WHAT TO LISTEN FOR directs the student's listening to the general listening goals of each part of the text. This feature reappears in each Listening Guide and is then specific to what to listen for in that guide.

PERFORMER PROFILE examines a composer or performer related to the music studied in the chapter.

PERFORMANCE PRACTICE focuses on how some aspect of the music studied in the chapter is performed now, was performed in the past, or the music's purpose.

In addition to these features the text contains margin callouts that direct the student to additional activities on the Dashboard website. These features link the student to further study, learning objectives, exercises, supporting videos, and other instructive material. Many of these features contain an activity or assignment for the student to complete. The text also offers the opportunity for students to build and share their playlists of works beyond the listening guides and provides a discussion board for sharing of ideas. Throughout all of these features students are encouraged to share their ideas, opinions, research, and results with others either through your own class website or course management site or through Dashboard.

Each chapter has a downloadable MP3 file of an accompanying lecture that covers the important points of the chapter.

Acknowledgments

In any endeavor the size of writing a textbook there are many people to thank. The assistance of those who have reviewed and tested the text at universities across the nation has been most helpful.

John Irish, *Angelo State University*
James McAllister, *Garden City Community College*
Debbie O'Connell, *Winston-Salem State University*
Gail Allen, *Averett University*
Robert Oakan, *Northwestern Connecticut Community College*
Kurt Gilman, *Lamar University*
Alex Powell, *Nashville State Community College*
Stephanie Lawrence-White, *Bennett College for Women*
Vaughn Roste, *Northeastern State University*
Johnson Frehner, *Oklahoma State University*
Douglas Mead, *Owens State Community College*
and thirteen reviewers who wish to remain anonymous.

I would also like to acknowledge the efforts of the Oxford University Press team: Richard Carlin, executive editor, music and art; Emily Schmid, editorial assistant, music and art; and Keith Faivre, production editor. The students at Arizona State University who tested the book have greatly contributed to the final text. And finally, I am most grateful to the ever-patient Gillian.

INTRODUCTION: LISTENING TO MUSIC

The life of the arts is far from an interruption, a distraction, in the life of a nation, it is close to the center of a nation's purpose—and is a test of the quality of a nation's civilization.
—JOHN F. KENNEDY

Music can be heard just about everywhere today—it is nearly impossible to avoid even if one wanted to do so. Never before has it been so easy and inexpensive to access music. You may spend more of your day with music playing than without it. The availability of personal listening devices and access to the Internet through personal computers and cell phones has made music even more available. And live performance is thriving! We still hear live music in concert halls and arenas, recital halls, in homes, in places of worship, on stage, and at most social and ceremonial occasions. Live music has both a utilitarian and an aesthetic purpose. It is hard to imagine a wedding without music, or a film with no soundtrack. And, the music of these events might be useful *and* evoke emotions at the same time. Despite all these opportunities to hear classical music, many people go through life without ever experiencing a Beethoven symphony or a Verdi opera. Perhaps this is because popular music is even more ubiquitous. Or perhaps it is because many people don't know what to expect at the opera house or concert hall, and therefore never consider attending. This text is structured around where we hear live music today. Each of the primary units presents the types of music that you might expect to hear if you went to a particular setting. Within the units the music of these different venues is presented in roughly an historical manner so that you can gain an overview of how music has developed in the last two thousand years in Western society.

© Svetlana Braun. Courtesy iStock.

Musical Labels

Music today is often divided into two very broad categories: popular music and art music. You may have also heard art music referred to as *classical* music. This division is not a particularly good idea. It tends to add stereotypical characteristics to both popular and art music and discourages people from the natural crossover listening from one type to the other. Popular music can be of high artistic quality and much art music has been, and is still, popular. Much of what we call art music was also popular music at the time it was written. And most popular styles and forms of today have developed from classical forms and systems. Listeners of past centuries would be puzzled by our categorization of music into popular or classical fields. Music to them was good or bad, pleasant or objectionable—not popular or classical. If we insist on making distinctions we might distinguish between popular music and classical music in the following manner: Popular music compositions are often shorter than classical music works. As such, popular music melodies rarely have the same kind of development of ideas that occurs in classical melodies. Because it is shorter, much popular music is usually more simply constructed than art music and is more easily understood on first hearing. Because classical music is usually longer and more complicated, it often takes more effort on the part of the listener to understand. Another difference is that much of popular music is presented at concerts and on recordings with the aid of electronic devices and theatrics, whereas most classical music is presented by acoustic instruments in a formal setting. Popular music and classical music both express the same types of ideas and emotions—the first just does it more quickly and on a simpler level. The two worlds are not as separated as many listeners think.

How Is Music Created?

The composer is the first of a three-link musical chain that also includes the performer and the listener. Sometimes a composer, the person who conceives of the music, writes a work because he is commissioned, or asked, to do so. The person commissioning, or paying for, the piece of music might suggest some boundaries or guidelines for the composer to work within. Much of music throughout history has been written to satisfy a commission. Other times a composer writes a work simply because he hears the musical idea in his head and feels compelled to work it into a musical composition. Regardless of why the music is created it is always based upon the inspiration and imagination of the composer. The composer's music comes from his own personal experiences and feelings and is shaped by when, where, and how he lives. The composition is the composer's attempt to convey those experiences and feelings in a way that will touch others.

The second element in the creative process is the performer who re-creates the composer's music. Performers take the composer's musical ideas and turn them into sounds. Performers are the intermediaries between the listener and the composer. The deeper the performer's understanding of the composer's original intent, the better the communication between the composer and the listener. And the better the technical ability of the performer, the easier it is for her to communicate the composer's musical ideas. The depth of aesthetic musicianship and the quality of technique is what distinguishes one performer from another, and what determines how successful she is in correctly performing the composer's intent.

The listener is the third link in the musical chain that begins with the composer and passes through the performer. Hearing music is not the same thing as actively listening to music. Music that serves as background to our lives is rarely experienced on an aesthetic level, nor is it intended to be so. It takes effort and some musical understanding in order to really appreciate the message and value of a particular piece of music. The more you know about the context and purpose of a work the better you will understand and enjoy it.

What to Expect at a Performance

At each type of live music venue (church, concert hall, recital hall, salon, or theater), your expectations should be different. Attending a formal concert, opera, or ballet is very different from attending a popular music concert in an arena. This text guides you through what you will hear in different settings and how the different events are structured, and each chapter provides information about concert etiquette at specific events.

In general, observing concert etiquette means you will need to understand the ticketing system, how to get the most out of reading the concert's program, and how the venue itself functions to present the music. This information will enhance your live performance experience.

First, there is always a specific time that you should arrive. There are no warm-up acts at art music events. If the event is to start at 8:00 P.M., do not arrive at 8:15. Doing so might cost you your seat or you may not be allowed to take your seat until the completion of a musical number. That might be several minutes. Most events have ushers to guide you to your seats and tell you when you can enter the hall. But generally speaking, if you are late, you should only enter the hall and go to your seats at the completion of the music being played. The same is true of leaving the event. You should not leave until the music is completed.

Once at your seat pay attention to the music being performed. Do not talk to your neighbor. Do not text or use your cell phone. Generally, do not do things that distract others from hearing the music. Art music concerts are considered social events just like popular music events. But unlike many popular music concerts, the socializing at art music events is done only at intermissions or before and after the event—never during the performance.

Art music venues also restrict what you can bring with you into the concert hall. In almost all cases no refreshments or water are allowed inside the hall during the event. You can usually bring binoculars or opera glasses, but recording devices and cameras are strictly prohibited. Flash photography is particularly frowned upon, as is video recording. These restrictions are not only a courtesy to the performers and others around you but are also designed to protect the composer's and performers' copyrights.

When to applaud at an art music event is a cause of concern for many first-time concert-goers. Generally, applaud when others do. At least when you first attend art music concerts, don't be the first to applaud. Since the musical compositions of art music are almost always longer than those in popular music, there is less opportunity to applaud. Rarely does the audience applaud in the middle of a work or to recognize a particular performer. For the most part applause is reserved for the end of an entire piece of music. This means that if a work is divided into movements or sections, the audience will not usually applaud at the end of each movement. Instead, it is customary to hold your applause until the entire work is completed.

How to Listen to Music

American composer Aaron Copland. © Copyright Bettmann/Corbis/AP Images.

In 1939 the American composer Aaron Copland wrote *What to Listen For in Music*. The principal material of the book was originally delivered in a series of fifteen lectures of the same title in 1936 and 1937 at the New School for Social Research in New York City. Copland outlined three ways of listening to music: the sensuous plane, the expressive plane, and the musical plane. Similarly, today we might think of listening to music in four ways: technical listening (similar to Copland's musical plane), sensuous listening, expressive listening, and musically aware listening.

- **Technical Listening.** In technical listening we are focusing on what it takes to perform the work. How fast is it? What is the range of the melody? How many people are performing? Professional musicians often listen to music in this manner when they consider whether or not they will be able to perform a particular work.
- **Sensuous Listening.** Sensuous listening means paying attention to how the music affects your senses—what, if any, physical effect it has on you. Does it relax you? Does it get your adrenaline running? Does it give you a headache? In this type of listening we let the music just wash over us not thinking much about its technical demands or how it is structured. Instead, we focus on how it affects our physical being.
- **Expressive Listening.** Expressive listening means appreciating the overall impression of the work. On this level of listening we allow the music to

affect our emotions. Contrary to common thought, music does not *express* emotions. Instead we react to music on an emotional level. Music can make us feel sad, happy, angry, joyous. But music itself is not expressing those emotions; as listeners, we relate certain sounds to those emotions because of our cultural training and experience.

- **Musically-Aware Listening.** Musically-aware listening is the deepest level of listening, and it involves all three of the other levels. We rarely listen to music only on one level. Most of the time we are multitasking when we listen to music, trying to understand it technically, allowing it to guide our mood, and relating to it in a cultural frame. To achieve this high level of listening is to understand a piece of music.

The first requirement for musically-aware listening is to remember what you have heard. In order to do that you must be able to identify what you hear and relate it to new sounds. Next, you must become a critical and attentive listener. Because of the constant barrage of music in our daily lives we often tune it out, use it as a background, and don't pay attention to it. Sometimes we do this on purpose. But in order to understand much of the music of this text we must truly listen to music, not just hear it. Finally, like anything at which we want to become more proficient, we must practice listening to music of a variety of styles. We must be open to honestly consider the expressive value of musical sounds that are new and foreign to us.

IN PERFORMANCE

The Fundamentals of Music

To discuss different aspects of music we need a common language. Music, like any other human activity, has a set of symbols, systems, and definitions all its own. We refer to these symbols as music notation, and systems as music fundamentals.

Notation refers to the symbols used by composers to represent sound. The musical notation system in existence today has roots in the Middle Ages and continues to develop as new music is written. Musicians learn to "read" music much the way we learn to read written words. And, music is structured similarly to prose or poetry. For example, music has rhythm, it is set in phrases, it has definite sounding stopping points, and it has a main subject. Composers and performers use symbols and terms to be able to communicate with one another.

The chapters of Unit 1 lead you through the fundamentals (sometimes also called the musical elements) of music and introduce you to the instruments of the orchestra. When listening to music it is not necessary that you be able to read music, and that is not the point of these opening chapters. What is important is that you be able to describe the sounds you hear in such a way that others can understand your ideas and feelings about the music. In order to do this we must learn what musicians call certain sounds and how different sounds are described. To enjoy listening to music is one thing, to understand what the composer means by the music and to be able to describe to another person that music's effect on you is quite another. Knowing music fundamentals gives voice to what you think and feel about music, and allows you to communicate with others.

In the instrument chapter you will learn about how sound is produced on musical instruments and how they are used in ensembles—groups of instruments such as bands, orchestras, and jazz bands. And, finally in this introductory unit, you will receive an overview of musical history since the Middle Ages. This summary overview is intended to give you a general idea of how music has changed over the past two millennia.

How We Construct Music

LEARNING OBJECTIVES

- Explain the characteristics of a melody.

- Recognize by listening example the different rhythmic meters.

- Demonstrate by listening examples an understanding of the difference between melody and harmony.

- Recognize the textural styles monophony, polyphony, and homophony.

- Recognize by listening example different textures and timbres of music.

- Identify by listening basic formal structures of music.

- Explain the relationship of musical tempo and dynamics in musical expression.

- Name the seven elements of music and explain the relationship among these elements.

Key Concepts: chord, dynamics, expression, form, harmony, homophony, melody, meter, monophony, polyphony, rhythm, scale, texture, timbre

Duration: A measurable length of time that a sound lasts.

Amplitude: In music, how loud or soft a musical tone is.

Tone: See **Pitch**.

Pitch: A quality of a musical sound, how high or low the sound is. To be musical, a pitch must have a measurable frequency.

Note: Name given to a specific musical sound, also called a tone or pitch.

Scale: A set of ascending or descending pitches arranged in a certain pattern and centered on one of the twelve pitches.

Tonal center: The most important pitch of a scale or musical work on which the work is based.

Key: See **Tonal Center.**

Melody: A series of tones or pitches that we understand as a recognizable unit.

Range: The distance between the highest and lowest notes of a melody.

Contour: The mix of rise, fall, and stasis in a melody.

Phrase structure (or phrases): The natural stopping and starting places of the melody.

Climax: The point in the melody where it reaches it highest intensity.

Dashboard

LISTEN

Why do we not perceive all sound as being music? Why are only certain tones thought of as musical? First, we tend to perceive something as musical if it has a definite pitch and a distinct duration. Pitch is simply how high or low the sound is. To be musical, a pitch must have a measurable frequency. **Duration** is how long a sound lasts. Another distinguishable characteristic of music is that it has **amplitude**; in other words, we can detect how loud or soft it is, and relate that to the pitch and duration.

Which sounds a listener perceives as musical depends on his or her cultural background. In Western art music, melodies are created by combining the twelve notes of a scale in different sequences. We use the words **tone** and **pitch** to mean musical **note** when discussing music. We label tones by using the first seven letters of the alphabet—A, B, C, D, E, F, G. A **scale** is a set of ascending or descending pitches arranged in a certain pattern and centered on one of the twelve pitches. This center is called the **tonal center** or **key** of a piece of music. Throughout most of the history of Western music this tonal center, or key, has been one of the most basic elements in the construction of any composition.

Music is made up of seven elements: melody, rhythm, harmony, texture, form, timbre, and expression. These elements are universally applied to music of all cultures, but they are treated differently in different eras and genres. Composers manipulate these elements in different ways to express their ideas and feelings.

Melody

What makes a sequence of sounds a melody?

Melody is a series of tones or pitches that we understand as a recognizable unit. Melody is what we usually first take note of in a piece of music and what we most often remember about it. After we hear a melody, we might repeat it by humming or whistling it, or simply hearing it in our head. Unlike other musical elements, each melody is unique. This unique quality is what makes a melody memorable. Melodies are also referred to as *tunes*, *themes*, and *motifs*.

All melodies have certain characteristics that distinguish them from one another. For example, every melody has a unique range, contour, phrase structure, and climax. The **range** is the distance between the highest and lowest notes. This varies greatly from melody to melody.

Melody is the linear aspect of music. The linear shape of the melody is called its *contour*. Melodies rise and fall in pitch, and sometimes remain static for a time. This mix of rising, falling, and stasis creates the **contour**. We hear melodies the same way we hear sentences and paragraphs in speech or lines in poetry. The natural stopping and starting of the melody is called its **phrase structure**. Just like in a novel or short story, a musical work is made up of melodic phrases, which contain sub-phrases. Each melody also has a climactic moment or **climax**. This is the point in the melody where it reaches its highest intensity. Composers tend to combine the musical elements in a work to reinforce the melodic climax.

Rhythm

How are rhythms constructed?

Rhythm is the movement of music through time. Musical notes all have distinct durations, and rhythm is created by the sequence of these durations. We call the basic rhythmic unit a **beat**. A beat is a regular pulse that helps divide the rhythm into understandable units. Not all beats have the same emphasis. Just like words in spoken language, some beats have more emphasis and some less. This emphasis of a beat is called an **accent**. The combination of regular beats and recurring accents creates meter.

Meter is an organizational device composers use to tell performers how the groupings or rhythms in a piece should sound. The most common meters in music are **duple meter**, **triple meter**, and **quadruple meter**. In each of these meters the accented pitches occur at different times within the regular grouping of pitches.

In duple meter every other beat is accented creating a pattern of "strong-weak," "strong-weak," etc. In the following examples the black arrows point to the strong beats and the gray arrows point to the weak beats.

In triple meter every third beat is accented. This creates a "strong-weak-weak," "strong-weak-weak," etc., pattern.

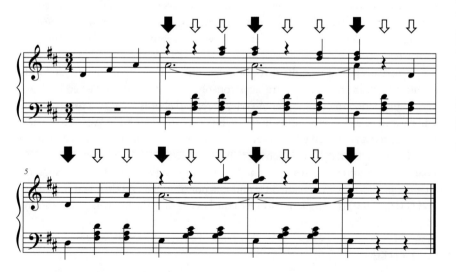

Quadruple meter is not always the same emphasis pattern. In our example we hear a pattern of "strong-weak-weak-weak," etc., beats.

Rhythm: The movement of music through time.

Beat: The basic rhythmic unit.

Accent: The placing of emphasis on a particular beat in a rhythm.

Meter: An organizational device composers use to tell performers how the groupings or rhythms in a piece should sound. Duple, triple, and quadruple meters are all common in music and refer to rhythmic groupings in pairs, trios, and quads, respectively.

Duple meter: A meter in which every other beat is accented, creating a pattern of "strong-weak," "strong-weak," etc.

Triple meter: In triple meter every third beat is accented. This creates a "strong-weak-weak," "strong-weak-weak," etc., pattern.

Quadruple meter: A meter in groupings of fours, for example "strong-weak-weak-weak," etc., beats.

When musical accents fall on weak beats or on a division of a beat, the rhythm is syncopated. **Syncopation** is very common, especially in jazz and popular music, and helps make rhythms interesting and varied. In the example below, the arrows point to the syncopated pitches.

Harmony

How does harmony differ from melody?
If melody is the linear aspect of music, then harmony is the vertical, as it lends depth of sound to a melody. **Harmony** might be described as the simultaneous sounding of two or more musical tones. Harmony in Western music is either **consonant** or **dissonant**. A consonant sound is at rest or stable—a sound that does not seem incomplete. A dissonant harmony is full of tension; it sounds like it is in motion and needs another harmony to complete it. This conflict between consonance and dissonance is one of the most important elements of Western music. The idea of contrast and conflict between harmonies helps create the form of Western music.

A **chord** is created anytime three or more tones sound simultaneously. Chords, because they are harmonies, are also consonant or dissonant. We tend to hear chords in relation to one another. A series of related chords is called a **progression**. Chords can be any combination of notes, but a common chord in Western music is a triad. A **triad** is created when three notes are sounded that are separated by notes that are not sounded. This is most easily understood by visualizing a piano keyboard. If we sound the notes C, E, and G we are playing a C chord, or C triad. Note that the pitch between C (called D) and E is not sounded and the pitch between E and G (labeled F) is also silent. (Refer to the keyboard in the following illustration.)

Texture

What are the three main types of texture found in music?
The interplay of melodies and harmonies is the **texture** of a musical work. The most basic form of texture is a single melodic line without any competing or accompanying musical sound. Such a texture is called **monophonic**. Much of the

Syncopation: Accents that fall on weak beats or on a division of a beat.

Harmony: The simultaneous sounding of two or more musical tones.

Consonant sound: A musical sound that sounds at rest or complete.

Dissonant sound: A musical sound that seems incomplete or creates tension.

Dashboard

LISTEN

Chord: Three or more tones sounded simultaneously.

Progression: In harmony, a series of related chords.

Triad: When three notes are sounded that are separated by notes that are not sounded.

Texture: The interplay of melodies and harmonies is the texture of a musical work.

Monophonic texture: A single melody sounding by itself.

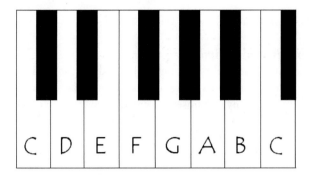

Names of musical notes as they are arranged on a piano keyboard.

earliest music, especially that of the early Christian church, was in this simple style. The music created when two or more melodic lines are heard simultaneously is **polyphonic**. Polyphonic music developed from monophonic music and first became important in the Middle Ages. A **homophonic** piece of music has a melodic line of great interest and importance that is accompanied or supported by a harmonic accompaniment. This accompaniment is usually a progression of chords that relates to the melodic contour and key. Today's music is a mixture of all three, but is primarily homophonic. A good deal of Western art music uses all three of these textural styles to create contrasts within a long work. Shorter pieces tend to be in one texture or another. These three types of music can be illustrated with the common melody *Row, Row, Row Your Boat*.

Polyphonic texture: The music created when two or more melodic lines are heard simultaneously.

Homophonic texture: Sound created when a single melody is accompanied by chords.

Dashboard

LISTEN

Timbre

How is music affected by timbre?

Timbre is the particular quality of a musical sound. Just as each person's voice is distinct, each instrument has its own sound or timbre. Also called **tone color**, this musical element is used by composers to create a vast palette of musical sounds. Timbre changes as a composer combines different instruments. The possibilities within a symphony orchestra or concert band are very large. In earlier eras it seems that the expressive quality of timbre was either not recognized by composers or it was simply not an important way to express their ideas. Today, timbral changes are frequent in works and a composer's style is often identified by his use of tone color.

Form

How is repetition and contrast used to create the form of a composition?

A musical composition adheres to a particular shape and structure that is called its **form**. Form is how the composer uses the melodic and harmonic structures in repetition, contrast, and/or variation. Most musical works have a planned form.

The central idea of form in each of the historical periods studied in this text is the use of contrast. The composer may contrast old ideas with new or develop old ideas to create the form of a work. Within the large form of a work are sections and phrases. Combining phrases into groups creates sections of a larger form. Sometimes a composer divides a long piece of music into **movements**. A movement is a distinct composition itself, and a group of movements are usually related in some musical way. For example, Ludwig van Beethoven's famous Symphony No. 5 consists of four movements that are all built upon the first four notes of the first movement. Each of the movements is a separate musical composition and together they make up the symphony.

In some time periods form has been central to the listening experience. For example, in the Classical era (1750–1820) the listener could predict the return of the first melody at a particular moment in the first movement of a symphony. In other eras, form has been less evident to the listener but is nevertheless a crucial aspect of the composition. The idea of form is used in all arts. The acts and scenes of a play, the rhythm and phrasing of a poem, or the structural design of a building are all examples of form in other arts.

Timbre: The particular quality of a musical sound. Sometimes referred to as tone color.

Tone color: See **Timbre**.

Form: A particular shape and structure of a musical composition.

Movement: A part of a larger musical work. A movement is a distinct composition itself and a group of movements are usually related by melodic, rhythmic, or tonal ideas.

The architectural scheme of the Chateau de Chambord visually demonstrates a rondo form of ABACABA. Courtesy nagelestock.com/Alamy.

Expression

How do composers use expression in music?

The term **expression** refers to a work's tempo and dynamics. The **tempo** is how fast or slow the beat is, while **dynamics** refers to how loudly or softly a musical sound is played. Composers indicate tempo and dynamics in their music as guides to performers as to how the piece should sound. Over the centuries composers have standardized certain words (often Italian) that indicate tempo and dynamics. For example, the Italian word *piano* indicates that the music should be played softly, while *forte* means loudly. There are many gradations between these two extremes. The same is true for tempo markings. The word **adagio** indicates a very slow tempo and **allegro** means fast or lively.

Composers use tempo and dynamics for expressive purposes. Over the years, composers have become more specific about these markings, and notation in general has become more specific as music has become more complex.

✓ **Audio Review:** Go to Dashboard to listen to Professor Bailey discuss the fundamentals of music.

✓ **How Am I Doing?** Go to Dashboard to test your understanding of this material by taking the chapter quiz.

Expression: A work's tempo and dynamics.

Tempo: The speed at which a musical composition is performed.

Dynamics: In music notation, the term refers to symbols and/or words indicating how loud or soft a passage of music should be performed.

Piano: When used as a word to guide performers, the term means the piece or section should be played softly.

Forte: In music, a word meaning a piece or section of music should be performed loudly.

Adagio: In music, a term meaning a slow tempo.

Allegro: In music, a term meaning a moderately fast tempo.

Dashboard

KEY TERMS

Accent	Form	Progression
Adagio	*Forte*	Quadruple meter
Allegro	Harmony	Range
Amplitude	Homophonic texture	Rhythm
Beat	Key	Scale
Chord	Melody	Syncopation
Climax	Meter	Tempo
Consonant sound	Monophonic texture	Texture
Contour	Movement	Timbre
Dissonant sound	Note	Tonal center
Duple meter	Phrase structure	Tone
Duration	*Piano*	Tone color
Dynamics	Pitch	Triad
Expression	Polyphonic texture	Triple meter

How We Make Music

LEARNING OBJECTIVES

- Name the four registers of the human voice and orchestral instruments.

- Explain the instrument classification systems used for Western and non-Western instruments.

- Recognize by sound the different instruments of the string, woodwind, brass, percussion, and keyboard families.

- Name the instruments of the string, woodwind, brass, percussion, and keyboard families.

- Explain how sounds are created on string, woodwind, brass, and percussion instruments.

Key Concepts: ensembles, families of instruments, method of production of sound on instruments, names and shapes of individual instruments, Sachs categorization system, voice registers

The Human Voice

What are the different registers of the human voice?

The human voice is the original natural musical instrument and many other instruments have been contrived to imitate its sound. As discussed in Chapter 1, timbre refers to the sound quality of an instrument or voice. The timbre of a human voice is determined by the person's gender, age, and the size of their vocal cords.

Voices are divided into four registers depending on their pitch. The higher two registers are usually female voices and are called **soprano** (highest) and **alto**. The two lower registers are most often male voices and are labeled **tenor** and **bass** (lowest).

Instrument Classifications

How are musical instruments classified around the world?

Western musical instruments can be grouped into families based largely on the materials from which they are constructed, and that is how they are discussed below. A more universal system of categorization developed by two scholars of instrument making, Curt Sachs and Erich von Hornbostel, divides all instruments into four categories: aerophone, chordophone, idiophone, and membranophone.

An **aerophone** uses air to create a sound. Instruments such as the flute, clarinet, and trumpet are aerophones. So are most organs, since they also use a column of air passing through pipes to produce their sound.

A **chordophone** produces a sound with the use of a vibrating string. The violin, viola, cello, bass, harp, and guitar are such instruments.

An **idiophone**'s body itself creates the sound. These instruments are usually struck with a stick, shaken, or clanged together. Examples of Western idiophones include many percussion instruments such as the xylophone, cymbals, and orchestra bells.

Membranophones are also usually considered percussion instruments. A player creates a sound on these instruments by striking a tightly stretched membrane with a stick or hand. The snare drum, bass drum, and timpani are membranophones.

Today there is a fifth type of instrument not considered in the Sachs categories—the electronic instrument. These instruments make use of computer generated and manipulated sounds to create tones.

Like the voice, instruments are also classified by register. For example, in the string family the violin is the soprano instrument; the viola is the alto; the cello is the tenor; and the string bass is the bass member.

Instrument Families

How are the instruments used in Western music grouped into families?

String Instruments

String instruments have strings that are bowed or plucked, sometimes both. When the instrument is bowed, a bow is drawn across the strings to set them vibrating. Alternatively, the strings can be plucked by the musician's fingers to

---

Soprano: The highest of the four registers of soprano, alto, tenor, and bass.

Alto: The second highest range in the four-range register system of soprano, alto, tenor, bass.

Tenor: The second lowest of the four registers of soprano, alto, tenor, and bass.

Bass: The lowest range in the four-range register system of soprano, alto, tenor, bass.

Aerophone: A musical instrument that uses air to create a sound.

Chordophone: A musical instrument that uses vibrating strings to create its sound.

Idiophone: A percussion instrument on which sound is created when the body of the instrument is struck with a mallet.

Membranophone: A percussion instrument on which the sound is produced by a mallet striking a membrane, skin, or plastic piece stretched across the body of the instrument.

The violin is the soprano voice of the string section. © chrisstockphoto/Alamy

EXPLORE

See videos of the instruments discussed in this chapter

Violin: A member of the string family in the soprano register.

create a sound. This plucking technique is called pizzicato. In Western music the primary bowed strings are the violin, viola, cello, and bass. The musician creates different pitches by changing the lengths of the instrument's strings that are allowed to vibrate. This is done by pressing a finger down on a string at a certain point on the fingerboard, thus stopping a portion of the string from vibrating.

The **violin** is the smallest of the string family that consists of violin, viola, cello, and double bass. It also has the highest range of the four string instruments. The violin can be played either by drawing a bow across its strings or by plucking them. The bow is held in the right hand and is a flexible and slightly curved stick that has very tightly strung horsehair. As the bow is drawn across the strings it sets them in vibration. The body of the violin acts as an amplifier to the sound. The left hand moves up and down the strings along the instrument to shorten or lengthen the amount of string vibrating. This creates different pitches. The violin is the most important instrument of the symphony orchestra and is often used to play the main melody of a piece of music or as a solo instrument.

The **viola** looks like a violin but is somewhat larger. It has nearly the same register and dynamic range of the violin but its timbre is different. It sounds a bit darker than the violin because the instrument is larger and the strings longer than those of the violin. We often refer to the violin as the soprano voice of the string family and the viola as the alto voice.

The **cello** (the c has a "ch" sound like in chair), more formally the violoncello, is the primary melodic instrument of the low strings because it has a dark and rich tone. It is a medium-sized instrument that cannot be held under the chin to be played. Instead the cellist places the instrument between his legs and uses the floor to support it.

The viola looks much like the violin but is slightly larger in size. Courtesy Milkovasa/Shutterstock.

Viola: A string instrument in the alto register.

Cello: A string instrument in the tenor register.

The cello is the tenor voice of the string family. Courtesy Ollyy/Shutterstock.

Double bass: A string instrument in the bass register.

The string bass is usually played standing up because of its size. Courtesy aodaodaodaod/Shutterstock.

Harp: A string instrument that is strummed and plucked.

Guitar: A string instrument that is strummed and plucked that has a resonating body.

The **double bass** (pronounced like "base") is the lowest and largest of the string family. As its name implies, it usually plays the bass line, or lowest part, in the orchestra. This is the only string instrument that is a regular member of the orchestra, concert band, and jazz ensemble. The instrument is large and is often played standing up, or sitting on a high stool. It is usually played with the bow in classical music and is most often plucked in jazz or popular music.

The most common plucked string instruments are the **harp** and the **guitar**. Notes on the harp are created by manipulating pedals, and plucking the strings with the fingers. The most common sound on a harp is called the arpeggio, which is created by the player rapidly moving across the strings of the instrument. The length of the string creates different pitches.

The harp has forty-seven strings and a very large range. The strings can change pitch by manipulation of one of the seven pedals, which the player plays with both feet. The harp also is a very versatile instrument and is heard today in symphony orchestras and in many movie soundtracks.

Woodwind Instruments

Wind instrument sounds are produced by a vibrating air column that passes through some kind of pipe. On all wind instruments other than the organ, the pipe has holes bored along its length, which the player covers with his fingers or some kind of key mechanism. To change the pitch of the instrument, the player uncovers more or fewer holes. The woodwinds as a section are much less homogeneous in sound than the strings. Each has its own identifiable tone quality and composers have used these instruments to create many different timbres.

The highest pitched woodwind instruments are the **flute** and its smaller cousin the **piccolo**. Flutes were once made of wood but today's flute is made of metal. The player blows across a tone hole near one end of the flute to produce the sound. The flute is a flexible instrument and is often used to play the melody in an ensemble. The flute is one of the most commonly played of the woodwind instruments. The flute has a very soft and sweet tone quality in its lowest register and a bright and sometimes shrill sound in its highest register.

The harp is played with both the hands and feet. Courtesy Ralf Siemieniec/Shutterstock.

Flute: A woodwind instrument in the soprano register usually made of metal and lacking a reed.

Piccolo: The smallest of the woodwind instruments.

The flute, though classified as a woodwind instrument, is made of metal. Courtesy Lana Langlois/ Shutterstock.

The piccolo is a member of the woodwind instrument family even though it is not usually made of wood. Wood was used to make early piccolos and some modern professional models, but they are usually made of metal. The instrument is one-half the length of the more common flute and plays an octave higher. The piccolo is the highest-pitched of the woodwind instruments and is very agile. The instrument changes pitch by the player opening or closing tone holes located along the body of the instrument. This lengthens or shortens the amount of the tubing that the air column passes through and changes the pitch. This concept of lengthening or shortening the instrument is used on all the woodwind instruments.

The **oboe** is made of wood and has an intricate system of keys and tone holes. The oboe's sound is created by two reeds controlled by the player's mouth. Since there are two reeds, the instrument is sometimes referred to as a double-reed instrument. The player's blowing vibrates the reeds and the oboe amplifies the reeds' vibrations. The oboe has a nasal and sometimes piercing tone quality.

The **clarinet** resembles the oboe but the inside of the body of the instrument (the bore) is larger. It, like the oboe, has many keys and tone holes. The clarinet is the most widely used woodwind in orchestras, bands, and jazz groups. It has a smooth tone quality and can play a large range of pitches. The clarinet's sound is created by one reed.

The clarinet is made in many different sizes. The most common sizes used are the B-flat clarinet, shown in the picture below, and the

The oboe is a double-reed instrument.
Courtesy Alenavlad/Shutterstock.

Oboe: A double-reed instrument in the woodwind family in the soprano register.

Clarinet: A single-reed instrument in the woodwind family in the soprano or alto register.

Benny Goodman, one of the leading jazz clarinetists of the 20th century. Courtesy Associated Press.

The bassoon. Courtesy mkm3/Shutterstock.

bass clarinet. The bass clarinet is a larger version of the B-flat clarinet and plays in a lower register.

The **bassoon** is the other double-reed instrument and its tone quality is a lower and darker version of the oboe's sound. It is the bass instrument of the woodwind family but has the ability to play high notes as well.

Bassoon: A double-reed instrument in the woodwind family that is in the bass register.

The **saxophone** is made out of brass and is the newest of the woodwinds, having been invented in the early 1800s by Adolphe Sax. The saxophone is a single-reed instrument like the clarinet, and has the same basic system of keys and tone holes as the flute. Soprano, alto, tenor, and baritone saxophones are standard members of concert bands and jazz ensembles. The saxophone is the most important woodwind instrument in jazz and is rarely used in orchestras.

Saxophone: A single-reed instrument in the woodwind family usually in the alto or tenor register.

Brass Instruments

All brass instruments' sounds are created in the same manner: a player creates a buzz by blowing an air column between their two lips. This buzz is amplified in the body of the instrument. The pitches are changed by lengthening the amount of tubing used to amplify the buzz and/or by changing the frequency of the buzz itself. The tubing is lengthened by a telescoping slide or by a valve system.

The **trumpet** is the soprano instrument of the brass family. It is an ancient instrument that historically was often used in ceremonies. It is made of metal. The sound of the instrument is produced by the

Trumpet: The highest pitched member of the brass family.

The alto saxophone is used in classical, jazz, and popular music. Courtesy Maksim Toome/Shutterstock.

Trumpeter Wynton Marsalis. Courtesy Associated Press.

player's lips buzzing into a cup-shaped mouthpiece. The trumpet's pitch is changed by the player changing the frequency of the buzz and by the player depressing one or more of its three valves. As each valve is depressed the air column passes through an ever-lengthening amount of tubing. The trumpet is the most versatile of the brass instruments and is used in orchestras, bands, jazz ensembles, popular music, and many other settings.

Horn: A brass instrument in the alto register.

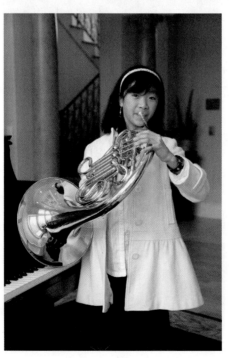

Trombone: A member of the brass family in the tenor register using a telescoping slide to produce different pitches.

The **horn** (sometimes called the French horn) is the alto instrument of the brasses. It developed from the hunting horn and conch shell horn of ancient times. In this curious-looking instrument the bell faces to the back of the player and away from the audience. The horn has a dark and mellow sound, but can also be brilliant and brassy in the upper register. Like the trumpet, it uses valves (most often four) to change the tubing length.

The **trombone** is one of the oldest of classical instruments. The trombone is the only brass instrument that does not require valves

The horn is often called the French horn.
© yenwen. Courtesy iStock.

The trombone is the only brass instrument that uses a slide instead of valves to change notes. Courtesy shyshak roman/Shutterstock.

to change tube length. Instead, the trombone has a telescoping slide that the player moves with his full arm to change the length of the tube. It is the tenor instrument of the brass family. The trombone has been important in instrumental music since at least the Renaissance era.

The **tuba** is the most recent member to join the brasses. It was developed in the early 1800s after many failed attempts at creating a bass brass instrument that sounded good. It has anywhere from three to six valves. Other commonly used members of the tuba family are the baritone,

Tuba: The lowest pitched member of the brass family.

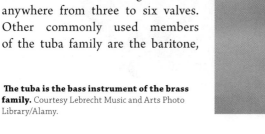

The tuba is the bass instrument of the brass family. Courtesy Lebrecht Music and Arts Photo Library/Alamy.

euphonium, and sousaphone. The baritone and euphonium look like small versions of the tuba. The sousaphone is used in marching bands. It wraps around the player's body so that it can be easily carried while marching and the bell is positioned above the player's head and faces front.

Percussion Instruments

Until the 20th century the percussion family's role in Western music was primarily to keep time. Over the past 50 years that role has grown significantly and today percussion instruments are also used as melodic instruments. They are particularly important in the creation of special timbres or tone colors in modern music. It is not possible to discuss all the instruments in the percussion family here. However, the traditional orchestral percussion sections have included four indefinite pitch instruments—the snare drum, bass drum, triangle, and cymbals, and three definite pitch instruments—the xylophone, timpani, and glockenspiel or bells. A member of the percussion section of an ensemble is expected to be able to play all of these instruments as well as the chimes, tambourine, castanets, tam-tam (gong), tom-tom (tenor drum), and a variety of other instruments.

Timpani: A low-pitched and tuneable membranophone.

The **timpani** are also sometimes called kettledrums because their shape resembles a large copper cauldron. Timpani are usually played in pairs of two or four drums and are membranophones. The player uses a pedal mechanism to tighten or loosen the head of the instrument, which changes the pitch.

Xylophone: An idiophone used in orchestras and bands.

A **xylophone** is a set of tuned bars (wood, metal, or plastic) arranged in the shape of a keyboard. The player strikes the bars with a pair of mallets to create the sound. The instrument is melodic in nature and is often used to contribute to a particular timbre or tone color.

Glockenspiel: Also called bells or orchestral bells, the instrument's sound is made by striking metal bars with a mallet.

The **glockenspiel**, or orchestral bells, is constructed and played similarly to the xylophone. The bars are always made of metal.

The timpani are sometimes called kettledrums. © johnhess. Courtesy iStock.

The xylophone. Courtesy Lebrecht Music and Arts Photo Library/Alamy.

The **snare drum** and **bass drum** are usually used in an ensemble to keep the beat and maintain a steady rhythm. The snare drum plays the most complicated rhythms in the entire percussion section and the bass drum usually plays the least complex. Both instruments consist of a shell over which two heads (usually made of plastic) are stretched (bottom and top of shell). Snares are strings or metal bands stretched across the bottom head that vibrate when the top head is struck with a stick. This creates the characteristic sound of the snare drum. The bass drum is usually struck with a soft stick, producing a much more resonant sound than the snare drum.

Snare drum: A small drum used to keep time by striking a head stretched across the body of the instrument.

Bass drum: A large drum used in ensembles to keep the beat.

A percussion section, showing bells, bass drum, timpani, and other percussion instruments.
Courtesy Norman Price/Alamy.

Crash cymbals. Courtesy Elvele Images Ltd/Alamy.

Cymbals: Metal plate, or plates, that are struck together or with a stick. A percussion instrument.

Triangle: A metal bar bent into the shape of a triangle and struck with a metal beater.

Harpsichord: A keyboard instrument on which the strings are plucked to create a sound.

Cymbals are large round brass plates that are struck together to create their sound. The "crashing" effect is often used to highlight a climactic moment or to gain the audience's attention. Cymbals are made in a wide variety of sizes from the very small finger cymbals to large plates. Cymbals can also be mounted on a stand and struck with a stick to create a rolling sound.

The **triangle** is a steel rod bent into the shape of a triangle and open at one corner. It is struck with a steel stick and the performer can create individual pitches or a roll on the instrument. The instrument gives off a high-pitched, brilliant tinkling sound quality.

Keyboard Instruments

The three most important keyboard instruments in Western music are the harpsichord, organ, and piano. The important difference between keyboard instruments and almost all others is that the keyboard allows the player to play more than one note simultaneously. None of these three keyboard instruments is a regular member of the orchestra or band, but all are used on occasion as special members, or as solo instruments.

The **harpsichord** was particularly popular in the Renaissance and Baroque eras. Its twangy sound is created by the string being plucked when the player depresses a key. The harpsichord has a much smaller dynamic range than the piano and organ. Its small size and sound made it a perfect match for the salon or small opera house.

The harpsichord was one of the primary keyboard instruments of the Renaissance and Baroque eras. Courtesy Linda Bucklin/Shutterstock.

The **pipe organ**'s sound is produced by pushing a column of air through a series of pipes. The keyboard and an intricate system of valves (called stops) determine which pipes the air passes through. The more stops that are employed, the louder the instrument plays. Each pipe has both a pitch and a tone color, allowing the organ to sound somewhat like a flute, bassoon, clarinet, trumpet, or other instrument. The organ often has multiple keyboards and a pedal-board that is played with the feet. Referred to as "The King of Instruments," the organ can produce a powerful sound. Pipe organs vary greatly in size, usually determined by the size of the building for which they are built. Because of their size, organs do not usually move from space to space.

The **piano** has been the most popular keyboard instrument since the late 1700s. It was originally called the pianoforte because of its ability to play both soft and loud. Sound is produced on a piano by the vibrations of strings that have been struck by small hammers connected to the keys on the keyboard. It can serve nicely alone or as the leader of a large concerto with a full symphony orchestra. A regular member of the jazz ensemble, it is also used by most other ensembles, chamber groups, and soloists as an accompanying instrument.

Electronic Instruments

Electronic instruments have played a significant role in music since about 1950. Today's computer technology makes it possible for just about anyone to try his or her hand at composing or performing. Three

The pipe organ is often a massive instrument built for a specific room or concert hall. Courtesy Pavel L Photo and Video/Shutterstock.

A grand piano. Courtesy Design Pics Inc./Alamy.

Pipe organ: In this text the term refers to a pipe organ on which sound is produced by passing a column of air through varying sizes of pipes.

Piano: A keyboard instrument on which the strings are struck by a keyed hammer to create a sound.

A synthesizer. © luminis. Courtesy iStock.

types of electronic devices have been used in music: the tape recorder, synthesizer, and computer.

The invention of the **synthesizer** in the 1950s radically changed modern music. A synthesizer not only modifies sounds, it creates them. Most synthesizers have a keyboard and are played much like a piano or organ. They are capable of producing both musical sounds and sound effects. Since synthesizers have internal memory storage, a musician can layer one sound on top of another much like in the recording studio to produce what can sound like an ensemble. Synthesizers became common in the 1970s as they became less expensive, and today many popular groups and movie studios use them.

The development of **musical instrument digital interface** (MIDI) allowed a synthesizer to be connected to a computer. In most computer music the composer generates all of the sounds on the computer. Today, many composers mix live musicians with electronic instruments to create a wide timbral palette.

Synthesizer: An electronic instrument that is used to record, manipulate, and play sounds.

MIDI: Musical Instrument Digital Interface allows synthesizers and computers to communicate.

Ensembles

How are the instruments and voices combined into different ensembles?

An ensemble is any combination of musicians making music together. The band, choir, and orchestra are the most traditional and common of ensembles. There are also many types of chamber and jazz ensembles.

Band: In this text this term refers to a concert band, an ensemble consisting of woodwind, brass, and percussion instruments.

The **band** is perhaps the oldest instrumental musical ensemble in Western music and has varied greatly in size over the centuries from four players to over one hundred. Today, the term refers to a group of woodwind, brass, and percussion instruments. Bands have a close association with the military and the entertainment industry. In the United States concert bands are particularly popular in schools and at colleges and universities. The concert band of today is a mixture of woodwind, brass, and percussion instruments of no standard size but often numbering about sixty players.

Choir: An ensemble of voices, usually consisting of all four voice ranges and both female and male vocalists.

The **choir** is the standard large ensemble for mixed voices. It can range in number from about twelve to several hundred, depending on the work being performed and the intent of the ensemble. Most groups include both men and women singing the four ranges of the voice: soprano, alto, tenor, and bass. Choirs are usually accompanied by a single piano or are unaccompanied (*a cappella*). Large choral

A concert band. Courtesy Ted Foxx/Alamy.

ensembles join symphony orchestras on occasion for special large works intended for the concert hall and in operas. Choirs are versatile in where they perform but are generally more effective indoors. They are regular ensembles at many church services and schools.

The **orchestra** is the large ensemble for which much of the great music of the Western world was written. It consists of strings, woodwinds, brass, and percussion instruments and varies in size from about twenty-five players to over one

Orchestra: An ensemble made up of string, woodwind, brass, and percussion instruments that sometimes includes one or more keyboard instruments.

A modern orchestra performing onstage. Courtesy Pavel L Photo and Video/Shutterstock.

hundred. Since the Baroque era, the orchestra has gradually increased in size and numbers of different instruments. The string section is the heart of the orchestra, with the woodwinds, brass, and percussion instruments being used for timbral and rhythmic purposes.

LISTENING GUIDE 2.1

The Young Person's Guide to the Orchestra
Benjamin Britten, composed 1946

This work is a showcase of each of the sections and primary instruments of the orchestra. In some versions there is also a narration in which the instruments are introduced. The work is a set of variations and fugue on a theme by Baroque era composer Henry Purcell. The original theme by Purcell was written as incidental music for the play *Abdelazer* by Aphra Behn. In addition to introducing each instrument the work is also an excellent example of varying textures including sections of polyphony and homophony. Britten wrote the work specifically to be performed for children.

Dashboard

HEAR STREAMING AUDIO ON DASHBOARD

What to Listen For

- Listen for the entrance of each section of the orchestra.
- Listen for the entrance and timbre of each major instrument.
- Listen for some special effects played by different instruments, including glissando and pizzicato.
- Note how Britten changes the character and mood of the theme with each variation.

TIMING	TEXTURE	FORM	WHAT TO LISTEN FOR
0:00	Full orchestra	Section 1	The entrances of each of the sections of the orchestra.
0:41	Woodwind section	Theme	
1:10	Brass section	Theme	
1:42	String section	Theme	
2:07	Percussion section	Theme	
2:25	Full orchestra	Theme	
3:00	Flute/piccolo	Section 2—Variations Theme variation	Flutes and piccolos play the theme in a fast, light, and soft style accompanied by harp and strings.
3:29	Oboe	Theme variation	Oboes play a lyrical version of the theme with string accompaniment.
4:31	Clarinet	Theme variation	Clarinets play a variation covering the range of the instrument with pizzicato strings and tuba accompanying.
5:15	Bassoon	Theme variation	Bassoons, with strings and snare drum accompaniment play a forceful and dramatic version of the melody.

6:12	Strings	Theme variation	The theme is played by the string instruments.
6:27	Violin	Theme variation	Violins play the theme in a sweeping fashion with brass accompaniment.
6:56	Viola	Theme variation	Violas play the theme more slowly and in a melancholy mood with woodwinds and brass as accompaniment.
7:45	Cello	Theme variation	Cello plays the theme in a lyrical style with clarinet, strings, and harp.
8:43	Double bass	Theme variation	Double bass plays the theme in short ascending notes with tambourine and woodwind accompaniment. The second half demonstrates the lyrical quality of the bass.
9:41	Harp	Theme variation	Harp plays the theme accompanied by percussion.
10:31	Brass section	Theme variation	The theme is played by the brass instruments.
10:53	Horns	Theme variation	Horns play the theme in a fanfare style accompanied by strings and harp.
11:12	Trumpets	Theme variation	Trumpets play the theme in a fast and light chase style accompanied by strings.
11:47	Trombones and tuba	Theme variation	Trombones and tuba play the theme in a dramatic fashion accompanied by woodwinds and high brass.
12:49	Percussion section	Theme variation	The theme is played by the percussion section in a waltz that changes style as the instruments enter. The instruments are introduced in groups in the following order: timpani, bass drum, and cymbals; timpani, snare drum, and wood block; timpani, castanets, and gong; timpani and whip; entire percussion section.
14:43		Section 3—fugue	A fragment of the original melody is turned into a fugue statement. The instruments play it in imitation in the same order as the variations.
14:43	Woodwinds		Woodwinds—piccolo, flute, oboe, clarinet, bassoon
15:22	Strings		Strings—first violin, second violin, viola, cello, bass, harp
16:02	Brass		Brass—horn, trumpet, trombone/tuba
16:21	Percussion		Percussion
16:31	Full orchestra		The full orchestra plays Purcell's original theme over the fugue.

If You Liked That, Try This

Bolero, Maurice Ravel
Peter and the Wolf, Sergei Prokofiev

YouTube video: search on keywords
"The Young Person's Orchestra"

Remember to add to your personal playlist any of these samples that you like.

Dashboard

✓ **Audio Review:** Go to Dashboard to listen to Professor Bailey discuss how we make music.

✓ **How Am I Doing?** Go to Dashboard to test your understanding of this material by taking the chapter quiz.

KEY TERMS

Aerophone

Alto

Band

Bass

Bass drum

Bassoon

Cello

Choir

Chordophone

Clarinet

Cymbals

Double bass

Flute

Glockenspiel

Guitar

Harp

Harpsichord

Horn

Idiophone

Membranophone

MIDI (Musical Instrument Digital Interface)

Oboe

Orchestra

Piano

Piccolo

Pipe organ

Saxophone

Snare drum

Soprano

Synthesizer

Tenor

Timpani

Triangle

Trombone

Trumpet

Tuba

Viola

Violin

Xylophone

How Music Has Changed over Time

LEARNING OBJECTIVES

- List the historical eras studied in this text and their approximate dates.
- Identify stylistic traits of historical eras.
- Identify names of important forms of music in historical eras.
- Identify important composer names and geographic centers of historical eras.

Key Concepts: composers of historical eras, dates, general style traits

Opening image: Illustration of Medieval musicians from *Songs of the Virgin Mary* attributed to King Alphonso the Wise of Spain. Courtesy Album/Art Resource, NY.

The music studied in this text is that of Western culture from approximately the year 450 to the current day. Throughout each of the chapters the history of specific composers and musical works is discussed within the context of performance. Your study of the history and development of music in Western culture is best undertaken when historical facts are combined with performance life situations that affected the creation of the music. Where a work was intended to be performed, why it was written, and for whom it was written are perhaps more important for you to understand than *when* a work was written. For example, the acoustics of cathedrals of the Middle Ages played a role in the development of the vocal forms studied in Unit 2 such as chant, motet, and Mass. The rise of the merchant class in the Baroque and Classical eras helped lead to public concerts and the development of the symphony. And, the popularity of literature and in-home music-making in the Romantic era contributed to the form and style of the art song. Learning the history of music within this performance context helps us understand the composer's intent and brings the music to life in our own time. In this way we can compare how music may have been used and received in one era with how it is heard today.

In order for us to discuss musical context it is important that we use accepted terms and names for time periods. Western music historians divide these years into six eras:

- The Middle Ages (450–1450)
- The Renaissance era (1450–1600)
- The Baroque era (1600–1750)
- The Classical era (1750–1820)
- The Romantic era (1820–1900)
- The Modern period (1900–today)

Of course, since musical styles continually evolve over years these are approximate dates and no clear lines separate one era from another. In this chapter we will briefly examine each period.

Music of the Middle Ages, 450–1450

- Key Stylistic Traits: primarily vocal, monophonic, polyphonic, sacred
- Key Forms: chant, organum, motet, Mass
- Key Places: France, especially the Cathedral of Notre Dame
- Key Composers: Hildegard of Bingen, Léonin, Pérotin, and Guillaume de Machaut

Sacred: Sacred music is music written for religious ceremony or to express religious belief.

Liturgy: The prescribed form of a traditional religious service—some of which is sung—both for special occasions such as marriages or funerals and for weekly rites.

Also called the Medieval period, or sometimes the Dark Ages, this period in Western music was dominated by the Catholic Church, as was society as a whole. Art music of this time was, for the most part, **sacred**—meaning it was written to express religious belief. Much of it was composed by men and women who served the church to be performed as part of church **liturgy**.

Liturgy refers to the prescribed form of a traditional religious service—some of which is sung—both for special occasions such as marriages or funerals and for weekly rites. Sacred music can be categorized into four types:

- music used in place of speaking in the church's liturgy
- music written as background music for pauses in the liturgy
- music written for use in the service for specific days or weeks of a religious year
- music written for outside the service but still about sacred topics.

The important music of this era was vocal, as instruments were only just developing and were not yet important or allowed in the church. As discussed in Unit 2, the sacred music of the early Middle Ages was primarily monophonic (a single melodic line without any competing or accompanying musical sound) or polyphonic (the music created when two or more melodic lines are heard simultaneously). And the important forms of music all stemmed from a need to enhance the liturgy of the church. The most significant forms still heard today include chant, organum, motet, and Mass.

- **Chant** is used to sing, rather than recite, sections of the church liturgy. Chants are nonmetrical with a free-sounding rhythm and a monophonic melodic line.
- **Organum** combines a chant and at least one other melody simultaneously.
- **Sacred motet** is based upon a chant and has at least three separate melodic lines. It can be polyphonic and/or homophonic in character, and is often polytextual—meaning that the motet contains both Latin and **vernacular** (native) languages.
- **Mass** is the most holy part of church liturgy. Parts of the Catholic Mass were sung in Latin till the middle of the 20th century. A musical Mass is a Mass delivered entirely by singing and playing of instruments. These special Masses were written for celebrations such as coronations, weddings, or funerals.

Each of these forms is discussed in more depth in Unit 2, Music of the Church.

We know little about the composers of this period. What we do know has come to us primarily through the Catholic church. Four important musicians of the period were Hildegard of Bingen, Léonin, Pérotin, and Guillaume de Machaut. Hildegard of Bingen (1098–1179), a nun who lived and worked in Germany, wrote over sixty-nine compositions—one of the largest surviving repertoires of Medieval music today. Léonin (?–1219?) and Pérotin (?–1238?) worked at the epicenter of art music at this time as choirmasters and composers at the Notre Dame Cathedral in Paris. These composers are credited with having contributed to the creation of organum in the Medieval period. Guillaume de Machaut (c. 1300–1377), among others, helped create the motet and is well known for his Masses, including the Mass of Notre Dame discussed in depth in Unit 2.

Although **secular** music—music written for everyday life or about nonspiritual events—would become more significant in the Renaissance court, **troubadours**, **trouvères**, *trovatore*, or **Minnesingers** (so called depending on whether the singers were in Spain, France, Italy, or Germany) would have sung love songs

Chant: A melody with a free-sounding rhythm, monophonic.

Organum: Music used in Catholic liturgy that combines a chant and at least one other melody simultaneously.

Sacred Motet: A form of three or more parts developed in the late Middle Ages based on a chant.

Vernacular: Language of the people of a particular country or geographic region.

Mass: The primary service of the Catholic Church consisting of two parts: the Ordinary and the Proper. Some portions of the Mass are sung rather than spoken. A musical Mass is a work for a special occasion and is entirely sung or played on instruments.

Secular: Refers to life outside religious life. In music this term refers to music that is not intended to express a religious belief.

Troubadour, trouvères, trovatore: From the Renaissance and Middle Ages; refers to amateur entertainers who sang and played instruments, usually at courts.

Minnesinger: See **Troubadour**.

for Medieval courts. A *jongleur* (juggler, acrobat, poet, animal trainer, and travel-ing musician) entertained those outside the court in town squares and pubs. It is most likely that the art music the public outside the court heard at this time was at church. Much of the music of the Middle Ages will sound unfamiliar and perhaps esoteric or cerebral compared to the music of today. However, our modern music has its roots in this ancient music, and some of this music has regained commer-cial popularity in recent years through the efforts of musicians such as Anony-mous 4, Chanticleer, and Cappella Romana.

Music of the Renaissance, 1450–1600

- Key Stylistic Traits: polyphonic and homophonic, imitative, vocal music more important than instrumental music, secular
- Key New Forms: chanson, madrigal
- Key Places: Italy
- Key Composers: Guillaume Dufay, Josquin des Prez, Palestrina, Tielman Susato, and Claudio Monteverdi

Chanson: Secular French love song of the Middle Ages and Renaissance.

Madrigal: A chamber piece for small vocal ensemble, usually four to six voices. Stemming from the Renaissance period the madrigal is a mix of polyphonic and homophonic styles.

Imitative: In music, the repetition of a melody by a different line either exactly or with some variation.

Word painting: Use of a particular musical sound to represent or bring to mind a particular word of text.

The important forms of the Medieval period continued into the Renaissance, in-cluding the chant, motet, and Mass, and while sacred music remained important, newly discovered Greek and Roman texts created an interest in these ancient civi-lizations that shifted the focus of the age to the individual and the secular. This humanism also contributed to the emergence of Protestantism and more diverse sacred music, now written for congregations to sing in the vernacular instead of Latin. The motet gradually developed a secular format with the addition of non-sacred and sometimes racy texts and was eventually equaled in importance by the **chanson** and **madrigal**, secular forms that took love, longing, and desire as their primary subjects. The madrigal became the dominant music of the Renaissance era, spreading from Italy (the geographic center of the Renaissance) all the way to Elizabethan England.

The texture of polyphonic music of the Renaissance is **imitative**, meaning a melody is repeated by a different voice (or by an instrument)—either exactly or with some variation—soon after it is introduced. Though not entirely new to Renaissance music, homophony (melody that uses chords to accompany a mel-ody) became more prevalent by the end of the period. The music of this time is closely tied to poetic texts with an emphasis on free-flowing harmony and the rhythms of natural speech. Composers used the technique of **word painting** to emphasize the importance of certain words. For example, "heaven" might be set to a high note or "surprise" might be accompanied by a sudden change in dynamics.

Like the Middle Ages, much of the music of the Renaissance period was written for voices. Both instrumental and vocal music had been important in the Middle Ages, but most *art music* prior to the Renaissance was vocal. Art music written for instruments—especially dance music—began to develop during the Renais-sance. Instrument-making technology was superior to that of the Middle Ages, and all our modern-day families of instruments of wind, brass, string, and percus-sion have precursors in the instruments of the Renaissance.

Art music was still performed mainly in courts and churches but much of it was now performed by amateur musicians as well as professionals and church men and women. Professional musicians worked not just as clergy but were also employed by towns and the powerful families who controlled Italy's city-states, such as the Medici family of Florence, introducing the **patronage system** where music was commissioned for specific courts or churches and was not readily available to the general public. Women played a more active role in performance in the Renaissance era because secular courtly music and music in the home became more common. Most members of the upper class learned to dance and sing as part of their education and were capable of playing several different instruments.

A woodcut by Hans Burgkmair of musicians of Emperor Maximilian. Courtesy Foto Marburg/Art Resource, NY.

We know the names of many composers of the time period since more of the population was literate and more records were kept than in the Middle Ages. Composers such as Guillaume Dufay (1397?–1474) introduced expressive harmonies and phrasing to the early Renaissance and was highly regarded in his own lifetime as an early composer of the homophonic motet. Josquin des Prez (c. 1450/1455–1521) wrote Masses and sacred motets for the court of Milan and the papal court in Rome, two centers of the artistic Renaissance. He also developed the chanson in the 16th century into an expressive form of vocal chamber music. Tielman Susato (c. 1510/1515–after 1570), a music publisher in the Netherlands, wrote some of the most renowned instrumental dance music of the Renaissance to accompany the great Renaissance interest in a variety of new dance forms. Palestrina (1525?–1594) reacted to Protestantism by bringing a simpler style to the music of the Catholic Church that led the musical style of the Counter-Reformation. And Claudio Monteverdi (1567–1643) used a more dissonant harmony, new to the time, as an expressive device filling his madrigals with elaborate ornamentation and moving musical style toward the drama of the Baroque era.

Patronage system: The commissioning of art for specific courts, churches, or cities usually to sponsor the living of a particular artist. Particularly important in the Renaissance and Classical eras.

Music of the Baroque Era, 1600–1750

- Key Stylistic Traits: increased importance of instrumental music, sudden and dramatic shifts in dynamics, elaborate displays of technical skill, energized rhythmic character, works that focused on one mood or emotion, predominant polyphonic texture

- Key Forms: orchestral suite, chorale, chorale prelude, cantata, oratorio, concerto, opera, fugue
- Key Places: Germany, Italy
- Key Composers: Claudio Monteverdi, Johann Sebastian Bach, George Frideric Handel

The Baroque era was more sacred in character than secular. Perhaps as a reaction to the humanism of the Renaissance, people in the Baroque turned their thoughts more to religion and an afterlife. The madrigal gave way to new forms that emphasized drama and religious fervor. Renaissance dance pieces were linked to create multi-movement **orchestral suites**, and many of the instruments of the **orchestra** as we know them today began in the Baroque with the development of such instruments as the violin and oboe. Instrumental music rose to the level of importance of vocal music. Sudden shifts in volume, the inclusion of dissonance, and elaborately ornamental displays of technical skill contribute to a sense of emotion. Baroque music was both polyphonic and homophonic, depending on the genre, but homophonic chord progressions become dominant in the Baroque and anchor even polyphonic compositions. Rhythm is perhaps the most important musical element of the time period. Baroque rhythm has a repetitive and driving character that energizes the music. Baroque music generally focuses on one mood or emotion in a musical work. This focus leads to repetition of melody and rhythm as a natural part of the composition.

The Mass continued to be important, as did the Protestant hymn (called a *chorale* in Germany in the Baroque period). Its simple, steady rhythms, four-part ranges (soprano, alto, tenor, bass) and vernacular language made it more singable than a chant or motet. Since hymns were usually accompanied by organs, organists of the day began to introduce the chorale to the congregation with a **chorale prelude** that embellished the hymn's melody with scales, trills, and other ornamentation in what became one of the most highly virtuosic forms of organ music of the period. Sacred music expanded to include such new musical genres as the **cantata**—a vocal form of Lutheran worship similar to the Mass that alternates between choir, soloists, and instrumentalists and is written for a specific Sunday based on the sacred text associated with that day's readings. Despite the sacred character of the era, or sometimes because of it, art music of the time also moved outside the church. The **oratorio**—a work with soloists, choir, and orchestra—tells a sacred story through singing rather than speech. Oratorios were composed not for performance in a church but to take advantage of the acoustics in a new venue, one that was usually larger than even the largest cathedral: the concert hall.

Concerts have existed since the beginning of music, but concerts in *public* concert halls as we know them today were first introduced in the Baroque era. With the establishment of a real middle class, music in the Baroque expanded past the court and church to become more available than ever before to the general public. New performance venues allowed the middle class access to art music, both sacred and secular, leading to the popularity of such new music genres as the orchestral suite, oratorio, and concerto—forms that would impact instrumental music for the next four hundred years.

The **concerto** is an instrumental composition that features one soloist. The form was first developed in the Baroque era and most composers of the time wrote

Orchestral suite: A piece of music popular in the Baroque era consisting of a series of short dance movements written for orchestra.

Orchestra: An instrumental ensemble consisting of string, woodwind, brass, and percussion instruments.

Chorale: Also called a hymn, a work originating in the Baroque era for use in the services of Protestant churches.

Chorale prelude: Originally an introduction to a chorale or hymn played on the organ, this type of music developed into a musical form intended to display the virtuosity of the organist.

Cantata: An extended work for use in the services of the Lutheran church based upon Bible texts. A cantata has multiple movements and is written for orchestra, chorus, and soloists.

Oratorio: A sacred work designed for the concert hall using choir, soloists, and orchestra.

Concerto: A multi-part work for instrumental soloists with ensemble accompaniment.

in this form. The most prolific composer of Baroque concertos was Antonio Vivaldi (1678–1741) who wrote over two hundred. The form of the concerto differs from other Baroque era works in that within its three-movement form different moods are musically explored.

The Baroque also saw the creation of **opera**, the earliest secular partnership of music and narrative in Western art music. Opera is a drama in which the characters sing their dialogue rather than speak it. Originally opera used only rhythmic sing-speech (called **recitative**). This was soon complemented by **aria** (solo song), and with aria came an era of musical stars, or **virtuosos**, that included women as professional musicians and composers.

The madrigalist Claudio Monteverdi (1567–1643) was the first well-known composer of opera, but the most important opera composer in the Baroque era was the German-born George Frideric Handel (1685–1759), who composed almost forty operas after he moved to London in 1712.

Much of the best instrumental music of the day was in the polyphonic form of **fugue**. In a fugue a primary melody (the **subject**) is introduced and then imitated by two or more melodies (that **answer** the subject). The subject is then taken up by each line while another melody—the counter-line, or **counterpoint**—is introduced. Interludes between the intermingling of the melody lines, called *episodes*, increase the audience's anticipation of the return of the melody.

Recognized as one of the greatest composers to have ever lived, Johann Sebastian Bach (1685–1750) is perhaps most closely associated with the fugue. His *Well-Tempered Clavier*—a book of forty-eight preludes and fugues for the keyboard—was written to train aspiring musicians in the Baroque and is still used today.

Music of the Classical Era, 1750–1820

- Key Stylistic Traits: melody-driven, elegant, balanced and restrained, full of humor and grace, symmetrical and regular, homophonic, secular
- Key Forms: concerto, symphony, string quartet, opera
- Key Places: Vienna
- Key Composers: Franz Joseph Haydn, Wolfgang Amadeus Mozart, Ludwig van Beethoven

Isaac Newton's discovery of the laws of gravity led to a scientific revolution that fundamentally changed the prevailing worldview. Reason was heralded over tradition (particularly church tradition) in almost all areas of life from medical practice to political reform. With the fall of monarchies and the continuing rise of the middle class, public concerts and concert halls became more important. For the first time in Western art music, secular music became more important than sacred music. The music of a period known as "The Age of Reason" would of course be balanced, elegant, restrained, and stately, and at the same time full of humor and grace. Classical era music has great variety and contrasts in mood and character within one musical work. Melodies were presented in symmetrical and regular phrases. The hard-driving rhythms of Baroque music were replaced with rhythmic structures that had regular accents. The texture of Classical era

Opera: A music drama using song rather than speech, developed in the early Baroque era.

Recitative: Used in oratorio and opera as a sort-of free rhythmical sung-speech. It is used to progress the drama forward much like dialogue in a play. It usually has a simple accompaniment without a steady rhythmic pulse.

Aria: A solo song with accompaniment used in opera to convey the thoughts and/ or emotions of characters. It usually has a full orchestral accompaniment.

Virtuoso: A highly skilled solo musician.

Fugue: A polyphonic piece of music created by imitation of a theme by all parts individually.

Subject: The primary melody of a fugue.

Answer: The subject of a fugue when repeated by voices subsequent to the initial presentation of the subject.

Counterpoint: A melody set in opposition to the subject of a fugue.

Episodes: Interludes between the intermingling of the melody lines of a fugue that increase the audience's anticipation of the return of the melody. See also **fugue**.

Composer Franz Joseph Haydn conducting an opera in the opera house at Esterházy Palace, Hungary. Courtesy SuperStock/SuperStock.

Dance suite: An instrumental form dating from the Renaissance era. The dance suite consisted of short, contrasting style dances often in pairs and was written for instruments.

Symphony: A multi-movement work for orchestra intended to be performed in the concert hall.

String quartet: Both a form in music similar to a symphony and an ensemble (two violins, viola, cello)

music is primarily homophonic; polyphony, so important from the Middle Ages through the Baroque, was much less used. The most important musical element was melody. Musical forms became longer and more complex through the development of melodic ideas.

The popularity of the opera continued into the Classical period, and it developed a comic style. The opera sinfonia (a sort of instrumental introduction to the main drama) and the orchestral **dance suites** of the Baroque evolved into the Classical multi-movement **symphony**. The orchestra became the most important musical ensemble of the period, and instrumental music was more important than vocal music, due in part to the popularity of the symphony and the continuing popularity of the concerto. Classical composers wrote symphonies, **string quartets** (for a group of four string players—almost always two violins, one viola, and one cello) and concerti to be performed at public concerts. In addition, new instruments in the Classical period made for the creation of new forms of music. The piano replaced Baroque keyboard instruments and solo piano sonatas and string quartets were performed not only in concerts but also in the home by amateurs—the ranks of whom had swelled as the Industrial Revolution and a population boom fueled the prosperity of a growing middle class.

The symphony of the Classical era was the focus of most composers' work and the growing importance of public concerts increased the need for such works. The Classical era symphony was most often a four-movement work contrasting in tempo and mood between the movements. In most cases the first movement of the symphony was fast and in a sonata form. The second movement was a slower movement in a contemplative or somber mood. Third movements of Classical symphonies were almost always in the dance form minuet and trio.

The finale, often a fast and energetic work, was similar in style and form to the opening movement.

Composers of the Austro-Hungarian Empire dominated in the early development of the symphony. Vienna was the unofficial musical capital of Europe in the mid and late 18th century, and composers such as Franz Joseph Haydn, Wolfgang Amadeus Mozart, and Ludwig van Beethoven became popular and important symphonic writers. The most important composers of the string quartet and symphony were Haydn, Mozart, and Beethoven.

Franz Joseph Haydn (1732–1809) served as an innovator—developing the symphony and string quartet into standardized forms—and was one of the first composers to be able to make a living from public performances of his works.

Wolfgang Amadeus Mozart (1756–1791) was an important contributor to almost all musical styles of his day, including symphonies, opera, concerti, keyboard music, and chamber music. There is hardly a genre that he did not influence.

Musicians consider Ludwig van Beethoven (1770–1827) to be one of the finest (if not *the* finest) composers of symphonies in the history of music. Like Mozart he spent much of his compositional life in Vienna. And, like Mozart, his virtuosity on the keyboard and violin made him popular. Unlike Haydn and Mozart, Beethoven never considered his music to be merely entertainment, and he spent a great deal of time perfecting a work before allowing it to be performed. This new style of composing meant that he wrote fewer symphonies than did his predecessors. Beethoven's works bridge the transitional period from the symmetry and refinement of the Classical era to the passion and fire of the Romantic age.

Music of the Romantic Era, 1820–1900

- Key Stylistic Traits: expressive, large-scale, nationalistic, dramatic, harmonic expansion, homophonic
- Key Forms: opera, symphony, program music, lieder, miniature forms, song cycles
- Key Places: Germany, Italy, Vienna, Paris
- Key Composers: Ludwig van Beethoven, Franz Schubert, Frédéric Chopin, Johannes Brahms, Richard Wagner, Pyotr Il'yich Tchaikovsky, Giuseppi Verdi, Gustav Mahler, and a host of others.

After Beethoven, music developed into a more expressive style referred to as *Romantic*. The Romantic spirit loved nature; it was expressive, passionate, and patriotic; it was interested in the exotic, the occult, even the macabre. Music of the time was dramatic, making use of wide dynamic ranges and expanded harmonies to express this spirit. Highly influenced by literature of the time composers used their music to be self-expressive. The orchestra expanded with the inclusion of new instruments like the tuba, piccolo, and harp, which composers were able to use in new combinations to create new tone colors. Most of the music of the time was homophonic in texture. Melodies became longer and lyrical with a wide range of pitches and dynamics.

Forms became both much longer, and at the same time, shorter compared with the Classical era. The symphony and opera still dominated music of the time. The great opera houses of Germany and Italy produced grandiose operas with larger sets, more spectacular costumes, and mythical plots. Likewise, the orchestra, which continued to be the most important "instrument" of composers, grew to over one hundred players as composers searched for new timbres and expressive gestures. The symphony grew into a work that could last for two hours and might consist of seven or eight movements. Much of the music of the time was programmatic in nature—meaning it sought to musically depict a narrative or inspire mental images in the listener. The orchestra became an important partner with the increasingly popular and expressive dance form, ballet. Both Romantic program music and ballet were often used to depict nationalism, so important to the Romantic spirit.

For entertainment many amateur musicians learned to play piano and sing at home. Composers began to write works for the salon that could be used to display their own compositional abilities and the technical abilities of the player. Salon culture saw its zenith in this time period, especially in Vienna and Paris. New forms emerged, such as the **lied** or **lieder** (a German art song based on a poetic text and created for a solo voice and piano) and the **song cycle**—a series of songs with a common poetic theme or a long story that runs throughout. These short songs and **miniature** piano pieces (that expressed one intense emotion and were performed in under five minutes) were important forms used by composers to express the Romantic spirit. Most miniature forms carried a title indicative of the nationality of the composer, and were often in popular or folk dance forms of different countries.

Two of the earliest composers of Romantic music, Franz Schubert (1797–1828) and Robert Schumann (1810–1856) developed both the art song and the song cycle. Others created miniature piano pieces as new forms, including Franz Liszt (1811–1886), Clara Wieck Schumann (1818–1896), and the French-Polish Frédéric Chopin (1810–1849), who settled in Paris after the Russian invasion of his homeland.

Italian composers, such as Giuseppi Verdi (1813–1901) and Giacomo Puccini (1858–1924), continued to write opera, just as Richard Wagner (1813–1883) became synonymous with opera in the new German Romantic style. Vienna remained a music center for many composers such as Wagner, Johannes Brahms (1833–1897), and Gustav Mahler (1866–1911). In France and Russia ballet emerged, especially with the works of Pyotr Il'yich Tchaikovsky (1840–1893).

Lied or **Lieder (pl):** The German word for solo song.

Song cycle: A set of songs that are connected in some manner, usually by the text.

Miniature: Refers to short forms popular in the Romantic era mostly written for solo piano and for performance in the home or recital hall.

Composer Franz Schubert shown playing the piano at a salon concert, by Moritz von Schwind. Courtesy INTERFOTO/Alamy.

Music of the Modern Era, 1900–Present

- Key Stylistic Traits: rhythmic complexity, emphasis on timbre and tone color, experimentation, eclecticism
- Key Forms: opera, symphony, musical theatre, jazz, "isms" of musical styles

- Key Places: Vienna, Russia, Paris, New York
- Key Composers: Claude Debussy, Maurice Ravel, Arnold Schoenberg, Igor Stravinsky, George Gershwin, Duke Ellington, Dmitri Shostakovich, Benjamin Britten, Charles Ives, Aaron Copland, Leonard Bernstein, Philip Glass, and many others

The experimentation that has existed in this time is like no other. Rocked by world wars in the first half of the 20th century, many composers turned away from the traditions of previous eras. Composers no longer wrote strictly in the forms of the Classical or Romantic eras, the harmonies of the past were rejected, and the importance of melody gave way to other musical elements. The system of tonality (the practice of writing a work around one scale or note center) begun in the Baroque era underwent a series of shockwaves that eventually led to its decline. Rhythm and tone color (the particular quality of a musical sound) became the most important musical elements as composers of the early 20th century no longer worked with set forms and works dominated by key. Even though forms like opera, symphony, string quartet, song, march, and so on, all continued to be written, form itself was no longer the unifying factor in music that it once was. Composers were free to write in any style, in any form, for any group of musicians they wished. Though influenced by one another, the 20th century composer is nothing if not an individual.

Impressionism, expressionism, serialism, minimalism, and a variety of "neo-" "isms" (neoclassicism, neoromanticism) emerge to make eclecticism perhaps the most distinguishing characteristic of this time.

- **Impressionism:** Unaccented floating rhythms and harmonies based on exotic scales give this style, championed by Claude Debussy (1862–1918) and Maurice Ravel (1875–1837), a lyrical, dreamy character.
- **Expressionism:** Clashing and dissonant tones and harmonies are used to express intense suffering and emotion. This style is most associated with Arnold Schoenberg (1874–1951), who used extreme dynamic ranges, melodies based on his own composition system, and harsh accents to create distorted and expressive sounds.
- **Serialism:** A compositional method that grew out of expressionism as a way to organize the twelve tones that are used in atonal music. In serialism all twelve pitches of the Western scale are ordered in a row without repetition such that one note is not emphasized over others.
- **Neoclassicism:** An effort to integrate the experiments of Impressionism and Expressionism into traditional Baroque and Classical musical forms—such major composers as Igor Stravinsky (1882–1971) have combined modern-era tonalities with early forms.
- **Neoromanticism:** A return to tonality and dramatic expression in music marks this style, which for the past three decades has dominated film music with its lush sound, sweeping rhythmic gestures, and memorable melodies.
- **Minimalism:** Emphasizing the repetition of melodic, harmonic, and/or rhythmic motifs with little or no variation over long periods of time, this style is found in the music of Philip Glass (b. 1937), who has brought minimalism to the film world in scores for such films as *The Truman Show.*

Impressionism: Unaccented floating rhythms and harmonies based on exotic scales. This style of music was inspired by the movement in visual art of the same name.

Expressionism: A style of music of the mid-20th century characterized by hyper-expression, abandonment of tonal centers, extreme ranges used in melodic structures, forceful accents and abrupt dynamic changes.

Serialism: A compositional technique of the mid-20th century led by composer Arnold Schoenberg that treats all twelve pitches of the Western scale equally. The technique is a highly organized style of writing music.

Neoclassicism: An effort to integrate the experiments of impressionism and expressionism into traditional Baroque and Classical musical forms.

Neoromanticism: Music of the 20th century in which composers returned to the formal and tonal structures of music of the Romantic era.

Minimalism: Music based upon the repetition of melodic, harmonic, and/or rhythmic motifs with little or no variation.

During the 20th century art music and popular music developed in different directions. As art music became more complex and esoteric, technology made popular music much more available. This created a chasm between the two styles and generations of listeners who heard one or the other style, but usually not both. Composers, open to experimentation, blended popular forms of music into their works. The American Charles Ives (1894–1954) and the British Benjamin Britten (1913–1976), among others, brought folk songs into compositions that included modernist compositional methods.

Jazz also had an impact on traditional classical music in the 20th century. From early in the 1900s some of the world's greatest composers were intrigued by this new genre. European composers such as Maurice Ravel, Claude Debussy, and Igor Stravinsky wrote music that blended jazz into their own compositional styles. The syncopations of the rhythmic structures of jazz seemed to be the most common element that classical composers incorporated into their works. In the United States George Gershwin (1898–1937) and Duke Ellington (1899–1974) successfully combined jazz and classical styles. Gershwin also wrote musical theater, film scores, and opera and made a determined attempt to bring the jazz idiom into the concert hall with works that fused the jazz, popular, and classical musical worlds such as his best-known work, "Rhapsody in Blue."

Finally, much music today is different from all of the other music studied in the text—it is not written for live performance. Computer programs and **synthesizers** make it possible for amateur musicians to compose and hear their own music. Popular and film music today is intended to be recorded in the studio. Composers today can use both live musicians and electronic sounds to create music. And, in rock concerts or films, the composer and producer can cause different sounds to be heard from different speakers in the movie theater or stadium. Film scores can contain acoustic music and sound effects, and both

Synthesizer: An electronic device that records and manipulates sounds electronically.

Composer Tod Machover in his electronic studio. Courtesy Boston Globe via Getty Images.

the electronic and live musician sounds can be manipulated by recording techniques to create sounds not heard in the live world.

The Modern era is a secular age and secular music continues to be more important than sacred music. The rise of technology has had a large impact not only on the delivery systems of music but on the composition of music as well. Music has never been more available than it is today, and more people than ever before make music a part of their daily lives.

✓ **Audio Review:** Go to Dashboard to listen to Professor Bailey discuss how music has changed over time.

✓ **How Am I Doing?** Go to Dashboard to test your understanding of this material by taking the chapter quiz.

Dashboard

KEY TERMS

Answer	Lied or Lieder	Sacred
Aria	Liturgy	Sacred motet
Cantata	Madrigal	Secular
Chanson	Mass	Serialism
Chant	Miniature	Song cycle
Chorale	Minimalism	String quartet
Chorale prelude	Minnesinger	Subject
Concerto	Neoclassicism	Symphony
Counterpoint	Neoromanticism	Synthesizer
Dance suite	Opera	Troubadour, trouvères,
Episodes	Orchestra	*trovatore*
Expressionism	Orchestral suite	Vernacular
Fugue	Organum	Virtuoso
Imitative	Patronage system	Word painting
Impressionism	Recitative	

UNIT 2

Music of the Church

Sacred music is performed today both in the concert hall and in places of worship. To be considered sacred music the work does not have to be originally written for use in a worship service. Generally, we label something a sacred work when its intent is to express a particular religious belief or if it was written for performance in a worship hall. All cultures have created music celebrating the spiritual and the physical aspects of life. In Western culture these musics are similar in style and come from the same roots.

Most Western art music and popular music owes much to the development of the early music of the Christian church. The chant, the Mass, and later—during the movement toward Protestantism—the hymn, have all come down to us from the Medieval, Renaissance, and Baroque periods. And they are still written and performed today. Most of the important forms of Western music that we study in this text have their roots in the liturgical music of the Catholic and Lutheran churches.

Music for Use in the Worship Hall

In the last four hundred or so years of the Middle Ages (1000–1400) great cathedrals and universities were founded across Europe. Much sacred music was originally written for and first heard in a place of worship. Its primary intent would have been either contemplative or uplifting—sometimes both. A good deal of the early music that we will study was written for large cathedrals. These buildings sometimes have special acoustical properties that composers use in their compositions. As we will see in this unit, the composers at St. Mark's Basilica in Venice exploited the church's acoustics and placement of the musicians as part of their compositions. Such works do not sound the same when performed somewhere

Opening image: Notre Dame Cathedral, Paris. © king_tut. Courtesy iStock.

Interior of St. Mark's Basilica, Venice. © rusm. Courtesy iStock.

else. Most large cathedrals or churches have choir lofts or stalls, organ lofts, and sanctuaries where music is performed. A choir loft is a special performance space where a choral group sings. In many cathedrals such a performance space exists at the front of the church near the altar. Many cathedrals and churches are built in the shape of a cross, affording the architect the opportunity to place choir lofts in four very distinct sections of the church. Most cathedrals have only one organ, sometimes a massive instrument with hundreds of wind pipes. These instruments can be placed anywhere in the church but many times are at the rear of the church, often over the main entrance. The organ keyboard and pedalboard are not always in the same location as the pipes. This allows for the special placement of some pipes of the organ or multiple keyboard stations. Disbursement of pipes around the cathedral is unusual; most often the pipes are at least grouped together by size, if not all in the same place. The sanctuary is a rather general term for the altar area and main congregation area of the church. In many cases musicians are placed at the front of the sanctuary so that the congregation can see them as well as hear them perform. The acoustical properties of large churches sometimes fool our eyes and ears. Seemingly, the music comes from a location in the church where there are no musicians. This use of acoustics in composition lends to the mystical quality that is present in much sacred music.

Some sacred music has been written that was not intended for performance as part of a worship service. This type of sacred music is studied in Unit 3 and most such works are written for large chorus and orchestra.

What to Listen for in Sacred Music

When listening to sacred music consider the following:

- Be aware of the effect of the acoustic "echo" that amplifies the music and contributes to a sense of grandeur.
- When listening to music in a place of worship, listen to the mood created by a particular piece of sacred music. Is it contemplative, uplifting, brooding?
- When in the church service does music appear?
- Who performs the music? In many churches both the musicians and the celebrant (priest, minister, etc.) perform music of different styles.
- What purpose is the music serving? Does it simply fill a place in the service where non-liturgical things are happening? Or, is it a focal point in the service?
- How is the music accompanied, or is it? What instruments are used?
- And, finally, what do the people attending the service do while the music is performed? Do they participate, or listen, or both?

Music of the Catholic Church

LEARNING OBJECTIVES

- Demonstrate an understanding of the development of chant, organum, motet, and Mass.

- Name important composers of early Catholic Church music.

- Explain the structure of the Mass as it pertains to musical form.

- Identify through listening examples monophonic, polyphonic, and homophonic music.

Key Concepts: chant, liturgy, Mass, melismatic, motet, organum, syllabic

Opening image: Example of the beauty of illustrated manuscripts of the Middle Ages. Courtesy
EmmePi Images/Alamy.

Front view and towers of Chartres Cathedral, France. Courtesy silky/Shutterstock.

Where It's Playing

Much of the music of this chapter was written for performance in a specific church and often the acoustics of the building played a role in how the composer structured the music. The great cathedrals of Europe are massive structures made mostly of stone. The soaring rounded ceilings combined with the hard surfaces of the stone create a special resonant acoustic. Often the sound in these cathedrals reverberates well after the initial sound production, creating overlapping layers of sound. Composers learned to make use of reverberation and echo within a space as part of their compositions. For example, the composers who worked at St. Mark's Basilica in Venice in the late Renaissance period created polychoral music, making use of the distance between the different choir lofts throughout the basilica to create echo effects. The music they created sounds very different outside the specific setting for which it was written.

The chant, motet, and Mass remain important in the great Catholic cathedrals. And, chant is still a part of most religious services of the Jewish, Christian, and Muslim religions. However, in most Christian churches today it is rare to hear the music studied in this chapter. It is more often heard in the recital or concert hall. Since these halls have special acoustics, the music retains more of its original sound there than it might in a modern community church, which usually does not have the acoustic qualities of a great cathedral. For an idea of the size and scope of a cathedral visit the textbook Helpful Resources page for Chapter 4 for a link to a site about cathedrals, or search the web for the home sites of cathedrals such as Chartres Cathedral, Salisbury Cathedral, St. Vitrus Cathedral, or St. Stephens Cathedral. Pay particular attention to the architectural plan of the cathedral and the size of the nave and the crossing. Note that all the surfaces are made of stone and that the ceilings are curved.

Sacred music has at least two purposes; to create a mood or atmosphere, and to deliver a religious message. Both of these caused many early composers to create music that has a mystical, serene quality; this is especially true of chant. When listening to chant, it is important to keep in mind the purpose of the music. Chant is simple in structure because the words were more important than the music. As you listen, note the smooth quality of most of the vocal lines, the limited range and lack of large leaps between notes, and pay attention to the dynamic range. Much of this music has a very limited dynamic range. Think about how the dynamics might have been impacted by the cathedrals in which the music was first performed. In addition to limited melodic and dynamic ranges, much of this music lacks an easily identifiable rhythmic pulse. This lack of a steady beat is another characteristic that adds to the mystical quality and provides long melodic lines that seem to float, rather than march along.

Noting these characteristics makes this early music much easier to understand and appreciate. These ancient Christian chants have their roots in earlier Muslim chants and Jewish cantors.

Chant—the Basis of Western Sacred Music

How did Catholic church music develop?

The music of the Catholic Church has had a great impact on Western European art music since the Middle Ages. Most of the basic notation and fundamental structures in our music today can be traced to music originally written for Catholic services. This early sacred music serves as the foundation for important forms of music to come, including the symphony, opera, song, and others.

The earliest example of Catholic music, and the oldest form of Western art music still practiced today, is the chant. Chant is the official music of the Catholic Church and is the basis for most Western sacred music. Chant, also called plainchant, is an unaccompanied monophonic vocal melody. Hundreds of chants were created in the early church and Pope Gregory I (540–604) and Pope Gregory II (669–731) are believed to have ordered them assembled, codified, and standardized. Because of this, chant is also often called **Gregorian chant**.

Gregorian chant: Specifically, chant for the Catholic Church liturgy named for Pope Gregory I.

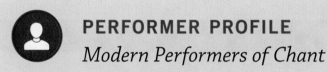

PERFORMER PROFILE
Modern Performers of Chant

Is chant ever performed outside a church service?

Chant was almost unheard by the everyday music listener after the Medieval and Renaissance eras. But, in the past two decades a revival of interest has occurred sparked by recordings. The Benedictine monks of Santo Domingo de Silos released a series of chant albums beginning in 1994, the first of which, *Chant*, topped at number three on the Billboard 200 charts. The Abbey of Santo Domingo de Silos, where the monks work and live, is located in northern Spain and traces its roots to the mid-900s. The album *Chant* was recorded as an LP in the monastery in 1973 and was re-released on CD in 1994, selling more than 6 million copies. The success of the CD led to others, including *Chant II* and *Chant Noel*. The monastery itself was an important center of learning in the Middle Ages, housing one of the leading and oldest libraries in Europe. The Chorus of Monks at the monastery began recording in 1957 and is recognized as one of the best male choirs in the Catholic Church.

Dashboard

RESEARCH

Church modes: A system of organizing the seven tones of a scale in varying sequences of half and whole steps.

Melismatic: A melody that has two or more musical notes per syllable.

Syllabic: A melody that has one music note per syllable.

Ordinary: Parts of the Mass that remain the same each day.

Proper: Parts of the Mass that change appropriate to the time of the liturgical year.

Dashboard

EXPLORE

Chant is used to sing, rather than recite, sections of the church liturgy. Chants are nonmetrical with a free-sounding rhythm. They are based not on our modern-day scales but on **church modes**, another system of organizing the twelve tones of the Western scale. Chants move in stepwise fashion with few leaps between adjoining notes, making them easy to sing. This monophonic vocal style, combined with a lack of rhythmic pulse and stepwise motion, creates an atmosphere of mysticism and contemplation that appropriately accompanies prayer.

Plainchants are either **melismatic** or **syllabic**. A chant that is syllabic has one note for each syllable. A melismatic chant has two or more musical notes per syllable.

Chants, like most music of the Middle Ages, were originally not written down. By the middle of the first millennium there were so many chants that a celebrant couldn't remember them all. Out of this need for a memory aid came the beginnings of our modern musical notation system.

Chants are used in the Catholic Church in two primary types of services: the offices and the Mass. The offices are a set of eight services said and sung by priests daily from sunrise to sunset. The Mass is a re-enactment of the Last Supper of Jesus Christ. Certain parts of the Mass, called the **Ordinary**, remain the same each day and other sections, called the **Proper**, change appropriate to the time of the liturgical year.

Chant is common in most cultures. It is commonly used in the Jewish and Islamic religions. In fact, much Christian chant is derived from Jewish music. Both religions use chanting of the psalms from the Old Testament. The text of the Koran is chanted in Islam. Chants were also common in the religious ceremonies of the American Indians. Chants were written by men *and* women who served the church.

LISTENING GUIDE 4.1

"RESURREXI, ET ADHUC TECUM SUM," *Alleluia from Mass for Easter*, *anonymous, composed unknown*

This chant is sung during the procession into the church. The text is taken from a psalm. The chant is mostly melismatic with four- or five-note melismas.

Dashboard

HEAR STREAMING AUDIO ON DASHBOARD

What to Listen For

- Listen for the limited range of the chant, making it easy for most people to sing.
- Listen for how the smooth and gentle tone quality, combined with the lack of regular rhythm, lends to the mystical sound of the music.
- Listen for the lack of dynamic change used in the chant.
- Listen for a mixture of syllabic and melismatic styles in this chant.

Following is a sample of the chant in modern notation:

TIMING	TEXT	TRANSLATION
0:00	Resurrexi, et adhuc tecum sum, alleluia	I arose and am still with thee, alleluia
0:23	posuisti super me manum tuam, alleluia	thou hast laid thy hand upon me, alleluia
0:50	mirabilis facta est scientia tua,	thy knowledge is become wonderful,
1:06	alleluia, alleluia	Alleluia, alleluia
1:26	Domine, probasti me, et cognovisti me	Lord, thou hast proved me, and known me
1:36	tu cognovisti sessionem meam,	thou knowest my sitting down
1:41	et resurrecctionem meam.	and my rising up.

If You Liked That, Try This

"O Greenest Branch," Hildegard of Bingen
"Vere dignum," from Mass on Whit Sunday
"Dies irae"

YouTube videos: search on keywords

Hildegard von Bingen—O pastor animarum (plainchant)
Chanticleer—Mysteria—Gregorian Chants
Chant—The Benedictine Monks of Santo Domingo de Silos
Gregorian—Losing My Religion

Remember to add to your personal playlist any of these samples that you like.

PERFORMANCE PRACTICE
Women in Early Music

Were there women musicians in the Middle Ages?

As you will note throughout this book there are few accounts of the music of women prior to the 20th century, especially when considering sacred music. This doesn't mean that women were not musicians. Instead, societal pressures and mores confined their work to the home and, in Hildegard of Bingen's (1098–1179) case, to the convent. Hildegard was born in Germany the tenth child of a noble Catholic family. Her parents gave her as a **tithe** to the Catholic Church at the age of eight and she took vows to become a Benedictine nun at fourteen or fifteen. She eventually became abbess of the convent by age thirty-eight. Her success as an abbess led to the construction of a new convent in Bingen, Germany, where she remained throughout her life. Hildegard was a mystic who claimed to have visions that related to her instructions and ideas of God. Her book recounting these visions, *Scivias*, was at the time influential enough that it was known by the pope and England's King Henry II. Though never officially canonized, in Germany she is considered a saint to this day.

As well as music, Hildegard also wrote poetry; scholarly treatises on science, theology, and medicine; and plays. She is credited with having written one of the earliest morality plays, *Play of Virtues*, a work extolling the virtues of charity, humility, chastity, and fear of God. Hildegard is the earliest composer to whom we can definitively credit a large body of musical works. She wrote over seventy chants. Her most famous work of music is a collection of religious poetry set to music called *Symphony of the Harmony of Celestial Revelations*.

Perhaps this tradition of male-dominated music performance and composition began with music of the Catholic Church. Though women composed and performed in convents and abbeys the Catholic Church's recognition of only male priests influenced its patronage of male composers over women. Churchmen were the leaders of choirs at the important cathedrals and most lay composers who worked for the church were men. Much of the history of the period was recorded by monks in monasteries, who were sheltered from contact with women. These factors all contributed to the general neglect of women in music in the beginnings of Western art music that continued for almost a thousand years. It seems to have taken until the mid-to-late 20th century before society began to accept women as important creators of music. It is no coincidence that this is also the century in which women gained political power, general economic freedom separate from men, and many basic legal rights.

Dashboard
RESEARCH

Tithe: One tenth of something. Often used as an expression of voluntary payment to a church.

Organum Grows from Embellished Chant

Was chant the only kind of music used in the early Catholic Church?

Church music developed and became more complex throughout the Middle Ages. An early musical development from chant is **organum**, a type of music used in Catholic **liturgy** (sacred rite spoken or sung within a service) that combines a chant and at least one other melody simultaneously. Music of this type that has more than one melodic line is generically called polyphony. The earliest type of organum used a second line starting on a different pitch and moving parallel to the chant. This type of music began sometime between 700 and 900 in France. Around 1100 the second melody became rhythmically independent of the chant, allowing for rhythmic variety between the two lines. In this form of organum the chant is usually the lower-pitched line. Léonin and Pérotin (ca. 1150–1200) were important early composers of organum and other polyphonic music who worked at Notre Dame Cathedral in Paris.

Organum: Music used in Catholic liturgy that combines a chant and at least one other melody simultaneously.

Liturgy: A sacred rite within a service, sometimes spoken and sometimes sung.

LISTENING GUIDE 4.2

"VIDERUNT OMNES,"
Léonin, composed date unknown, late 12th century

This example of two-part organum was written for performance on Christmas day in the Notre Dame Cathedral in Paris. The piece has a triple meter feel, which refers to the Holy Trinity of the Catholic Church.

Dashboard

HEAR STREAMING AUDIO ON DASHBOARD

What to Listen For

- Listen for how the low voice drones the chant as the high voice sings melismas on the same word.
- Listen for how the two voices change syllables simultaneously.
- Listen for the pure tone quality of the vocalists. This kind of singing lacks **vibrato**.

Vibrato: An audible pulsation on a particular tone not intended to produce a rhythm but instead to give color to the tone by slightly altering the intonation of the note higher and lower.

TIMING	TEXT	TRANSLATION
0:00	Viderunt omnes fines terrae	All the ends of the earth have seen
1:28	Salutare Dei nostril	the salvation of our God.
1:41	Jubilate Deo omnis terra.	Make a joyful noise unto the Lord, all the earth.

If You Liked That, Try This

"Rejoice, Virgin Mary," Pérotin
"Alleluia: Diffusa est gratia," Pérotin

YouTube videos: search on keywords
Léonin: organum duplum
Léonin: viderunt omnes

Remember to add to your personal playlist any of these samples that you like.

Motet Develops Outside the Liturgy

How did church music influence music outside the church?

Motet: A three or more part form developed in the late Middle Ages based on a chant.

With the development of organum, composers and performers realized that more complicated works were possible. Soon the **motet** was created, a polyphonic choral work usually with a Latin text. The text used for motets is traditionally not part of the Ordinary of the Mass but some other sacred text. The motet became one of the most important vocal forms of the Middle Ages and was used in both sacred and secular music. The secular motet was important in the development of the Renaissance madrigal, which is discussed in Unit 4. Motets were performed in churches and courts and were more important in secular music than in sacred.

The motet has at least three separate lines, or melodies, usually more. It is based upon a chant, but the chant is often disguised by a slow rhythmic pattern or obscured by the complexity of the other voices. Two or more voices sing above the chant. Sometimes these voices use different texts (polytextual), and they often are in different languages (polylingual). The chant itself is always in Latin. The upper lines of a motet are usually highly melismatic and complex.

***Procession in St. Mark's Square*, by Bentile Bellini.** Courtesy Erich Lessing/Art Resource, NY.

Motet developed in France in the late Middle Ages in a time referred to in musical history as the **Ars Nova**—about 1300–1450. The leading composers of motet were Philippe de Vitry (1291–1361), Guillaume de Machaut (1300–1377), and Guillaume Dufay (ca. 1400–1474).

Who were the important composers of early music?

Guillaume de Machaut

Machaut is one of the first composers of whom we have dependable information. He was born in France and was well recognized in his day as both a poet and a musician. He was a theologian but worked mainly for courts. Perhaps because of his travels around Europe as musician to King John I of Bohemia, his music became widely known. Machaut was also a writer of courtly poetry, much of which he used in his vocal music. He is thought to be the first composer to regularly sign his name to musical compositions. Hence, today we know more of his works than others of the time. Machaut was primarily prominent as a composer at Notre Dame Cathedral in Rheims and served two kings of France. Machaut was the leading composer of the Ars Nova period of the late Middle Ages, when rhythm, harmony, and counterpoint were developed from music that sounds ancient and foreign to us into music that still influences today's sounds. He wrote one of the best-known works of his time, the Notre Dame Mass.

Ars Nova: Literally "new art," commonly referred to as the years ca. 1300–1450 during which time music was in transition from the style of the Middle Ages to that of the Renaissance.

Machaut receiving from Nature three of her children: Sense, Rhetoric, and Music. Courtesy Snark/Art Resource, NY.

Guillaume Dufay with fellow composer Gilles Binchois from Martin LeFranc's poem *Le champion des dames*. Courtesy Hipix/Alamy.

Guillaume Dufay

Guillaume Dufay was born in a part of France that is in modern-day Belgium. He spent a good deal of his professional life in Italy but ended his career at the French cathedral of Cambrai. Some of his works abandon the more polyphonic and imitative style of the early motet for a homophonic sound. In the High Renaissance period (beginning around 1500) that followed Dufay's work, the motet became primarily homophonic in character. The focus of these works was on a single melodic line with harmonization, creating a much more choral and choral-sounding composition than the early polyphonic motets. Dufay was an early important composer of the homophonic motet.

LISTENING GUIDE 4.3

"AVE MARIS STELLA,"
Dufay, composed date unknown

This hymn-like work is based upon the chant "Ave maris stella" and the piece begins with a statement of the chant. The setting alternates between plainchant and harmonized chant through six stanzas. The music for stanzas 2, 4, and 6 (the stanzas that Dufay harmonized) is the same with different text. The text was well known in the Renaissance because it was in praise of the Virgin Mary, who by that time had become a major figure in the church's year.

Dashboard
HEAR STREAMING AUDIO ON DASHBOARD

What to Listen For

- Listen for the top voice in the harmonization. It is an embellishment of the original chant.
- Listen for how the setting alternates between the free rhythm of the chant and the regular rhythm of the harmonized stanzas.

The work ends with an "Amen," which became typical of later hymns.

TIMING	FORM: STROPHIC	TEXTURE	TEXT	TRANSLATION
0:00	Stanza 1	Plainchant	Ave maris stella	Hail, star of the ocean
0:06			Dei Mater alma,	bountiful Mother of God,
0:10			Atque semper Virgo,	And ever a Virgin
0:14			Felix coeli porta.	Our blessed portal to heaven.
0:20	Stanza 2	Harmonized chant	Summens illud Ave	May that blessed "Ave"
0:26			Gabrielis ore,	From Gabriel's mouth
0:30			Funda nos in pace	Grant us peace,
0:34			Mutans Hevae nomen.	Giving Eva a new name.

STANZA 3	STANZA 4	STANZA 5	STANZA 6	STANZA 7	AMEN
0:42	1:02	1:23	1:44	2:06	2:26
Plainchant	Harmonized chant	Plainchant	Harmonized chant	Plainchant	

If You Liked That, Try This

"Deo gratias," by Johannes Ockeghem
"Vasilissa, ergo gaude," by Dufay
"Vergena bella," by Dufay

YouTube videos: search on keywords
Guillaume Dufay (1397–1474)—Vasilissa, ergo gaude
Guillaume Dufay (1397–1474)—Missa se la face ay pale: Kyrie
Sanctus—Ockeghem (1420–1497)—Requiem

Remember to add to your personal playlist any of these samples that you like.

Josquin des Prez

Josquin des Prez was another important composer of motets later in the Renaissance era. He was born in northern France (now part of Belgium), but worked as a composer in the court of Milan and the papal court in Rome, two centers of the artistic Renaissance. In his time Josquin was the best-known composer in Europe. His works were published (unusual at the time) and widely distributed. Despite the interest in his music in his own time little is known about his life. Even his birth year is an educated guess. Music historians have only recently discovered that his family surname was Lebloitte and that des Prez was a sort of nickname. Josquin wrote in all the important forms of his time but he is best known today for his Renaissance Masses and sacred motets. He also developed the chanson in the 16th century into an expressive form of vocal chamber music. Josquin's "Ave Maria . . . Virgo Serena" is an example of the polyphonic motet style.

Flemish composer Josquin des Prez.
Courtesy World History Archive/Alamy.

LISTENING GUIDE 4.4

"AVE MARIA . . . VIRGO SERENA,"
Josquin, composed ca. 1475

This polyphonic motet has a varied texture of two to four voices. Much of the work is imitative in style and Josquin uses imitation between single voices and pairs of voices. The motet is in three sections in an ABA' form. The first and third sections are in duple meter and have a peaceful quality. The middle section is much more animated and is in triple meter. At times the voices move in a homorhythmic fashion, in contrast to the more prevalent polyphonic style.

Dashboard

**HEAR STREAMING AUDIO
ON DASHBOARD**

What to Listen For

- Listen for the change of meter between sections 1 and 2, and 2 and 3.
- Listen for the imitation between voices.
- Listen for the closing section in which the voices are not imitative and move in unison rhythms in a homophonic style.

TIMING	FORM: ABA'	TEXT	TRANSLATION	WHAT TO LISTEN FOR
0:00	A	Ave Maria, gratia plena dominus tecum, Virgo serena	Hail Mary, full of grace, the Lord is with you, serene Virgin.	The beginning section is in duple meter and is primarily imitative in style.
1:21 1:44		Ave cuius conceptio, solemni plena gaudio, coelestia terrestria nova replete laetitia.	Hail, whose conception, full of solemn joy, fills Heaven and Earth with new joy.	
2:23 2:49		Ave, cuius nativitas nostra solemnitas, ut Lucifer lux oriens, verum solem praeveniens.	Hail, whose birth brought us joy, like Lucifer, the morning star, went before the true sun.	Pairs of voices in imitative style.
3:26		Ave, pia humilitas. Sine viro fecunditas, cuius annuntiatio nostra fuit salvatio.	Hail, pious humility, without original sin, whose Annunciation was our salvation.	Some homorhythmic texture.
4:11	B	Ave, vera virginatas, immaculata castitas, cuius purificatio nostra fuit purgatio.	Hail, true virginity, immaculate chastity, whose purification was our cleansing.	The B section is set in triple meter with much regular homorhythmic style.

4:46	A′	Ave praeclara omnibus angelicis virtutibus, cuius assumptio nostra glorificatio.	Hail, first in all angelic virtues, whose Assumption was our glorification.	The A′ section returns to duple meter and is in a more imitative, polyphonic style.
6:09		O mater Dei, memento mei.	O Mother of God, remember me.	Pause followed by a brief homophonic section that ends with an "Amen."
6:33		Amen.	Amen.	

If You Liked That, Try This

"Exsultate Deo," Giovanni Pierluigi da Palestrina
"Sicut servus," Palestrina
"Quant en moi," Machaut

YouTube videos: search on keywords
Josquin des Prez "Qui habitat"
Johannes Ciconia—Latin Motets (4/5) Venetia mundi splendor

Remember to add to your personal playlist any of these samples that you like.

The Secular Motet

Begun as a sacred piece of music in the Middle Ages, the motet was transformed by Guillaume Machaut and the Renaissance composer Josquin des Prez into a secular form of vocal chamber music. A motet is usually for four voices and is polyphonic and imitative in style. Unlike most other vocal forms, the motet sometimes has two or more texts sung simultaneously (polytextual), sometimes in different languages. The development of secular vocal music owes much to the motet. Begun as a sacred form based on chants of the Catholic Church, this form gradually developed into a secular genre with the addition of nonsacred and sometimes racy or suggestive texts. These new texts set in motet form were the beginning of secular vocal art music. However, by the early to mid-Renaissance the motet had returned to its sacred roots as the madrigal supplanted it as the important secular vocal form.

LISTENING GUIDE 4.5

"QUANT EN MOI,"
Guillaume de Machaut, composed unknown

"Quant en moi" is a polyphonic motet set for three voices. The lowest voice is a fragment of a chant and it is usually played by an instrument but could also be sung. The top two voices are love poems and they use different texts. The motet uses two compositional devices, the **hocket** and **isorhythm**. Each of the stanzas of this motet has a different melody but all have the same overall rhythm.

Dashboard

**HEAR STREAMING AUDIO
ON DASHBOARD**

Hocket: A compositional device in which one voice rhythmically and melodically imitates the other in alternation. Often described as a musical hiccup.

Isorhythm: The compositional technique of using the same rhythmic pattern with different melodies.

What to Listen For

- Listen for how Machaut combines two poems—one in the alto voice and another in the soprano. The poems are sung simultaneously.
- Listen for the lowest voice, a portion of a chant taken from Easter time. Most motets, including secular ones like this, included a chant fragment as one of the lines. The text is in Latin, "Amara valde."
- Notice how the melodies of the different stanzas are not the same, but contain similar rhythmic structure from stanza to stanza. This compositional technique is called isorhythm.
- Listen for the echo sections between the two upper voices. These sections are called hockets and are part of the isorhythmic scheme. The hockets provide places where the melodies coincide and interact rather than compete.
- Listen for the type of rhythm used in the motet. The swaying, almost singsong rhythm continually rushes forward but does not produce the sort of beat that we encounter in today's vocal secular music.

TIMING	FORM	TEXT	TRANSLATION	WHAT TO LISTEN FOR
0:00	Stanza 1	*Voice 1* Quant en moi vint premierement	When I was first visited by	The soprano and alto poems use different texts and melodies that begin simultaneously. They are accompanied by the chant fragment in long notes. The vocalists present a smooth, clear tone quality even on the complex rhythms.
		Amours, si tres doucettement	Love, he so very sweetly	
		Me vost mon cuer enamourer	Captured my heart;	
		Que d'un regart me fist present,	He gave me a glance as a gift.	
		Et tres amoureus sentiment	And with amorous sentiments.	
		Me donna avuec doulz penser,	He presented me with this sweet idea:	

		Voice 2 Amour et biauté partaite	Thanks to love and consummate beauty	
0:30	Hocket 1	*Voice 1* Espoir, d'avoir *Voice 2* Doubter, celer	To hope, to have Fearing, concealing	The hocket is an echo two-note rhythmic pattern in which the two voices interact.
0:35	Stanza 1 cont.	*Voice 1* Merci sans refuser Mais onques en tout mon vivant Hardement ne me vost donner *Voice 2* Me font parfaitement.	Grace, and no rejections But never in my entire life Was boldness a gift he meant for me. Are what entirely consume me.	
0:54	Stanza 2	*Voice 1* E si me fait en desirant Penser si amoureusement Que, par force de desirer, Ma joie convient en tourment Muer, se je n'ay hardement, Las! et je n'en puis recourvrer *Voice 2* Et vrais desir, qui m'a fait	And if, in my passion, He makes me think so amorously That, thanks to desire My joy becomes torment Must turn, since I am not bold. Alas! I cannot save myself And true desire, that has made me	The rhythmic structure remains like that of stanza 1 but the melodic lines differ.
1:25	Hocket 2	Qu'amours, secours De vous, cuer doulz	For love, no help Love you, dear heart	The hocket rhythm is the same but the melodic pitches are new.
1:29	Stanza 2 cont.	*Voice 1* Ne me vuet nul preseter, Qui en ses las si durement Me tient que n'en puis eschaper. *Voice 2* Amer sans finement,	Will lend me Love, who holds me so tightly In his grasp that I cannot escape. For ever and ever.	

If You Liked That, Try This

"De ma dolour," Machaut
"Fine amor," Machaut
"Quam pulchra es," John Dunstable

Remember to add to your personal playlist any of these samples that you like.

Mass: The Most Important Sacred Music Form

How is the music of the Mass structured?

Liturgy refers to the traditional religious services as practiced publicly and regularly, both for special occasions such as marriages or funerals, and for weekly rites. In the Christian church some of this ritual is sung rather than spoken. The musical sections of the liturgy might be sung by the celebrant alone, by a choir of the church, and/or by the congregation.

The Mass is the primary service of the Catholic Church and most Protestant church services are modeled on it. As a religious ceremony, it consists of two main parts: the Ordinary (unchanging) and the Proper (changing based upon the church calendar). As a musical form, a Mass can be written for either of these two parts, but it is most commonly written for the Ordinary. In the Ordinary there are five prayers that are sung by the celebrants: the Kyrie, Gloria, Credo, Sanctus, and Agnus Dei. The Kyrie and Gloria are sung one after the other but the other three are separated by spoken liturgy. Texts of all but the Kyrie are in Latin; the Kyrie text is in Greek.

The Proper also is divided into five sections: Introit, Gradual, Alleluia, Offertory, and Communion. Composers write music for each section to create a Mass. Each Mass contains chant as part of the musical sections and most Masses are a mixture of chant and polyphonic music. Music for the Mass is the most important form of music in the Catholic liturgy.

The Mass began in the Middle Ages and was developed to a high musical level at Notre Dame. The earliest known composer of this musical form was Machaut, and his Notre Dame Mass is a Medieval masterwork that is still heard today. This Mass is an early example of polyphonic writing.

A Renaissance depiction of a performance of the Mass of the Dead. An engraving by Philip Galle, after J. Stradanus from 1595, *Encomium musices.* Courtesy bpk, Berlin/Musikinstrumenten-Berlin/Dr. Otto/Art Resource, NY.

LISTENING GUIDE 4.6

Dashboard

**HEAR STREAMING AUDIO
ON DASHBOARD**

KYRIE FROM NOTRE DAME MASS,
Guillaume de Machaut, composed ca. 1350

This setting of the Mass is the only example from the Medieval period that we know was written by a specific composer. In it Machaut sets the plea for mercy three times. (The number three is of special significance in Christian church liturgy.) Machaut added three voices to an existing chant to create the Kyrie. The Kyrie is the only part of the Mass that is not taken from Latin. The original of the Kyrie is in Greek.

What to Listen For

- Listen for the contrast between the florid fast-moving lines of the upper parts in contrast to the longer notes of the lower parts.
- Listen for the hockets early in the first section of the work.
- Listen for the syncopation of the rhythmic lines.
- Listen for the chant presented in the tenor part in long notes.

	TEXT	TRANSLATION
0:00 0:58 1:16	Kyrie eleison (sung three times)	Lord have mercy upon us.
2:17 2:32 3:23	Christe eleison (sung three times)	Christ have mercy upon us.
3:39 4:18 4:35	Kyrie eleison (sung three times)	Lord have mercy upon us.

If You Liked That, Try This

Gloria from Pope Marcellus Mass, Palestrina
Kyrie from Pange lingua Mass, Josquin des Prez
Sanctus from Eternal Gifts of Christ Mass, Palestrina

YouTube videos: search keywords
Palestrina—Gloria
The Tallis Scholars sings Palestrina
Gloria-Messe de Notre Dame, Guillaume de Machaut. Ensemble Organum
Guillaume de Machaut—Messe pour Notre Dame

Remember to add to your personal playlist any of these samples that you like.

CULTURAL CONNECTION: ISLAMIC CHANT

The styles of monophony, polyphony, and homophony developed in the Middle Ages served as building blocks for subsequent composers. The early forms of chant, motet, and Mass were copied and altered in the secular world to create forms that could be used outside the church. As you will learn in this text, the symphony, opera, oratorio, solo song, and even string quartet and keyboard music can all be traced to the music notation and fundamental systems of this early sacred music.

✓ **Build Your Own Playlist:** The works studied in the chapter Listening Guides serve as examples of different styles of early Catholic church music. Now, build your own playlist from those works listed in each IF YOU LIKED THAT, TRY THIS list, or from other works you find. Share your playlist with others by posting it to your class discussion board or on Dashboard.

Dashboard

✓ **Audio Review:** Go to Dashboard to listen to Professor Bailey discuss music of the Church.

✓ **How Am I Doing?** Go to Dashboard to test your understanding of this material by taking the chapter quiz.

KEY TERMS

Ars Nova	Liturgy	Proper
Church modes	Melismatic	Syllabic
Gregorian chant	Motet	Tithe
Hocket	Ordinary	Vibrato
Isorhythm	Organum	

CHAPTER

5

Protestant Church Music

LEARNING OBJECTIVES

- Define the terms *cantata* and *hymn*.
- Explain the use of the cantata and hymn in Protestant church services.
- Name important composers of the cantata and hymn.
- Recognize by listening example strophic form.

Key Concepts: cantata, hymn, strophic

Opening image: A church choir performing in a service. Courtesy Bob Daemmrich/Alamy.

65

Where It's Playing

The music of this chapter was originally written to be performed as a regular part of the Protestant church Sunday service, and it can still be heard there today. It is also used in settings outside the church, including the concert and recital hall, and informal gatherings of all kinds.

The popularity of the new Lutheran sacred work called the **cantata** (an extended work in multi-movement form written for orchestra, chorus, and soloists) in the Baroque era led composers to write them for both the church service and secular settings. The sectional structure of the cantata lent it to theatrical style productions similar to opera. These secular cantatas were performed in coffeehouses, universities, city squares, and secular meeting places. Today the secular cantata is most often performed in a recital hall.

The **hymn** is a very versatile form of sacred music. It is closely related to, and serves as one of the roots for, the popular music of today called **gospel**. Many gospel works use hymns as musical and textual foundations.

When listening to sacred music of any kind the most important thing to listen for is the text. The words convey the meaning of the work and most composers take great pains to carefully create melodies, harmonies, rhythms, and other musical elements that they believe enhance and highlight the text.

Cantata: An extended work for use in the services of the Lutheran church based upon Bible texts. A cantata has multiple movements and is written for orchestra, chorus, and soloists.

Hymn: A short, strophic work designed for use in a Protestant church service. Hymns are usually four-part with easily singable melodies.

Gospel: Christian music structured similarly to a hymn usually featuring one singer.

The Protestant Hymn

Why was the hymn created for Protestant services?

With the Protestant Reformation came a need for music to serve the liturgy of the new non-Catholic Christian church. To distinguish their music from that of the Catholic faith, Protestant composers, for the most part, abandoned the use of chant as a basis for sacred compositions. They also wrote their works in the vernacular language of the congregation, and much Protestant music was written for the congregation to take part in.

The earliest important form of music for the Protestant church service was the hymn. In Germany in the Baroque era this form was called the chorale. Hymns began in the Lutheran church and the great religious reformer Martin Luther himself wrote some of the most popular hymns still used today. Luther believed that the congregation should be allowed to participate in the worship service and one way to do this was to make the music simple enough to be sung by all. Hymns are generally syllabic in character and have steady, regular rhythms. They are written in four-part harmony (soprano, alto, tenor, bass) and are usually accompanied by an organ. In most churches the choir is capable of singing all four parts and since the melody is in the top voice it is easy to hear. This all makes a hymn much

Renaissance church reformer Martin Luther. Courtesy Georgios Kollidas/
Shutterstock.

more singable for the average member of the congregation than a chant or motet.
Hymns and chorales are in **strophic** form, meaning that there is one melody with
multiple verses of text. This also lends to their simplicity and makes it easier for
the congregation to learn the music since it does not change from verse to verse.

Strophic: A form in music in
which multiple verses of text are
set to the same music.

LISTENING GUIDE 5.1

"A MIGHTY FORTRESS IS OUR GOD,"
Martin Luther, composed ca. 1527

This chorale is, perhaps, the most famous of all Protestant hymns. Believed
to be written by Martin Luther, its text is taken from Psalm 46 of the Bible.
The chorale is also used as the eighth movement of Cantata No. 80 by J. S.
Bach for chorus and orchestra. In most settings today the hymn is sung by
the congregation and accompanied by a church organ. A hymn is used to
help congregation members proclaim faith during a worship service.

Dashboard
**HEAR STREAMING AUDIO
ON DASHBOARD**

What to Listen For

- Listen for a four-part structure that has a clearly heard top voice that sings the melody of the hymn.
- Listen for how the voices move together in a homorhythmic style.
- Listen for how regular the rhythm remains throughout the chorale.

TIMING	FORM: STROPHIC	TEXT	TRANSLATION	WHAT TO LISTEN FOR
0:00	Stanza 1	Ein' feste Burg ist unser Gott, Ein gute Wehr und Waffen; Er hilft uns frei aus aller Not, Die uns jetzt hat betroffen.	A mighty fortress is our God, a bulwark never failing; Our helper he amid the flood of mortal ills prevailing.	The choir and congregation sing in rhythmic unison the main melody of the hymn. The choir sings in four-part harmony.
		Der alt' böse Feind, Mit Ernst er's jetzt meint, Gross' Macht und viel List Sein' grausam' Ruestung ist, Auf Erd' ist nicht seingleichen.	For still our ancient foe doth seek to work us woe; his craft and power are great, and armed with cruel hate, on earth is not his equal.	The second part of the primary melody is sung in unison as well.
0:58	Stanza 2	Mit unser Macht is nichts getan, Wir sind gar bald verloren: Es Steit't fur uns der rechte Mann, Den Gott hat selbst erkoren.	Did we in our own strength confide, our striving would be losing, were not the right Man on our side, the Man of God's own choosing.	The choir also sings in four-part harmony on this stanza.
		Fragst du, wer der ist? Er heist Jesu Christ, Der Herr Zebaoth, Und ist kein andrer Gott, Das Feld muss er behalten.	You ask who that may be? Christ Jesus, it is he; Lord Sabaoth his name, from age to age the same; and he must win the battle.	

If You Liked That, Try This

"Crown Him with Many Crowns," Matthew Bridges
"Faith of Our Fathers," Henri F. Hemy and James G. Walton
"Rock of Ages," Thomas Toplady

YouTube video: search on keywords
A Mighty Fortress Is Our God (with words)— Martin Luther

Remember to add to your personal playlist any of these samples that you like.

Lutherans Develop the Cantata

***Besides the hymn what other form of Protestant
sacred music is important?***

A moderate-scale vocal form that was in some ways similar to the Mass was called
the cantata. The cantata was most important in the Baroque era in Lutheran
church services and was also used as a form of secular entertainment in coffeehouses, homes, and theaters.

A cantata is usually written for soloists, choir, and small orchestra. Its text, if
sacred, is taken from the Bible or popular and familiar hymns. In the Lutheran
Church, each Sunday and religious holiday requires special readings, similar to
those in the proper of the Mass. A cantata was written for a specific Sunday and
its text was associated with that day's readings and sermon. If the cantata was for
secular use the text was much like the libretto of an opera or the script of a play.
Subjects for secular cantatas were most often current topics of the time or political
satire. For example, J. S. Bach, an important composer of cantatas, wrote secular
cantatas for inauguration of city council members in Leipzig, to celebrate elec-
tions in Mühlhausen, and to poke fun at the popularity of a new drink in Europe
in his time—coffee. Many cantatas of the Baroque era were about thirty minutes
long and were in several movements that alternated between choir, soloists, and
instrumentalists. Composers also borrowed the **recitative** and **aria** from opera
and incorporated them into their works.

The most important composer of cantatas was Johann Sebastian Bach (1685–
1750). Because of his position in Leipzig, Germany, he had to provide music for
each week of the church year and he wrote many cantatas for this purpose. Ultimately, he wrote about 295 cantatas, both sacred and secular. In many he made a
familiar hymn the anchor of the work, much the same way a Catholic composer
would have based a work on a chant. Bach's works represent the height of advance-
ment of the cantata.

Recitative: Used in oratorio and
opera as a sort-of free rhythmical
sung-speech. It is used to progress
the drama forward much like
dialogue in a play. It usually has a
simple accompaniment without a
steady rhythmic pulse.

Aria: A solo song with
accompaniment used in opera
to convey the thoughts and/or
emotions of characters. It
usually has a full orchestral
accompaniment.

Dashboard

EXPLORE

How Was Early Music Performed?

Is music performed the same today as it was hundreds of years ago?

We hear a lot today about "authentic" performances of music from the Middle
Ages, Renaissance or Baroque periods. As you look at print ads for concerts you
might see this mentioned, or the phrase "performed on original instruments" as a
selling point for the concert. Many recordings have been made by ensembles that
specialize in "period," "authentic," or "original instrument" performances. But
what does this mean? Wouldn't any ensemble try to create an "authentic" performance? Why would it be better to play on an instrument made over four hundred
years ago than on a new model?

One of the primary goals of performers is to re-create a piece of music as the composer intended it to sound. That is easier to do with new music or with music by a
living composer. Musical notation can tell a performer only so much about a work,
and it was considerably less specific prior to the mid-1800s. Many composers, like
Bach, wrote in a sort of musical shorthand because they knew they would be performing their music themselves and could use the score as a memory aid as much

as a specific road map for performance. It is up to the musical intuition and study of the performer to interpret the composer's meaning and bring a work to life. This is one of the reasons that we still value live performances over recorded ones. Hearing a work performed by one artist one night and then by another a second night shows us that musical notation is not a specific system. Both performances may be beautiful and appropriate and still sound different from one another.

Over the centuries musicians continue to discover more about old music through musicians' letters, writings, and records. As this occurs, performance practice changes when musicians put new information about a work or composer into their performances. This use of information from the time of the composer is what makes a performance a so-called "authentic" performance. In other words, the performer is trying to perform the work using the musical rules and guidelines of the composition's time rather than of our own time. Such information might affect the tempo the performer chooses, or the range of dynamic she uses. It could also change the number of players used to perform a work or the timbre that they try to create on their instruments.

The use of old or "period" instruments is easier to understand. These instruments are used either because they sound better than modern instruments or because the players want some specific technique that is easier to create on them than with modern instruments. For example, it is generally thought that some of the best violins ever produced were made in the Baroque era by makers such as Antonio Stradivari, Nicolo Amati, or Andrea and Guiseppe Guarneri. These instruments seem to have a special tone quality prized by musicians and are difficult and expensive to acquire. When such an instrument comes for sale it draws much international attention and the instruments are often sold for millions of dollars.

Dashboard

EXPLORE

Johann Sebastian Bach

Johann Sebastian Bach is recognized today as one of the greatest composers of all time. Born in Eisenach, Germany, he worked as a performer and composer in the courts and churches of Germany. At eighteen he became church organist in the town of Arnstadt where he became a virtuoso performer, which eventually led to a better position in Mühlhausen. In 1708 Bach achieved a still more important position as the organist to the court in Weimar, where he also served as concertmaster of the court orchestra. This experience led him to the position of court music director at Cöthen, where he composed almost exclusively secular music.

Bach's final post was as cantor at St. Thomas Church in Leipzig, a Lutheran church, where he oversaw the music of four churches. He worked in Leipzig for twenty-seven years and wrote some of his most memorable music for this church and city. One of his compositional tasks was to write a work for choir, orchestra, and soloists for each Sunday of the church year. During his own lifetime Bach was not well known outside the immediate area, yet he was one of the most prolific composers of his time.

His works have been extremely influential since they were "rediscovered" and presented to the public in the early 1800s. Besides being a great composer and organist, Bach was also a gifted improviser.

Baroque era master composer Johann Sebastian Bach.
© Maxim Anisimov. Courtesy iStock.

Organists of the time were expected to improvise music on the spot during church services, and Bach excelled at this type of performance.

The music of Bach is everywhere today. He wrote in every genre of the time except opera, and he had to write a good deal of music simply to meet the musical demands of his positions. Much of his music is of a polyphonic texture in which more than one melody occurs at the same time. His music is imitative in style, and in many works he elaborates on one melody throughout the piece. Rhythmic drive is important in most of Bach's works, as it is in much of the music of the Baroque.

Dashboard

RESEARCH

LISTENING GUIDE 5.2

"AWAKE, A VOICE IS CALLING US," from Cantata 140,
J. S. Bach, composed 1731

The work consists of seven movements and is based on a chorale tune of Bach's time, "Wachet auf" or "Awake." The first movement is in an AAB structure with nine inner phrases, although phrases 3 and 9 are identical and phrase 5 repeats phrase 4. The movement is in **ritornello** form, meaning that an orchestral section (ritornello) alternates with the vocal sections. The cantata is written for chorus, soloists, and orchestra. The movement structure of the cantata is as follows:

Dashboard

**HEAR STREAMING AUDIO
ON DASHBOARD**

Ritornello: An Italian term meaning return. In music the term is used to indicate a form in which one short section of music, usually performed by an orchestra, alternates with longer sections often performed by orchestra and voices together.

> Movement 1: Chorus and orchestra, uses the first A section (stanza) of the chorale.
> Movement 2: Recitative style for solo male voice (tenor) and orchestra.
> Movement 3: Duet of soprano and bass with small orchestra accompaniment.
> Movement 4: Male chorus voices (tenors) and orchestra, uses the second stanza (A) of the chorale.
> Movement 5: Recitative style for bass solo and orchestra.
> Movement 6: Second duet for soprano and bass with small orchestra.
> Movement 7: Chorus and orchestra using the B section of the chorale.

The chorale tune follows.

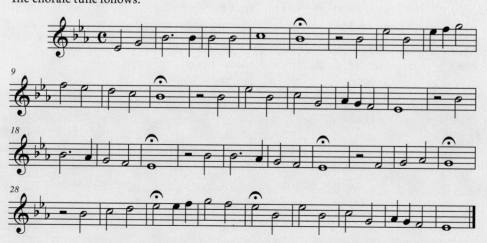

What to Listen For

- Note the simplicity of the chorale melody. This was necessary to enable the congregation to easily sing the hymn.
- Listen for how the phrases are segmented by the orchestral interludes, called ritornellos.
- Listen for the imitative style of the chorus parts.
- Listen to the quality and character of the orchestral introduction, which creates a feeling of anticipation. Bach uses fast scales and dotted rhythms to create a sense of urgency in both the orchestral and vocal parts.

Movement 1

TIMING	FORM: RITORNELLO	TEXT	TRANSLATION	WHAT TO LISTEN FOR
0:00	Introduction			Introduction—the movement opens with a brief orchestral introduction that introduces three short rhythmic/melodic motifs that are used in ritornello fashion throughout the movement. The first is a repeated note rhythmic figure, the second an ascending scale in a halting rhythmic figure, and the third a sequential fast note scale pattern.
0:31	A Chorale phrase 1	Wachet auf, ruft uns die Stimme	Awake, a voice is calling	The chorus is set in imitative style
0:48	Orchestral ritornello 1			
0:55	Chorale phrase 2	der Wächter sehr hoch auf der Zinne	From the watchmen from high in the tower	
1:13	Orchestral ritornello 2			
1:22	Chorale phrase 3	wach auf, du Stadt Jerusalem!	Awake, city of Jerusalem!	
2:14	A Chorale phrase 1	Mitternacht heisst diese Stunde	Midnight is the hour	The A section repeats in the same order with new text. The section begins with the same orchestra introduction used this time as a ritornello.
2:31	Ritornello 1			

Time	Section	German	English	Notes
2:38	Chorale phrase 2	sie rufen uns mit hellem Munde	They call us with a high, clear voice	
2:57	Ritornello 2			
3:07	Chorale phrase 3	wo seid ihr Ikugen Jungfrauen?	Where are the Wise Virgins?	
3:27	B Ritornello in a varied form, orchestra.			
3:51	Chorale phrase 4	Wohl auf, der Bräut'gam kömmt,	Get up, the Bridegroom comes	Imitative section for chorus
4:05	Ritornello 1			
4:11	Chorale phrase 5	steht auf, die Lampen nehmt!	Stand up and take your lamps!	
4:29	Chorale phrase 6	Alleluia	Hallelujah	Imitative section for chorus
5:10	Ritornello 1			
5:20	Chorale phrase 7	Macht euch bereit	Prepare yourselves	
5:30	Ritornello 2			
5:37	Chorus phrase 8	zu der Hochzeit	For the wedding	
5:53	Ritornello 2			
5:56	Chorale phrase 9	ihr müsset ihm entgegen gehn.	You must go forth to meet him.	
6:16	Ritornello			All three parts restated as a coda to the movement.

If You Liked That, Try This

"Nun komm, der Heiden Heiland," BVW 62, Bach
"Christ lag in Todes Banden," BWV 4, Bach
The Coffee Cantata, BWV 211, Bach

YouTube video: search on keywords
Bach—Coffee Cantata

Remember to add to your personal playlist any of these samples that you like.

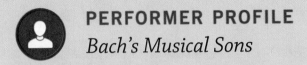

PERFORMER PROFILE
Bach's Musical Sons

With his first and second wives, J. S. Bach had twenty children, ten of whom lived to adulthood. Of these, four became well-known composers in their own right: Wilhelm Friedemann Bach, Carl Philipp Emanuel Bach, Johann Christian Bach, and Johann Christoph Friedrich Bach.

Wilhelm Friedemann (1710–1784) was an exceptional organist and a fine composer. Of the four sons he was the least financially successful, apparently due to his temperament. He worked as organist in Dresden and Halle, Germany. Wilhelm Friedemann's compositions are contrapuntal and in the style of his father, which by his adulthood had begun to go out of fashion.

Johann Christian Bach (1735–1782) was the youngest and is sometimes referred to as "the London Bach" where for a time he served as master of music to Queen Charlotte, wife of King George III. His works are, perhaps, the most different from his father's of the four sons. Johann Christian lived and worked in the Classical era whereas his father's music is of the Baroque. Unlike his father, Johann Christian wrote opera as well as instrumental music and sacred music. He too was a skilled organist.

Johann Christoph Friedrich Bach (1732–1795) is the least known of the four composer sons. In his lifetime he was known best as a harpsichord virtuoso and Konzertmeister of the court at Bückeburg. His works possess characteristics of both the Baroque and Classical era styles. A prolific composer he wrote in most genres of the time including a good deal of keyboard music, oratorios, and orchestral works.

The most famous of the Bach sons was Carl Philipp Emanuel Bach (1714–1788). Known as C. P. E. Bach today, he was a composer of the early Classical era and is viewed as an important bridge figure between the Baroque and Classical eras. His most important and influential position was as composer to Frederick the Great of Prussia, a well-known lover of music and talented flutist himself. Bach's book *An Essay on the True Art of Playing Keyboard Instruments* is an important guide to the style and performance practice of the early Classical era. C. P. E. Bach was one of the leading composers and performers of his time and his works were influential to those by Haydn, Mozart, and Beethoven.

Learn more about the family life and legacy of Johann Sebastian Bach by an Internet search of his family tree. How did the musical backgrounds and family association of both of his wives impact their children's future vocations? Did Bach stay in Leipzig so long because of the educational opportunities for his children? Given his sons' musical success, why was the music of the father neglected for so many years? Report your findings to your class discussion board or the book's Dashboard.

✓ **Build Your Own Playlist:** The works studied in this chapter are examples of different styles of Protestant church music from different eras. Now, build your own playlist from those works listed in each IF YOU LIKED THAT, TRY THIS list or from other works you find. Share your playlist with others by posting it to your class discussion board or on Dashboard.

✓ **Audio Review:** Go to Dashboard to listen to Professor Bailey discuss Protestant Church music.

✓ **How Am I Doing?** Go to Dashboard to test your understanding of this material by taking the chapter quiz.

Dashboard

KEY TERMS

Aria	Hymn	Strophic
Cantata	Recitative	
Gospel	Ritornello	

UNIT 3

Music of the Concert Hall

With today's easy access to recorded music some might question the continued need for the concert hall. But no matter how interesting a recording may be, there is nothing as exciting as a live concert in a concert hall shared with hundreds of other people. The live concert provides visual and social stimulation that a recording cannot. The unpredictability of live performing is an interesting and unique aspect of a concert—the same piece of music doesn't sound the same in two different live performances even when performed by the same person. In today's society it is easy to find many varied live music options.

This unit focuses on the music most often heard in a concert hall, works written over the past 400 years for large concert ensembles (bands, choirs, and orchestras). As you hear the Listening Guides and study the What to Listen For features, try to imagine sitting in a concert hall with hundreds of other people listening to an orchestra of about sixty musicians playing this music. But, first let's see how and why public concerts and concert halls developed and how a concert unfolds.

Development of the Concert Hall

Concerts have existed since the beginning of music, but concerts in *public* concert halls as we know them today were rare until about the late 18th century. First introduced in the Baroque era (approximately 1600–1750) they gained popularity in Europe with the beginning of the rise of a real middle class. As discussed in Chapter 3, until the late 1700s most composers worked within the patronage system and their music, produced for specific courts or churches, was not readily

Opening image: Exterior of Disney Hall, Los Angeles. Courtesy Gerry Boughan/Shutterstock.

77

available to the general public. With the demise of the aristocracy in Europe in the late 1700s and early 1800s, and advent of the Industrial Revolution of the 1800s, more people had leisure time and some disposable income to spend on music. Public concerts were a natural outgrowth of these societal changes.

The idea of public performances began, perhaps, with opera. In 1637 the Teatro San Cassiano opened to the public in Venice. Because Venice was a trading center, merchants from all over Europe carried this public performance idea home with them. By the mid-1600s the public could attend the opera in London, Vienna, Paris, Prague, and Hamburg.

The first regularly scheduled type of concert was called the subscription concert and was common in European capitals in the Classical era (approximately 1750–1820). These subscription concerts were prepaid ticketed events usually sponsored by an impresario or the composer/performer himself and open to anyone with the price of admission. This seems normal to us today, but at the time it was a new way for the average person to hear great art music outside the church.

These early public concerts usually focused on one performer—often a piano or violin virtuoso who most often presented his own compositions. They were long, often three hours or more. By the late 1800s concerts were a common part of life in Europe. Cities built concert halls, middle-class businessmen and politicians formed and paid for orchestras and opera troupes, and writing about music (music criticism) began to help the public judge quality and availability of music. Today, concerts are so common that it is difficult to imagine them not being so. Access to live music is a regular part of most people's lives.

The Concert Hall

Concerts are most often given in halls that have been specifically designed for that purpose. Some halls serve multiple purposes, but many of the great orchestras of the world perform in halls that were built specifically to highlight the acoustical properties of the orchestra and the music.

Inside the concert building there are four primary areas: the lobby, the house, the stage, and the backstage. In the lobby is the ticket office where patrons can purchase or pick up tickets they have ordered (referred to as "will call"). There is also often a souvenir store and refreshment bar, though most concert halls do not allow refreshments to be taken into the hall itself.

The seating space, or house, is divided into at least three seating areas called orchestra, box seating, and balcony. Orchestra seating is on the main floor. Box seats are special small, and usually isolated, areas that are at balcony level. These seats are usually the most expensive and have some of the best views of the stage (though not always the best sound). The best seats in a concert hall are rarely directly in front of the stage, but usually in the middle of the hall (referred to as the house) about halfway back from the stage. The front rows of the balcony are often equally good seats. Concert halls have two primary seating plans, American and Continental. The Continental plan has aisles only on the sides and the American plan has a middle aisle as well to make it easier to get to seats.

Interior of a concert hall. © gnagel. Courtesy iStock.

The stage is, of course, restricted to the performers. In a concert hall it is usually wider than it is deep. The front of the stage, or proscenium, extends the stage a few feet into the house seating area. The stage is raised above the seating area so that the performers can be more easily seen and heard by the audience.

The backstage consists of storage areas for instruments and personal effects of players, dressing rooms, and a good deal of mechanical equipment that helps the concert happen. This area is rarely seen by audience members. Stage crew members who set up the stage, work the lights and curtain, operate the sound equipment, and assist the performers are stationed backstage.

What to Expect at the Concert Hall

When entering the concert hall, patrons are given a program listing the works to be performed. It also lists the composers' names and often the dates that they lived, and sometimes provides historical notes about the pieces on the

---

Program

Carnival Overture, opus 92   Antonin Dvorak
                                                                  (1841-1904)

Symphony No. 6 in F major,   Ludwig van Beethoven
opus 68 ("Pastorale")   (1770-1827)

    The Awakening of Cheerful Feelings upon Arrival in the Country
    Scene by the Brook
    Village Festival – The Merry Gathering of Country Folk
    Tempest, the Storm
    Shepherd's Song – Happy and Thankful Feelings after the Storm

~ Intermission ~

Don Quixote, opus 35   Richard Strauss
                                                                  (1864-1949)

    Fantasy-like Variations on a Theme
    of a Chivalrous Character

                    Thomas Landschoot, violoncello
                        Katherine McLin, violin
                           Nancy Buck, viola

A sample program.

concert. These program notes often give clues to the composer's thinking about the work, why it was written and what to listen for. Most concert halls have ushers at the hall doorways to assist patrons in finding their seats and to distribute the programs. These ushers also remind concertgoers of guidelines of etiquette and enforce the hall's rules concerning latecomer seating. Today, concerts will be about two hours in length and will have one fifteen- to twenty-minute intermission. If there is a soloist she will probably appear on the first half of the concert if she is an instrumentalist and probably in both halves of the concert if she is a vocalist.

Once the programs have been distributed and the audience has been seated the concert hall lights will be dimmed. The ensemble is already seated on the stage and is warming up—a process that sounds chaotic since it is done individually and collectively. Often the primary instrumentalist of the ensemble (called a concertmaster in an orchestra) enters the stage last, quiets the ensemble, and indicates that it is time for the ensemble to tune. At this point one member of the ensemble sounds a lone pitch. All the other members match this pitch to ensure that the basic tone of each instrument matches the others, which makes the music sound much better, even to the inexperienced ear. Once the ensemble has tuned, the conductor will enter the stage. Usually he bows as the audience applauds and often acknowledges the other musicians on the stage. Most often at this point in the concert the conductor does not speak to the audience. Instead he steps onto the podium (a small raised platform at the front of the ensemble that aids the players in seeing the conductor) and starts the music.

Music of the Concert Hall

Much of the music of this unit will be familiar to you from its use in movies, television, cartoons, or as background music in elevators, lobbies, or waiting rooms. Most of the music heard in a concert hall is not new music, but dates from the Baroque, Classical, or Romantic eras. Musicians speak of the traditional canon of literature that makes up a standard repertory, and they spend a good deal of time studying these two hundred or so pieces. Prior to the mid-1800s there was no traditional or standard repertory that all musicians knew and practiced. Much like popular music of today the art music of the past was composed, performed for a few months, and often put away and forgotten. Not so today.

A concert of a symphony orchestra or wind band usually contains a variety of the musical forms and styles studied in this unit. A typical orchestra concert in a concert hall consists of works played only by the orchestra (symphonies, overtures, and program music studied in Unit 3) and pieces in which the orchestra accompanies a soloist. Some concerts contain a single piece of music in which the orchestra combines with a large choir and/or soloist.

What to Listen for in Concert Music

- Listen for how the composer uses different instruments. Are some instruments usually playing the melody while others accompany them? Or does the melody move throughout the ensemble in a shared manner?
- Most music performed in a concert hall is performed by a large ensemble: a band, choir, or orchestra. This makes it difficult to focus on a particular instrument or voice. In fact, the blend of the voices and/or instruments is one of the most important aspects of ensemble music. The listener focuses on the overall sound of the group and how it changes at different times in the music, or in different pieces of the concert. This blending of the different instrument sounds should change from piece to piece and often within one work.
- The sound blend is determined by the instruments the composer has specified at particular moments in the piece and it is a rare piece when all instruments play the entire time. This differs from most popular music ensembles today, where blend is not usually an important musical element in popular music. As such, it takes your specific attention at an art music concert to focus on this element.

- Most musical works contain sections that alternate between full ensemble playing and solo performers playing. Listen to this exchange as a musical dialogue.
- Finally, the order of the program is important. The pieces were put in a particular sequence to create an overall effect for the entire concert. Usually, the program will provide changes in speed, intensity, and volume so that the concert has a varied content. Concert program ordering is similar to the production of recordings. If an artist puts eight songs on a CD she spends a good deal of time determining what order is most likely to produce the desired effect on the listener. The same is true for program order at concerts.

Music for Soloists with Orchestra—The Concerto

LEARNING OBJECTIVES

- **Explain the form and characteristics of the concerto.**
- **Demonstrate an understanding of the differences between a solo concerto and a concerto grosso.**
- **Name important composers of the concerto.**
- **Recognize a solo cadenza by listening examples.**

Key Concepts: accompaniment, cadenza, form of the concerto, ritornello

Where It's Playing

The concerto was written for concert performance. Today we usually hear a concerto in a concert hall as part of an evening-long orchestral concert. Such a concert might include the concerto, a symphony (studied in Chapter 7), and other incidental orchestral music. Often the concerto is performed immediately before intermission, and for many people in the audience, hearing the soloist is the reason they attended the concert.

Unlike music for orchestra alone we rarely hear a concerto used in television ads, movies, or cartoons as background music. However, we often hear a concerto played in smaller venues than the concert hall. Most concertos are written for soloist with full orchestra accompaniment. But composers and arrangers often take the orchestral accompaniment and rearrange it so that it can be played on the piano. This rearrangement makes the concerto playable outside the concert hall by just the soloist and one pianist serving as the accompaniment in place of the orchestra. This presentation of concertos is at least as common today as versions with full orchestra and usually occurs in recital halls, churches, or venues smaller than the concert hall.

One of the most important features of a concerto is the concept of contrast between the soloist and the full orchestra. The changing texture between soloist alone, orchestra alone, and both together, in tandem or opposition, makes the concerto interesting to the listener.

When listening to a concerto, try to focus on the musical conversation that occurs between the soloist and the orchestra. Listen to how the composer uses the orchestra to make dramatic statements and allows the soloist to embellish these statements into virtuosic showpieces. Listen also to the **cadenza**, (a brief interlude in a concerto in which the soloist plays alone), to the way the soloist takes a melody from the concerto and embellishes and enhances it. Does the cadenza sound free and improvised, or does it seem prepared in advance? One way to tell this is by the number of stops the performer makes in the cadenza movement's? Perhaps these are brief moments of thought before the performer continues. How many of the movement's melodies are used in the cadenza? Perhaps the fewer that are used the more planned the cadenza because developing an idea usually takes more planning than stating a new one.

Finally, if you are hearing the concerto in a live performance, watch the interaction between the orchestra's conductor and the soloist. Who is the leader and who the follower? Does the soloist indicate when to start movements or sections by some body movement

Cadenza: A brief interlude in a concerto in which the soloist plays alone. Cadenzas are often improvised.

Virtuoso: A musician considered among the finest performers in the world on his or her instrument.

Concerto: A showpiece written for a single instrument accompanied by an ensemble, usually orchestra or band. The concerto is often in three movements.

Dashboard

ATTEND AND REPORT

or gesture? You may see a violinist's bow arm or a pianist's head give such a gesture.

Characteristics of the Concerto

What is the form and important characteristics of the concerto?

Many orchestra or band concerts in concert halls include at least one work in which a soloist joins the ensemble. This is usually an instrumentalist, often a violinist or pianist. This soloist is usually a well-known **virtuoso** musician, and many times the concert has been publicized around the performance of this one musician. The most common form of music played by a soloist or group of soloists with orchestral or band accompaniment is called the **concerto**.

The concerto is the most important form of solo instrumental music for the concert hall. It is usually written to display the virtuosity of the soloist and the flexibility of the instrument. A concerto can be written for one or more soloists, but is most commonly designed to be played by one solo performer. The concerto is usually divided into three separate sections called **movements** that are contrasting in tempo in a fast, slow, fast sequence. The primary idea of these individual smaller forms that combine to make up the concerto is **thematic development** and the contrast and repetition of **themes** (melodies) or **motifs** (fragments or roots of melodies). At the completion of a movement the orchestra stops momentarily. The next movement is usually of a contrasting speed and style.

The first movement of a concerto is usually a fast work in sonata form. The **sonata form** of the Classical era is characterized by melodic development and the idea of contrast versus repetition. It usually contains two primary melodies and is in three sections. The first and third sections (called respectively the **exposition** and **recapitulation**) are similar, if not identical, and usually contain two themes in contrasting style. The middle section of the sonata form is called the **development** section and is used to extend, break up, recharacterize, and generally develop these melodic ideas.

The second movement could be a number of different forms, but is often a lyrical movement containing song-like melodies.

The final movement of the concerto is most commonly written in a sonata form or a **rondo** form. The rondo, like the sonata form, is a form based upon contrast and return to original material. Unlike the sonata form there is no development of previous melodic material in a rondo—instead additional melodies are presented and alternate with the original idea. To visualize this form think of each melody as being represented by a letter. The first melody is represented by A, the second by B, and so on. At the completion of each new melody the original melody returns, resulting in a form of A B A C A D A, and so on, depending on how many new melodies are presented. The work always returns to the original melody.

At least one of the movements often contains a short unaccompanied section of music called a cadenza, which allows the soloist to display even more virtuosity and is sometimes improvised, or created on the spot, near the end of a movement. The player takes melodic or rhythmic motifs from the main body of the concerto and presents them in a segmented manner that builds tension toward the return

Movement: While a complete piece of music in itself, it is usually part of a larger work such as a symphony or string quartet.

Thematic development: Manipulation or variation of a theme, often used in the development section of a sonata form.

Theme: A melody.

Motif: A fragment of a melody or rhythm on which a larger melody or rhythmic structure is built.

Sonata form: A short work for orchestra usually used as the first and/or last movements of a symphony. The sonata form is a three-part form based upon the development and expansion of melodic ideas.

Exposition: The opening section of a sonata form in which the primary melodies of the work are presented.

Recapitulation: The third part of a sonata form in which the primary melodies of the exposition are restated.

Development: The middle section of a sonata form in which the primary melodies of the work are altered, enhanced, or manipulated through melodic fragmentation, variation, or some other compositional device that recharacterizes the melodies.

Rondo: A form consisting of contrasting melodies with one of the melodies used as a unifying return theme. Each time a new melody is presented and completed, the original rondo theme returns. Perhaps best illustrated by the letters ABACADA, where A represents the original melody and B, C, and D represent new melodies.

of the accompaniment. One of the most important aspects of the concerto form is contrast—contrast of tempos between movements and contrast of dynamics and timbre between the accompaniment and soloist.

The Baroque Concerto

What is the difference between a concerto grosso and a solo concerto?

Concertino: A group of soloists featured in a concerto.

Concerto grosso: A concerto in which a group of instruments serve as the featured performers and are contrasted with a larger group.

Terraced dynamics: Sudden changes in volume.

Solo concerto: A concerto designed to display the virtuosity of one player.

The concerto form began in the Baroque era (1600–1750) and is still an important form written by composers today. The idea of music alternating between a full orchestra, or tutti, and a small group of players, or **concertino**, is the central concept of the Baroque concerto. This early form of concerto is now referred to as the **concerto grosso** to distinguish it from the solo concerto which features just one soloist. In a concerto grosso the musical sections alternate between the full group (tutti), and the smaller ensemble (concertino). This type of alternation exploited two ideas important to instrumental music of the Baroque: **terraced dynamics** and timbral change. Baroque music often uses terraced dynamics, in which the volume changes abruptly from loud to soft, or vice versa. And, during the Baroque era the idea of timbre began to be important in instrumental music. Rather than keeping the instrumentation the same throughout a work, composers began to alter the mix of instruments used in each section. The concerto is ideally suited to express these two concepts. J. S. Bach's six Brandenburg Concertos are in this form. These six concerti grossi were written for Margrave Christian Ludwig of Brandenburg. Each features a different set of instruments in the concertino.

The other form of concerto established in the Baroque era was the **solo concerto**, which displays the virtuosity of one player. This form is still commonly composed today.

Antonio Vivaldi. Courtesy World History Archive/Alamy.

Dashboard

EXPLORE

Antonio Vivaldi

The best-known composer of the solo concerto in the Baroque era was the Italian Antonio Vivaldi (1678–1741). A priest, he became the head of music instruction at a school for orphaned children in Venice and wrote much of his music for performance at the school. Vivaldi's father was a violinist, which may be why over two hundred of his more than five hundred total concertos were written for the violin. Vivaldi became well known throughout Europe as a virtuoso himself and his concertos were performed regularly. He also wrote operas, a good deal of chamber music for instruments, cantatas, and one oratorio. Visit Dashboard for a link to a brief video on virtuosic performance.

Of Vivaldi's works none are more famous than the four violin concertos that make up *The Four Seasons*. Each concerto represents a season and contains three movements. The work was an early form of **program music**, much like that de-scribed in the chapter on program music. Each movement is accompanied by a poem, and Vivaldi actually wrote lines of the poem into sections of the musical score. The music at those points is constructed to convey the atmosphere and feel-ing of the poetry.

Program music: Instrumental music that is suggestive of a mood, story, poem, or phrase.

LISTENING GUIDE 6.1

"SPRING," from *The Four Seasons*, mvt. 1,
Antonio Vivaldi, composed 1725

Dashboard

HEAR STREAMING AUDIO ON DASHBOARD

What to Listen For

In the first movement of "Spring" listen for musical sounds that evoke im-ages of birds, thunderstorms, running water, and wind. Vivaldi uses a light texture combined with energized rhythms and bright, airy melodies to create the feel of spring.

- Listen for the alternation between solo violin and orchestra.
- Listen for the driving rhythms so characteristic of Baroque era concertos.
- Listen for the terraced dynamics.
- Listen for the **ritornello** theme.

Ritornello: The portion of the melody that recurs throughout the concerto.

TIMING	TIMBRE	FORM	POETRY	MUSICAL PROGRAM
0:00	Orchestra	Ritornello	Joyful Spring has arrived.	
0:35	Soloists	Episode 1	The birds greet us with a happy song.	Solo violins play high trills and scales to emu-late the sounds of birds.
1:10	Orchestra	Ritornello		
1:18	Soloists	Episode 2	And the streams in the gentle breezes flow with a sweet murmur.	Violins play soft scales in a kind of undulating rhythm to evoke a running stream.
1:42	Orchestra	Ritornello		
1:50	Soloists	Episode 3	The sky is covered with a black cloak.	Low strings play tremolos to produce thunder-like sounds, alternating with high strings play-ing fast, ascending scales and violin solo to produce a thunder-and-lightning type of music conversation.

(continued)

TIMING	TIMBRE	FORM	POETRY	MUSICAL PROGRAM
2:18	Orchestra	Ritornello		Orchestra plays the closing phrase of the ritornello in a minor key.
2:28	Soloists	Episode 4	When they have quieted, the birds resume their song	The violin trills and repeated notes of Episode 1 return to represent the birds.
2:47	Orchestra	Ritornello		Orchestra plays the closing phrase of the ritornello.
2:59	Soloists	Cadenza		The ritornello is interrupted by the solo violin, which presents a short cadenza based on the theme.
3:15	Orchestra	Ritornello		Orchestra plays the ritornello to close the movement.

If You Liked That, Try This

Brandenburg Concerto no. 2 in F, BWV 1047, J. S. Bach
"The Tempest at Sea," from Concerto for Flute, Strings, and Basso Continuo, op. 10, no. 1, Vivaldi
Concerto no. 1 in B-flat major for Oboe, HWV 301, G. F. Handel

YouTube videos: search on keywords
Vivaldi Four Seasons Summer Sand Animation film Ferenc Cakó
Bach Brandenburg Concerto 2, 1st movement

Remember to add to your personal playlist any of these samples that you like.

The Classical Concerto

How was the concerto used in the Classical era?

The concerto became the most important solo form in instrumental music in the Classical era (1750–1820). In this period it was almost always a solo concerto. The orchestral parts alternate between sections that state the main melodic ideas and strictly accompanimental music that supports the soloist. This creates the timbral and dynamic contrast so important to the concerto. The first movement is almost always the longest movement because the orchestra first states the entire exposition of the movement followed by a restatement of it by the soloist. The soloist usually plays more complicated versions of the initial exposition. The movement ends with a virtuosic cadenza for the soloist. The finale is usually the fastest and often the shortest movement. As stated above, it is often in rondo or sonata form. The Classical era concerto is, like the symphony, about fifteen to thirty minutes in length.

During the Classical era composers wrote concertos for each of the instruments of the orchestra as well as for keyboard instruments. For example, Haydn's Concerto in E-flat was written for the keyed bugle and is played today on the trumpet. Wolfgang Amadeus Mozart helped establish the piano as the leading instrument of the Classical concerto. His own virtuosity at the instrument and ability to improvise exciting cadenzas contributed to the popularity of these works at public concerts. The fortepiano, a predecessor of today's modern piano, became the leading concert keyboard instrument of the time and some of the most famous concertos were written for it. It is a smaller and somewhat more muted instrument than our modern piano, but it was capable of more nuanced performance than the organ or the Baroque harpsichord.

Wolfgang Amadeus Mozart

One of the greatest writers of concertos, operas, and symphonic music was Wolfgang Amadeus Mozart (1756–1791). Born in Salzburg, Austria, his short life was marked by great successes and failures. His father, Leopold Mozart, a well-respected composer in his own right, taught Wolfgang to compose and play the violin and harpsichord. By the age of eight he had written a symphony and by twelve he had composed oratorio and opera. Leopold Mozart took Wolfgang and his sister Nannerl on a tour of the European courts to show him off to the kings and queens of Europe. This tour made him an international superstar as a child.

Wolfgang Amadeus Mozart with his sister Maria Anna and father Leopold. Mozart's mother is depicted in the background portrait. Courtesy World History Archive/Alamy.

PERFORMANCE PRACTICE
Improvisation

How was Mozart similar to a modern-day jazz artist?

Mozart was a very popular performer on the harpsichord and fortepiano (a predecessor of the modern piano). He could entertain guests after dinner by improvising entire pieces, or making up his own versions of pop tunes of the day. He also used this skill in the performance of cadenzas in his concertos. Like today, many of the musicians of Mozart's time wrote out their cadenzas and played essentially the same cadenza at each performance. In fact, each edition of a concerto often includes one or more cadenzas that the editor/arranger feels are appropriate stylistically to the concerto. In some cases Mozart wrote out his cadenzas for his piano concertos and some of them are published today. However, in many cases Mozart used his ability to extemporaneously compose in order to improvise a cadenza while performing a concerto. This made each of his performances different and different from other musicians who played his works. Today's musicians who have a similar talent are often jazz performers who improvise a good deal of the music they perform. A cadenza is usually an embellishment or development of one or more of the melodic ideas of the concerto. In jazz a performer usually does the same to a melody, embellishing and developing it. Called cadenzas in concertos, these improvised sections are called solo choruses in a jazz tune.

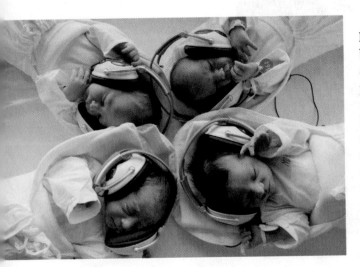

The "Mozart effect." Four babies listen to classical music in a test to determine its effect. Courtesy Getty Images.

Unfortunately, Mozart found less success in his own lifetime as an adult. Though today we consider him to be one of the greatest musicians and composers, his adult life was marred by frustration. This was due in part to the fact that his lifetime spanned the end of the old patronage system and the beginning of the free-lance composer who made a living by touring, teaching, and giving public concerts. Mozart's father was a court musician and composer at the court of the archbishop in Salzburg. Though he tried in many places, Wolfgang was never able to gain such a stable position. Instead he produced his works in public concerts and opera houses, mainly in Vienna. Finally, in the last decade of his life he was successful in Vienna due in large part to the popularity of his operas. During the same period he wrote some of the most beautiful concertos and symphonies ever composed.

Mozart was a versatile composer, able to write for large orchestra, opera, concerto, and chamber music. Throughout this text hardly a genre will be discussed which he did not influence. Mozart was, along with Franz Joseph Haydn, the master of the Classical era compositional style of refinement, symmetry, and melodic invention.

Dashboard

RESEARCH

LISTENING GUIDE 6.2

CONCERTO NO. 23 IN A MAJOR FOR PIANO, K. 488, mvt. 1,
Wolfgang Amadeus Mozart, composed 1786

Dashboard

**HEAR STREAMING AUDIO
ON DASHBOARD**

What to Listen For

- Listen for the changes in mood that Mozart signals by shifts between major and minor keys.

Theme A

- Listen for a new theme in the development section, an unusual idea in a Classical era sonata form.

- Listen for the piano cadenza near the end of the first movement. Mozart wrote out this cadenza, which was unusual because cadenzas are usually improvised by the performer.
- Note that there are two expositions in this solo concerto. Though common by this time in the Classical era this was not the case when solo concertos first became popular in the Baroque era.
- Note the graceful melodies, and how natural they sound on the piano.
- Listen for how the orchestra responds after a technical passage by the solo piano. It almost sounds like an orchestral cheer for the pianist. And listen to how the orchestra always seems to prepare the entrance of the solo part by becoming more agitated and coming to a full stop just before the piano plays.

TIMING	TEXTURE	FORM: SONATA	WHAT TO LISTEN FOR
0:00	Orchestra	Exposition 1 Theme 1	The work begins with the first theme stated without introduction by the orchestra.
0:17			The theme is repeated in the winds.
0:35	Orchestra	Response theme	This bridge-like theme is used several times to lead to a new idea.
0:59	Orchestra	Theme 2	The second theme is presented softly by violins and bassoon. It is a gentle, scalar melody and is repeated with the addition of the flute.
1:30	Orchestra	Closing theme	In this section the orchestra presents material that is full of tension. The section gets louder and ends with a brief pause after orchestral unison chords.
2:10	Soloist	Exposition 2 Theme 1	Theme 1 presented by solo piano with limited orchestral accompaniment.
2:26	Soloist	Theme 1	Theme 1 repeated by piano with some variation.
2:39	Orchestra and piano	Response theme	Theme stated by full orchestra. Piano plays a series of scalar runs.
3:11	Piano	Theme 2	Theme 2 stated by piano.
3:27	Orchestra	Theme 2	Theme 2 is restated by orchestra.
3:42	Soloist	Closing section	The piano plays more scalar runs with gentle orchestral accompaniment. The piano ends its portion of the section with a trill.
4:26	Orchestra	Response	Response theme stated by the orchestra comes to an abrupt stop.
4:39	Orchestra and piano	Development theme	A new theme is stated by the orchestra and picked up by the piano in an ornamented form.
5:05	Orchestra and piano		Development theme is developed in small fragments stated first by clarinet, then flute, then woodwinds. In each case after the fragment is stated, the piano answers with a showy section of its own in a dialogue manner. The fragments alternate between minor and major keys.
6:10	Soloist		Development section ends with a piano solo that resembles a cadenza but is accompanied. It ends with an ascending scale.
6:29		Recapitulation	
6:29	Orchestra	Theme 1	
6:44	Piano	Theme 1	Theme 1 is restated and developed in the piano. The development is ornamentation of the melody and use of more scales in the piano.
6:58	Orchestra	Response theme	Followed by a lengthy section of running scalar notes in the piano.
7:28 7:43	Orchestra and soloist	Theme 2	Stated by piano and repeated by woodwinds.

7:58	Orchestra and soloist		Piano and orchestra play a section that is similar in function to the closing section of the second exposition. The material builds tension by alternating between piano and orchestra, shifting between major and minor keys, and by the piano playing running scales. The section ends with a sudden stop.
8:33	Orchestra and soloist	Development theme	Piano plays the development theme, which is repeated by the woodwinds while the piano plays more showy and fast runs. The section becomes more and more exciting and ends with a trill in the piano that leads to the response theme.
9:17	Orchestra	Response theme	
9:30	Orchestra	Development theme	This section ends with the orchestra getting slower and louder, leading up to a held chord and pause before the cadenza.
9:46	Soloist	Cadenza	Piano solo that ends with a long trill.
11:03	Orchestra	Response theme material	Full orchestra ends the movement with response theme-like material that gives way to a short melodic phrase from the end of the orchestral exposition.

If You Liked That, Try This

Concerto in E-flat major for Trumpet, Hob.VIIe:1, Joseph Haydn
Concerto no. 3 in E-flat major for Horn, K. 447, Mozart
Concerto no. 5 in A major for Violin, K. 219, Mozart

YouTube video: search on keywords
Horowitz plays Mozart piano concerto 23 1st movement
Wynton Marsalis Haydn Trumpet Concerto part 1

Remember to add to your personal playlist any of these samples that you like.

The Romantic Concerto

How did the concerto change from the Classical era to the Romantic period?

The virtuosity of the Classical era concertos demonstrated in Mozart's piano concertos increased in the Romantic era. Public concerts became increasingly popular in the late Classical era and throughout the Romantic period. These concerts gave rise to the traveling virtuoso, who played a set repertory of works, mainly concertos, at public concerts throughout Europe. Many concertos of the late

Dashboard

COMPARE AND CONTRAST

Classical and Romantic time periods were written for specific performers skilled at particular techniques.

During the 19th century the concerto form remained three movements of alternating speeds. Cadenzas are common in both the first and last movements, and the technical demands of the works are generally greater than in earlier periods. Most composers of the period wrote in this form, beginning with Beethoven. His piano concertos are still considered some of the finest examples of the form ever written. Felix Mendelssohn, Johannes Brahms, and Pyotr Il'yich Tchaikovsky all wrote concertos for violin and/or piano that are part of the standard concerto repertory today.

PERFORMER PROFILE
Cellist Yo-Yo Ma

Cellist Yo-Yo Ma. Courtesy Associated Press.

Born in Paris to Chinese parents, cellist Yo-Yo Ma calls the United States home. But, he is the world's musician. Having mastered the classical cello solo repertory he has also recorded with such diverse musicians as vocalist Bobby McFerrin, fiddle player Mark O'Connor, jazz trumpeter Chris Botti and in such wide ranging musical genres as Argentinian tango and African music of the Kalihari Desert. Yo-Yo Ma also performed solos for the film soundtracks of *Memoirs of a Geisha* and *Crouching Tiger, Hidden Dragon*. Born in 1955, he began the cello at age four. Both of his parents were musicians. After his family moved to the United States he performed at age seven in a special concert for President Kennedy conducted by Leonard Bernstein. He has won fifteen Grammy awards for his more than seventy-five albums, and has performed concertos with most of the world's major orchestras.

In 1998 he founded the Silk Road Project with the aim of using music as a means of communication and migration of ideas between cultures. The project promotes study of cultural and artistic traditions existing along the trade routes of Eurasia of the Silk Road. The Silk Road Ensemble, of which Yo-Yo Ma is a regular member, has performed worldwide, and presents multimedia events as well as concerts. In addition to his musical studies at the Juilliard School in New York, he also earned a Bachelor of Arts degree in humanities in 1976 from Harvard University. In 2006 the United Nations appointed him U.N. Messenger of Peace and in 2011 he was awarded the Presidential Medal of Freedom.

Go to the Helpful Resources section for Chapter 6 for links to websites about Yo-Yo Ma. Create a list of musicians whose names you recognize that have performed with Yo-Yo Ma. What styles of music did they perform together? Share your research with your class on your course discussion board or on the textbook Dashboard.

Felix Mendelssohn

German-born Felix Mendelssohn (1809–1847) was another child prodigy, a piano virtuoso by nine and an accomplished composer of symphonies, concertos, songs, and sonatas by thirteen. His sister, Fanny, appears to have been equally talented but, due to traditions of the time, her music was not made public. Like Mozart's sister, Nannerl, Fanny's life was one of family and home rather than fame through music. Mendelssohn is widely credited with rediscovering the music of J. S. Bach when he presented Bach's Passion According to St. Matthew to the Romantic-era public. Mendelssohn had a successful career as a pianist, composer, and conductor. In 1842 he founded the Leipzig Music Conservatory, which set the standard curriculum for a program of study in music. Prior to that time music study was taken individually, usually in a master–student setting. Most music schools today retain curricula modeled on the Leipzig school. His violin concerto is one of the most often played and virtuosic pieces of the Romantic era.

Composer Felix Mendelssohn-Bartholdy.
© Grafissimo. Courtesy iStock.

LISTENING GUIDE 6.3

CONCERTO IN E MINOR FOR VIOLIN, op. 64, mvt. 1,
Felix Mendelssohn, composed 1844

Dashboard

**HEAR STREAMING AUDIO
ON DASHBOARD**

What to Listen For

In this work, and in most Romantic era concertos, the solo part begins immediately and states the themes.

Theme A

Theme B

Cadenzas in many concertos, especially those written prior to the Romantic era, were usually improvised. In this work Mendelssohn writes out the cadenza for the violinist and places it near the middle of the movement.

TIMING	TEXTURE	FORM: SONATA	WHAT TO LISTEN FOR
0:00	Soloist with orchestra	Exposition Theme A	The A theme is presented by violin in the high register of the instrument.
0:30	Soloist with orchestra		Violin plays fast running notes answered by *forte* chords from the orchestra.
0:46	Soloist with orchestra		Violin plays fast, ascending octaves.
0:54	Orchestra	Theme A	Theme A is played by the orchestra.
1:20	Orchestra	Bridge theme	Orchestra presents a new theme that is used to connect the two main melodic sections of the exposition. It continues the lyrical style of theme A.
1:26	Soloist with orchestra	Bridge theme	The violin plays this new theme.
1:35	Soloist with orchestra		Following much display of virtuosity over the range of the violin, the solo part comes to a calm rest at the end of the section.
2:34	Orchestra	Theme B	The second theme is played by woodwinds in a major key. The mood is less hurried and the tempo is slower.
2:49	Soloist with orchestra	Theme B	Violin plays the second theme.
3:51	Soloist with orchestra	Theme A	Theme A returns in solo violin, this time in a major key. Violin continues display of virtuosity through fast runs and use of the full range of the instrument.
4:40	Orchestra and soloist	Development	The themes are fragmented and developed.
5:00	Soloist with orchestra		The violin plays an altered version of theme 1.
6:29	Soloist	Cadenza	
8:01	Orchestra	Recapitulation Theme 1	The orchestra plays the first theme. The violin plays virtuosic broken chords.
8:48	Orchestra	Theme 2	The woodwinds state the second theme.
9:03	Soloist with orchestra	Theme 2	The violin states and extends the second theme.
10:50	Soloist with orchestra	Cadenza-like	Virtuosic passage by the violin. Violin plays in the very high register. This section sounds somewhat like a cadenza with limited accompaniment.

11:13	Soloist	**Coda**	The transition theme of the exposition is stated by solo violin.
11:30	Soloist with orchestra		Violin plays a running passage that leads to a full orchestra close to the movement.

If You Liked That, Try This

Concerto no. 5 in E-flat major for Piano, op. 73 ("Emperor"), Ludwig van
  Beethoven
Concerto in D major for Violin, op. 77, Johannes Brahms
Concerto in D major for Violin, op. 35, Pyotr Il'yich Tchaikovsky

YouTube videos: search on keywords
Sarah Chang: Mendelssohn Violin Concerto mvt.1 part1
Lang Lang plays Tchaikovsky Piano Concerto no. 1 1M

Be sure to add to your playlist any samples that you like.

Coda: A brief ending section of a musical work that often makes use of fragments of the primary melody of the work and has a repeated rhythmic figure.

✓ **Build Your Own Playlist:** The works studied in the chapter Listening Guides serve as examples of different styles of concertos from different eras. Now, build your own playlist from those works listed in each IF YOU LIKED THAT, TRY THIS list or from other works you find. Share your playlist with others by posting it to your class discussion board or the textbook Dashboard.

✓ **Audio Review:** Go to Dashboard to listen to Professor Bailey discuss music of the concert hall.

✓ **How Am I Doing?** Go to Dashboard to test your understanding of this material by taking the chapter quiz.

Dashboard

KEY TERMS

Cadenza	Exposition	Solo concerto
Coda	Motif	Sonata form
Concertino	Movement	Terraced dynamics
Concerto	Recapitulation	Thematic development
Concerto grosso	Ritornello	Theme
Development	Rondo	Virtuoso

The Symphony

LEARNING OBJECTIVES

- **Explain similarities and differences between orchestral suite and symphony.**
- **Demonstrate by listening examples an understanding of the styles and tempos of the standard four-movement forms of a symphony.**
- **Contrast the characteristics of the Classical era and Romantic era symphonies.**
- **Name important composers of the symphony.**

Key Concepts: development of the symphony, form of the symphony, orchestral suite's influence on the symphony

Opening image: Courtesy Ferenc Szelepcsenyi/Shutterstock.

Where It's Playing

The symphony is one of the most important and popular of all art music forms written for the concert hall, so much so that many written as early as the 1700s are still performed regularly today. If you attend an orchestra concert in a concert hall it is very likely that a symphony will be on the program. The word *symphony* is used both to indicate a form of music and sometimes to mean an orchestra. In this text it is used to indicate a form of music.

We hear symphonies in many places in our daily lives, often as background music in some public place. Because many symphonies in the standard repertory were written over one hundred years ago, they are in the public domain and can be recorded or presented without incurring copyright fees. This makes them convenient and inexpensive to use in movies, television commercials, and cartoons.

In order to hear a symphony live, you will need to go to a concert hall. If you are taking this class on a college or university campus you can most likely hear a symphony played sometime during the academic year presented by your own college or university student orchestra. Or, perhaps there is an amateur or professional orchestra near where you live. Many areas too small to maintain a professional orchestra have orchestras made up of amateur musicians from the community.

The Development of the Symphony

What are the similarities and differences of orchestral suite and symphony?

The rise of public concerts in the late 18th century helped popularize the **symphony**, a large-scale instrumental work lasting anywhere from twenty minutes to over two hours today. In the 18th century concerts were often longer than today and could be three hours or more in length. Since a symphony is usually divided into four or more movements, the symphony was the perfect form to help fill the time. Some early symphonic composers wrote hundreds of these works, but by 1820 most composers wrote ten or fewer.

The symphony as a form has its roots in dance music of the 1500s and 1600s. **Dance suites** of the Renaissance era (ca. 1450–1600) were often sets of popular dances of the time such as the **pavane**, **saltarello**, and **galliard**. When combined, these dance movements form a longer sectional work. The suites were originally performed in private concerts at homes or at courts, or sometimes as dinner or ceremonial music. These early dance suites influenced an important ancestor of the symphony and one of the earliest types of music written

Dashboard

ATTEND AND REPORT

Symphony: A large-scale work usually for full orchestra dating to the Classical era and still in use today. Often divided into at least four contrasting movements. The term is derived from Greek and means "to sound together."

Dance suite: An instrumental form dating from the Renaissance era. The dance suite consisted of short, contrasting style dances often in pairs and was written for instruments.

Pavane: A slow dance in duple meter often used as a processional, thought to have originated in France.

Saltarello: An Italian dance in triple meter. The dance is characterized by a jumping step.

Galliard: A fast dance originating in France in triple meter. It, like the saltarello, contains a jump step that ends in a pose. The galliard is often paired with the pavane.

for orchestra, the **orchestral suite**. Instrumental music of the Renaissance and early Baroque was closely associated with dance, and the first concert pieces for orchestra alone were taken from dances. The orchestral suite is a multi-movement work usually consisting of a series of dances in contrasting tempos. Most often the dances are in the same key and are in a two-part form (AB), with both sections played twice.

   Most Baroque era composers wrote in this form, but the suites of Johann Sebastian Bach (1685–1750), George Frideric Handel (1685–1759), and Georg Phillip Telemann (1681–1767) are the best examples of this style. The fact that Telemann wrote about 125 orchestral suites speaks to the importance and usefulness of this form of music in Baroque life. Bach wrote four suites for orchestra and most likely heard them performed by student orchestras in Leipzig coffeehouses. Listening Guide 7.1 is not a symphony, it is a dance suite, and is useful to hear as a predecessor of the symphony.

Orchestral suite: A large-scale work for orchestra consisting usually of a set of contrasting dances in movements. The suite was used in the Baroque era and is considered a predecessor of the Classical era symphony.

LISTENING GUIDE 7.1

AIR FROM SUITE NO. 3 IN D FOR ORCHESTRA, BWV 1068,
J. S. Bach, composed 1730

Bach's Orchestral Suite no. 3 in D (1730) is written for strings, two oboes, three trumpets, two timpani, and harpsichord. This work is in five movements; an overture and four dances (in order: Air, Gavotte, Bourree, and Gigue). Each of the four dance movements is in the dance form of AABB. The Air contains one of Bach's most famous melodies. This movement is scored for violins, viola, and continuo. The **continuo** part would have been played by two instruments, one capable of playing chords and the other playing a bass line. Often the pairing was harpsichord and cello or double bass.

Dashboard

HEAR STREAMING AUDIO ON DASHBOARD

Continuo: A part of the score usually in music of Baroque era. The continuo part was a way of notating music in a sort-of shorthand fashion using chord symbols (numbers) and what looks like a bass line. The part is played by two players, one being an instrument capable of creating chords such as the harpsichord, organ, or lute. The written bass line might be played by cello, double bass, or bassoon. The instruments used to play the part varied greatly and the choice was left to the discretion of the performers.

What to Listen For

- Listen for the bass line that gently pulls the rhythm of the work along in a walking style and tempo. The bass part is a series of two-note motifs.
- Listen for the long, high pitches of the melody that seemingly float above the bass line.
- Listen for the contrast of the rhythmic variety of the melodies with the repetitive quality of the bass line.
- Listen for the use of sequence in the B sections. Bach uses this repetitive device to lend organization to the work and forward direction to the phrase.
- Listen for the two primary themes of the Air.

Theme A

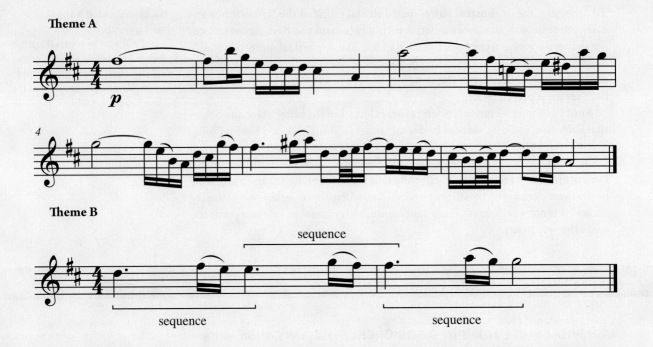

Theme B

TIMING	TEXTURE	FORM	WHAT TO LISTEN FOR
0:00	Homophonic, Melody in upper strings, counter-lines in viola and second violin	A	Theme A begins without an introduction. The walking bass line descends with a regular and gentle beat. The melody floats smoothly.
0:44	Same as A	A	Theme A repeats with minor embellishment.
1:30	Same as A	B	Theme B moves with a quicker melodic rhythm with the same kind of walking bass line. It makes wide use of sequence. The B section is twice as long as the A section.
3:00	Same as A	B	Theme B repeats.

If You Liked That, Try This

Suite no. 2 in D major ("Water Music"), HWV 349, G. F. Handel
Suite in A minor for Orchestra, TWV 55:a3, G. P. Telemann
Suite in D major no. 4, for Orchestra, BWV 1069, J. S. Bach

YouTube videos: search on keywords
Handel: Music for the Royal Fireworks 1/2 (Ouverture)
Handel: Water Music (Opus Arte)
Telemann—Suite part 1

Remember to add to your personal playlist any of these samples that you like.

The Classical-Era Symphony

What are the styles and tempos of the standard four-movement forms of a symphony?

While the orchestral suite is a form of orchestra music from the Baroque era that is related to the symphony, the symphony became the dominant form of orchestral music in the Classical era, and remains so today.

In the Classical era the symphony's movements developed into a predictable format:

- Movement 1, Sonata Form
- Movement 2, Theme and Variations or ABA Form
- Movement 3, Minuet and Trio
- Movement 4, Rondo or Sonata Form

The movements often are related through the use of common tonal centers (or keys) and/or melodic material.

Like the concerto, the first movement is usually in sonata form and features two main contrasting melodies. The second movement of the symphony is usually slow in tempo and could be a number of different forms, but the theme-and-variation form was common in the Classical era. **Theme and variation** relies on the strength of one melody and the ability of the listener to recognize it even after much alteration. The original melody is changed through alterations, embellishments, or varied restatements of the original melody. Sometimes these variations are complex and designed to obscure the original theme. The idea is to create numerous moods or styles using the same melodic material.

The third movement of the Classical era symphony is the **minuet and trio**. Although the minuet can be danced, this was originally a Classical era dance form intended for listening rather than dancing. Such works as the minuet and trio are called *stylized dances*. The minuet was originally popular at the court of Louis XIV of France and became fashionable throughout the courts of Europe during the Classical era. The minuet is in triple meter and is a contrast to the duple meter movements that surround it in the symphony. This movement is in a three-section format of minuet-trio-minuet. The first section minuet is repeated to create the third section. The trio section of a minuet and trio is often slightly slower in tempo than the minuet and usually has a more lyrical melody and is set in a different key than the minuet.

The final movement of the symphony is most commonly a sonata or rondo. Sometimes a work has a short ending section called a coda. A coda usually contains one of more fragments of the primary melody of the work and often has a repetitive rhythmic pattern that helps solidify the key of the piece.

Theme and variations: A form of music in which one melody is presented and followed by embellishments, enhancements, or developments.

Minuet and trio: Originally a dance form, the minuet and trio is a three-part form often used as the third movement of a symphony.

The Romantic-Era Symphony

How do the Classical era and Romantic era symphonies differ?

Composers throughout the 19th and 20th centuries continued to write in the symphonic form but few achieved the quantity and quality of the symphonies written by Haydn, Mozart, and Beethoven. Still, many wrote excellent works that

PERFORMER PROFILE
Trevor Pinnock and the English Concert

Have orchestras always sounded like they do today?

Classical musicians don't just perform classical art music. Most spend a good deal of their careers also performing music in the popular and jazz genres. And, some classical musicians specialize in art music of a particular time period. One such musician is conductor and keyboardist Trevor Pinnock (b. 1946) who is best known for his performing, conducting, and writing about music of the Baroque and Classical eras. An English musician, Pinnock studied at the Royal College of Music in London. In 1972 he formed the English Concert, an orchestra dedicated to performance of music from the Baroque and early Classical periods. One of the distinctive aspects of this orchestra is that its members perform on instruments made in the Baroque and Classical eras. Through scholarly research, the players also attempt to perform the music using the same techniques as might have been used when the music was new. This usually entails special bowing techniques by the string players and specialized dynamic and articulation performance by all. Often the ensemble is led by one of the performers in the orchestra as would have been the case during the Baroque and early Classical eras.

Pinnock is also one of the world's foremost harpsichordists, specializing in music of the early Classical and Baroque periods. For more information on Pinnock and the English Concert visit his website or that of the English Concert.

British conductor and early music specialist Trevor Pinnock.
Courtesy Hermann Wüstmann/picture-alliance/dpa/AP Images.

have become part of the standard canon of literature played each year by orchestras around the world.

Following Beethoven's style, symphonic music became more expressive, ushering in a new period referred to as the Romantic era (approximately 1820–1900). The great writers of symphonies of the Romantic era transformed the form and the ensemble playing it by making them more dramatic and larger. Throughout the Romantic era the symphony was altered to fit the expressive requirements of the time. In terms of length and sentiment, symphonies became the musical equivalent of the novel in literature. By the end of the 1800s, symphonies were no longer written only in four movements. The form had become longer and less predictable. What began as a four-movement work that might last twenty-five minutes changed into a work that could last two hours and might consist of seven or eight movements. While early symphonies could be played by approximately thirty musicians, the late Romantic orchestra might require over one hundred players with several new instruments and larger sections of traditional instruments. The typical Romantic orchestra included 3 flutes, 3 oboes, 3 or more bassoons, 3 clarinets, occasionally a saxophone, 4 horns, 3 or 4 trumpets, 3 trombones, a tuba, and a large percussion section. Composers called for more and more strings in the violin, viola, cello, and bass sections.

The interior forms of the symphony's movements also changed. No longer were they movements of a dance character. The **scherzo**, which is similar to the old Classical minuet and trio form but more agitated and dramatic in character, replaced the minuet-trio, and the song form became more common than the theme and variation. Many symphonic movement forms became much more free in form and less dependent upon the contrast and repetition patterns so important in the Classical symphony. Melody, which had been succinct and regular in the Classical symphony, became longer, more disjunct and expressive, and at the same time more lyrical. Harmonies of the Romantic symphony were more dissonant and expressive than those of the Classical era, and composers used the larger orchestra to create much more dramatic changes in dynamics and tone color.

Scherzo: A three-part form usually in triple meter used in Romantic era symphonies as the third movement, replacing the Classical minuet and trio. The work is usually faster and more agitated in style than its predecessor.

Most composers of the Romantic era composed symphonies. Sometimes these works took on other names such as the symphonic poem or program symphony studied in Chapter 8, but the idea of a long and dramatic work for large instrumental forces continued throughout the century.

Throughout the 18th, 19th, and 20th centuries many composers wrote symphonies for orchestras and bands. And some of the composers studied in this book wrote symphonies that are part of the standard orchestral repertory today, including Franz Schubert, Robert Schumann, Pyotr Il'yich Tchaikovsky, Charles Ives, Antonin Dvořák, Sergei Prokofiev, and Aaron Copland. And the symphony continues today as an important form of orchestral music. While it is true that fewer composers today focus their creative energies on the symphony as their primary compositional output, many Modern era symphonies exist.

Important Composers of Symphonies

Who were the most important composers of the symphony?

Franz Joseph Haydn

One of the earliest of the important writers of symphonies of the Classical era was Franz Joseph Haydn (1732–1809). Haydn was born in Austria, the son of a wheelwright, and at age eight was accepted into the boys choir at St. Stephen's Cathedral in

Classical era composer Franz Joseph Haydn. Courtesy GL Archive/Alamy.

Vienna. Here he stayed and worked as a freelance musician and teacher until he won the position of music director for the court of Prince Esterházy of Hungary. The prince was a legendary patron of music and provided Haydn with the musicians to perform his music. For Esterházy, Haydn managed the musicians, wrote music for the prince's chapel and opera house, and composed music for the prince's orchestra and chamber musicians. Mostly for this court, Haydn wrote an incredible amount of music including 104 symphonies, more than 20 operas, 83 string quartets, oratorios, and many works for individual instruments or small groups. The prince regarded Haydn as a high-level servant, which was typical of the era's patronage system, in which most successful composers wrote almost exclusively for one wealthy aristocrat or church. Today's best composers are freelancers who accept commissions to write their works.

Word of his compositional mastery spread throughout the great houses of Europe, and in the late 1700s Haydn left his position and wrote works on commission. By the end of his career public concerts were becoming popular and Haydn was one of the earliest composers able to make his living presenting his compositions across Europe.

Some of the most famous works from this time in his life were six symphonies written for concerts in Paris and twelve symphonies written for a concert tour to London. Haydn was also a successful composer of oratorios and wrote two popular ones near the end of his life, *The Creation* and *The Seasons*. In the Classical era Haydn served as an innovator, developing the symphony and string quartet into standardized forms. Much of his music is highly dependent on rhythmic ideas and is energetic and full of joy.

Esterházy Palace, where Haydn worked for almost thirty years. Courtesy mauritius images GmbH/Alamy.

LISTENING GUIDE 7.2

SYMPHONY NO. 94 IN G MAJOR, Hob.1:94, mvt. 2,
Franz Joseph Haydn, composed 1792

One of Haydn's best-loved symphonies is his Symphony no. 94 in G Major, the "Surprise Symphony," so-called because of a sudden very loud chord that sounds at the ends of some phrases in the second movement. Written in 1792 its orchestra consists of violin, viola, cello, bass, two flutes, two oboes, two bassoons, two horns, two trumpets, and timpani, which had become the standard orchestra used in the early Classical era. The second movement is an audience favorite and illustrates the use of the theme and variation form as a second movement of a symphony. Like most second movements of the time, it is slow in tempo. The work has four variations of the original theme. Typical of themes used for variation settings, it has two parts of contrasting nature. The first part is **staccato** (meaning the notes are separated from one another and often sound short) and light and simply outlines the notes of a C major chord (C-E-G). The second part is a disjunct melody and sounds more lyrical in nature. Haydn's wit shows throughout the movement in his modifications of the melody and sudden changes of style.

Dashboard

HEAR STREAMING AUDIO ON DASHBOARD

Staccato: Indication to play notes separated from one another or short.

What to Listen For

- Listen for the theme in two phrases, each of which is repeated.
- Listen to how graceful yet folk-like the theme seems. One can imagine a light stepping dance matching with the music.

A Section of the Theme

B Section of the Theme

- Listen for the "surprise"—the loud chord at the end of the repeat of the first section. Haydn doesn't overuse the surprise, it appears only once at this point in the theme.
- Listen to the change in style and quality of each of the four variations on the original theme.

TIMING	TEXTURE	FORM	WHAT TO LISTEN FOR
0:00	Homophonic Strings	Theme A part	The primary theme of the movement is a folk-like melody that has a dance quality to it. The form of the movement is a theme with four variations and coda.
0:19	Strings	Theme A part repeats	The repeat of the theme is softer and sets up the surprise *fortissimo* chord that ends the first A section.
0:38	Strings	Theme B part	The B section of the theme begins with a contrast in style with the strings playing slurred notes. The end of the B section returns to the initial thematic material and style of the A section.
0:57	Woodwinds and horn added	Theme B part repeats	Theme B repeats.
1:15	Strings and flute	Var. 1 A	As the lower strings play the theme, Haydn adds a counter-line in faster notes in the high strings and flute. Each of the phrases begins with a suddenly *forte* chord rather than ending with one.
1:33	Strings	Var. 1 A repeat	Repeat of Var. 1 part A material.
1:50	Strings	Var. 1 B	First violin continues a similar embellishment using faster scalar pitches.
2:08	Strings	Var. 1 B repeat	Repeat of Var. 1 part B material.
2:25	Strings and woodwinds	Var. 2 A	Variation 2 is in C minor rather than the original key of C major and is much more dramatic in character than the original. The melody is much louder.
2:42	Strings and woodwinds	Var. 2 A repeat	A section repeats.
3:00	Strings and woodwinds	Var. 2 A part developed	This time the A section material is developed rather than presenting a full B section. Strings and bassoon play a series of descending scales while flute and oboe play a doubled version of material similar to the B section. Variation 2 ends with violin alone.
3:39	Strings woodwinds	Var. 3 A part	The theme begins softly with sixteenth notes outlining the theme rather than eighth notes as in the original.
3:55	Strings flute, oboe	Var. 3 A repeat	The A section repeats with a lyrical countermelody added in flute and oboe.
4:13	Strings flute, oboe	Var. 3 B	The flute and oboe duet continues to dominate the tone quality.
4:31	Strings flute, oboe, horn	Var. 3 B repeat	Horns are added.

4:48	Full orchestra including the first entrance of trumpets and timpani	Var. 4 A	The theme is presented accompanied by agitated strings and accented offbeats. Variation 4 is both a rhythmic and dynamic variation. This variation is the climax of the work and is the loudest and most dramatic. The use of louder dynamics and full orchestra create this change in style and sound.
5:06	Strings and bassoon	Var. 4 A repeat	The melody is changed to a lyrical line in an altered rhythm with offbeat accompanying chords.
5:24	Strings and bassoon	Var. 4 B	The lyrical feel continues.
5:42	Full orchestra	Var. 4 B repeat	The section is played in a loud, full orchestra version. It ends with a four-measure extension leading to a loud and dramatic fermata.
6:11	Full orchestra	Coda	The primary theme returns with some new accompaniment and a repeated timpani note beneath it. The movement ends quietly with repeated tonic chords—a stereotypical ending of symphonic movements.

If You Liked That, Try This

Symphony no. 45 in F-sharp minor ("Farewell"), Haydn
Symphony no. 103 in E-flat major ("The Drumroll"), Haydn

YouTube videos: search on keywords
Leonard Bernstein conducting Haydn's Symphony no. 88

Remember to add to your personal playlist any of these samples that you like.

Wolfgang Amadeus Mozart.
Courtesy FineArt/Alamy.

Wolfgang Amadeus Mozart

If Haydn's music is the beginning of the Classical style, Wolfgang Amadeus Mozart's music is the zenith. Mozart (1756–1791) was a versatile composer, able to write symphonies, operas, concertos, keyboard music, and chamber music. His symphonies represent the culmination of development of the classical style. In his own time Mozart was perhaps best known as a composer of keyboard music and opera, and as such we will discuss his life and work further in chapters devoted to those genres.

LISTENING GUIDE 7.3

SYMPHONY NO. 40 IN G MINOR, K. 550, mvt. 1, Allegro molto,
Wolfgang Amadeus Mozart, composed 1788

**HEAR STREAMING AUDIO
ON DASHBOARD**

The Symphony no. 40 in G minor is the next-to-last symphony written by Mozart and is one of the most recognized symphonies still today. It was written in 1788, near the end of his life, and has a much darker character than much music of the Classical era.

The first movement is characteristic of much Viennese Classical style in that it is made up of a melodic line with homophonic accompaniment. The movement is a fast sonata form that has two themes that are both played twice in the opening section of the sonata form (the exposition). The opening theme in the key of G minor has a driving and persistent rhythmic pattern that pushes the work forward with urgency. This theme is contrasted with a lyrical second theme in B-flat major, and Mozart divides the sections of the theme between the string instruments and the woodwinds to create even more contrast. The middle section of the movement (the development) can only be described as manic, feverish. The themes are broken into small pieces and taken through a number of key centers quickly. The return of the original material (the recapitulation) is altered in that both themes are presented in the original minor key center, creating an impression of sadness and remorse. The Symphony no. 40 in G minor, K. 550, is an example of the height of Classical era symphonic style and is still popular today.

What to Listen For

- Listen for the persistent quality of the rhythmic pattern of the first theme. The rhythm of this theme is often described by musicologists as throbbing because of its repetition of a three-note figure. The effect is one of tension and urgency.

Molto Allegro

- Listen for the question and answer quality of the phrases of the theme. The themes are structured in clearly heard phrases. The opening theme creates this effect, with the first two measures of the three-note theme being answered by a descending scale on the same rhythm.

- Listen for the contrast in style between the first and second themes. Theme 1 is a forward-moving theme that has rhythmic drive and is as much a rhythm as it is a melody. Theme 2 produces just the opposite effect in that the longer pitches sound halting.

TIMING	TEXTURE: HOMOPHONIC	FORM: SONATA	WHAT TO LISTEN FOR
0:00	Strings alone	Exposition Theme 1	The primary theme appears softly first in the violins and contains a rhythmic urgency. The theme is in G minor.
0:23	Full orchestra		This theme is repeated by the full orchestra with an added part in woodwinds.
			There is a momentary pause before the second theme begins.
0:52	Strings and woodwinds	Theme 2	The second theme is a lyrical melody in B flat major. It is presented first by strings and woodwinds at a soft dynamic.
1:02	Strings and woodwinds		The theme is restated by strings and woodwinds playing in reverse order.
1:20	Full orchestra	Closing	The exposition ends with a brief section that sounds developmental. Mozart uses the first three notes of the theme 1 to toss back and forth between different instruments of the orchestra.
1:47			The section ends with the full orchestra playing short descending scales and cadences in a major key.
2:01		Repeat of the exposition	
		Development	
4:04	Woodwinds then strings add Full orchestra	Theme 1	First part of the development section uses the theme in different ranges of the orchestra.
4:21	Full orchestra		The second part of the development is suddenly louder with the full orchestra. While the main theme is played by the upper strings, the lower strings and woodwinds play a fast scalar accompaniment that adds to the manic quality.

(continued)

TIMING	TEXTURE: HOMOPHONIC	FORM: SONATA	WHAT TO LISTEN FOR
4:49	Full orchestra		In the third part of the development section Mozart segments the three-note motif of theme 1 and passes it among the instruments. This section is in three short phrases that alternate suddenly between soft and loud playing. This section descends directly into the recapitulation of the movement.
			Note that only theme 1 is developed. Mozart gradually diminishes theme 1 in this section to the three-note motif, first deleting the upward leap, then leaving off the last note of the theme, and finally just playing the three notes.
		Recapitulation	
5:23	Strings only	Theme 1	Theme 1 is restated much the same as in the beginning of the work.
5:45	Strings and woodwinds		Theme 1 begins as if to be restated but is altered this time. The remainder of this section is a series of sequential patterns that ascend and heighten the tension.
6:36	Strings and woodwinds	Theme 2	The second theme is stated this time in a minor key, giving it a sadder feeling than originally stated. It too is varied from its original form and ends with a downward scale that leads into the closing section.
7:19	Full orchestra	Closing	This closing section is much like that in the exposition in that it sounds somewhat developmental of the three-note motif of theme 1. Mozart bats the motif around between instruments before ending the section with a series of descending scales.
7:50	Full orchestra	Coda	The movement ends with a short coda section that contains a brief statement of theme 1 and a full orchestra cadence at the *forte* level in G minor.

If You Liked That, Try This

Symphonies no. 39 and 41, Wolfgang Amadeus Mozart
Symphony no. 103 in E-flat major, "The Drumroll," Haydn

YouTube videos: search on keywords
Mozart—Sinfonia no. 41 "Jupiter"—VPO Bohm (1 de 4)

Remember to add to your personal playlist any of these samples that you like.

Ludwig van Beethoven

Perhaps the best-known of all writers of symphonies was the German-born Ludwig van Beethoven (1770–1827). Like Mozart he was something of a child prodigy, serving as an organist at court by age eleven and publishing compositions a year later. At twenty-two he moved to Vienna, then the music capital of Europe, and caught the city's imagination with his incredible virtuosity as a pianist and violinist. Though he had wealthy supporters, Beethoven did not work under the formal patronage system for one employer. Instead he was a freelance musician who made his living by teaching, performing, and mostly by composing. Music publishing had developed sufficiently by this time that he could earn money through the sale of his works for individuals to perform.

Around age twenty-nine Beethoven began to go deaf, a condition that he much feared would end his career as a composer. Consequently, he tried to hide it from the world and for the most part withdrew from society. Beethoven's life was one of personal struggle and great fame. At his death he was the best-known and most highly regarded composer in Europe. Over twenty thousand mourners attended his funeral. Many of his works are still thought of as some of the best music ever written, and he is revered as one of the greatest and most influential composers of all time.

Composer Ludwig van Beethoven at his desk. © HultonArchive. Courtesy iStock.

Beethoven's symphonic music was, perhaps, the first to go beyond entertainment in its purpose. His works bridge the Classical and Romantic time periods in music and exhibit some traits of both eras. He used and developed Classical era forms, but his music is more self-expressive than that of his predecessors, and more emotional and dramatic, all Romantic traits. His works express human emotions through syncopations, dissonances, range, and dynamics. They are full of interruptions—sudden stops and starts. These elements create a sense of urgency in many of his works. Much of the music of his early career sounds heroic. Beethoven expanded the size of the orchestra and lengthened the timing of the symphony.

Beethoven completed nine symphonies; the Third, Fifth, and Ninth are three of the most famous of all time. He also wrote thirty-two piano sonatas, five piano concertos, one opera, two masses, and a great deal of chamber music. His string quartets are considered some of the finest of the repertory.

LISTENING GUIDE 7.4

SYMPHONY NO. 5 IN C MINOR, op. 67, mvt. 1, Allegro con brio,
Ludwig van Beethoven, composed 1808

Dashboard

**HEAR STREAMING AUDIO
ON DASHBOARD**

One of the best-known and loved symphonies is Beethoven's Symphony no. 5 in C minor, op. 67. The work was composed in 1808 and has become so ubiquitous that it is hard to get through one day of American life without hearing a few measures somewhere on the radio, in elevators, in cartoons or movies, or in its original symphonic form. The opening four notes serve as an idea (motif) that Beethoven referred to as "fate knocking at the door." This motif dominates the first movement and is developed throughout the first movement sonata form. This single rhythmic device is transformed and repeated as three short notes followed by a long note and is used throughout the symphony. The first movement is a series of arresting devices that build up tension that does not truly end until Beethoven turns the struggle and tension of the minor first movement theme into a major key center and joyous final fourth movement.

Each of the final three movements sounds like a response in one way or another to the tension and defiance of the opening movement. The slow second movement is written in variation form. It presents both a graceful and noble melody that is interrupted by a second theme in **fanfare** style that seems to rudely break the pastoral mood. The third movement is a scherzo. Like the minuet it is in three parts, but the style is not dance-like. Instead the scherzo creates a mysterious and dark mood. The fourth and final movement of the work is a joyous release of the tension of the first movement. It is also in sonata form. It is longer than the first movement (unusual at the time) and brings back the "fate knocking at the door" motif from movement one, but this time it conveys a sense of victory. The Fifth Symphony is, along with the Third and Ninth, the most commonly heard of Beethoven's symphonies. Professional orchestras around the world schedule these three symphonies on a regular basis. The powerful Fifth and Ninth symphonies are ringing endorsements for live performance over recordings. Their full impact is best experienced in a concert hall played by a live orchestra and shared with members of your community.

Fanfare: A musical form used to announce or introduce an event. Often played by brass instruments.

What to Listen For

- Listen for the development of the so-called fate motif of the first four notes of the symphony.

- Listen for how Beethoven uses the repetition and sequence of this rhythmic motif to build tension throughout the movement.
- Listen for how Beethoven uses the pause in the music as part of the theme to make it more dramatic. The stopping and restarting of the music adds to the tension.
- Listen for the use of dynamics, especially sudden loud ones, to create dramatic effects.
- Listen for the change of style of the second theme of the exposition.

- Listen for the oboe cadenza in the recapitulation of the movement.

- Listen for a new theme in the coda section of the work, an unusual device for Beethoven's time. This theme looks and sounds a bit like theme 2.

TIMING	TEXTURE: HOMOPHONIC	FORM: SONATA	WHAT TO LISTEN FOR
0:00	Full orchestra	Exposition Theme 1	The "fate" theme consisting of a four-note rhythmic idea presented in a minor key.
0:05	Strings first then joined by woodwinds. All by end of the section	Theme 1	The motif is used in a sequential manner and passed among various sections of the orchestra to create an urgent and driving rhythm.
0:43	Horns	Bridge	At this bridge section between themes Beethoven uses the motif in horn to change key and as a transition into the second theme.

(continued)

TIMING	TEXTURE: HOMOPHONIC	FORM: SONATA	WHAT TO LISTEN FOR
0:46	Strings alone then joined by woodwinds	Theme 2	The second theme is more lyrical than the first and is in a major key. Beethoven includes the four-note rhythmic motif as an accompaniment in the bass.
1:07	Full orchestra	Closing theme	This section is based upon the original motif and is used as a closing section to the exposition.
1:26		Exposition repeated	
2:54	Horn and clarinet, then woodwinds and strings	Development Theme 1	Theme 1 is developed, announced by the horn and clarinet sections. The four-note motif is presented in a sequence that descends.
3:31	Full orchestra but rarely all together	Bridge	The bridge theme is developed first in a descending manner through the string section, then in fragments alternating between low notes in strings and high notes in wind instruments.
4:12	Full orchestra		The horn call theme used to return to original idea of the movement.
4:17	Strings and woodwinds	Recapitulation Theme 1	Theme 1 in full orchestra played loudly.
4:36	Oboe solo		Oboe cadenza.
4:51	Strings joined by winds	Bridge	Bridge theme returns.
5:14	Bassoons, then full orchestra	Theme 2	Theme 2 is introduced by horns and then played in bassoon.
5:42	Full orchestra	Closing theme	Closing theme returns and continues in a triumphant fashion into the coda.
6:00	Full orchestra	Coda	Theme 1 material repeated.
6:41	Full orchestra		The new theme is march-like, presented in building fashion.
7:06	Full orchestra		Beethoven plays a sort of joke on his listeners at this point. Following the final fate motif and full stop of the music it sounds like he is returning once again to the exposition of the sonata. Instead he interrupts this with powerful and dramatic closing chords on the original rhythmic motif.

If You Liked That, Try This

Symphonies no. 6, 7, and 9, Ludwig van Beethoven
Symphonies no. 3 and 4, Felix Mendelssohn

YouTube videos: search on keywords
Beethoven Symphony no. 5, 1st mvt—Arturo Toscanini/NBC Symp
Beethoven, Symphony no. 7, II Karajan, Berliner Phil

Remember to add to your personal playlist any of these samples that you like.

PERFORMANCE PRACTICE
Conductors

What does a conductor do?

When you go to a concert hall today to hear an orchestra it will almost certainly be led by a conductor. As Maestra Marin Alsop, music director of the Baltimore Symphony Orchestra points out, it is her job to "project a vision . . . to them [the orchestra musicians] . . . the role of the conductor is the ultimate authority figure." The conductor chooses the music to be performed, decides on how the rehearsals will be run, and is the public face of the orchestra. And the conductor does not play an instrument in the orchestra. This has not always been the case. Early orchestras in the Baroque era and some in the Classical era did not have conductors at all. Instead, the orchestra was led by a member of the ensemble, usually the best violinist or a keyboard player. This person would often make large gestures, sometimes with their body or head instead of their arms to cause the orchestra to start or stop playing. Early conductors used rolled up pieces of paper instead of batons to indicate the beat. In the Baroque era a famous composer named Jean-Baptiste Lully kept the orchestra on beat by pounding a large staff on the floor while the orchestra played. As music became less rigid in phrase structure and rhythm the conductor became more important to the success of a performance. By the middle of the 1800s orchestras were commonly led by musicians who did not perform an instrument in the ensemble. Today, some small orchestras (called chamber orchestras) function without conductors, but most large ensembles (bands, choirs, and orchestras) perform exclusively with a conductor as musical leader.

Dashboard

EXPLORE

American conductor Marin Alsop. Courtesy Associated Press.

Johannes Brahms

Johannes Brahms (1833–1897) was born in Germany into a musical family, and became one of the most-loved composers of symphonies despite the fact that he wrote only four. He is usually viewed by music historians as a traditionalist rather than an innovator. He seems to have made no real attempt to develop music's harmonic language or formal structure. Instead Brahms turned back to the style, and to some degree the harmonic language, of the earlier Viennese masters: Mozart and Beethoven. He wrote music in the Classical forms and to a great extent within the scope and size of the Classical era. His music, especially the

Johannes Brahms at the piano. Courtesy North Wind Picture Archives/Alamy.

orchestral works, exudes warmth, making use of dark, rich timbres.

At a young age Brahms became friends with the famous composing couple, performers, and music critics Robert and Clara Schumann, and they assisted his establishment as a composer. Brahms was a champion of the at-the-time largely forgotten music of Bach, Handel, and Mozart. He was well known as a performer and conductor of his own works and spent the second part of his life in Vienna. Brahms wrote a good deal of chamber music and vocal music but not opera. One of his best-known works is *A German Requiem* written for orchestra, vocal soloists, and large chorus.

LISTENING GUIDE 7.5

SYMPHONY NO. 3 IN F MAJOR, op. 90, mvt. 3, Poco allegretto
Johannes Brahms, composed 1883

Dashboard

HEAR STREAMING AUDIO ON DASHBOARD

Brahms's Symphony no. 3 in F major, op. 90 is a four-movement work. Its movements are connected by recurring melodic material. While using the Classical symphony structures, the piece is Romantic in its lyricism and sweep of melodies. The first movement is a sonata form and makes use of a Brahmsian melodic idea; the pitches F–A flat–F, which stood for "Frei aber froh" (Free, but happy), Brahms' personal motto. The second movement is also a sonata form, an unusual choice. The third movement is not a scherzo as would have been common for symphonies at the time of its composition. Rather, Brahms wrote a sort-of waltz in a more relaxed tempo than was normal for symphonic third movements and for less than full orchestra. Its melody is a mysterious tune, full of Romantic yearning. The finale is the third sonata form of the work and contains dramatic changes of style and mood.

What to Listen For

- Listen for the unhurried style of the movement. Unlike his contemporaries, Brahms did not use a frantic scherzo for the third movement of this symphony. Instead, he wrote a waltz that is much more relaxed and similar in character to the minuets of the Classical era symphonies.

- Listen for how Brahms creates a sense of yearning and passion by present-ing the waltz in a minor key and then lightens the mood when he plays it in a major key.
- Listen for how Brahms uses the horn to carry the melody and make it sound expressive. Use of horn as an instrument of passion and expression was common in the Romantic era.
- Listen for the primary theme of the work.

TIMING	TEXTURE: HOMOPHONIC	FORM: ABA'	WHAT TO LISTEN FOR
0:00	Strings, flute, and bassoon	A	Theme A is played first by the cello section in C minor.
0:27	Strings, clarinet, and bassoon		Violins repeat the theme, cello plays a descending scale that sounds like a musical sigh.
0:52	Strings, clarinet, and bassoon		The cello section presents a new motif that the violins take up.
1:28	Full orchestra		Theme A returns played first in flute, oboe, and horn.
1:58	Woodwinds and cello	B	The first theme of the B section is a waltz in a major key that is played by woodwinds, but it doesn't sound like a regular waltz because of the rhythmic placement of the melodic lines. These placements and entrances of instruments create a sort of off-beat waltz.
2:31	Strings		Strings play an interlude melody between the major state-ments of the B section waltz. This expressive line leads into the second statement of the melody.
2:53	Full orchestra		Winds play the B section waltz again.
3:10	Strings joined by winds at end of section.		Strings play the interlude again and this phrase ends with the woodwinds playing a fragment of the first theme of section A.
3:46	Full orchestra	A'	Horns play Theme A.
4:15	Full orchestra		Oboe repeats Theme A.
4:41	Full orchestra		First bassoon and clarinet, then strings play a lyrical interlude between two statements of Theme A.
5:18	Full orchestra		Theme A returns played by violin and cello.
5:45	Full orchestra	Coda	Winds and then strings play a short ending to the movement using the rhythmic pattern of Theme A.

If You Liked That, Try This

Symphony no. 8 in G major, op. 88, Antonín Dvořák
Symphony no. 1 in C minor, op. 68, Johannes Brahms

YouTube videos: search on keywords
Brahms, Symphony no. 2—BRSO—M. Jansons 1/5
Dvořák, Symphony no. 8 mvt. I—Mehta—1/4

Remember to add to your personal playlist any of these samples that you like.

Exotic: A term used within the larger scope of Nationalism in music. A work is considered to be exotic if the composer creates a work based upon folk material from a country other than that of his origin and/or creates a work to sound like music of a country other than his homeland.

CULTURAL CONNECTION: THE GAMELAN

Czech composer Antonín Dvořák (1841–1904) was brought to the attention of the musical public by the more famous symphonist Johannes Brahms. Championed by Brahms, he was invited to present his symphonies in concerts in England and in 1892 traveled to the United States to become director of the National Conservatory of Music in New York.

While in America, Dvořák spent a summer in Spillville, Iowa, and there was influenced by the sounds and landscape of America's heartland. Dvořák's Symphony no. 9 in E minor, op. 95 ("From the New World"), was written in 1893 and contains some of his best-known melodies. Though often labeled nationalistic it is actually a form of what was called **exotic** music because it makes use of not just the composer's home country folk traditions but also the music of another country. This work makes use of scales that are prevalent in folk music and expresses the size and landscape of the United States through its melodic expansiveness. It is cyclical in nature in that themes from the first movement are used in all movements and the final movement brings back melodic material from the first three. The primary theme of the second movement is a very recognizable melody to which the words of the song "Goin' Home" are often sung in a spiritual style.

LISTENING GUIDE 7.6

SYMPHONY NO. 9 IN E MINOR, op. 95, mvt. 2,
Antonín Dvořák, composed 1893

HEAR STREAMING AUDIO ON DASHBOARD

What to Listen For

• Listen for the plaintive tone quality of the English horn as it plays the first theme. The instrument and the shape of the melody give it a sort of nostalgic quality.

- Listen for how Dvořák uses *cresendi* and *diminuendi* to create tension and release in the movement.
- Listen for the way the woodwinds are used in this movement. They are both carriers of the melody and instruments that create tone color.

Pizzicato: Technique of plucking a string on a string instrument rather than using a bow to produce the sound.

TIMING	TEXTURE: HOMOPHONIC	FORM: ABA′	WHAT TO LISTEN FOR
0:00 0:28	Winds alone Strings added	Intro	A slow introduction with brass and woodwinds playing soft chords that gradually crescendo followed by a soft string section.
0:41	Strings and English horn	A	Theme A is presented by the English horn. The theme is in three sections.
2:19	Woodwinds Brass and timpani added		Chords of the introduction return first in woodwinds, then in a crescendo in the brass ending with a loud timpani roll.
2:48	Strings only		Soft and lyrical section played by strings sounds like it was derived from the main theme.
3:45 3:58	Strings and English horn Other winds added		The English horn plays the third phrase of the melody again. The section ends with a soft French horn playing the initial notes of the theme.
4:49	Strings and woodwinds	B	Theme B begins with a descending scale played in oboe and flute. The theme is faster and sounds hurried or urgent to move forward.
5:21	Strings and woodwinds		Clarinets play a slower melody with string basses playing **pizzicato** notes as accompaniment. The melody then moves to flute and oboe.
6:10 6:45	Strings and woodwinds Strings and clarinet		The violins join in this melody but move it forward in intensity and speed. The orchestra gets louder through this section and more intense. This section builds in intensity until the strings begin a long downward sequence of sound that returns to the clarinet theme in section B.
7:26	Strings		Strings play the clarinet theme from earlier in section B.
8:29	Full orchestra	Bridge	The bridge begins with short high and fast notes in the oboe and flute.
8:55			The section crescendos with full orchestra playing much faster than any other section of the movement and adding a melody from movement 1.
9:24	Strings and English horn	A′	Theme A returns played by the English horn again.

(continued)

TIMING	TEXTURE: HOMOPHONIC	FORM: ABA′	WHAT TO LISTEN FOR
9:49	Strings only		Strings play part of theme A and Dvořák adds pauses between sections of the theme that break up the rhythm.
10:19	Strings and woodwinds		Theme A is presented simply by violin and cello soloists, and full strings and clarinet play the ending of the melody, gradually getting softer and softer.
11:22	Brass and bassoon Woodwinds Strings		Brass play the chords from the introduction softly at first, then louder. Strings end the movement with soft sustained chords.

If You Liked That, Try This

Symphonies no. 4 and 5, Pyotr Il'yich Tchaikovsky
Symphony no. 8 in G major, Antonín Dvořák

YouTube videos: search on keywords
Dvorak—Symphony No. 9 "From the New World"—II (part 1)
Tchaikovsky Symphony No. 4, 4th mvmt

Remember to add to your personal playlist any of these samples that you like.

✓ **Build Your Own Playlist:** The works studied in the chapter Listening Guides serve as examples of different styles of symphonies from different eras. Now, build your own symphony playlist from those works listed in each IF YOU LIKED THAT, TRY THIS list or from other symphonies you find. Share your playlist with others by posting it to your class discussion board or on Dashboard.

✓ **Audio Review:** Go to Dashboard to listen to Professor Bailey discuss the symphony.

✓ **How Am I Doing?** Go to Dashboard to test your understanding of this material by taking the chapter quiz.

Dashboard

KEY TERMS

Coda	Galliard	Saltarello
Continuo	Minuet and trio	Scherzo
Dance suite	Orchestral suite	Staccato
Exotic	Pavane	Symphony
Fanfare	Pizzicato	Theme and Variations

Program Music

LEARNING OBJECTIVES

- Explain similarities and differences of program music and symphony.
- Define four different types of orchestral program music.
- Name important composers of program music.
- Demonstrate an understanding of characteristics of program music by listening examples.

Key Concepts: absolute music, concert overture, incidental music, nationalistic music, program symphony, pure music, symphonic poem

Opening image: Cartoon of Berlioz conducting. Courtesy Pictorial Press Ltd/Alamy.

123

Where It's Playing

Program music is some of the most often heard music today. Like the symphony, we hear program music in the concert hall played by an orchestra. But, you are much more likely to hear live program music than a symphony in your everyday life. Any piece of music that is used to introduce or set the scene for an event that follows can be called program music. We hear this kind of live music today at graduation ceremonies, political rallies, and many civic events. And, most film scores are program music. Program music is also heard in the recital hall, most often played by a solo piano.

Program music is more accessible to many listeners today than is absolute music. The assistance of a program or title to help guide one's imagination is appealing to many concertgoers. When attending a concert that contains program music, it is best to pay close attention to the title and/or the accompanying program. While the music plays, allow your mind to freely associate the musical sounds you hear with ideas that the title or program suggests. Listen to how the composer uses tempo and dynamic changes to create distinct sections and to dramatize aspects of the program. Listen for melodies or rhythms that seem to be associated with particular instruments or groups of instruments. This will help you understand the composer's use of timbre and tone color to shape the overall work.

In the concert hall today program music is often used to create theme concerts, which focus on a particular event or composer. Such concerts may revolve around a holiday like Halloween, Christmas, or the Fourth of July, or be based on a country theme or genre, like Russia, space, or American patriotic or jazz-influenced music. The descriptive and evocative nature of program music makes it ideal for creating an overall mood or design for a concert. As you hear instrumental music of any kind during your day, pay attention to its effect on you. Is it suggestive of a scene or story to you? If so, it is program music.

Dashboard

ATTEND AND REPORT

Types of Program Music for the Orchestra

How does program music differ from other types of orchestral music?

During the Romantic era composers found that audiences increasingly wanted music that was descriptive. The result was a great increase in **program music**, which sets a mood or scene, depicts an emotion, or tells a story. Program music became the most important type of music for the concert hall in the mid-1800s and remained so for fifty years. All music can be said to be either pure music or program music. **Pure music**, also called absolute music, has no allegorical or pictorial

Program music: Instrumental music that is suggestive of a mood, story, poem, or phrase.

Pure music: Also called absolute music. Music that has no allegorical or pictorial meaning.

meaning. Program music can be appreciated as absolute music if the listener does not associate the work with any particular scene or emotion but enjoys it solely for its compositional craft and structure. An early example of program music from the Baroque era is Antonio Vivaldi's *The Four Seasons* studied in Chapter 6. This work is a set of four concertos that depict the seasons of the year.

Most program music is written for orchestra or piano. Program music is suggestive music. Often the title of the work suggests the idea of the program (notes from the composer explaining the idea of the work), as with Berlioz's *Symphonie Fantastique*. The title might also be suggestive of another art form such as a poem or novel, with the sections often corresponding to characters or events in the poem or novel. Sometimes the composer writes an accompanying note about the piece to guide the listener. Other times, program music accompanies a dramatic work such as a play or film. Program music is more than merely imitative, not simply the musical imitation of car horns, wind, or other sounds in nature. Music can be made to represent these things but this alone does not make it program music. The music must be evocative of characters, scenes, and emotions, not simply a series of sound effects.

During the Romantic era composers developed four major musical forms of program music for the concert hall. These four types include the **symphonic poem**, the **program symphony**, **incidental music**, and the **concert overture**. Many works from this period are still in the standard repertory of orchestras and are heard regularly today.

Symphonic poem: A long piece of program music for orchestra in which the music depicts a story, scene, or mood.

Program symphony: Multi-movement work similar to tone poems and symphonic poems in intent. Each movement or section of the symphony contains its own program.

Incidental music: Music written to accompany a play or drama, usually for orchestra in the Romantic era.

Concert overture: A one-movement piece usually in sonata form, similar to the overture played at an opera prior to the raising of the curtain.

The Program Symphony

The program symphony is a multi-movement work, often made up of longer and more movements than the traditional four-movement Classical era symphony. These works are usually composed for very large orchestras, making it possible to create a great number of timbres by different combinations of instruments. Most often the symphony is a work of absolute music, but in the Romantic era the desire for expression extended into this form as well. The movements were usually titled or had accompanying programs in addition to the overall title and theme of the work. The Romantic era composer used form freely in the movements, which no longer followed a predictable pattern or sequence as they had in a Classical era symphony.

Hector Berlioz

Berlioz (1803–1869) was one of the first great masters of innovative instrumentation, the art of combining instruments purposefully to create different timbres. Like his Romantic contemporaries, he was inspired by literature, especially that of Shakespeare and Goethe. Berlioz was also one of the earliest great conductors. During his life, his music was thought of as unconventional and was not received well by the public or critics.

About his music Berlioz wrote, "Qualities of my music are passionate expressiveness, inner fire, rhythmic drive, and unexpectedness."

Hector Berlioz. Courtesy GL Archive/Alamy.

"Witches' Sabbath" by Francisco de Goya. Courtesy Erich Lessing/Art Resource, NY.

His use of large dynamic ranges, multiple tempo changes, and reliance on percussion and wind instruments made him a Romantic composer ahead of his time. He wrote long melodies that were not regular in their construction. Timbre was one of the most important musical elements in his compositions. These same elements would be used by most of the great late Romantic era composers in their operas and symphonic works for dramatic effect, but they were unusual in Berlioz's time.

Berlioz wrote works monumental in length that required considerable resources to perform. He combined large numbers of instrumentalists and vocalists as no other composer. A work for band and chorus entitled *Grand symphonie funèbre et triumphale* was performed by more than 1,500 musicians! Berlioz also wrote opera, overtures, incidental music for plays, and most other large-scale forms of the Romantic era. Berlioz based portions of his *Symphonie fantastique*, written in 1830, on his own life. He became obsessed with an actress named Harriet Smithson. His unrequited love for her inspired the primary melodic theme of the work—the **idée fixe**. This musical motif unifies the five movements in varied tempos, dynamics, timbres, rhythms, and harmonies.

Idée fixe: A primary idea of a work, literary or musical, which repeats throughout the work.

LISTENING GUIDE 8.1

"MARCH TO THE SCAFFOLD," from *Symphonie fantastique*, mvt. 4,
Hector Berlioz, composed 1830

Dashboard
**HEAR STREAMING AUDIO
ON DASHBOARD**

Movement 1, "Reveries, Passions," opens with a long, slow introduction that is followed by a loosely structured sonata form. The idée fixe is the primary melodic material of the movement and it, like Berlioz himself, is transformed from love-sick to "volcanic love" to "religious consolation." Berlioz provided the following program for the first movement: "First, he remembers the weariness of the soul, the indefinable yearning he knew before meeting his beloved. Then, the volcanic love with which she at once inspired him, his delirious suffering, his return to tenderness, his religious consolation."

Movement 2, "A Ball," is a waltz, one of the most popular dances in the 19th century. The movement is in three parts and the idée fixe is presented in two of these sections. Compared with the other movements, "A Ball" provides the simplicity required in a long orchestral journey. Of this movement Berlioz wrote: "Amid the tumult and excitement of a brilliant ball he glimpses the loved one again."

Movement 3, "Scene in the Fields," is a **pastorale** movement that is intended to create "sorrowful loneliness." This movement is also in three-part form and is slow in tempo. Romantic composers often tried to express their love of nature in program music. The oboe is commonly used as a melodic instrument in pastorales and Berlioz presents the idée fixe in English horn, a relative of the oboe. The program for this movement states: "On a summer evening in the country, he hears two herders calling each other with their shepherd melodies. The pastorale duet in such surroundings, the gentle rustle of the trees softly swayed by the wind, some reasons for hope which had come to his knowledge recently—all unite to fill his heart with a rare tranquility and lend brighter colors to this idea. But his beloved appears again, spasms contract his heart, and he is filled with dark premonitions."

Pastorale: A work of music that evokes images and feelings associated with nature.

Movement 4, "March to the Scaffold," is the most popular and best-known of the work. In this movement the dreamer "dreams that he has murdered his beloved, that he has been condemned to death and is being led to the scaffold. At the end, the idée fixe returns for a moment like a last thought of love interrupted by the death blow." Berlioz stated that the "March to the Scaffold" was even more frightening when he heard it for the first time than he had imagined it. The movement has two themes; Berlioz calls the first "somber and fierce" and the second "brilliant and solemn." The work is **march**-like in style and ends with a loud chord—suggesting the executioner's ax, followed by descending pizzicato notes in the strings to evoke the head bouncing down the stairs of the scaffold.

March: A piece of music often associated with the military that has a steady and repetitive beat, making it easy to march to.

Movement 5, "Dream of a Witches' Sabbath," is a mixture of witch's dance and funeral music. It is intended to be macabre and fantastic, and it meets its goal. The program states, "He sees himself at a witches' Sabbath in the midst of a hideous crowd of ghouls, sorcerers, and monsters of every description, united for his funeral. Unearthly sounds, groans, shrieks of laughter, distant cries, which other cries seem to answer. The melody of the beloved one is heard, but it has lost its character of nobleness and timidity; it is no more than a dance tune, ignoble, trivial, and grotesque. It is she who comes to the Sabbath. The funeral knell, burlesque of the 'Dies irae,' Witches' dance."

The opening is a number of musical cries and events in an otherwise slow section. The section is eerie, with the cries interjected into soft tremolos in the strings. The second section presents the idée fixe as a dance melody showing that the beloved is actually a witch. Bells toll in a funereal fashion, followed by the "Dies irae" (the "Day of Wrath" chant, which evokes the Last Judgment). The movement becomes a musical nightmare as it crescendos and builds to a huge finish of orchestral sound. The idée fixe is a typical Romantic-era melody in that it is long, has a large range of pitches from highest to lowest, contains numerous dynamics shifts, and uses tempo **rubato** to express yearning and longing. The various settings of the motif throughout the work demonstrate Berlioz's mood swings.

Rubato: The intentional changing of tempo within a work to highlight certain climactic moments.

What to Listen For

- Listen for the use of musical sounds to represent the execution.
- The rhythm of the opening measures and theme B represent the solemn procession to the scaffold.

Theme A represents the anguish of the condemned.

- The idée fixe at the end of the march played by clarinet representing the beloved.

- The loud full orchestra chord that interrupts the idée fixe signifying the executioner's blade.
- The pizzicato chords that follow the execution representing the rolling severed head.
- The cheers of the crowd represented by the final full orchestra chords.

TIMING	TEXTURE: HOMOPHONIC	FORM: MARCH	WHAT TO LISTEN FOR
0:00	Percussion, horns and low strings Woodwinds added	Intro	The movement begins with a repeated rhythmic pattern in timpani and a soft but gradually growing pattern in horns. The music immediately gives the impression of a solemn procession.
0:28	Cello and string bass	Theme A	The first melody is presented suddenly and loudly by low strings. The melody is a descending minor scale that suggests an anguished cry.
0:40	Cello, string bass and bassoon		Theme A is repeated with bassoons playing a short marching accompanimental theme.
0:52	Strings and percussion		Theme A is repeated in violins.
1:17	Strings and bassoon		Theme A is restated by pizzicato strings with bassoon scalar line played staccato.
1:36	Woodwinds, brass and percussion	Theme B	Brass introduce the march-like theme B loudly.
2:25	Full orchestra is used	Theme A developed	Theme A is briefly reintroduced played by a combination of instruments. Short phrases of the melody are played by different sections as the theme descends.
3:33	Full orchestra	Theme B	Theme B is restated by brass and woodwinds. Strings play a wild sounding flurry of accompanimental scales.
4:03	Strings and woodwinds Full orchestra	Theme A	Theme A returns first in pizzicato strings, then in brass.
4:14	Full orchestra	Theme A	Theme A is restated by full orchestra.
4:38	Full orchestra		Theme A scale is presented by full orchestra in reverse, this time ascending. Theme B is reintroduced.
5:25	Full orchestra		Full orchestra begins a harried, excitement-filled section. Less melodic than rhythmic, the section is driven forward by a faster tempo and a dotted rhythmic pattern with rapid scales in strings. Tension builds to the solo clarinet.
6:04	Clarinet	Idée fixe	The idée fixe is presented by solo clarinet.
6:14	Strings		It is interrupted by a short and loud full orchestra chord meant to represent the falling of the guillotine blade. String pizzicato pitches suggest the bouncing head.
6:16	Full orchestra		The movement ends with repeated chords by full orchestra playing loudly.

If You Liked That, Try This

The Sorcerer's Apprentice, by Paul Dukas
Till Eulenspiegel's Merry Pranks, by Richard Strauss

YouTube videos: search on keywords
Berlioz Symphony Fantastic Simon Rattle DVD Quality
Walt Disney—Fantasia—Mickey The Sorcerer's Apprentice

Remember to add to your personal playlist any of these samples that you like.

The Symphonic Poem

Most important of the four types of program music is the symphonic poem, developed in the 1840s by composer and pianist Franz Liszt (1811–1886). Symphonic poems are similar to program symphonies in purpose and intent. But, there is no standard inner form to symphonic poems that composers need follow. This freedom of form also matches well with the depiction of scenes from literary works. These pieces usually exhibit large dynamic ranges and include many changes of tempo—traits of Romantic era music that carried into the early 20th century and that would have been uncommon in a Classical era orchestral work. Symphonic poems lent themselves easily to new styles of music such as impressionism.

Franz Liszt. Courtesy INTERFOTO/Alamy.

Tone poem: A late-Romantic era term for symphonic poem.

Franz Liszt

In his time Liszt was one of the world's greatest concert pianists and an exceptional showman. Liszt was Hungarian and spent his student life in Vienna and his early adult years in Paris. His early compositional life focused on piano works, most of them incredibly virtuosic and considered at the time to be unplayable by anybody but him. Desiring more recognition as a composer he accepted a position as court conductor in Weimar. Here his career focused on orchestral music, primarily program symphonies and symphonic poems. Liszt wrote twelve symphonic poems including works based on Greek myths and Shakespeare plays. Perhaps his most famous is *Les préludes*, written in 1853. The work is typical of symphonic poems in that it is in one long movement with multiple sections that change character and mood. It is based on a poem by Alphonse de Lamartine called *Méditations poétiques* and generally depicts the moods, emotions, and events of that work. In 1861 Liszt changed careers again when he moved to Rome to take holy orders. In Rome he wrote primarily oratorios and masses.

The symphonic poem remained an important form of orchestral music throughout the Romantic era. Late in the time period it was renamed the **tone poem**. The most important late Romantic composer of the symphonic or tone poem was Richard Strauss.

Richard Strauss

Strauss (1864–1949) was German and was the son of a professional musician. He began composing at six and was a famous conductor most of his adult life. His work as conductor of the Vienna State Opera orchestra is probably what led him to focus much of his composing on opera. Strauss's understanding of how to use the orchestra to create specific sounds and timbres in a representational manner made him the master of the tone poem. His tone poems *Don Juan*, *Death and Transfiguration*, *Ein Heldenleben*, and *Also sprach Zarathustra* are among the best-known and most often heard in the concert hall today. *Zarathustra* has become an iconic

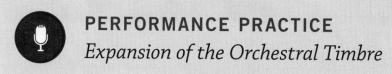

PERFORMANCE PRACTICE
Expansion of the Orchestral Timbre

Why were more instruments added to the Classical era orchestra?

In the Romantic era the size of the orchestra increased dramatically compared to that of the Classical era. As new instruments were created, and old ones were refined, composers tried out new combinations of instruments to create a wider timbral palette. Unlike in the Classical era, there was not a standard orchestra size throughout much of the 19th century. Composers in different countries used different instruments in the orchestra. In France program music was often used for political purposes and to celebrate national occasions at outdoor events. Berlioz wrote a number of works for these types of events and often used massive forces to perform them. His masterwork for band *Grande symphonie funèbre et triomphale* was scored for over two hundred players and was performed at least once by over 1,500 musicians. His *Grande Messe des morts* was written for an orchestra of about 170 players, four brass choirs, and a large choir of at least 210. In the score to this work Berlioz stated that if space permitted, the choir and orchestra numbers could be doubled or tripled!

In addition to widening the timbral palette available, adding large numbers of performers to orchestral music also had to do with the dramatic effect of loud musical sounds. The more brass and percussion instruments added to the orchestra, the louder it could be, and therefore more dramatic. Composers writing program music required an extremely wide dynamic range in order to create effects. This increase in size of the orchestra continued in the symphonic forms until World War I when financial issues made it impossible to maintain large orchestras.

piece of music in the modern era, used to represent space travel, as in the 1968 movie *2001: A Space Odyssey*.

Paul Dukas

One of the most recognized and best-loved of all symphonic poems is *The Sorcerer's Apprentice* by Paul Dukas (1865–1935). Dukas was a French composer and teacher who wrote a good deal of music, but nothing as well known as this tone poem. The work was based on a 1797 ballad by Goethe, *Der Zauberlehrling*, and told the story of an apprentice who found a shortcut to his work through the magic of his master. The apprentice cast a spell that he was unable to control and ultimately had to be saved by the sorcerer. This symphonic poem was used prominently in the 1940 Walt Disney film *Fantasia*, to which it owes much of its popularity.

LISTENING GUIDE 8.2

THE SORCERER'S APPRENTICE,
by Paul Dukas, composed 1897

Dashboard
**HEAR STREAMING AUDIO
ON DASHBOARD**

The work is a scherzo in one movement with many sections. Dukas's witty use of the low reed instrument, the bassoon, to represent the relentless marching theme demonstrates his mastery of orchestration. True to its form, the tone poem contains numerous shifts in mood, tempo, and dynamic ranges. The scherzo is a large two-part form in which the second part is a varied repeat of the material of the first part. The work contains four primary melodic ideas: the "swirl motif," first theme, second theme, and fanfare. The work ends with a short Coda section that returns to the sound of the beginning of the work.

What to Listen For

- Listen for how Dukas uses woodwinds and brass to introduce many of the important ideas of the work. Some instruments, like the bassoon, actually take on a character. This is particularly true in the use of the work in the Walt Disney movie *Fantasia*.

- Listen for how Dukas uses the strings and their ability to make sweeping fast passages sound like water or wind. The sounds actually seem to go uphill and downhill.

- Listen for how Dukas uses the instruments to build up to one climactic moment after another and follows them with an abrupt change in volume.

TIMING	TEXTURE: HOMOPHONIC	FORM: AA′ CODA	WHAT TO LISTEN FOR
0:00	Strings and woodwinds	Introduction	Very soft strings play a descending slurred scalar line. This is the "swirl" motif. Flutes play a fast repeated rhythm, and clarinet and oboe introduce theme 1.
0:36	Strings and woodwinds		The ideas repeat.
1:10	Strings and woodwinds		A sudden change to a fast and short outburst in the woodwinds foreshadows theme 2. The strings interrupt with another hushed shimmering sound while a flute and then horn play a fragment of the first theme.
1:43	Full orchestra		A second sudden fast outburst, longer this time, ends as abruptly as it starts with a huge bang from the timpani.
2:07	Woodwinds	A	Introduction to theme 1 in low winds played as short "droplet" notes.
2:25	Bassoon with strings	Theme 1	Theme 1 is presented by solo bassoon.
2:40	Strings and horns Woodwinds added		Swirl theme fragments in the strings alternate with theme 1 in horns.
3:07	Full orchestra		A long descending chromatic scale in the strings leads to a return of Theme 1.
3:10	Full orchestra		Theme 1 returns in the strings and trumpet.
3:30	Woodwinds, strings, and bells Full orchestra added	Theme 2	Theme 2 appears in full form for the first time played by the upper winds and bells.
3:54	Full orchestra	Theme 1	Theme 1 reappears stated in the brass.
4:06	Full orchestra		Strings play a fragment of theme 1 in a section that builds up to an abrupt drop of volume.
4:19	Strings and woodwinds Full orchestra adds	Theme 1	Theme 1 is played by the strings and then by the woodwinds.
4:35	Strings and woodwinds	Theme 1	Theme 1 is presented by the violins, this time in a lyrical fashion.
4:52	Full orchestra	Theme 2	Theme 2 reappears in its original fashion.
5:10	Strings and woodwinds Full orchestra adds	Theme 1	Theme 1 is stated by low winds and strings, and then by horns.
6:09	Brass Full orchestra	Fanfare	Fanfare theme is stated by brass and is used in fragmentation and repetition to build up to a climactic fanfare in the trumpets to end the A section.
6:48	Strings and low woodwinds	A′	The section begins much like the original A section, starting hesitantly and seeming to wind itself up.
7:03	Bassoon and strings	Theme 1	Theme 1 is played by bassoon.
7:15	Woodwinds and strings	Theme 1	Theme 1 is repeated by clarinet and viola.
7:26	Full orchestra	Theme 2	Theme 2 is stated by woodwinds and violins in a lyrical style.
7:34	Full orchestra		Themes 2 and 1 are fragmented and combined by full orchestra.

(continued)

TIMING	TEXTURE: HOMOPHONIC	FORM: AA′ CODA	WHAT TO LISTEN FOR
8:01	Horn and trumpet solos with woodwind and string accompaniment	Fanfare	Fanfare theme is stated by horn and then by solo trumpet.
8:07	Full orchestra	Theme 1	Theme 1 is restated by low winds and strings. Fragments of theme 2 and the fanfare are played.
8:13	Full orchestra		Theme 1 is played by trumpet.
8:34	Full orchestra		The swirl motif returns and is combined with ascending fast low string and wind scales.
8:52	Full orchestra		Fragments of theme 1 along with the swirl motif create a section that gains in volume and intensity to a climactic return of the Fanfare theme.
9:09	Brass with string and woodwind accompaniment	Fanfare	Fanfare theme is stated in brass, bringing the A′ section to an abrupt end.
9:42	Strings and woodwinds	Coda	The swirl motif appears in strings sounding like the beginning of the work.
10:06	Strings and woodwinds		Woodwinds play fragments of theme 1.
10:32	Full orchestra		Full orchestra plays one final rhythmic fragment of theme 1 at a full volume.

If You Liked That, Try This

Don Juan, Richard Strauss
Les préludes, Franz Liszt
Dance macabre, Camille Saint-Saëns
Also sprach Zarathustra, Richard Strauss

YouTube videos: search on keywords
2001 A Space Odyssey Opening
Mitropoulos conducts Liszt—Les préludes

Remember to add to your personal playlist any of these samples that you like.

Incidental Music

Incidental music is music written to accompany or precede a theatrical or literary performance. It is considered secondary in importance to the play, hence the name "incidental." Essentially the music can be in any form. It is usually sectional and contains many shifts in moods, both being a practical way to match the music to the openings or interludes in a play. Incidental music is written for many different types of ensembles but the kind that concerns us here is for orchestra. Like the other types of program music in this chapter much incidental music is written for large orchestra to take advantage of the many different colors or timbres that can be created by various instrument combinations. These timbres assist the composer in bringing to mind a character or emotion of the play, or to help set the scene. Much of this music is also considered to be in the form of a concert overture. And, much of film music can be considered incidental music since it sets scenes and emotions but remains secondary to the drama. One of the best examples of incidental music for orchestra is 19th century composer Felix Mendelssohn's music for Shakespeare's *A Midsummer Night's Dream*. This music contains the famous "Wedding March" often used in American weddings.

LISTENING GUIDE 8.3

OVERTURE TO *A MIDSUMMER NIGHT'S DREAM*,
Felix Mendelssohn, composed 1826

Mendelssohn wrote his incidental music for Shakespeare's comedy *A Midsummer Night's Dream* at two different times in his life. The overture in this listening guide was written when he was just seventeen years old and was not written for any particular performance of the play. He returned to the work in 1842 when asked to do so by the King of Prussia. Mendelssohn added marches (including the Wedding March), intermezzos, dances, and songs for a production of the play at the king's New Palace in Potsdam in October 1843. The overture is intended to inspire in the listener images of an enchanted forest containing fairies and other magical creatures. The play mixes a fantasy world with real-world characters, and Mendelssohn's melodies represent these characters. The work is a mix of Classical and Romantic era ideas. The form of the overture is a sonata but contains five primary themes.

Dashboard

HEAR STREAMING AUDIO ON DASHBOARD

What to Listen For

- Listen for how each of the five themes matches a character or scene in the play.

Theme 1, a magical scene

Theme 2, fairy theme of Oberon and Titania, rulers of the fairy world

Theme 3, a dramatic and loud theme for Theseus, ruler of the human world

Theme 4, theme of the human lovers, Lysander and Hermia, and Demetrius and Helena

Theme 5, theme of the weaver Bottom who has the head of an ass

The themes are designed to match some aspect of the character or scene which they depict. Theme 1 consists of long notes played very softly by woodwinds in their upper register. This creates a mysterious, yet unforeboding sound representing the magic of the forest. Theme 2 represents the fairies—light and playful creatures who move quickly. This theme appears in high strings and is played softly and lightly. Theme 3 is most often played by full orchestra at a loud dynamic. It represents the king of the humans, Theseus, and is intended to be pompous. Theme 4, representing the lovers is lyrical and is played by soft woodwinds. Theme 5 represents the fool of the play, Bottom, who appears as an ass head. The theme is played by full orchestra and is designed to imitate the braying of an ass.

TIMING	TEXTURE: HOMOPHONIC	FORM: SONATA	CHARACTER/SCENE RELATIONSHIP
0:00	Soft woodwinds	Exposition Theme 1	Fantasy world of the forest
0:12	Soft strings played staccato	Theme 2	Fairies
1:08	Full orchestra	Theme 3	Theseus, the human leader
2:13	Woodwinds, then strings	Theme 4	The pairs of lovers
3:13	Full orchestra	Theme 5	Bottom
3:42	Full orchestra	Theme 3	Theseus
4:09	Strings, woodwinds add	Development Theme 2	Fairies
5:51	Strings	Theme 4	Lovers
6:42	Woodwinds, strings add	Recapitulation Theme 1	Fantasy world
7:02	Strings	Theme 2	Fairies
7:46	Woodwinds, then strings	Theme 4	Lovers
8:48	Full orchestra	Theme 5	Bottom
10:01	Full orchestra	Theme 3	Theseus
10:32	Strings, woodwinds added	Theme 2	Fairies
11:25	Strings	Theme 4	Lovers
12:15	Woodwinds	Theme 1	Fantasy world

If You Liked That, Try This

Egmont Overture, Ludwig van Beethoven
L'Arlésienne Suite, Georges Bizet
In the Hall of the Mountain King, Edvard Grieg

YouTube videos: search on keywords
In the Hall of the Mountain King (Peer Gynt) by Edvard Grieg
Wedding March—Felix Mendelssohn

Remember to add to your personal playlist any of these samples that you like.

The Concert Overture

Another type of program music is the concert overture, a one-movement piece that is usually in sonata form. It is similar in nature to the overture that is played at an opera (to be discussed in Chapter 15) prior to the raising of the curtain in that it is a one-movement work, usually with contrasting styles and tempos. In fact the form grew from the tradition of performing opera overtures as part of concerts.

Most composers of the Romantic era used this form of program music at some time, often when called upon to produce a work of ceremonial or heroic nature. Johannes Brahms wrote his *Academic Festival Overture* for a ceremony in 1880 at the University of Breslau where he was granted an honorary doctorate.

Pyotr Il'yich Tchaikovsky (to be studied for his ballets in Chapter 17) wrote his famous *1812 Overture* as a commission to commemorate the 1882 Moscow Exhibition and for a ceremony consecrating the Cathedral of Christ the Savior, which was built to give thanks for Russia's victory over Napoleon in 1812. The work premiered on August 20, 1882, and has been popular ever since. Starting in the mid-1970s with the Boston Pops Orchestra, it has become a favorite finale and accompaniment to fireworks exhibitions at Independence Day celebrations across America.

Tchaikovsky's *1812 Overture* prominently features the trumpet. Prior to the mid-1800s horns and trumpets could only play in certain keys and were often left out of music simply because the instrument couldn't play the right notes. With the invention of the rotary and piston valves in the 1830s the instruments became much more widely used. Berlioz was an early champion of the new instruments that are still in use today. Visit Dashboard for a link on the instrument's development. Note how the trumpet has changed through the years as instrument makers attempted to make it a more versatile instrument for the orchestra.

Dashboard

EXPLORE

LISTENING GUIDE 8.4

1812 OVERTURE, op. 49,
Pyotr Il'yich Tchaikovsky, composed 1882

Dashboard

HEAR STREAMING AUDIO ON DASHBOARD

What to Listen For

- Listen for programmatic elements that Tchaikovsky used to tell the story of the failed French invasion of Russia in 1812.
- Listen for the sixteen cannon shots that are part of the music.
- Listen for the use of the French national anthem, "La Marseillaise."

- Listen for the national anthem of Czarist Russia, "God Preserve Thy People," which represents the spirit of the Russian people.

- Listen for music that sounds first like chase music and then is used as a triumphal hymn called "God Save the Czar."
- Listen for music in the middle section that sounds like Russian folk music.

TIMING	TEXTURE: HOMOPHONIC	FORM: CONCERT OVERTURE	WHAT TO LISTEN FOR
0:00	Strings only	Section 1	Theme 1 is the Russian Orthodox Church hymn "God Preserve Thy People."
1:29	Strings, woodwinds, and horns added		Theme 1 material passes between strings and woodwinds, getting louder and becoming agitated.
2:17	Oboe solo, woodwinds, and strings	Section 2	Theme 2 is a Russian folksong in C minor and begins in the oboe like a plaintive cry. This section depicts the approach of French troops to Moscow. The theme is repeated and fragmented as it grows louder and more agitated. The brass section becomes prominent as the music becomes more exciting.
3:15	Brass added		
3:41	Full orchestra		The section is brought to a climactic and abrupt halt by two loud, full orchestra chords followed by a restatement of theme 2 in strings.
4:09	Woodwinds and strings	Section 3	Theme 3 is perhaps the most famous music of the work. It is march-like and fanfare-like at the same time. Stated first in woodwinds and horns, it becomes a dominant and triumphant melody later in the work.
4:20	Brass and strings		As the theme repeats, the strings add a soaring lyrical line above the march. The music gradually diminishes and comes to a complete halt before section 4.

(continued)

TIMING	TEXTURE: HOMOPHONIC	FORM: CONCERT OVERTURE	WHAT TO LISTEN FOR
5:09	Woodwinds and strings	Section 4	Theme 4 is an agitated melody designed to create tension and conflict.
5:34	Brass and percussion added		The melody, presented in the strings, gets louder and more intense throughout the section.
5:48	Full orchestra	Section 5	The important melodic material of this section is the French anthem "La Marseillaise." The horn first presents the material, which is to represent the French marching into battle.
5:55	Full orchestra		The trumpet continues the line while violins play sweeping scales above it.
6:24	Full orchestra		Theme 4 returns in strings at a fast tempo.
6:39	Full orchestra		Theme 5 returns in one trumpet statement and the tempo gradually slows.
7:07	Strings and woodwinds	Section 6	Theme 6 is a lyrical Russian folk lullaby played first by strings in a minor key.
7:31	Strings and woodwinds		The melody is a sweet and flowing line. The second half of the theme moves the rhythm forward.
7:53	Strings and woodwinds		Theme 6 is repeated by winds with string accompaniment. The melody shifts to a minor key and ends with a rhythmic figure that foreshadows the melody of section 7. Sections 6 and 7 are meant to represent the Russian soldier thinking of his home during the long winter encampment.
8:39	Flute, clarinet with string and tambourine Bassoon added	Section 7	Theme 7 is a Russian folk dance played first by flute and clarinet with a tambourine providing rhythmic accompaniment.
9:15	Full orchestra	Section 8	The section begins with overlapping statements of theme 4 and theme 5. It continues by adding themes 6 and 7 while theme 5 plays on. The fragmentation of the themes in this section evokes the battle scene where one army gains, then loses, and then gains again. The full orchestra is used as if in a conversation with the various themes. The section ends in the strings with a slowing similar to that in section 5.
10:50	Full orchestra	Section 9	Theme 1, the hymn returns in strings as a faster lyrical version with triangle accompaniment.
11:34	Strings, percussion, and woodwinds		Theme 7 is restated by strings and tambourine.

11:50	Brass and strings	Section 10	This section of the work opens with a statement by the horns of the French anthem.
12:04	Woodwinds added		The section gains in speed, volume, and intensity to an augmented statement of the anthem. Following this statement of "La Marseillaise," the strings repeat a rhythmic pattern that gradually slows to the presentation of the czar's theme.
13:14	Full orchestra		Theme 8, "God Save the Czar" is presented by full orchestra with lots of chimes and bells. The chimes represent the bell towers of the churches of Russia. This section builds to final statements of the triumphal march themes.
14:46	Full orchestra		Theme 3 is presented as a victory march in the upper brass while the czar's theme is simultaneously presented in low brass. The section contains cannon shots and more bells. Theme 8 represents the Russian army's triumphant reentry into burned Moscow. The work ends loudly in an excited and triumphant fashion.

If You Liked That, Try This

Academic Festival Overture, Johannes Brahms
Festive Overture, op. 96, Dmitri Shostakovich
Romeo and Juliet, Pyotr Il'yich Tchaikovsky
Hebrides Overture, Felix Mendelssohn

YouTube videos: search on keywords
A Capitol Fourth 2007 | PBS
Tchaikovsky "1812 Overture" with 105mm Cannons 20071020
Shostakovich Festive Overture Op 96 Live @ Nobel Prize Concert 2009

Remember to add to your personal playlist any of these samples that you like.

Nationalistic Music

The *1812 Overture* is also a type of program music called nationalistic music. Nationalistic music expresses pride in, or love for, one's country. Nationalistic composers based their orchestral works for the concert hall on songs and dances that evoked images of their country and its people. Many traveled their native

Lady Liberty Leading the People, **Eugene Delacroix.** Courtesy Ivy Close Images/Alamy.

countryside collecting folk music and trying to transfer the style and sound of folk songs into their works for orchestra. Folklore, legends, and tales became the programs of much symphonic music in the nationalistic style. And composers attempted to represent the landscape of their countries through music. In some countries this music became a political tool, sometimes inspiring revolution. Much nationalistic music appeared in the form of symphonic poems, ballets, and operas.

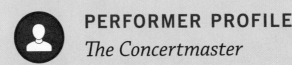

PERFORMER PROFILE
The Concertmaster

When you attend an orchestra concert you will probably notice that one violinist seems to enter the stage late, and that the audience applauds for his or her entrance. This is the orchestra's concertmaster, and he or she is not late to the stage. Instead, tradition dictates that this musician, who is the leader of the string section, be recognized for his or her virtuosity.

The concertmaster is the best violin player in the orchestra and is usually a very experienced performer. In addition to playing whatever violin solos are in the music the concertmaster also helps the orchestra tune and decides on the bowing technique for the string section. To understand bowing technique you must watch the arms and bows of the string players. They all move together in the same direction and change directions at the same time. This synchronicity does not just happen naturally—it must be organized by the concertmaster. And, this bowing direction is so important that it actually changes the accents and phrases of the music. The concertmaster organizes the bowings for the section by indicating the direction the bow should move—either as a down bow where the arm pulls the bow in a downward motion or an up bow in which the arm pushes the bow upward. He or she does this by making small marks on the music. Each orchestra has slightly different bowings for each piece of music in the standard repertory and sometimes a conductor asks for the concertmaster to change the bowing technique to achieve a different type of sound.

Dashboard

EXPLORE

Nationalistic music was strongest in the Romantic era in countries where foreign art music had been previously dominant. For example, composers from Poland, Bohemia, Finland, Spain, and Russia all developed strong nationalistic musical traditions during the 19th century. This music was less prominent in countries whose music had dominated the Western art world for centuries such as France, Germany, Austria, and Italy.

Nationalism in symphonic music continued well into the 20th century. The so-called *Les Six* of France, which included Darius Milhaud, Francis Poulenc, and Arthur Honegger, were popular nationalist composers. English composers Ralph Vaughan Williams, Percy Grainger, and Benjamin Britten contributed to a resurgence in folk music of the British Isles. Two prominent composers of this style in the 20th century were the Hungarian Béla Bartók (1881–1945) and American Aaron Copland (1900–1990).

✓ **Build Your Own Playlist:** The works studied in the chapter Listening Guides serve as examples of different styles of program music from different eras. Now, build your own playlist from those works listed in each IF YOU LIKED THAT, TRY THIS list or from other works you find. Share your playlist with others by posting it to your class discussion board or on Dashboard.

✓ **Audio Review:** Go to Dashboard to listen to Professor Bailey discuss program music.

✓ **How Am I Doing?** Go to Dashboard to test your understanding of this material by taking the chapter quiz.

Dashboard

KEY TERMS

Concert overture	Pastorale	Rubato
Idée fixe	Program music	Symphonic poem
Incidental music	Program symphony	Tone poem
March	Pure music	

Isms for Orchestra

LEARNING OBJECTIVES

- Explain the similarities and differences of the five isms of orchestral music studied in this chapter.

- List new compositional techniques used by composers of orchestral isms in the Modern period.

- Name important composers associated with each of these orchestral styles.

- Recognize by listening example the different musical styles of the chapter.

Key Concepts: expressionism, impressionism, minimalism, neoclassicism, neoromanticism

Austrian composer Alban Berg (left) with his friend and teacher Arnold Schoenberg (right).
Courtesy DEA/A. DAGLI ORTI/Contributor/Getty Images.

Where It's Playing

Like other music for full orchestra the music of this chapter is most often heard today in the concert hall. In most of the styles of music studied in this chapter composers used a large percussion section to create new timbres and intricate rhythms. The space required for these percussion sections (added to the already large orchestral string and wind sections) makes it necessary to perform on a large stage. Some music of this chapter is not written for the concert hall but still is often heard there. For example, neoromantic orchestral music is the dominant style of film music. As such, this music is recorded (performed) in a film recording studio and heard in movie theaters and on soundtrack recordings and is often played in the concert hall as a suite.

Two isms studied in this chapter, **impressionism** and **expressionism**, are styles of music used in instrumental chamber ensembles and for solo instruments like the piano as well as full orchestra. In the case of impressionism and expressionism we hear much of this music in the recital hall, specifically in the recital halls of colleges and universities where experimental music has been fostered throughout the past century. As 20th century art music became more experimental it became distanced from the tastes of the general public. Since professional ensembles such as orchestras exist at least in part based upon ticket sales, it became difficult for orchestras to program new and experimental music that was unpopular with the concertgoer. This forced composers to the academic world where they became professors of music theory and composition, and where they could write and perform new music without the burden of having to make money from a concert. This trend continued as electronically-generated music came into being. For the past seventy years the most experimental new music has been performed on college campuses.

Impressionism: Influenced by visual art, impressionistic music is suggestive of mood or atmosphere.

Expressionism: A style of music of the mid-20th century characterized by hyper-expression, abandonment of tonal centers, extreme ranges used in melodic structures, forceful accents, and abrupt dynamic changes.

Dashboard

RESEARCH

Symphonic Music in the Modern Period Becomes More Diverse

What are the important styles (isms) of orchestral music in the Modern period?

In the late 19th and early 20th centuries composers began to experiment with new systems of tonality and abandoned the set forms and instrumentations of the Classical and Romantic eras. For most of the 20th century Western art music can best be described as eclectic and lacking in any standard or universal style. This chapter focuses on five of the most important styles in orchestral music, the names of which each end with the suffix "ism."

After about 1910 the symphony lost ground as the leading type of music composed for orchestras. Economic problems brought on by the two world wars of the 20th century caused some composers to write for smaller ensembles. The state economies of some European countries during this time caused the governments to provide less support for large orchestras and opera companies. Many such organizations in France, Germany, and Russia either ceased to exist or scaled back the number of concerts given and the number of musicians employed.

As composers of the early 20th century turned away from set forms and works dominated by key center relationships, the symphony as a form fell into disuse. Of course, there are notable exceptions. The Russians Sergei Prokofiev and Dmitri Shostakovich wrote important symphonies, as did the American Charles Ives. And, near the end of the century the form was revived by composers turning to a neoromantic style.

Impressionism in Painting Influences Music

What innovative compositional techniques contributed to the sound of impressionism?

Early in the 20th century music and painting forged an artistic alliance of influence. The impressionistic painters Claude Monet, Edgar Degas, and Auguste Renoir and the symbolist poets Stéphane Mallarmé and Paul Verlaine influenced composers such as Claude Debussy (1862–1918) and Maurice Ravel (1875–1937). Their music, called impressionism, began in France as composers looked for alternatives to the 19th century system of major/minor key structures. Impressionism uses other scales, sometimes older church modes, and scales and modes from non-Western music to create a new tonality.

Whole-tone scale: A seven-note scale consisting entirely of whole steps.

Impressionistic composers made use of all twelve tones of the chromatic scale in their works and explored use of scales heretofore rarely used in Western music such as the **whole-tone scale**. These innovations created music that lacked the sound of a strong pull and progression toward a particular central pitch of a piece that had been important in all Western music since the Middle Ages. Chords often moved in parallel fashion in impressionistic music, an idea before considered incorrect in traditional Western music. Timbre and tone color became important, and composers used instruments in less traditional ranges and dynamics, often creating a shimmering sound. Rhythm in impressionistic music was more fluid, seeming to glide rather than be marked by regular and recurring strong and weak beats. The forms of works were shorter than other styles of the time and less regular in pattern. Composers such as Maurice Ravel (1875–1937) and Claude Debussy (1862–1917) were important in this style.

Claude Debussy. Courtesy Image Asset Management Ltd./ Image Asset Management Ltd..

Claude Debussy

Claude Debussy was the leader of musical impressionism and the most important French composer of his time. Debussy spent most of his life working in Paris and was profoundly influenced by what he heard and saw at the Paris International Exposition in 1889. There he heard music of Asia and Spain, and incorporated their scales and harmonies into his own works. Following the production of his opera *Pélleas et Mélisande,* he became an internationally recognized composer. Debussy led a colorful personal life in Paris. He knew and moved among the greatest writers and artists of his age. His expensive tastes left him constantly in search of commissions and public appearances.

Debussy's works, like those of the impressionist painters and symbolist writers, evoke moods and create atmospheres. Tone color is the most important musical element in his works and the use of woodwinds to create atmosphere pervades his works. He wrote a number of works for solo piano that are miniature masterpieces and over fifty songs for solo voice. Some of his orchestral works have become repertoire standards, such as *La Mer, Three Nocturnes,* and *Prelude to the Afternoon of a Faun.* Though his works are tonal, he once said, "One must drown the sense of tonality." To accomplish this, he made much use of the **pentatonic scale** and the whole-tone scale, which he heard in Javanese music at the Paris Exposition. In his music, rhythm is undefined by accent, creating a floating feeling.

Pentatonic scale: A five-note scale.

LISTENING GUIDE 9.1

PRELUDE TO THE AFTERNOON OF A FAUN,
Claude Debussy, composed 1894

Prelude to the Afternoon of a Faun was written in 1894 to musically evoke the ideas of Stéphane Mallarmé's poem *The Afternoon of a Faun.* In the poem the faun (a half-man, half-goat figure) dreams of two beautiful nymphs while he plays his flute. The work is symphonic poem-like in nature. The exotic scales combine with dynamics and a pulse that ebbs and flows to create a sensuous work. Debussy's music is characterized by a rich palette of tone colors, as this work illustrates.

HEAR STREAMING AUDIO ON DASHBOARD

What to Listen For

- Listen for the lyrical melodies created on nontraditional scales. The melodies use chromatic, whole-tone, and pentatonic scales. This creates a mystical, sensuous, almost cloudy sound.

- Listen for the use of combinations of winds and strings to create a rich palette of tone colors.
- Listen for the use of an ebb-and-flow rhythm that adds to the sensuous feeling. There is never a feel of a steady beat.
- Listen for the use of the harp, clarinet, oboe, flute, and soft horn as solo instruments, which each helps evoke the sounds of nature.

TIMING	FORM: ABA′	WHAT TO LISTEN FOR
0:00	A	The A section begins with a solo flute melody based on a chromatic scale.
0:19		Horn calls and harp glissandos answer the flute.
0:43		Flute melody returns with string accompaniment.
1:01		Oboe takes over the flute melody and hands it to the orchestra, which gradually increases in volume and intensity. The section ends with a lone clarinet that hands off the line to the flute.
1:35		Flute melody returns.
2:50	Interlude	After a short interlude of chromatic flourishes by the orchestra, a second melody is introduced by the oboe.
3:16		Oboe hands the melody off to the strings. The orchestra gets faster, louder, and more exciting, only to fall back again by the end of the section without a climax.
4:18	B	A new theme is introduced by the clarinet. The melody is based upon a pentatonic scale.
5:08		Strings repeat the clarinet melody in lush, full tones, becoming more intense.
5:44		Once again the music subsides gradually and horns and clarinets lead into the original melody.
6:24	A′	The first theme is restated by flute.
7:00		Oboe restates the theme with harp accompaniment, creating wave-like sounds.
7:40		Flute restates the melody with antique cymbals accompanying amid a growing orchestral base.
8:46		Oboe closes the theme.
9:10		Horns state the opening of the theme.
9:21		Flute makes one final statement of the opening with antique cymbals and harp.

If You Liked That, Try This

Bolero, by Maurice Ravel
La Mer, by Claude Debussy
"Sails," from *Préludes*, Book 1, by Claude Debussy

YouTube videos: search on keywords
Debussy—"Prélude à l'après-midi d'un faune"
Torvill & Dean—1984 Olympics—Bolero—HQ
Blast! Bolero

Remember to add to your personal playlist any of these samples that you like.

***The Scream*, Edvard Munch.** Courtesy Album/Oronoz/Album.

Dashboard
EXPLORE

Expressionism and the Second Viennese School

What are the characteristics of expressionistic music?

During the early 20th century composers throughout the Western art world began to question the further usefulness and development possibilities of the tonal system on which music had been constructed since the Middle Ages. In Vienna during 1905 to 1925 composers led by Arnold Schoenberg (1874–1951) created a new style of music called expressionism. Much of this music was written for small instrumental ensembles or keyboard and is most at home in the recital hall, but some of Schoenberg's early works were for full orchestra. This so-called Second Viennese School of composers (the First Viennese School included Haydn, Mozart and Beethoven) included Schoenberg and his students Anton Webern (1883–1945) and Alban Berg (1885–1935). These composers, highly influenced by German and Austrian expressionistic painters and writers, stressed extreme emotionalism and inner feelings. No expressionistic painting better demonstrates this approach than *The Scream* by Edvard Munch. Works in this style are often distorted or grotesque and depict madness and death.

Expressionistic music is characterized by abandonment of tonal centers (atonality), extreme ranges used in melodic structures, forceful accents and abrupt dynamic changes, and dissonant sounds that do not resolve to consonances. The use of exaggeration and distortion of musical elements is common in expressionistic music. The intent of expressionism in art is to reveal the deepest, and sometimes darkest, of human emotions.

Arnold Schoenberg

Schoenberg was born in Vienna in 1874 and began his musical career conducting an amateur choir. He began to teach composition in the early 1900s and Berg and Webern became his disciples. His early works were met with hostility and derision by critics and the public. It was not until he was past fifty that he developed the system of composition that would make him, along with Igor Stravinsky, one of the two most important and controversial composers of the 20th century. Because of his Jewish faith, Schoenberg was forced to immigrate to America in the late 1930s. Here he was employed to teach composition first at the University of Southern California and then at the University of California at Los Angeles. Schoenberg's most important and most often performed work is *Transfigured Night* (1899). His *Chamber Symphony, Five Orchestral Pieces,* and *Survivor from Warsaw* are all concert works. Schoenberg developed a new manner of delivering text, called Sprechstimme, in which text is spoken on specific pitches, creating a combination singing and speaking. He also experimented with what he called **klangfarbenmelodie**, a system of varying tone color on each pitch of a melody.

Klangfarbenmelodie: A system of composition in which each pitch of a melody has a distinct tone color.

Sprechstimme: A vocal delivery that is a sort of mixture of singing and speaking.

PERFORMANCE PRACTICE
New Performance Techniques

What new performance techniques were developed in music of the 20th century?

In the 20th century composers began to expand the types of performance techniques required to create the sounds of their music. These "extended techniques" occur in music for strings, winds, keyboards, and voice and include anything out of the ordinary methods of creating sound with an instrument or voice. For example, Schoenberg used a technique for vocalists in expressionistic music called **Sprechstimme**, which is a sort of mixture of speech and singing. This sung-speech technique is used in *Pierrot Lunaire*. Late 20th century composers such as Henry Cowell, George Crumb, and John Cage extended the technique of playing the piano to include plucking or striking the strings by hand or with a mallet from inside the piano, use of the keyboard cover as a percussion instrument, and "preparing" the piano by placing objects on or between the strings to create new timbres. String players have been asked by contemporary composers to strike their strings with the wooden back of their bows (called *col legno*), tune their strings to pitches other than what is usual, create a scratch tone by using excessive pressure on the bow, snap the strings against the fingerboard (wooden piece under the strings), and many other techniques. In contemporary music wind players often disassemble their instruments and play on only parts of them, produce more than one tone at a time (multiphonics), and make clacking noises with their keys. All these techniques expand the range of sounds possible from which a composer can choose. Visit the textbook website section Helpful Resources for Chapter 9 for more information on Schoenberg's *Pierrot Lunaire*.

Serialism: A compositional technique of the mid-20th century led by composer Arnold Schoenberg that treats all twelve pitches of the Western scale equally. The technique is a highly organized style of writing music.

In order to free his music from tonality, Schoenberg created the twelve-tone system, which came to be called **serialism** later in the century. In this system of composing music tones are organized in a new way. The system does not emphasize one pitch, as did tonality. Instead it gives equal importance to all twelve pitches of the Western scale. The pitches in a twelve-tone work are ordered in a special way called the *tone row*, which is different for each piece of music. The row is the source for all melodies and chords in a work and can be presented in retrograde, inversion, or retrograde inversion. None of the twelve pitches can occur more than once in any tone row. The melody is created by manipulating the row, and the row can be transposed to begin on any of the twelve pitches of the scale. Thus, the row can exist in forty-eight versions.

One of Schoenberg's best-known works of expressionism is *Pierrot Lunaire*, set for female voice and chamber ensemble of violin/viola, cello, flute/piccolo, clarinet/bass clarinet, and piano. Written in 1912, this work is based on twenty-one strange poems by the symbolist poet Albert Giraud that revolve around an Italian "comedy of the arts" character named Pierrot, a sad clown. (In other works in other languages, this character is called Petrouchka or Pagliacci.) Schoenberg created a 20th century song cycle in three parts in this work. In the first part Pierrot drinks too much wine and becomes obsessed with the moon. Part two is a nightmare involving death and guilt. In part three Pierrot becomes more playful and sobers up. The music generally lacks what at the time would have been called melody or tune. The overall effect is unsettling.

LISTENING GUIDE 9.2

"PERIPETIE," from *Five Orchestral Pieces*, op. 16, mvt. 4,
Arnold Schoenberg, composed 1909

Dashboard
**HEAR STREAMING AUDIO
ON DASHBOARD**

Written in 1909 and first published in 1912 *Five Orchestral Pieces*, op. 16, for full orchestra was a break with the symphonic traditions of the time. In a letter to a contemporary composer, Richard Strauss, Schoenberg stated that the work was "absolutely not symphonic, quite the opposite— without architecture, without structure. Only an ever-changing, unbroken succession of colours, rhythms and moods." The pieces were premiered at the summer "Proms" concerts in London in 1912 and left the audience bewildered and hostile. The five movements each have a title that Schoenberg added simply to please his publisher.

1. Vorgefühle (Premonitions)
2. Vergangenes (The Past)
3. Farben (Chord-colors)
4. Peripetie (Peripeteia)
5. Das obligate Rezitativ (The Obbligato Recitative)

Schoenberg does not connect the movements, or even the form within the movements, with standard symphonic devices of related key centers or recurring themes. Movement 1 is a series of motifs that Schoenberg continuously develops at a fast and energetic pace. Movement 2 is slow with expressive melodies that create a dream-like atmosphere. To 21st century ears this movement's chromatic harmony does not surprise or shock, in fact we hear it repeatedly in film music. But at the time it was composed, the lack of thematic development around one key confused its first listeners. Movement 3 is, perhaps, the most innovative of the five in that it is wholly not melodic in character and has only one single chord throughout. It has been described as "still" but Schoenberg accomplishes movement and change by continuously altering the instrumentation of this single chord. Many scholars believe this to be an early example of klangfarbenmelodie, a technique also developed by Schoenberg. Movement 4, like the first piece, is a fast and frantic outburst of motifs. This piece repeatedly erupts in sound and is quickly reined in, creating a halting and continually restrained, almost frustrated rhythmic energy. The fifth piece sounds like an unraveling of a single melody that is made expressive by wide dynamic and pitch ranges. The movement is polyphonic throughout. It seems to simply stop without building to any specific climactic moment or resolving any of the tonal and timbral issues of the piece.

What to Listen For

- Listen for wide leaps, extreme and rapid dynamic range shifts, fast changes of timbre, and sudden shifts in tempo. These are all characteristics of expressionistic music and are prevalent throughout this piece.
- Listen for the overlapping of melodic ideas.
- Listen for how Schoenberg uses abrupt changes of speed to make the work more dramatic and expressive. The actual pulse of the work does not change much but the rhythms are written such that it sounds like the piece is constantly speeding up and abruptly slowing.

The title of this movement means "episode." Listen to how the short melodic fragments match with this definition.

TIMING	FORM: THREE-PART	WHAT TO LISTEN FOR
0:00	Section 1 (m. 1–19)	Schoenberg presents the seven melodic ideas of the movement in the first twenty measures of the movement. This section is itself in three parts: m. 1–6, 6–18, 18–20. Schoenberg creates this aural division by presenting the first three motifs loud, fast, and harsh. They are played at increasing levels of *forte*—*f*, *ff*, *fff*. The next four motifs are soft, slower sounding, and lyrical. They are all played at the lower dynamic levels increasing from pianissimo to piano to mezzo piano. The fourth, fifth, and sixth motifs overlap to create a sort-of second part that sounds softer and slower. The seventh motif sounds like a return to the style of the opening—faster and with wider dynamic changes.
0:00	Motif 1—mm. 1–3	The motif is dominated by wind instruments, first the low reeds, then the brass, and finally the high woodwinds creating three distinct timbres in three measures of music. Each uses very wide ranges, fast rhythms, and loud dynamics to create a harsh opening to the movement.
0:04	Motif 2—mm. 3–5	Horns play the second motif very loudly and with harsh accents. Their motif is made up of wide leaps and fast pitches within the same timbre.
0:07	Motif 3—mm. 5–6	The brass and high strings begin the motif with very loud repeated notes. This rhythmic figure is echoed softly by high woodwinds. In one measure Schoenberg creates two distinct timbres and changes dynamics from *fff* to *pp*.
0:09	Motif 4—mm. 6–13	Again played by only the horns this motif sounds slow. It is actually at the same tempo as the first three motifs but its rhythm creates a slower beat. This is the first of four soft motifs and it is chordal.
0:12	Motif 5—mm. 8–13	Motif 5 is stated in low woodwinds and overlaps and works with motif 4. It too is very soft but has a brief swell in dynamics.
0:15	Motif 6—mm. 10–18	Motif 6 also overlaps 4 and 5 and is stated by solo clarinet. Schoenberg uses wide leaps and a large range to create an expressive melody. It is the longest of the motifs and is played softly.
0:28	Motif 7—mm. 18–20	The final primary melodic idea of the work is presented in low strings. It, like the clarinet solo is very expressive, making use of wide leaps and quick dynamic changes. It sounds like a return to a faster tempo. But, like all seven of the motifs, it is the same basic beat as the others.
0:29	Section 2—mm. 19–58	In the second section of the piece Schoenberg develops and manipulates the seven primary motifs. Like Section 1, this section is also in three smaller parts. Each section develops one or more of the motifs and overlaps.
0:29	mm. 19–38	Development of each of the seven motifs except number 4 in the following order: 7, 1, 2, 3, 5, 6 The section begins as an overlap of the previous section. The section builds in dynamics and intensity throughout, ending abruptly. The strings end the section with a lush, ascending version of motif 6.
1:00	Motif 4—mm. 37–44	Motif number 4 is stated by horns beginning a section that sounds slower, softer, and much less frantic.
1:12	Motifs 1, 2, 7—mm. 44–58	Motifs 1, 2, and 7 are played in that order by bassoon, trumpet, and cello. The brief section builds in dynamics and intensity.

1:40	Section 3—mm. 59–end	The final section is a restatement of most of the original motifs in an altered fashion.
1:40	mm. 59–64	Motifs 1, 3, 4, 6, and 7 are stated simultaneously as the piece builds to a frantic and loud climax.
1:54	Motif 2—mm. 64–66	Motif 2 is stated very softly by clarinet, horn, and low strings to end the work. The piece sounds like it just stops without conclusion or finality.

If You Liked That, Try This

Wozzeck, Alban Berg
Five Pieces for Orchestra, op. 10, Anton Webern
A Survivor from Warsaw, Arnold Schoenberg

YouTube videos: search on keywords
Pierrot Lunaire
Arnold Schoenberg: A Survivor from Warsaw. cond. Simon Rattle
Alban Berg—Wozzeck

Remember to add to your personal playlist any of these samples that you like.

Neoclassicism

What makes a work neoclassical rather than just Classical?

During the first half of the 20th century, from about 1910 to 1950, some composers wrote in a style based upon the emotional restraint and balance of the Baroque and Classical eras. This style is called neoclassicism. The music is intended to be absolute music, without a program. Much of the music is polyphonic in texture and composers returned to using older forms such as the fugue, dance suite, and Classical era symphony. Composers of this style tended to use smaller size orchestras than was common in the late Romantic era and early 20th century. The works are more concise than Romantic works and are lighter in texture with generally fewer instruments in the orchestra. Despite their forms and style these works do not sound like copies of Baroque and Classical music—they sound like music of the modern era. Neoclassical style is a rejection of the overly emotional and individualistic music of the Romanticists and the atonality of the expressionists. Like impressionism, neoclassicism was influenced by other arts, especially painting and architecture.

Important composers of neoclassical music include Paul Hindemith (1895–1963), Sergei Prokofiev (1891–1953), Aaron Copland (1900–1990) and Igor Stravinsky (1882–1971). An early work in the neoclassic style is Stravinsky's music to the ballet *Pulchinella*, written in 1920. Stravinsky's ballet collaborator Sergei Diaghilev commissioned him to rescore some music of the 18th-century composer

Sergei Prokofiev **by Pyotr Konchalovsky.** Courtesy Lebrecht Music and Arts Photo Library/Alamy.

Giovanni Pergolesi (1710–1736) for a ballet. Stravinsky reworked the Pergolesi music utilizing its form and melodies set in Stravinsky's modern style. Perhaps one of the best examples of the neoclassical style is the "Classical" Symphony no. 1 by Prokofiev.

Sergei Prokofiev

Sergei Prokofiev was a Russian composer whose life and works were greatly influenced by the political issues of his homeland. Perhaps because of the conservative bias of the Soviet government his most important works are in the neoclassical style and include the very popular music to the ballet *Romeo and Juliet* and the children's piece *Peter and the Wolf*. His film scores for *Lieutenant Kijé* and *Alexander Nevsky* are considered among his finest work. He reworked both of these scores into an orchestral suite and a cantata, respectively.

Prokofiev was a gifted pianist and following the 1917 Russian revolution he toured the United States and much of Europe for twenty years as a performer and composer. In his early years his works were considered to be dissonant and experimental but by 1937 his reputation as a neoclassicist earned him an invitation to return home to Russia. He remained there until his death, like his compatriot Dmitri Shostakovich, in and out of favor with the Soviet government much of his life.

LISTENING GUIDE 9.3

"GAVOTTA," from Symphony no. 1 in D major, op. 25 ("Classical"), mvt. 3,
Sergei Prokofiev, composed 1917

Symphony no. 1 in D major, op. 25 by Prokofiev is better known by the title "Classical Symphony." It premiered in 1918 in St. Petersburg, Russia, conducted by Prokofiev and is one of the earliest works, along with Stravinsky's *Pulchinella*, of the neoclassical style. The work is an imitation of the style of Haydn. The orchestra for this work is of Classical-era proportions with pairs of flutes, oboes, clarinets, bassoons, horns, and trumpets in addition to the strings. The work is in four movements in the standard forms and tempos of symphonies of the Classical era. The symphony is Classical in form, instrumentation, and style yet modern in terms of harmonies.

The Gavotta is the third movement of the symphony. A gavotte is a French folk dance usually with four beats in each measure. Prokofiev's gavotta is unusual in that each of the phrases begins on beat three of a four-beat measure rather than on beat one.

Dashboard

**HEAR STREAMING AUDIO
ON DASHBOARD**

What to Listen For

- Listen for the symmetrical phrases of the work in the style of a Classical dance movement.
- Listen for the sparse and clear instrumentation of the work.
- Listen in the B section of the work for the accompaniment drone sound, which lends a folk-like quality to the work.
- Listen for the sense of restraint in dynamic levels, rhythmic regularity, and sound of the theme.

TIMING	FORM: ABA ROUNDED BINARY	TEXTURE	WHAT TO LISTEN FOR
0:00	A, phrase 1	String melody, woodwinds double	Listen for the light style of the melody and the restrained and regular rhythm.
0:23	phrase 2	String melody, woodwinds double	Listen for the abrupt changes in dynamics—a characteristic of the Baroque era.
0:31	phrase 3	Full orchestra	Listen for the regularity of the phrases; each is four measures long. Listen for the tonal sense of the piece capped by a tonic D major chord at the end of the section.
0:38	B, phrase 1	Woodwind melody, string accompaniment	Listen for the folk-like quality of this section of the work. Prokofiev creates this sense by placing a graceful melody in soft woodwinds accompanied by a drone sound in the strings and percussion.
0:53	phrase 2	Melody in strings, light staccato line in oboes	Listen for the transfer of the melody from the woodwinds to the strings and the addition of a counter-line in the oboes.
1:08	a, phrase 1	Melody in flute and clarinet, string accompaniment	Listen for the reprise of the opening melody played softly by the woodwinds. Note that this A section does not repeat as it did in the original statement.
1:16	phrase 2	Melody in flute and clarinet	Note that this time the melody continues at the soft dynamic rather than changing to forte as it did in the original statement.
1:23	phrase 3	Strings with limited clarinet and bassoon	Listen for the slight slowing in tempo in the last measures of the work.

If You Liked That, Try This

Symphonies of Wind Instruments, Igor Stravinsky
Symphony of Psalms, Igor Stravinsky
Appalachian Spring, Aaron Copland

YouTube videos: search on keywords
Martha Graham's Appalachian Spring Part 1/4
Peter And The Wolf 1 of 2

Remember to add to your personal playlist any of these samples that you like.

Minimalism

Does minimalism continue the emphasis on contrast and repetition to create form?

Minimalism: Music based upon the repetition of melodic, harmonic, and/or rhythmic motifs with little or no variation.

Chance music: Music of primarily the 20th century in which at least some of the work is left to chance or the performer's discretion.

Minimalism is a style of concert music often written for orchestra that developed in the second half of the 20th century. Based upon the repetition of melodic, harmonic, and/or rhythmic motifs with little or no variation over long periods of time, this music can create a trance-like effect. It is based on understatement and its harmonic structure is usually tonal and clear. The music is a reaction to the complex and esoteric style of compositions of the first half of the 20th century by such composers as Schoenberg, Berg, Boulez, and to the randomness of **chance music** composers like John Cage.

Like other isms of this chapter, minimalism is also apparent in other art forms. The work *64 Copper Squares* by visual artist Carl Andre is sixty-four copper plates laid out on the floor in a square. Andy Warhol's piece *Green Coca-Cola Bottles* is a painting of nothing but green Coke bottles. In music, minimalistic elements include the use of drones, repetition of rhythmic and melodic material, and very small and gradual changes over time. Important composers of minimalism include Americans Steve Reich (b. 1936), Philip Glass (b. 1937), and John Adams (b. 1947).

John Adams

John Adams is an American composer who writes, among other styles, minimalistic music. He is a clarinetist and studied composition at Harvard University with David del Tredici. He won the 2002 Pulitzer Prize for Music for his work *On the Transmigration of Souls*, a choral work in honor of the victims of the attacks on September 11, 2001. Adams is a prolific composer who has written operas, works for orchestra, choral works, chamber music, film scores, and electronic music. Much of his music incorporates elements of Americana, popular music, and world ethnic musics; and unlike other early minimalists his works often incorporate motivic development.

Adams directed the New Music Ensemble at the San Francisco Conservatory of Music throughout the 1970s and has served as a composer for the Los Angeles Philharmonic. He has conducted his works with many professional orchestras around the world. For more on Adams's music search the web for his homepage, called "earbox."

American composer John Adams. Courtesy ZUMA Press, Inc/Alamy.

LISTENING GUIDE 9.4

SHORT RIDE IN A FAST MACHINE,
John Adams, composed 1986

Dashboard
**HEAR STREAMING AUDIO
ON DASHBOARD**

Adams's minimalist work *Short Ride in a Fast Machine* for orchestra and synthesizers was written as a concert-opening piece, though it is actually a piece of minimalist program music. The work is about four minutes long and makes use of repeated rhythmic figures to create a steady yet driving pulse. Adams said of the work "You know how it is when someone asks you to ride in a terrific sports car, and then you wish you hadn't?" The work was commissioned by the Great Woods Festival for the Pittsburgh Symphony Orchestra. American conductor Michael Tilson Thomas led the premiere of the work at Great Woods in Mansfield, Massachusetts, on June 13, 1986.

The work is so popular with audiences that it was the most frequently performed work for orchestra by an American composer in the last decade of the 20th century. The work has been transcribed for wind ensemble and synthesizer.

What to Listen For

- Listen for sections that remind you of machine sounds or the sense of riding in a fast car. For example, the loud bass drum and snare notes might be an engine backfiring. The opening woodwind repeated rhythm might be the sound of the wind as the machine races along. The work-long crescendo in volume and intensity suggests building excitement. The walking bass line of Section 3 could represent a larger car that pulls up alongside.
- Listen for how Adams uses the repetitive rhythms to generate a work of extended building excitement.
- Listen for how the percussion is used not as a rhythmic pulse, but in an episodic manner.

TIMING	FORM: SECTIONAL	WHAT TO LISTEN FOR
0:00	Section 1	The piece begins with a rhythm played by wood blocks followed by repeated rhythmic patterns (called *ostinato*) by woodwinds and synthesizer.
0:10		Trumpets add a fanfare rhythm that is picked up by other brasses.
0:26		Snare drum and brass play offbeat and harshly accented pitches.
1:01	Section 2	Strings enter and bass drum plays loud pitches. Brass continue chords on repetitive rhythm.
1:28		The section crescendos in volume and intensity, adding more percussion, including cymbals, and horn ripping notes.

(continued)

TIMING	FORM: SECTIONAL	WHAT TO LISTEN FOR
1:40	Section 3	The section begins suddenly softer and a walking bass line enters played by cellos and basses.
2:06		More accented snare drum and brass chords are added to the texture as in Section 1.
2:30		Trumpets continue with repeated *ostinato* rhythm, and trombone and tuba share a two-note motif.
2:46	Section 4	The music is suddenly softer again, followed by a loud trumpet fanfare line. Horns later add their own fanfare to the trumpets, followed by the low brass, until the entire brass section is playing loud separate lines.
3:50	Section 5	From the fanfares of the brasses of Section 4, the trumpets emerge triumphantly with their original *ostinato* fanfare rhythm from section 1. The snare drum adds what can only be described as gunshots or car backfire sounds and the brass bring the work to an end.

If You Liked That, Try This

Music in Twelve Parts, by Philip Glass
Six Pianos, by Steven Reich
In C, by Terry Riley

YouTube videos: search on keywords
Short Ride In a Fast Machine

Remember to add to your personal playlist any of these samples that you like.

Neoromanticism and Modern Orchestral Music

In what way(s) is modern orchestral music similar to that of the Romantic Era?

For almost two hundred years the symphony was the leading form for orchestra in the concert hall. From its roots in the dance suites and concerto grossos of the Baroque era, it grew in length and complexity to a point where composers of the 20th century could develop the form no further. The form relied upon contrast and repetition of melodic ideas in a set order and made use of a set sequence of key centers. The Romantic composer expanded the orchestral piece in length and added to the size of the orchestra that played it. Melodies became longer and less regular and predictable. And perhaps most important, the tonal ideas of the Romantic composer needed a wider range of choices than those of the Classical era.

In the 20th century composers rejected set forms and predictable contrasts and repetitions. They also expanded the harmonic language such that key centers were either obscured or simply no longer of importance in the musical form. For a time between the two world wars, it also became too costly in many countries to maintain full-sized orchestras. These factors all contributed to both the development and the decline of the large symphonic form in the 20th century as the leading type of music written by composers.

In the past two decades some composers have returned to the symphony and large orchestral form as a viable means of expression both for orchestra and concert band. However, the symphony no longer has a set number of movements or forms within the movements. The size of the orchestral forces needed to perform modern symphonies also varies greatly from composition to composition. Composers such as Libby Larsen, David Maslanka, and John Corigliano have used their experiences in writing film music, opera, sacred music, and popular music to write symphonies for bands and orchestras in the last two decades.

Neoromanticism is a term used in music throughout the 20th century and is a recent trend in orchestral music for the concert hall. Like minimalism, neoromanticism is a reaction to the atonal and electronic music of the late 20th century. Neoromantic music marks a return to tonality and expression in music. Works are often scored for large orchestra to take advantage of the expressive qualities of the timbres of the orchestra. Leading composers in this style include Dmitri Shostakovich, Aaron Copland, David del Tredici, George Rochberg, Howard Hanson, Samuel Barber, Ellen Taaffe Zwilich, and Libby Larsen.

Neoromanticism: Music of the 20th century in which composers returned to the formal and tonal structures of music of the Romantic era.

Libby Larsen

Libby Larsen is an American composer born in 1950. One of the best-known and respected musicians of her generation, she has written operas, songs, dance works, and works for large band and orchestra. Her music is usually characterized as neoromantic, full of the lush extended harmonies of the late Romantic era mixed with contemporary sounds of the 20th century. Her works are melodic and accessible to even the inexperienced art music listener. She is a champion of music education in the schools and has held numerous artist-in-residence positions at educational institutions and with professional symphony orchestras. For more information on Libby Larsen search the web for her homepage.

American composer Libby Larsen.
© Ann Marsden.

LISTENING GUIDE 9.5

"ONE DANCER, MANY DANCES" from *Solo Symphony*,
Libby Larsen, composed 1999

Symphony no. 5, *Solo Symphony*, is in four movements entitled I. Solosolos; II. One Dancer, Many Dances; III. Once Around; and IV. The Cocktail Party Effect. The work calls for a large percussion section and electric bass in addition to the standard orchestra. It was commissioned by the Colorado Symphony and premiered by conductor Marin Alsop when Larsen was serving as composer-in-residence with the orchestra. This style of music is closely related to film music, which will be discussed in Chapter 18. Libby Larsen says of the work:

Dashboard
**HEAR STREAMING AUDIO
ON DASHBOARD**

What is solo? Is it the effort of one and only one, such as a solo violin, a solo flight? Is there such a thing as a solo effort? Is the "man on the moon" a solo effort? Amelia Earhart's solo flights were only solos in that she was in the plane alone. But her ground crew was as responsible for each flight as she was.

A solo is a group. The effort of many becomes the effort of one to produce a unified sound, a unified music. This symphony is about the one and the many.

"Solo-solos," the first movement, presents a flow of short melodies played by trumpet, clarinet, oboe, horn and bassoon alone. These same melodies are then played in unison by the strings, then combined with the solo instruments, creating a musical fabric which is unified, but any given moment is a solo moment.

"One dancer, many dances." A single melody seen through the lens of different dances, including funk, waltz, swing, square dance, tango, and jig.

"Once around" is a brash dash through the choirs of the orchestra.

There is a feature of human hearing called the "cocktail party effect." It is the ability to pick out and hear a single voice amidst chaos. This final movement treats the cocktail party effect as a listening game, a kind of musical "Where's Waldo?" In this case, Waldo is a melody. Introduced by a snare drum at the beginning of the movement, from then on Waldo is hidden amidst the other music.

This is a listener's symphony, as well as a solo display. In fact, the listener is the true soloist. ("One Dancer, Many Dances," libbylarsen.com)

This is the second movement of the four-movement symphony written for full orchestra. The work is a theme with variations—the variations being in the style of different dances including funk, waltz, swing, square dance, tango, and jig. The theme is first presented by solo trombone in a "jazzy" style.

What to Listen For

- Listen for the use of different styles of contemporary dance music used to create each variation.
- Listen for the two cadenzas used to break up the variation form.

TIMING	FORM: VARIATION	WHAT TO LISTEN FOR
0:00	Theme	Trombone plays a solo in free cadenza style.
0:18		Trombone is joined by string accompaniment.
0:55	Percussion interlude 1	An intricate rhythm is begun by bongos and imitated in conga drums, tom tom, and finally timpani. This section leads into the funk rhythm that follows.
1:34	Variation 1—Funk	The theme is presented in a funk rhythm by horns.
2:18		Trumpets join horns in a funk version of the theme in diminution.
2:43		Clarinet plays the theme.

3:15		Flutes play the theme in augmentation.
3:30	Variation 2—Waltz	The clarinet plays the theme in a waltz style and rhythm.
3:41		Oboe joins clarinet.
3:52		Violins continue the theme in waltz rhythm and solo flute ends the phrase.
4:15	Percussion interlude 2	The material from the first percussion interlude returns, leading into a swing section.
4:40	Variation 3—Swing	The ensemble plays the theme in swing style introduced first by clarinet. Note the walking bass line that contributes to this style change.
5:17	Violin cadenza	A solo violin plays thematic material in a free cadenza section.
5:58		The clarinet returns to the swing style.
6:15	Percussion interlude 3	Material from the first percussion interlude returns, this time to accompany the trombone and tuba in another jazz presentation of the theme.
6:41	Variation 4—Square dance	The entire ensemble combines to play a "hip" square dance. Note the walking bass line here again that contributes to the jazzy sound within a square dance.
7:32	Flute cadenza	A solo flute plays a free cadenza on thematic material.
7:59	Variation 5—Tango	The entire ensemble combines again to set up a tango rhythm.
8:10		The cellos play the theme in tango rhythm.
8:47		Upper woodwinds continue the theme.
9:19		The work ends with a short return to the solo trombone.

If You Liked That, Try This

Symphony no. 3, John Corigliano
In Wartime, David Del Tredici

YouTube video: search on keyword
Circus Maximus—J. Corigliano—1/4—CIM La Armonica de Buñol—
El Litro—Mano a Mano 2009.avi

Remember to add to your personal playlist any of these samples that you like.

PERFORMER PROFILE
Composer John Corigliano

One of the most influential and popular composers of symphonies today is John Corigliano (b. 1938). His Symphony no. 2 won a Pulitzer Prize in 2001 and he has won several Grammy awards. In 1997 he won an Academy Award for his musical score to the film *The Red Violin*. He has also composed opera, string quartets, concertos, oratorio, works for wind band and other forms of orchestral music. He studied composition with neoromantic composers Vittorio Giannini and Paul Creston. Corigliano's music for orchestra is influenced by neoromanticism and is almost always tonal. Many of his works call for large forces, allowing him to create a wide palette of timbres and dramatic effects allowed by loud dynamic levels.

Corigliano grew up in New York City. His father was the concertmaster of the New York Philharmonic and his mother was a pianist. He studied composition at Columbia University and now teaches at the Juilliard School in New York City. In an interview with the *New York Times* he described his duty as a composer in this way: "It has been fashionable of late for the artist to be misunderstood. I think it is the job of the composer to reach out to his audience with every means at his disposal. . . . Communication of his most important ideas should be the primary goal." He is one of a few contemporary composers whose music appeals to the fans of both the traditional and the avant garde. To listen to Corgliano talk about composing the orchestral music for *The Red Violin* go to the video section of his homepage.

American composer John Corigliano. Courtesy Associated Press.

✓ **Build Your Own Playlist:** The works studied in the chapter Listening Guides serve as examples of different styles of orchestral music from different eras. Now, build your own playlist from those works listed in each IF YOU LIKED THAT, TRY THIS list or from other works you find. Share your playlist with others by posting it to your class discussion board or on Dashboard.

✓ **Audio Review:** Go to Dashboard to listen to Professor Bailey discuss isms for orchestra.

✓ **How Am I Doing?** Go to Dashboard to test your understanding of this material by taking the chapter quiz.

Dashboard

KEY TERMS

Chance music	Klangfarbenmelodie	Pentatonic scale
Expressionism	Minimalism	Serialism
Impressionism	Neoromanticism	Whole-tone scale

Orchestra and Voices

LEARNING OBJECTIVES

- List the components of large-scale choral/orchestral works such as the oratorio, passion, nonliturgical Mass, and requiem.

- Explain similarities and differences of oratorio, passion, and nonliturgical Mass.

- Name important composers of the oratorio, passion, and nonliturgical Mass.

- Recognize the use of word painting by listening.

Key Concepts: form and use of oratorio, nonliturgical Mass, passion, word painting

Where It's Playing

The concert hall stage may be best suited for large ensembles of instruments, but a great repertory of music including voices is performed there as well. From the Baroque era to the present, composers have written works for full orchestra and large chorus. The music of this chapter was all written for performance in the concert hall despite the fact that it is sacred in nature. The **oratorio** and **passion** were originally developed to be performed during Lent and Advent, especially in England where Puritan doctrine forbade theatrical or concert performances. While the public might not be able to attend their usual evening amusements they could still go to the concert hall to hear an oratorio during Lent and Advent, since it had a religious subject. Today, the oratorio, passion, and large choral/orchestral work are heard in both the concert hall and the church. However, if performed in a church these works are part of a special event and are not part of the service.

Contrast is the thing to listen for in an oratorio, passion, or large-scale choral/orchestral work. And you can't miss it. Composers mix the use of soloists, choruses, orchestra alone, and chorus and orchestra together in these works to create an interesting and constantly changing texture.

- Listen for the order of these different textures. Is there an inner form created by the alternation of soloist, chorus, orchestra, etc.?
- Listen for how these sections are tied together. Does the music just stop, followed by a pause and then a restart? Or, is there an interlude between these sections? If there is a connecting piece of music what instrument(s) play(s) this interlude?
- Listen for how the orchestra is used. In most works of this nature the orchestra is both a featured ensemble and an accompanist. Try to determine at what kinds of times the orchestra is used by itself.

Watch the soloists. Do they interact? Why do they stand up to sing? Why don't they use music when the orchestra and chorus does? Does the chorus stand throughout the work, or do they sit when they are not singing? If they sit, how do they know when to stand up? Each of these questions is worthy of your notice while you hear a live choral/orchestral work and is interesting to discuss with your classmates.

Oratorio: A long work for orchestra and voices, usually with large chorus, intended for the concert hall. Similar to an opera except it lacks scenery, costumes, and acting.

Passion: A large work for choir, soloists, and orchestra the text of which is taken from the biblical account of the crucifixion of Jesus Christ.

Dashboard

RESEARCH

The Oratorio

How is an oratorio structured?

The oratorio is a large-scale work that originated in the Baroque era and makes use of both vocalists and instrumentalists. It usually involves a large orchestra, chorus, and vocal soloists. The oratorio tells a story through singing rather than speech. It is sacred music, but it is not intended for performance in church. Oratorios were written for concert performances. They are long works, often the only work on an evening's program. Similar to an **opera** in size and scope, the oratorio also has a sung story like opera, but no sets, scenery, or costumes, and little or no acting. The oratorio is a multi-movement work sometimes divided into acts or scenes that contain several musical numbers. The text is usually taken from biblical stories. Composers contrast solo voice with orchestral accompaniment (called an **aria**) to both orchestra sections alone and vocal ensemble or large chorus pieces. The chorus of an oratorio plays a much larger role than the chorus when used in an opera. This variety of presentation not only helps move the story forward in an interesting manner, but can be used to depict different scenes. The action is often helped along by a narrator who, through a sort of sung-speech called **recitative**, connects the individual sections. The chorus comments on events and the soloists usually portray various characters. The oratorio form was used in both the Classical and Romantic eras and is still composed today. Composers such as Vivaldi, Haydn, Mendelssohn, Igor Stravinsky, and John Adams have all written important works in this form. The most important early composer of oratorio was George Frideric Handel.

Opera: A large-scale drama set to music using costumes, scenery, music, and acting.

Aria: A song for solo voice. In an oratorio the aria is usually accompanied by the orchestra.

Recitative: Used in oratorio and opera as a sort-of free rhythmical sung-speech. It is used to progress the drama forward much like dialogue in a play. It usually has a simple accompaniment without a steady rhythmic pulse.

Dashboard

RESEARCH

George Frideric Handel

Handel (1685–1759) was best known in his lifetime as a composer of oratorio and opera. He was born in Halle, Germany, and began his career in Hamburg. Handel became a famous composer of opera while working in Italy. Handel served the Elector of Hanover as his court composer and when the Elector became King George I of England in 1714 Handel went to England as well. He spent the last fifty years of his life in England, where he founded the Royal Academy of Music for the sole purpose of performing opera. When this organization failed financially nine years later as Italian opera went out of style in London, Handel used his composing and promotion skills to make the oratorio a major form of vocal music of the Baroque era. His oratorios on biblical subjects, *Israel in Egypt*, *Jephtha*, *Saul*, *Judas Maccabaeus*, and *Messiah*, were all extremely popular with the English public. Handel was unquestionably the most popular musician in England in his own time, perhaps in all of Europe.

Like much music of the Baroque, Handel's music is marked by a driving, rhythmic force. He used the full combined forces of the orchestra and chorus to create massive sounds unheard in earlier works. The chorus is the most important group in Handel's oratorios, serving both as a spectator/commentator and as a main

George Frideric Handel holding the score to *Messiah*, by Thomas Hudson. Courtesy FALKENSTEINFOTO/Alamy.

character. Handel was a prolific composer of instrumental music as well, and his *Water Music* and *Music for the Royal Fireworks* along with keyboard works are standards of the repertory. Ludwig van Beethoven said about Handel, "He is the greatest composer that ever lived. I would uncover my head and kneel before his tomb."

LISTENING GUIDE 10.1

"HALLELUJAH CHORUS," from *Messiah*,
G. F. Handel, composed 1742

Dashboard

HEAR STREAMING AUDIO ON DASHBOARD

Handel's most famous work is the oratorio *Messiah*. Premiered in Dublin in 1742, this oratorio uses text from both the Old and New Testaments. Part 1 tells of the prophecy of the Messiah, part 2 describes the redemption of mankind by the death of Jesus, and part 3 establishes the afterlife made possible through Christ as redeemer.

The work has more than fifty sections and is performed at both Christmas and Easter times but we hear it most often around Christmas. It is traditional for audience members to stand at the beginning of the playing of the "Hallelujah Chorus." The tradition began at a performance in 1743 when King George II supposedly rose at the opening bars of the chorus. Others in attendance also rose, of course! Today, *Messiah* is often performed by a community sing-in where members of the community are invited to attend and sing the work rather than just listen to it. Many of these "Messiah Sings" are accompanied by full orchestra and have hundreds of community members singing the piece.

Audience members sing along with orchestra to Handel's *Messiah* in a community performance. Such community sings of this work have become common. Photographer Tim Curtis. Courtesy of Symphonicity.

What to Listen For

- Listen for the primary rhythmic pattern of the work, derived from the English pronunciation of the word "hallelujah."

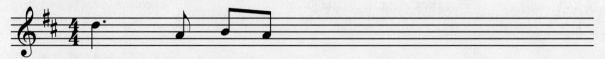

- Listen for how Handel mixes monophony, polyphony, and homophony in this chorus.
- Listen to the repetition of words, typical in a chorus. Note that the original text is in English.
- Listen for **word painting**.

Word painting: Use of some musical device to enhance or represent the meaning of a word.

TIMING	FORM: ABCD	TEXTURE	TEXT	WHAT TO LISTEN FOR
0:00	Introduction	Orchestra homophonic		The work begins with a brief orchestral (strings) introduction based upon the primary rhythmic figure of the work.
0:06	A	Homophonic	Hallelujah	The primary theme of the chorus is presented in a four-part homophonic style by full mixed chorus on the word "hallelujah."
0:14		Homophonic	Hallelujah	The theme is repeated. Trumpets and percussion added.
0:23		Monophonic	For the Lord God Omnipotent reigneth.	Orchestra accompaniment in strings and bassoon.
0:29		Homophonic	Hallelujah	A brief homophonic answer on Hallelujah.
0:34		Polyphonic	For the Lord God Omnipotent reigneth. Hallelujah 2 texts together	A repeat by women voices of "for the Lord God Omnipotent reigneth." This begins an imitative section with short fragments of both melodic and rhythmic ideas presented thus far.
1:09	B	Homophonic	The kingdom of this world is become the Kingdom of our Lord and of His Christ.	Full orchestra accompaniment. Chorus melody is punctuated by timpani rhythm on the repeat.
1:26		Polyphonic	and He shall reign for ever and ever	This section begins with men's voices. The text is presented throughout all voices of the choir in a polyphonic fashion. The orchestra both doubles the voices and at times participates in the polyphony.

(continued)

TIMING	FORM: ABCD	TEXTURE	TEXT	WHAT TO LISTEN FOR
1:48	C	Monophonic	King of Kings, and Lord of Lords for ever and ever	This section combines three parts of the text used thus far. It begins with high voice and high trumpet and ascends.
2:01		Homophonic	King of Kings Hallelujah	The women's voices begin a monophonic ascending line on "King of Kings," answered by orchestra and homophonic men's voices with "Hallelujah." This line builds in volume and intensity.
2:28	D	Polyphonic	And he shall reign for ever and ever.	Men begin the section with a polyphonic restatement at first accompanied only by strings and double reeds. This quickly becomes a dense polyphonic statement of the same material with all voices participating.
2:39		Monophonic Polyphonic	King of Kings Hallelujah	The line is interrupted by a loud statement by the men of "King of Kings." This section is the climactic section of the chorus. Throughout the section the imitative polyphony becomes more complex and involves all voice parts and orchestra. The section builds up to a dramatic and sudden full stop on the repetition of the word "Hallelujah."
3:19	Coda	Homophonic	Hallelujah	The full chorus and orchestra present one final augmented, homophonic "Hallelujah" as the climactic ending of the chorus.

If You Liked That, Try This

Judas Maccabeus, HWV 63, Handel
The Creation, Hob. XXI:2, Franz Joseph Haydn
Israel in Egypt, HWV 54, Handel
Elijah, Felix Mendelssohn

YouTube video: search on keywords
Handel: Messiah, Hallelujah (Sir Colin Davis, Tenebrae, LSO)
William Christie—Haydn, The Creation

Remember to add to your personal playlist any of these samples that you like.

PERFORMANCE PRACTICE
Male Sopranos

Who sang the highest voice parts in early oratorios?

One of the most unusual performance practices in all of music was the use of the castrato singer in opera and oratorio in the 16th to 19th centuries. The early Catholic church did not allow women to participate in the liturgy or perform as musicians. However, composers still wanted all vocal ranges available to them for their works. First, they used boys whose voices had not yet changed to sing the alto and soprano lines. This practice continues in some choirs to this day. Beginning in the mid-1500s the practice began of using castrated adult males to sing these high vocal parts. The surgery took place prior to puberty so that the vocal chords did not stretch and lower the voice. In addition to being able to sing in a high voice, a second physical attribute of the castrato was large breath capacity. This was caused by the fact that castration tended to cause limbs and ribs to lengthen more than in a normal adult male. This allowed for larger lung capacity.

Castrati were used throughout the Baroque era in opera and oratorio and were some of the most popular vocalists of their day. By its height in the early 18th century over 4,000 boys each year were castrated in Europe for musical purposes. Many poor parents believed this to be a way for their musically talented son to have a successful life. The practice lingered on into the 20th century until Pope Pius X finally put an official end to it in 1903. The last of the castrati, Alessandro Moreschi, died in 1922.

Dashboard

EXPLORE

The Musical Passion

How does the passion differ from the oratorio?

A passion is a work large in scope for choir, soloists, and orchestra. The text is taken from the Bible and describes the crucifixion of Jesus Christ. Like oratorios, passions were originally designed to be performed at important times in the Protestant church year, usually Easter and Christmas, when other forms of popular entertainment were banned. Passions were most popular in the Baroque era. Though often originally written to be performed in a concert hall, they are sometimes heard today in churches as a special event, not part of the service. In Bach's and Handel's time oratorio and passions were particularly popular during Lent. Today they are performed throughout the concert season.

J. S. Bach was the most important composer of this form of music and his *Passion According to St. Matthew* is a masterwork. Mendelssohn re-presented it to the world in 1829, signaling the revival of Bach's works. It had not been heard for over one hundred years and most of Bach's music was unknown at the time.

Bach wrote four passions, two of which have survived: his Passion According to St. Matthew and his Passion According to St. John.

The St. Matthew Passion is based on the text of the Gospel according to St. Matthew. It is oratorio-like and makes use of recitative and aria forms. The work is structured in two parts, both containing multiple movements.

LISTENING GUIDE 10.2

EXCERPT FROM PASSION ACCORDING TO ST. MATTHEW, "O Haupt voll Blut und Wunden," BWV 244,
J. S. Bach, composed 1727

Dashboard

HEAR STREAMING AUDIO ON DASHBOARD

Bach wrote the Passion According to St. Matthew in 1727 and it may have been first performed on Good Friday that year, April 11, at St. Thomas in Leipzig where Bach worked. The work was revised at least twice and the 1746 version is what we hear today. The text used comes from Chapters 26 and 27 of the Gospel of Matthew in the New Testament of the Bible. The work calls for soloists, double choir, and double orchestra. The Evangelist narrates through recitative and soloists (Jesus, Judas, Pontius Pilate and his wife, Peter, two priests, two witnesses, and two maids) sing the words of St. Matthew in arias and duets. A chorus is also required but may have been constituted in Bach's time by the soloists joining together. The work alternates between recitative, solo sections, and chorus movements.

The following chorale is from part 2 of the Passion and, along with the chorale "O Mensch, bewein dein Sunde gross" (O Man, weep for your great Sin), is perhaps the best-known music from the Passion. This is an excellent example of a homophonic, **homorhythmic** chorale. The chorale may be set in this style so that the words are easily heard and understood. The chorale "O Haupt voll Blut und Wunden" (O Sacred Head Now Wounded) is a strophic work with two verses. It is used as numbers 17 and 54 in the Passion.

Homorhythmic: Unison rhythmic movement of multiple parts or lines.

What to Listen For

- Listen for the four-part voicing of the chorale with the clearly heard melody line in the top voice.
- Listen for how the instruments of the orchestra double the choral parts. This produces a clear and powerful basis for the text. This also produces a work that has no real contrast. Composers may have used this unified structure to symbolize the unity of the faithful.

- Listen for the homorhythmic style of the chorale.

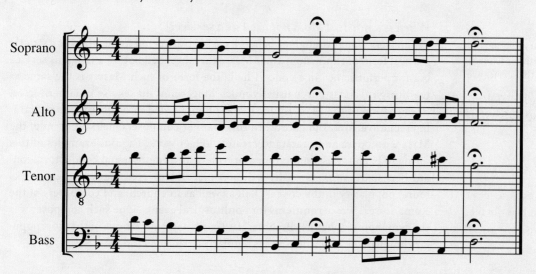

TIMING	TEXT	TRANSLATION
	Stanza 1	
0:00	O Haupt voll Blut und Wunden voll Schmerz und voller Hohn.	Oh head covered with blood and wounds full of pain and full of insults!
0:16	O Haupt, zu Spott gebunden mit einer Dornenkron.	Oh head, wreathed for mockery with a crown of thorns!
0:32	O Haupt, sonst schön gezieret mit höchster Ehr und Zier	Oh head, once beautifully adorned with highest honor and reknown,
0:47	zetzt aber hoch schimpfiret, gegrüsset seist du mir.	but now outrageously abused, let me hail thee!
	Stanza 2	
1:07	Du edles Ange Sichte,	Thou noble countenance
1:14	vor dem sonst schrickt und scheut	at which shrank and cowered
1:21	das grosse Welt gerichte, wie bist du so bespeit.	the mightiest of the world.
1:37	Wie bist du so erbleichet	How art thou spat on!
1:45	wer hat dein Augenlicht.	How pallid thou art!
1:53	dem sonst kein Licht niet gleichet,	Who has so shamefully reduced the light of thine eyes
2:01	so schändlich zu gericht.	which no other light can equal, to such a sorry state?

If You Liked That, Try This

"O Mensch, bewein dein Sunde gross," BWV 622, Bach
"Awake, a Voice Calls to Us," Bach

YouTube video: search on keywords
Bach's St. Matthew Passion, by Kurt Masur

Remember to add to your personal playlist any of these samples that you like.

Nonliturgical Mass and Requiem

Mass: The primary religious service of the Catholic Church. Certain parts of the service are often set to music.

When is a musical Mass not used as a service?

Composers of many religious beliefs have been attracted to the **Mass** as a strictly musical form of expression. Their Masses are intended not for a religious service but for performance in a concert hall. The form of such Masses is the same as the liturgical Mass but is usually much longer and makes use of larger forces. Each section of the Mass is longer and often divided into subsections containing recitative, aria, and chorus. In this manner composers meld the form of the Mass with opera and cantata to create a longer work. Famous examples of this form are Bach's Mass in B minor and American composer and conductor Leonard Bernstein's *Mass* (actually a theater piece). However, many of these works found popularity in the concert hall as well as in church, and composers of the Romantic era wrote **requiems** for nonliturgical events. One such composer was the symphonist Johannes Brahms. His *German Requiem* is one of the most popular choral/orchestral works and is regularly performed today.

Requiem Mass: A Mass for the dead.

LISTENING GUIDE 10.3

"HOW LOVELY IS THY DWELLING PLACE," from *A German Requiem*, op. 45, mvt. 4,
Johannes Brahms, composed 1868

Dashboard
HEAR STREAMING AUDIO
ON DASHBOARD

The work is written for orchestra, chorus, and soloists and is in seven movements that create an arch in overall form. Brahms creates this arch form by connecting the music of movement 1 to that of 7, 2 to 6, and 3 to 5. The fourth movement keystone of the work, "How Lovely Is Thy Dwelling Place," is based upon Psalm 84. The *German Requiem* differs from other Requiems in that Brahms intended it to offer consolation to the living and promote acceptance of death. As such, it does not use the traditional Requiem Mass liturgy from the Catholic Church, which focuses on prayers for the dead. Brahms chose as the text for the work sections of the Lutheran bible. The work underwent several years of revision before this final version was published. A near-complete six-movement version of it was performed on Good Friday, 1868, in Bremen Cathedral. The complete work was premiered in Leipzig in 1869. This movement is set in a rondo form.

What to Listen For

- Listen for word painting. The word "lovely" is emphasized throughout.
- Listen for the interaction between the vocal material and the instrumental lines. The orchestra is not merely accompanimental.
- Listen for how the lyricism of Brahms's melodies creates an ethereal feeling to match the text.

This movement is the centerpiece of the entire Requiem. Connections exist between movements 1 and 7, 2 and 6, 3 and 5, leaving movement 4 to stand alone.

- Listen for how Brahms reverses the first melody to create a new theme. The opening woodwind introduction to the movement is an inversion of the chorus's first melody.

TIMING	FORM: RONDO	TEXT	TRANSLATION	WHAT TO LISTEN FOR
0:00	Intro			A brief introductory line in the woodwinds descends to the initial chorus entrance. The line is the inversion of the chorus's melody.
0:07	A	Wie lieblich sind deine Wohnungen Herr Zebaoth!	How lovely is thy dwelling place O Lord of Hosts!	Theme A is stated by the full chorus.
0:29		deine Wohnungen Herr Zebaoth!	thy dwelling place O Lord of Hosts!	Woodwinds repeat this ascending fragment of the opening melody.
0:44		Wie lieblich sind deine Wohnungen Herr Zebaoth!	How lovely is thy dwelling place O Lord of Hosts!	A second melodic idea is used for the same words as those of theme A. This theme begins with longer notes but has an ascending line much like that of theme A.
1:00		Wie lieblich sind deine Wohnungen Herr Zebaoth!	How lovely is thy dwelling place O Lord of Hosts!	Brahms repeats the words "how lovely" in imitation in the voices, emphasizing them.
				Strings play a brief pizzicato line introducing the B section.
1:25	B	Meine Seele verlanget und sehnet sich	My soul longs and faints for thee	The B theme is stated in imitation and in a minor key.
1:46		nach den Vorhöfen des Herrn.	courts of the Lord.	The work builds to a dramatic volume and the phrase ends with a soft statement of the words "for the courts of the Lord."

(continued)

TIMING	FORM: RONDO	TEXT	TRANSLATION	WHAT TO LISTEN FOR
				Oboe plays an echo of the chorus.
2:00		Mein Leig und Seele freuen sich	My body and soul rejoice	The chorus begins a section that accents specific words of the text including "body" and "soul" as part of the text "My body and soul rejoice in the living God."
2:16		In dem lebendigen Gott.	In the living God.	The line repeats to end the section.
2:45	A	Wie lieblich sind deine Wohnungen	How lovely is thy dwelling place	Theme A is reintroduced by the downward line, this time presented by strings. Theme returns as it sounded at the beginning.
2:53		Herr Zebaoth! Herr Zebaoth!	O Lord of Hosts! O Lord of Hosts!	
3:07		deine Wohnungen Herr Zebaoth!	thy dwelling place O Lord of Hosts!	
3:34	C	Wohl denen, die in deinem Hause wohnen,	Blessed are those who dwell in thy house	A homophonic setting of the text.
3:50		die loben dich immerdar.

die loben dich immerdar. | who praise Thee evermore.

who praise Thee evermore. | An imitative section begins on the words "who praise thee evermore." The tempo moves faster in this poly-phonic section. The section builds in intensity and volume and suddenly draws to a close with low long tones on the word "evermore." |
				Woodwinds play the descending introductory line again as a bridge to Theme A.
4:45	A'	Wie lieblich Wie lieblich	How lovely How lovely	Theme A once more emphasizes the words "how lovely."
5:06		Wie lieblich sind deine Wohnungen	How lovely is thy dwelling place.	The chorus swells in volume and intensity once more on the words "how lovely is thy dwelling place."
5:24				The orchestra brings the movement to a soft and gentle close.

If You Liked That, Try This

Manzoni Requiem, by Giuseppe Verdi
Gloria, by Francis Poulenc
Requiem, by Maurice Duruflé

YouTube videos: search on keywords
Brahms German Requiem Mvt 1
Dies irae, Requiem, Verdi. Zubin Mehta

Remember to add to your personal playlist any of these samples that you like.

PERFORMER PROFILE
Robert Shaw

American conductor Robert Shaw (1916–1999) was one of the most respected choral conductors of the 20th century. Shaw was the conductor and music director of the Robert Shaw Chorale, a professional mixed chorus that performed and recorded with the country's major symphony orchestras and toured for the U.S. State Department. During his career he won fourteen Grammy awards and conducted choruses all over the world. In 1991 he was a recipient of the Kennedy Center Honors. Shaw was also an orchestral conductor serving as music director of the San Diego Symphony, associate conductor of the Cleveland Orchestra, and music director of the Atlanta Symphony Orchestra.

Shaw spent a good deal of his energy working with amateur choruses across the United States working to raise the performance level of American choirs and it is perhaps for this that he will be best remembered. Dismayed at the general level of choral singing in America, Shaw traveled the country guest conducting college/university choruses and community choirs in an attempt to raise their musicianship. Successful especially in the nation's colleges and universities, he was mentor and teacher to generations of American choral conductors.

Choral conductor Robert Shaw. Courtesy Associated Press.

✓ **Build Your Own Playlist:** The works studied in the chapter Listening Guides serve as examples of styles from different eras. Now, build your own playlist from those works listed in each IF YOU LIKED THAT, TRY THIS list or from other works you find. Share your playlist with others by posting it to your class discussion board or Dashboard.

✓ **Audio Review:** Go to Dashboard to listen to Professor Bailey discuss orchestra and voices.

✓ **How Am I Doing?** Go to Dashboard to test your understanding of this material by taking the chapter quiz.

Dashboard

KEY TERMS

Aria	Passion	Requiem Mass
Mass	Recitative	Word painting
Oratorio		

Music for Wind Bands

LEARNING OBJECTIVES

• **Name important composers of band music.**

• **Explain similarities and differences of timbre between the band and the orchestra.**

• **Recognize by listening example the tone quality of a band.**

Key Concepts: history of bands, instrumentation of the concert band, march form

Opening image: A concert band is made up of woodwind, brass, and percussion instruments.
Courtesy Ted Foxx/Alamy.

Where It's Playing

Concert bands give concerts in concert halls—and many other places. In fact, bands are heard in more different types of venues, including outdoors, than any other ensemble. Most serious concert band music is played in the concert hall, just like an orchestra. The large band, sometimes called a "wind ensemble" usually has a larger percussion section than an orchestra and thus requires a concert hall–size stage. However, concert bands also regularly give concerts outdoors. This is much more common for bands than orchestras because wind instruments are not as sensitive to weather as are string instruments. Many communities sponsor summer outdoor concerts on a regular basis.

The University of Michigan Marching Band forms the traditional "Block M" at pregame ceremonies in Ann Arbor, Michigan. Courtesy MMB Photography—www.umichbandphotos.com.

Bands also often perform in stadiums at athletic events. These marching bands are not concert bands but they still often perform art music. The primary difference between a concert band and a marching band is that in the marching band the members move while they play. There are some minor differences in instrumentation between the two bands and the marching band percussion section is usually larger than that of the concert band. It is common for university marching bands to have over 250 members. This very large number is required in order to produce enough volume of sound when playing in a stadium.

Bands are rarely used to accompany opera but they have appeared on Broadway. The recent Broadway production *Blast* is a Broadway show of what amounts to a marching band performance.

Attending a band concert in a concert hall is much the same experience as attending an orchestra concert. Essentially, the same concert traditions are observed by both. The differences between a band and an orchestra concert are primarily in the types of music played by the two ensembles and the timbral qualities of the two groups. When you attend a band concert there will probably be more pieces on the program than at the orchestra concert you attend. Generally speaking, band works, especially those written before the last two decades of the 20th century, are shorter than orchestral pieces. And there is a good deal more music written for band that is of a lighter character than orchestral music. Most band concerts offer a wider range of musical styles than orchestra concerts. This sort of variety concert dates back to the touring professional bands, which presented a varied fare of music from opera arias to marches to popular songs set for band.

Dashboard

EXPLORE

The varying timbres of a band are, perhaps, its most interesting aspect. Listen for the wide range of sounds produced in contemporary wind band music. Composers have learned to exploit the combinatory tonal qualities of the wind band's instruments to create many new timbres. Listen to the dynamic ranges presented by the ensemble. The band is capable of very dramatic effects due to the volume and accents it is capable of producing. The band can easily arouse emotions.

Before the Beatles, before the Rolling Stones, before Glenn Miller, the E Street Band, or U2, the most famous and popular band in the world was a concert band—the Sousa Band, a professional touring concert band. For nearly thirty years the Sousa Band traveled the world as the musical ambassadors of the United States. The concert band was the most often-heard ensemble of the first thirty years of the 20th century.

As stated in Chapter 2, a concert band is made up of wind and percussion instruments and is generally divided into woodwind, brass, and percussion sections. In the United States bands far outnumber orchestras, and chances are much better that you have heard a band perform live than an orchestra. Today, there are four types of concert bands in America: military bands, school bands, community bands (bands of amateurs who were in high school and/or college bands and wish to continue playing their instruments), and college/university bands.

Band Instrumentation

How do the makeup of the band and orchestra differ?

The wind and percussion instruments used in orchestras and bands are, for the most part, the same, the notable exception being the saxophone, which is a regular member of the band, but not the orchestra. However, the numbers of each instrument used in these two ensembles differs greatly. The chart below shows the typical numbers of wind instruments in the concert band and the orchestra.

INSTRUMENT	CONCERT BAND	ORCHESTRA
Piccolo	1	1
Flute	5–9	2
Oboe	2	3
English horn	1	1
Bassoon	2	2
B flat clarinet	6–24	2
Bass clarinet	1–4	0–1
Alto saxophone	2–4	0
Tenor saxophone	1–2	0

(continued)

INSTRUMENT	CONCERT BAND	ORCHESTRA
Baritone saxophone	1	0
Horn	4–8	2–4
Trumpet	3–13	2–4
Trombone	3–9	3
Euphonium	1–4	0
Tuba	1–4	1
Timpani	1	1
Percussion	Often 6	Usually no more than 3
Piano	1	1
Harp	1	1

Dashboard

COMPARE AND CONTRAST

The orchestra's string instruments are replaced by multiples of wind instruments in the band. In most band works the clarinet, oboe, and flute parts are similar in purpose and style to those of the violin in the orchestra. The trombone and euphonium sections of the band play parts much like those of the cello in the orchestra and the tuba in the band replaces the string bass of the orchestra. When thought of this way the numbers of these wind instruments in the band correspond closely to the numbers of violin, cello, and bass in the orchestra. Bands and orchestras often play the same piece of music. In most cases this is a work originally written for orchestra that has been arranged for the band's instrumentation.

Early Development of Bands

How have bands developed over the time periods studied in this text?
Bands of wind instruments have been used in Western music throughout each of the style periods discussed in this book. In fact, during the Medieval and Renaissance eras they were much more important and popular than ensembles of string instruments. These early bands were used in watchtowers to warn of fire or invasion, for public ceremonies, and for dances. In the Medieval and Renaissance periods most bands, professional and amateur, were very small, often only four to ten members. Large bands (meaning fifty players or more) did not come into general use until the late 1790s. After the French Revolution Paris's French Revolutionary Guard Band became the model for larger bands throughout Europe. It included multiples of each of the wind instruments and totaled about seventy-five players. The Guard Band was used for political, ceremonial, and military purposes and this utilitarian use became the norm for the next 175 years.

Throughout the 19th century most bands were attached in some manner to the military. This influenced the type of repertoire that developed for bands. For the most part the early band repertoire was music that could be played outdoors and was ceremonial in some manner. Most bands performed marches, arrangements of orchestral music called transcriptions, and music of a light, uplifting character as the primary part of their repertoire.

In America wind bands became very popular with the general public after the Civil War, during which bands were used by both sides to recruit, move, and entertain troops. Upon returning home many former soldiers helped form a vast number of amateur town bands. The resulting interest in band music throughout the United States led to the development of professional touring bands. Bands led by Patrick Gilmore, John Philip Sousa, and Edwin Franko Goldman toured the country for over seventy years presenting a wide variety of music. However, these bands all but died out with the development of radio. The focus of band performance then shifted to the public schools, colleges, and military service bands. By the 1940s most colleges had band programs even if they didn't have orchestras or music schools. College bands became closely associated with college athletics, further determining the style of music performed.

Dashboard

ATTEND AND REPORT

John Philip Sousa

The best-known composer of band music is John Philip Sousa (1854–1932). Sousa's father was a member of the United States Marine Corps band in Washington, D.C., and he apprenticed Sousa to the band at the age of thirteen when Sousa tried to run away to join the circus. In 1880 Sousa was appointed director of the Marine Band, and he shaped it into the finest band in the world. It remains among the most outstanding musical ensembles of any kind. In 1892 Sousa left the Marine Band to form his own professional touring ensemble, which he led until his death. The band toured the United States and the world to great critical and public acclaim.

   Though a composer of many styles of music, Sousa is best known for his marches. Known as the "March King," he wrote over 130 marches during his career and many have become iconic in American culture. The most famous is "The Stars and Stripes Forever," now America's official march. Sousa wrote the march in 1896 as he and his wife sailed back from a European vacation. It contains two of the most recognized melodies in all of American music—the melody of the trio section, and its piccolo countermelody. Sousa died shortly after conducting a rehearsal of the Ringgold Band in Pennsylvania. The last piece of music he rehearsed was "The Stars and Stripes Forever."

American band conductor and composer John Philip Sousa.
© Copyright Bettmann/Corbis/AP Images.

LISTENING GUIDE 11.1

"THE STARS AND STRIPES FOREVER,"
John Philip Sousa, composed 1896

"Suddenly, I began to sense the rhythmic beat of a band playing within my brain. It kept on ceaselessly, playing, playing, playing. Through the whole tense voyage, that imaginary band continued to unfold the same themes,

Dashboard

HEAR STREAMING AUDIO ON DASHBOARD

echoing and re-echoing the most distinct melody. I did not transfer a note of that music to paper while I was on the steamer, but when we reached shore, I set down the measures that my brain-hand had been playing for me," John Philip Sousa recounted, of the composition now known the world over as "The Stars and Stripes Forever." It was written on a voyage home from a European vacation. The work is in standard American march form of Introduction, A, B, C, Breakup strain, C—a form which Sousa developed. The melodies of this work are well known in the United States and the march is often heard live, especially at patriotic events. It is the official march of the United States of America.

What to Listen For

- Listen for the introductory theme. These few bars are so familiar to many in the United States that they immediately recognize the march.

- Listen for the contrasting styles of melodies typical of an American march. The first two melodies, or strains, are generally martial and rhythmic. The third melody, played in the trio section, is almost always lyrical.

- Listen to the tone quality of the band. Notice that the clarinets, flutes, and trumpets take the melodic role of the violin section in an orchestra.
- Listen for the traditional short last note, called the "stinger" or "bump" note. The tradition of ending marches in this manner is thought to relate to the folk dance habit of ending some folk dances with a leap in the air and a clicking of one's heels together.
- Listen to how the trumpets and trombones seem to battle one another for melodic supremacy in the "Breakup strain." Band directors call this section the "dogfight" because the music is segmented and imitative, often between high and low brass instruments.

TIMING	FORM: AMERICAN MARCH FORM	WHAT TO LISTEN FOR
0:00	Introduction	Some of the most recognizable measures of music in all of America serve as the introduction to this march. The stately introduction sets up the rhythmic pulse of the march.
0:04	A—Strain 1	The first melody is a rhythmic line of short, accented quarter notes. The melody, like almost all march melodies, is presented by the upper woodwinds and trumpet. The slurred phrase-ending measures break up the scalar character of the melody.
0:19		The strain repeats. This is typical of a march form. On most repeated sections the band alters some aspect of the music such as dynamics or instrumentation.
0:33	B—Strain 2	Melody 2 is made up of longer pitches and has a more lyrical, singable quality.
0:49		The strain repeats.
1:05	C—Trio section	The C section of a march is traditionally referred to as the "Trio section." The key changes in the trio of a march, adding one flat to the key signature. Melody 3 is the most famous melody of this march, a lyrical melody introduced by woodwinds.
1:36	Breakup strain	This section is also called the "dogfight." The melody alternates between the low brass and the upper brass. First introduced by the low brass, it is interrupted by two short chords in the upper brass. The melodic fragments move back and forth from high to low instruments. The section ends with a descending scale played in unison rhythm by the full band.
2:00	C—Trio section	The trio section is repeated. On the repeat of the trio, Sousa added the now-famous piccolo countermelody. This melody is traditionally played by one piccolo player as a soloist who stands to play the line.
2:31	Breakup strain	The end of the repeat of the dogfight traditionally slows down in tempo.
2:57	C—Trio melody	The final statement of the trio melody is played in a martial style by full band but featuring the trumpets. The march traditionally ends with a special drum cadence heard underneath the final measures.

If You Liked That, Try This

"Americans We," Henry Fillmore
"Semper Fidelis," J. P. Sousa
"The Melody Shop," Karl King

YouTube videos: search on keywords
Henry Fillmore—The Circus Bee
Karl King—Barnum & Bailey's Favorite

Remember to add to your personal playlist any of these samples that you like.

CULTURAL CONNECTION: TURKISH MEHTER BANDS

Many composers of orchestral and vocal music of the 20th century also wrote for concert bands including Arnold Schoenberg, Igor Stravinsky, Darius Milhaud, and Aaron Copland. Two especially important band composers of this type were Australian-born Percy Grainger (1882–1961) and Gustav Holst (1874–1934) of England. Both were well-known composers of orchestral music who dedicated part of their time to composing original band music. One of the most influential and best-loved band pieces is Holst's First Suite in E-flat. This work, written in 1909, served as a model for generations of band composers. In three movements, each melody is related to the opening pitches of the "Chaconne."

LISTENING GUIDE 11.2

"CHACONNE," from First Suite in E-flat for Military Band, mvt. 1,
Gustav Holst, composed 1909

This piece for concert band was written in 1909, though it is unknown what is was written for or when it was first performed—unusual for a piece by a composer as famous as Holst was at the time. The work is set in three movements: "Chaconne," "Intermezzo," and "March." All melodies of the three movements are based upon the first three notes of the piece. The first movement is set in a variation form as a theme and fifteen variations.

HEAR STREAMING AUDIO ON DASHBOARD

What to Listen For

- Listen for the manner in which Holst changes the chaconne melody. In two instances he inverts the melody. Most of the variations are variations of style or articulation.

- Listen for the tone quality of the band sound. It is a very different timbre than that of the full orchestra.

TIMING	FORM: THEME AND VARIATIONS	WHAT TO LISTEN FOR
0:00	Theme—Chaconne	The piece begins without introduction. The chaconne melody is stated in the low brass and is structured on a note pattern of short-long, short-long. The tune is a very lyrical melody.
0:17	Variation 1	Variation 1 for brass adds both harmony to the original and an important counter-line in trumpet. It, like the original, is lyrical, subdued, and soft.
0:33	Variation 2	Variation 2 is played by woodwinds. This variation is made up of three other woodwind lines that weave in and out of the original.

0:48	Variation 3	Variation 3, for mixed brass and woodwinds, is a stylistic variation. Holst adds fanfare-like short woodwind and brass material to the lyrical original.
1:03	Variation 4	Variation 4 is played by full band, including percussion. It continues the overall crescendo begun in Variation 3. This variation is in the same style as Variation 3 and sounds like a continuation of that Variation, with more forces involved.
1:18	Variation 5	Variation 5 is the high point of the first half of the movement. Holst creates the variation by shortening the length of notes of the original, harmonizing the theme in brass, and combining this with woodwind continuous scales.
1:32	Variation 6	Variation 6 is primarily for brass. The variation is again created in two ways: by harmonization of the original and by the addition of a running bass line. The end of this variation serves as a transition into a return to the more lyrical and brooding character of the original, when Variation 7 begins.
1:45	Variation 7	Variation 7 has a new countermelody in clarinet to accompany the horn solo line of the original.
1:59	Variation 8	Variation 8 is a duet between flute and oboe and a rhythmic variation.
2:15	Variation 9	Variation 9 is the first of two inversion variations in a minor key. It is a literal inversion of the original theme and amazingly lyrical and melodic, a true melody equal to the original.
2:30	Variation 10	Variation 10 continues the minor inversion in brass and adds a bass line.
2:43	Variation 11	Variation 11 returns to the original chaconne melody, slightly varied in accompaniment.
2:57	Variation 12	Variation 12 returns to the true original theme. This section begins the buildup to the second climax of the movement in Variation 14.
3:11	Variation 13	Variation 13 is for full ensemble. Combined with variation 12, it creates a sixteen-measure crescendo in dynamics and intensity to Variation 14.
3:26	Variation 14	Variation 14 is the climactic section of the second half of the movement. Scored for full ensemble, it contains four lines that serve as counter-lines to the original.
3:41	Variation 15	Variation 15 contains the work's largest climax. The upward resolution of the tension on the final chord provides a surprisingly brilliant end to the movement.

If You Liked That, Try This

Folk Song Suite, by Ralph Vaughan Williams
Lincolnshire Posy, by Percy Grainger
William Byrd Suite, by Gordon Jacob

YouTube video: search on keywords
Air Force Concert Band Plays Lincolnshire Posy by Grainger

Remember to add to your personal playlist any of these samples that you like.

PERFORMER PROFILE
Military Band Musicians

Colonel Michael Colburn is the 27th director of the United States Marine Corp band, "The President's Own." Colburn joined the band as a euphonium player in 1987 and was appointed director in July 2004 and retired from the position in July 2014. The commander of the Marine Band in Washington, D.C., has a demanding and interesting job. In addition to regularly conducting "The President's Own" band at White House ceremonies, around Washington, D.C., and on tour of the United States, Colburn also oversaw the musical operations of the White House and other Marine musicians. He also was the music director of Washington's Gridiron Club, the oldest journalistic organization in the U.S.

Col. Michael Colburn conducts the United States Marine Corp band. Courtesy Associated Press.

Each of the branches of the U.S. military has bands stationed in Washington, D.C., and throughout the world. Many of the musicians are cross-trained in another aspect of military service. Most of the service bands tour the country presenting free band concerts in community centers and concert halls.

Visit the website of the United States Marine Band for a history of the band.

Modern Concert Band Music

Throughout much of the 20th century, especially the first fifty years, communities all over America held weekly summer band concerts in local parks. The concerts became important social events for small communities and did much to further the spread of art music in the United States. These types of concerts continue today in lesser numbers but are still important social events in the lives of many small, rural communities. The bands in these concerts are made up of amateur players from the community. To find a community band in your area, visit the website of the Association of Concert Bands, the international organization for these bands.

Beginning in the second half of the 20th century, bands, mostly led by college band directors, began to take on a more serious repertoire. More and more original music was written for band, replacing the transcriptions of the past as the primary repertoire. Today, the repertoire is a mixture of marches, traditional arrangements for band, and original compositions for band. Though a few professional ensembles like the Dallas Wind Symphony exist, the highest level of band performance remains at colleges and in military bands.

Courtesy ZUMA Press, Inc./Alamy.

Today's bands are mostly flexible in instrumentation and size. And they use a very wide range of music to make up their repertoire. Still largely associated with the military or colleges, bands now commission some of the world's greatest composers to create original works for them. One such composer is American Frank Ticheli (b. 1958), who writes music for many different ensembles but seems especially intrigued by the timbral possibilities of the modern wind ensemble.

Dashboard

EXPLORE

LISTENING GUIDE 11.3

POSTCARD,
Frank Ticheli, composed 1991

Postcard is a work for modern day wind ensemble. It was commissioned in 1991 by H. Robert Reynolds, then director of bands at the University of Michigan. The symphony band at Michigan gave the work its first performance in 1992. Reynolds intended the work to be an elegy for his mother. Ticheli wrote a short work in ABA form that has great energy.

Dashboard

**HEAR STREAMING AUDIO
ON DASHBOARD**

What to Listen For

- Listen for the dance-like quality of the melodies.
- Listen for the rhythmic energy. The mixture of meters contributes to this.
- Listen for how Ticheli uses different wind and percussion instruments in combination to create interesting timbres.

TIMING	FORM: ABA	WHAT TO LISTEN FOR
0:00	A	The work opens with the theme presented in a fast offbeat fashion in the clarinet and flute.
0:10		The theme is restated by oboe and bassoon with variations.
0:29		The theme is fragmented and developed. A lyrical motif is introduced.
1:05		Horns play long pitches loudly leading into an imitative statement of the theme in saxophone, oboe, and flute.
1:20		Full band statement of the theme.
1:36		Brass restate the theme.
1:57		Section ends with a soft percussion and flute transition.
2:07	B	The B theme is stated in euphonium and is a lyrical melody. The accompaniment continues the same quality as the A theme. The B section continues with many brass interjections. The line moves in a frenzied fashion between choirs of instruments.
3:02		The flutes and oboes play a lyrical statement of theme B.
3:19		Brass interrupt with a syncopated rhythm and woodwinds answer with short material that is in the same style as the A theme.
3:50		Woodwind runs lead into a section of quickly-changing dynamics and repeated notes in the brass.
4:03	A	The A theme returns in brass.
4:11		Woodwinds answer with the theme in the low register. Material from the original A section is presented in basically the same order and style as before.

If You Liked That, Try This

Kingfishers Catch Fire, John Mackey
Moon by Night, Jonathan Newman
Ecstatic Waters, Steven Bryant

YouTube video: search on keywords
Mackey: Kingfishers Catch Fire, TMEA

Remember to add to your personal playlist any of these samples that you like.

✓ **Build Your Own Playlist:** The works studied in the chapter Listening Guides serve as examples of different styles of band music from different eras. Now, build your own playlist from those works listed in each IF YOU LIKED THAT, TRY THIS list or from other band works you find. Share your playlist with others by posting it to your class discussion board or Dashboard. Remember to add to your personal playlist any of these samples that you like.

✓ **Audio Review:** Go to Dashboard to listen to Professor Bailey discuss music for wind bands.

✓ **How Am I Doing?** Go to Dashboard to test your understanding of this material by taking the chapter quiz.

Dashboard

Music of the Recital Hall and Salon

M any classical musicians are not performers in large orchestras, bands, or choirs like those discussed in Units 2 and 3. Instead they make music as soloists or as members of small groups of musicians called chamber ensembles. Their performance venues are recital halls, salons, or intimate spaces with smaller audiences.

The type of music performed in a recital hall differs from that of the concert hall. Not only is it designed for soloists or chamber ensembles, but it also often contains sections that are much quieter or more contemplative than music for the concert hall. The forms of music are also different. A symphony is usually not performed in a recital hall. Instead a string quartet might be heard. Rather than a concerto with orchestral accompaniment, you might hear an instrumental sonata or a song. The recital hall is also where a good deal of experimental and electronic music is presented.

The experience of attending a concert in a recital hall is much like the experience in the large concert hall. The physical aspects of the recital hall and concert hall are similar—there is still a backstage area, a stage, and a house. The recital also has a printed program, usually distributed by ushers, and the performers in a recital hall act much like those performing in a large concert hall. The primary difference between these two performance spaces is one of size. The recital hall is smaller, it seats fewer audience members, its stage is smaller (since it needs to accommodate fewer musicians), and its backstage area is much smaller. The recital hall is designed to enhance the sound of soloists or a chamber group, so its acoustics are different from those of a concert hall. Since the performers are closer to the audience, with no orchestra pit separating them, and since the audience is smaller, the performers in a recital hall can interact more closely with the audience than in a large concert hall.

Opening image: A chamber ensemble rehearses on stage of a recital hall.
© Courtesy ZUMA Press, Inc / Alamy.

Moreso than concert halls, recital halls tend to be associated with educational institutions. Most cities have at least one concert hall, but fewer have recital halls. In addition, since most recital halls are associated with not-for-profit organizations, recitals are more often free than are concerts.

The Recital

A recital usually lasts from one to one and one-half hours with a short intermission. Unlike the concert hall, a recital hall lobby rarely offers shopping or refreshments. This, along with a smaller audience size, usually makes the intermissions of recitals shorter than concert hall performances. The recital will typically consist of four or five works if an instrumental concert and ten to fifteen songs if a vocal recital. A recital printed program usually offers less information than a concert program. It generally lists the performers and the works in order of performance, but does not contain notes describing the works, performer biographies or pictures, or sponsor advertising. For a vocal recital with songs in foreign languages the program will normally include translations of the texts of the songs.

Music for the Recital Hall or Salon

In two of the chapters of Unit 4 you will listen to music written for solo voice or solo keyboard. Much of this music is very passionate and emotional, and was written in the 19th century. A good deal of it was popular music of the 1800s and, like our popular songs today, many of the works are brief and are focused on one emotion or idea. Romantic-era composers wrote a huge amount of this type of music for solo voice or solo keyboard, perhaps because it was often intended for performance in a home by amateurs.

Much of the music of this unit was written for amateur entertainment at gatherings of families and friends, or just in the living room after dinner. This inspired composers to write a great deal of music that we call art song or character music. Music of this time period was closely related to literature, especially poetry. The solo keyboard music of this unit was mainly of two types; study pieces (called etudes) designed for teaching the instrument or virtuosic showpieces created to display the abilities of a particular performer.

The art song and the piano pieces are the staple of recitals at colleges and universities and are still used as teaching pieces in music schools. Young pianists all over the world learn the etudes of the composers of this unit. Just like when they were written, these works are also still heard in living rooms as keyboard students develop their skills.

Chamber music is also often performed today in recital halls and is music written for small groups, in the case of instrumentalists most often four or five players. Vocal chamber ensembles are more varied in size and usually range from four to twelve singers. This type of music is some of the oldest music because much of it was written for entertainment and amusement during and after dinner or for ceremonies. Over the years the styles and forms have changed but not the intent. Chamber music is intimate music, music to be shared with a small audience or sometimes just performed for the enjoyment of the performers and friends. From the Middle Ages to the advent of radio and television in the 20th century families and friends joined together in salons to perform chamber music together for their own pleasure. By the end of the 19th century any young person of even modest social standing would have been expected to be able to sing and/or play an instrument well enough to participate in this amateur music-making.

Composers of each of the musical eras also wrote serious art music for chamber ensembles of professional musicians. Over time, the types of chamber ensembles changed as instruments changed. This music was written for performance at concerts in formal halls and in the living rooms (salons) of wealthy patrons of the arts.

Works written for the salon or for home entertainment were meant to be performed with an audience in close proximity to the performers. They were intended for small rooms with intimate acoustics. And, they were often experimental works being tried out by a composer on his/her friends and patrons to see what might work in a larger scale piece of music.

What to Listen for and Observe at a Recital

- As noted above, recitals are performed by small groups of people—sometimes just one or two. Observe the close communication between the musicians, their facial expressions and other nonverbal communication. Their interactions resemble a musical conversation.
- It is also interesting for audience members to consider the order of the program. Why is it presented in this order? What seems to be the hardest piece for the performers? Which seems easiest? Which is most difficult for the audience to understand?
- The careful observer might also note occurrences in the hall that could distract the performers. The intimacy of the space means that the performers can see what the audience does, and vice versa. Recital performers are generally much more aware of their audiences than those performing in a large concert hall.

Vocal Music for the Recital Hall and Salon

LEARNING OBJECTIVES

- **Compare the art song to popular song of today.**
- **Explain the relationship of the piano and voice in an art song.**
- **Summarize the forms commonly used in art song.**
- **Name important composers of art song and madrigal.**
- **Explain the differences between solo song and part song.**

Key Concepts: a cappella, ballett, lied (lieder), madrigal, piano and voice relationship in art song, strophic and through-composed forms, song cycle, word painting

Opening image: ***The Concert* by James Tissot.** Courtesy Manchester City Art Gallery, Manchester, Great Britain/HIP/Art Resource, NY.

A solo vocalist accompanied by piano at a recital. Courtesy Design Pics Inc./Alamy.

ATTEND AND REPORT

Where It's Playing

Songs are perhaps the most prevalent type of expression in the history of music. Before any musical instrument that could produce a melody was created, the human voice sang. You probably heard a song from one of your parents when you were a baby, to help you sleep. And, whether or not you can play an instrument, it is most certain that you have sung a song at some time in your life. Many people, even those who are not musicians, sing somewhere every day, in the shower, or along with the car radio on the way to work, or at a ballgame. Chances are good that your favorite piece of popular music is a song. Singing seems to be one of those things that is natural to human beings.

The type of songs we focus on in this chapter are heard specifically in two places: the recital hall and in intimate gathering places like homes or meeting halls. In the Renaissance a great number of songs were written for the pleasure of singing. Large homes of the time served as resting places for noble travelers and hosted guests. Family members and guests performed music called madrigals for one another's entertainment during and after dinner in such estates. Romantic era art songs were very personal expressions of one's own feeling and thoughts. These songs were often created for informal gatherings in a friend's home where literature was discussed, poetry was read, and music was performed among friends. While this tradition may still exist, it is no longer common. Today, art song is performed most frequently in the recital hall. This smaller concert space still allows to some degree the intimacy between audience and performer that would have been experienced in a salon setting. The art song is a perfect type of music for the recital hall in that it heightens the emotional experience of the listener through the intimacy of the setting. Song recitals are most common on college and university campuses. Vocal students, and their teachers, present recitals of art song on a regular basis on American campuses every year.

The Madrigal

What makes a song a part-song?

We often sing informally together or for one another at sporting events, in church, at home, at clubs or karaoke bars for fun and entertainment. We usually sing a song in unison. For example, when we sing "The Star Spangled Banner" at a sporting event we all sing the same notes, rhythms, and words. But in the **madrigal**, each singer has a different part to sing. This part-singing is one of the things that distinguishes solo song from vocal chamber music.

Madrigal: A secular part-song popular in the Renaissance era.

The madrigal was the most important type of vocal music of the Renaissance era and, like art song, it is well suited to the recital hall because it inspires intimacy between audience and performer. The madrigal originated in Italy around 1520 as a secular form that soon spread from Italy throughout Europe, and was especially popular in England. It was the most popular form of vocal music until about 1620. It was intended as entertainment at dinners or other social occasions and to be sung by amateurs. The invention of movable type enhanced its popularity, as it led to widespread distribution of printed music. Literally thousands of madrigals were written and published during the Renaissance era, and most members of the upper classes learned to sing and play instruments as part of their education. After dinner educated people were expected to participate in the evening's music-making.

The words of a madrigal were usually taken from a short poem and most often dealt with love or longing, but texts were also humorous and satirical, sometimes political, and often filled with double entendres. **Word painting** was a common expressive device in madrigals. Madrigals were written for four to six individual voices. Sometimes instruments either doubled the singers or played a part by themselves. The texture of the madrigal was a mixture of polyphony and homophony, and the individual parts were imitative of one another.

A Concert **by Lorenzo Costs.** Courtesy National Gallery © National Gallery, London/Art Resource, NY.

Most composers of the time wrote madrigals. Among the best were Italians Luca Marenzio (1553–1599) and Carlo Gesauldo (1560–1613) and English composers William Byrd (1543–1623), Thomas Morley (1557–1602), and Thomas Weelkes (1576–1623). However, the composer who brought the madrigal to culmination was Claudio Monteverdi (1567–1643).

Word painting: A compositional device in which a particular sound is created to evoke an idea or represent a specific word in a song.

Claudio Monteverdi

Claudio Monteverdi was born in Cremona, Italy, and his life spanned the years between the end of the Renaissance and the beginning of the Baroque. He wrote important vocal music in at least two genres: madrigal and opera. Monteverdi spent over twenty years working as a musician and composer at the important court of Mantua, where he developed opera as a vocal form. He is best known as the music director of St. Mark's Basilica in Venice, one of the most important churches in Europe. In Venice he wrote all styles of vocal music including sacred and secular.

Monteverdi's madrigals were especially emotional, filled with word painting. He used a dissonant harmony, new to the time, as an expressive device and his madrigals were filled with elaborate ornamentation. Monteverdi's music was the earliest to emphasize the highest and lowest parts as the most important. This idea became central to the compositional style of the Baroque era and may have developed because madrigals were written for amateurs. If the lowest part was played on an instrument and one fine singer could perform the highest part, lesser singers

Claudio Monteverdi. Courtesy GL Archive/Alamy.

could fill in the inner parts. Monteverdi wrote nine books of madrigals and was the most influential composer of his time.

The madrigal was extremely popular in the English courts of Elizabeth I and James I. Elizabeth I, a fine musician herself, maintained an excellent household of music, instruments, and musicians. In 1588 a set of madrigals translated into English was published in London and this began a thirty-year period of popularity of the genre. English composers like Morley, Weelkes, and John Farmer (ca. 1570–1601) were leading composers who published many madrigals. The English madrigal was generally a bit simpler and often more humorous than the madrigals of Italy, and contained less word painting.

LISTENING GUIDE 12.1

"HERE, NOW, THE WAVES MURMUR," from *Second Book of Madrigals*,
Claudio Monteverdi, composed 1590

HEAR STREAMING AUDIO ON DASHBOARD

"Here, Now, the Waves Murmur" was written for five voices and published in 1590 as part of Monteverdi's *Second Book of Madrigals*. The work uses word painting to represent waves, rustling leaves, birds, and the wind. The work is imitative in style and demonstrates the new clear distinction between high and low voices.

What to Listen For

- Listen for the mixture of melismatic lines, imitative polyphony, and homophonic choral sounds.
- Listen for the clear distinction between high and low voices.
- Listen for the use of word painting to portray certain aspects of the text including waves, leaves, birds, wind, a heavy heart.

TIMING	FORM: SECTIONAL	TEXT	TRANSLATION	WHAT TO LISTEN FOR
0:00	Section 1	Ecco mormorar l'onde	Here are the waves murmuring	Word painting begins immediately as the low voices softly and quickly change dynamics and direction to imitate waves. The quick-moving scalar line of the second line of text evokes rustling leaves. The third line of the text is set with higher voices and a fast, lyrical melisma to indicate a morning breeze.
		e tremolar le fronde a l'aura matutina e gli arborscelli	And the leaves and shrubs quivering In the morning breeze.	
0:31				
		Ecco mormorar l'onde	Here are the waves murmuring	

1:13	Section 2	e sovra i Verdi rami i vaghi augelli cantar soavemente e rider l'oreinte.	And on the tree-branches the pretty birds sing softly and the East smiles.	High voices in imitative polyphonic style sing descending scalar lines to imitate bird calls.
1:41	Section 3	Ecco già l'alba appare e si specchia nel mare	Here, the dawn looms And is reflected in the sea,	The tempo is quicker and the rhythm more steady as the imitative polyphony continues. Each of the "and . . ." lines is set in an ascending line.
2:01		e rasserena il cielo e imperla il doce gielo e gli alti monti indora Oh, bella e vag' aurora.	And brightens the sky And the gentle frost impearls the fields. And gilds the tall mountains. O beautiful and gentle dawn.	
2:41	Section 4	l'aura è tua messaggiera, e tu de l'aura	The gentle breeze is your messenger, and you the breeze's	The imitative polyphony continues. The music accompanying the text "breeze" is set with a fast crescendo, or swell of sound to imitate wind. The final section is suddenly in much longer notes without melisma as Monteverdi uses word painting to indicate a heavy heart. The section is primarily homophonic.
3:08		ch'ogni arso cor ristaura!	Which refreshes every heavy heart.	

If You Liked That, Try This

"Fair Phyllis," John Farmer
"As Vesta Was from Latmos Hill Descending," Thomas Weelkes
"Alone and Pensive," Luca Marenzio

> **YouTube videos: search on keywords**
> NYRF 2007—The Crown Madrigals: El Grillo
> King's Singers—Madrigal History Tour—Now is the month of
> King's Singers—Madrigal History Tour—Fine knacks

Remember to add to your personal playlist any of these samples that you like.

Fa La La—The Ballett

Ballett: A form similar to the madrigal but usually homophonic and light in character.

A form similar to the madrigal that developed in England was the **ballett**. This form was usually dancelike and was almost always homophonic, with the melody in the highest voice. (The madrigal usually contained both polyphonic and homophonic sections.) The form began in Italy but was cultivated in England. It was characterized by a refrain section using the syllables "fa-la-la" in place of words. The ballett was humorous and playful or flirtatious in style. Being dance-like, it had an easily recognizable rhythmic beat.

LISTENING GUIDE 12.2

"NOW IS THE MONTH OF MAYING,"
Thomas Morley, composed 1595

"Now Is the Month of Maying" is a strophic ballet with a fa-la chorus. This type of work is very similar in style to the madrigal but is always in a humorous, satirical, or happy mood. These works were most popular in England and are often associated with a time of the year such as spring or Christmas.

Dashboard

HEAR STREAMING AUDIO ON DASHBOARD

What to Listen For

- Listen for the form of the work. Within the strophic form, the melody is divided into two parts, each of which repeats.
- Listen for a change in texture from homophonic to polyphonic at the end of the second part of each phrase of the melody.
- Listen for the dance-like character of the melody and the way Morley makes the music as flirtatious as the text.

TIMING	FORM: STROPHIC	TEXT	WHAT TO LISTEN FOR
0:00	Stanza 1	Now is the month of Maying, When merry lads are playing. Fa la etc.	The first part of the melody, a, is repeated with a fa-la chorus at the end. Each phrase ends this way. The dance character is produced by the repetitive and accented rhythms and the light singing style of the vocalists.
0:08		Now is the month of Maying, When merry lads are playing. Fa la etc.	
0:16		Each with his bonny lass, Upon the greeny grass. Fa la, etc.	The second part of the tune, b, is also repeated with a fa-la chorus to end the section. This chorus is in a polyphonic style, in contrast to the homophonic quality of the rest of the melody.

0:24		Each with his bonny lass, Upon the greeny grass. Fa la, etc.	The ensemble repeats the phrase at a softer dynamic.
0:34	Stanza 2	The spring, clad all in gladness, Doth laugh at winter's sadness. Fa la, etc.	The ensemble sings the first line of each phrase at a higher dynamic level than its answer.
0:43		The spring, clad all in gladness, Doth laugh at winter's sadness. Fa la, etc.	The ensemble continues the alternation of loud and soft statements.
0:51		And to the bagpipe's sound, The nymphs tread out their ground. Fa la, etc.	
1:00		And to the bagpipe's sound, The nymphs tread out their ground. Fa la, etc.	
1:10	Stanza 3	Fie them why sit we musing, Youth's sweet delight refusing? Fa la, etc.	In this stanza the ensemble alternates dynamics between the verse and the Fa la la chorus.
1:19		Fie them why sit we musing, Youth's sweet delight refusing? Fa la, etc.	
1:27		Say, dainty nymphs, and speak, Shall we play barley break? Fa la, etc.	
1:36		Say, dainty nymphs, and speak, Shall we play barley break? Fa la, etc.	

If You Liked That, Try This

"My Bonny Lass She Smileth," Morley
"My Bonny Lass She Smelleth," Peter Schickele (aka P. D. Q. Bach)

YouTube video: search on keywords
"My Bonnie Lass She Smelleth"—PDQ Bach

Remember to add to your personal playlist any of these samples that you like.

The Rise of the Art Song

How is the art song similar to popular songs today?

By the middle of the 19th century many families owned a musical instrument, often a piano. Young women were especially encouraged to develop musical skills, usually singing and playing the piano. Perhaps because of the appetite for amateur performance, Romantic era composers wrote a huge amount of this type of music for solo voice and piano. The art song became popular in the Romantic era, partly because the piano became a common instrument in many homes at this time, which made in-home music-making easier.

Much of the music of the 19th century is passionate and emotional, and music of this time period was closely related to literature, especially poetry. German poets Johann Wolfgang von Goethe and Heinrich Heine were leading Romantic poets. Their works, as well as those of the English poets Lord Byron, William Wordsworth, and John Keats served as inspiration to the songwriters of the Romantic era. In many cases the same poetry was set to music by different composers. The **art song**, also known in German as **lied** (or plural, **lieder**), is a musical setting of literature or the musical expression of some sentiment. A good deal of it was also popular music of the 1800s, and like our popular songs today, the works are often brief and focused on one emotion or idea.

Art song: A musical setting of a work of literature for solo voice and piano in which the piano and voice are equal partners.

Lied (plural **Lieder**): German term for song.

A Musical Conversation

What is the relationship between the voice and the piano in an art song?

An art song is a work for solo voice and piano in which the piano is an equal partner in making the music, not just an accompaniment. Perhaps the most important thing to listen for in art song is the interplay between the vocal and piano parts. Unlike most songs of previous centuries, in art song the keyboard instrument (in this case the piano) has a real part to play in the telling of the story. The vocalist and pianist are having a musical conversation, much like the conversation between a concerto soloist and the orchestra as they trade musical lines back and forth. The piano and vocal parts work together, alone, and against one another in an art song—sometimes a duet and sometimes a duel. Many art songs express yearning, unrequited love, or sadness. The music reflects the mood of the text, and specific words are often represented by musical sounds—a compositional technique called word painting.

The piano often sets the mood and character of the text that follows. This is also true of piano postludes in which the piano closes the song with a final phrase that usually supports in style, or even repeats, the final phrase of the vocal part. The characterizations that the vocalist uses, and the expressions in the body language, help tell the story. One of the best aspects of hearing art song in a recital hall or salon is being close enough to the performers to be able to see what their bodies and faces express from the song. You should be able to feel as if they are performing the song just for you. The piano is also used to enhance the words, with special chords, dynamic changes of tempo, or accent in the piano part that can represent a word or make the text more effective.

Forms Used in Art Songs

What forms are most commonly used in art song?

Art songs usually take one of two standard forms: strophic or through-composed. A **strophic** art song has one melody with numerous verses. The same music is repeated for each verse of the text. This musical form is also used in Protestant church hymns. In a **through-composed** song the music changes with each verse. This type of song is more flexible in terms of expressing the changing moods of a poem and allows more word painting to be applied to important points in the text. It allows the composer to better mirror the text with the music than in a strophic form.

Sometimes art songs are grouped into **song cycles**. A song cycle is a set of songs that are connected in some manner, usually by the text. A cycle might be made up of a series of songs with a common poetic theme or a long story that runs throughout the songs. The art song is a form still written today and is one of the central parts of a vocalist's training while in music school.

Strophic: A form that uses the same music for each stanza of the song.

Through-composed: A form which uses different music for each stanza of a song.

Song cycle: A set of songs that are connected in some manner, usually by the text.

PERFORMANCE PRACTICE

How does a vocalist choose the songs she sings on a recital?

Or, how does any artist choose the order of the works on a CD recording? Much time and thought goes into both of these decisions. In many ways a CD recording is like a recital except that it is a lasting performance rather than a one-time recital. When making repertory choices for performances or recordings a singer might first consider the range of the song—can he or she sing all the notes, both high and low? The technique required is also a consideration—how fast is the song, how complex are the rhythms and other musical elements? The language in which the song was written might be a factor. While most art song performers can sing in Italian, French, German, Russian, and English they usually have one or two languages in which they feel most comfortable with pronunciation and diction. The intent and emotional effect of the song is important and most musicians choose to perform works that speak to them on a personal level.

Getting the order of a group of songs right, whether it be on recital or on a recording, can enhance the overall impression of the performance. Performers might group songs together by tempo, either contrasting or similar. Songs might be grouped into song sets by composer or by topic. Or, a performer could choose to alternate songs in terms of language. Whatever the structure the performer puts together a song order that he or she believes creates the appropriate effect for the recital or recording as a whole.

You probably also make such considerations in putting together your personal playlists. The songs you have in your playlists are most likely in a particular order, either by artist, type, or perhaps in an order that creates some emotional effect for you.

Dashboard

RESEARCH

Song Composers

Who were the important composers of art song?

Franz Schubert

Composer Franz Schubert. Courtesy GL Archive/Alamy.

Dashboard

SHARE

One of the first great composers of art song was Franz Schubert (1797–1828). Schubert was born in Vienna and was recognized early by his schoolmaster father as having special musical gifts. He was sent to be a choirboy in the Imperial court chapel and school, and became a member of the now-internationally-famous Vienna Boys Choir. Schubert first became a schoolteacher, but this career was short-lived.

Schubert loved the new poetry of Romanticism and at the age of eighteen wrote a masterwork of art song, "The Erl-King." The success of this song with the public was immediate, and that same year he wrote over 140 songs. The following year Schubert wrote 179 works, including many art songs, an opera, a mass, and two symphonies. Schubert was an incredibly prolific composer, writing over six hundred art songs and many instrumental works.

Schubert's interest in poetry and literature soon led him to associations with other artists, many of whom came to love his music. These associates supported him (he rarely had money and did not hold a position) and often shared their homes with him. Schubert's life was troubled, and—like a typical Romantic—he felt this helped him create his best songs; he said, "That which I have written in my greatest distress is what the world seems to like best." He spent many nights performing in private homes at salon concerts of his own works. These evenings became known as "Schubertiads," and he usually played the piano while other artists sang. A good deal of his music was written for these evenings.

Schubert's music serves as a bridge between the styles of the Classical and Romantic eras, much like the early music of Beethoven. His symphonic works and instrumental chamber music are Classical in style, but his songs and piano pieces are distinctly Romantic in nature. Much of his instrumental music evokes his song style with its long, lyrical melodies. The texts he chose for his songs usually concerned love or nature. Though there is no evidence he ever met Beethoven (odd, since they lived in Vienna at the same time), their symphonic works are comparable in style and intensity.

LISTENING GUIDE 12.3

"THE ERL-KING,"
Franz Schubert, composed 1815, poetry by Johann von Goethe

"The Erl-King" is an excellent example of early Romantic song. The work is based upon a poem of the same name by Goethe, in which a father rides through the night with his sick boy. As they ride, the child becomes

Dashboard

**HEAR STREAMING AUDIO
ON DASHBOARD**

delirious and has visions of the legendary king of the elves, the Erl-King, the bringer of death. Schubert's music clearly portrays the four characters of the poem: the narrator, the father, the boy, and the Erl-King. The rhythm of the piano even evokes images of the horse galloping through the night. The boy's fears are demonstrated through a high melodic line accompanied by dissonant chords. The father responds in a soothing voice in the low register. The elf's music is a sort of sing-song, enticing style. At the end of the poem the riders arrive home, but the boy is dead.

The work is through-composed, allowing the music to follow and portray the action. Nevertheless, most listeners will probably hear the work in four or five sections (**strophes**) because the rhythm stays very much the same throughout, the melody is only somewhat varied each time, and Schubert presents the child's cry motif four times. Following each outcry the father offers a soothing response that is answered by an enticing verse by the Erl-King. The inner vocal structure thus becomes son, father, Erl-King. This order of verse happens three times. At the fourth cry the father has no soothing response. The narrator appears only to begin and end the tale.

Strophe: A section composed of two or more lines that are repeated as a unit.

What to Listen For

- Listen for how Schubert portrays the four characters of the poem.

  The cries of the boy with increasingly high melodic line.
  The soothing of the father in a melody in the low register.
  The Erl-King in the middle register in a sing-song style.
  The narrator, in a minor key, to evoke the sad quality of the narrative.

- Listen for how Schubert sets the mood of the work immediately in the rhythm and timbre of the opening piano line.

- Listen for the return of the child's cry motif, which helps give shape to the work.

TIMING	STROPHE	CHARACTER	TEXT	TRANSLATION	WHAT TO LISTEN FOR
0:00	Intro, piano only				The fast and repetitive rhythm combined with the minor key center set the dark and urgent mood of the work immediately.
0:23	1	Narrator	Wer reitet so spät durch Nacht und Wind? Es ist der Vater mit seinem Kind: Er hat den Knaben wohl in dem Arm, Er fasst ihn sicher, er hät ihn warm.	Who rides so late through night and wind? It is a father with his child: he holds the boy tight in his arm, he holds him safely, he keeps him warm.	The melody is in a minor key. The narrator sings in the middle register in a declamatory manner setting the stage.
0:56		Father	Mein Sohn, was birgst du so bang dein Gesicht?	My son, why do you hide your face in fear?	Melody is in the lower range of the voice in a smoother style.
1:04	2	Son	Siehst, Vater, du den Erlkönig nicht? Den Erlenkönig mit Kron' und Schweif?	Father, do you not see the Erl-King? The Erl-King with his crown and train?	The melody is in the high range and is a bit more tense-sounding than the father's.
1:20		Father	Mein Sohn, es ist ein Nebelstreif.	My son, it is a wisp of mist.	The father's answer is stated in the low range.
1:29		Erl-King	Du liebes Kind, komm, geh mit mir! Gar schöne Spiele spiel' ich mit dir, Manch bunte Blumen sind an dem Strand, Mein Mutter hat manch gülden Gewand.	You dear child, come with me. I'll play lovely games with you. There are many colorful flowers on the shore; my mother has many goldenrobes.	The melody is soft and higher. It is in a major key and is sung in an enticing manner.
1:51	3	Son	Mein Vater, mein Vater, und hörest du nicht, Was Erlenkönig mir leise verspricht?	My father, my father, do you not hear the Erl-King whispering promises to me?	The melody is in the high range in a minor key sung *forte* as if a cry.

2:04		Father	Sei ruhig, bleibe ruhig, mein Kind	Be calm, stay calm my child:	The melody is again sung in a calming manner in the low register.
			In dürren Blättern säuselt der Wind.	it is the wind rustling in the dead leaves.	
2:14		Erl-King	Wilst, feiner Knabe, du mit mir gehn?	My fine boy, do you want to come with me?	The melody is in a major key, sung softly in a playful manner.
			Mein Töchter sollen dich warten schön	My daughters will take care of you;	
			Mein Töchter führen den nächlichen Reihn	my daughters lead the nightly dance,	
			Und wiegen und tanzen und singen dich ein	and will rock and dance and sing you to sleep.	
2:31	4	Son	Mein Vater, mein Vater, und siehst du nicht dort	My father, my father don't you see	The son answers with a high and dissonant outcry in a minor key.
			Erlkönigs Töchter am düstern Ort?	the Erl-King's daughters over there in the shadows?	
2:44		Father	Mein Sohn, mein Sohn, ich seh' es genau	My son, my son, I see it clearly,	The father's answer, as always, is set in the low range and sung in a reassuring style.
			Es scheinen die alten Weiden so grau.	it is the gray shimmer of the old willows.	
3:00		Erl-King	Ich liebe dich, mich reizt deine schöne Gestalt	I love you, your beautiful form delights me!	The melody begins pleasantly but by the end becomes more tense and insistent.
			Und bist du nicht willig, so brauch' Gewalt.	And if you are not willing, then I shall use force.	
3:12	5	Son	Mein Vater, mein Vater, jetzt fasst er mich an!	My father, my father, now he is grabbing me!	The boy cries in a terrified manner, sung loudly in the highest range of the voice yet.
			Erlkönig hat mir ein Leids getan!	The Erl-King has hurt me.	
3:26		Narrator	Dem Vater grauset's, er reitet geschwind,	The father shudders, he swiftly rides on:	
			Er hät in Armen das ächzende Kind,	he holds the moaning child in his arms,	

(continued)

TIMING	STROPHE	CHARACTER	TEXT	TRANSLATION	WHAT TO LISTEN FOR
			Erreicth den Hof mit Mühe und Not	he reaches the farmyard wary and afraid.	
3:45					The piano stops as the ride ends and the narrator sings in a recitative style.
3:47		Narrator	In seinen Armen das Kind was tot.	in his arms the child is dead.	

If You Liked That, Try This

"Der Wanderer," Schubert
Die schöne Müllerin, Schubert
"Die Forelle," Schubert

YouTube video: search on keywords
Schubert—Die schöne Müllerin, part 1/8

Remember to add to your personal playlist any of these samples that you like.

Dashboard

COMPARE AND CONTRAST

Robert and Clara Schumann

Perhaps the composer who most embodied the Romantic spirit was Robert Schumann (1810–1856). Along with his wife Clara Wieck Schumann (1819–1896) and Franz Schubert, he developed both the song cycle and the Romantic piano miniature piece (to be discussed in Chapter 13) to the height of expression.

Schumann was born in Zwickau, Germany, and studied law as a young man. At twenty years of age he gave up the law and turned to literature and music, especially the piano. He worked hard to become a concert pianist, but an injury to his right hand caused him to turn to composition and the new field of music criticism. Schumann launched the *New Journal of Music*, which became influential in promoting new music and composers. In the 1830s, while studying piano, he met his future wife Clara, the young daughter of his teacher Friederich Wieck. Clara had a profound influence on his compositions and was an excellent composer and well-known pianist in her own right. Upon their marriage in 1840, they moved to Leipzig, where Clara premiered many of Robert's works and became his best-known interpreter. Despite his success, Robert struggled with depression for several years. After an attempted suicide in 1854, Clara was forced to commit him to a mental institution, where he died two years later.

Clara lived another forty years, raised their seven children (one died as an infant), and continued to perform music. She became a close friend of Robert's protégé Johannes Brahms. Possibly due to the fact that it was difficult for a woman composer to have her work performed at the time, she eventually gave up composing and focused on teaching and concertizing throughout Europe.

Robert Schumann wrote impassioned piano music and art song. He also wrote four symphonies that are still performed regularly today, some choral works, an opera, incidental music for plays, and some instrumental chamber music. His best works, however, are his piano character pieces and art songs, especially his song cycles. Most of his songs deal with love, and much of his music contains dance rhythms and an improvisatory element in the piano parts. Like other Romantic composers, Schumann sought to create a musical picture of the song's lyrics. As he said, "The painter turns a poem into a painting; the musician sets a picture to music." Schumann's most famous song cycle is *Dichterliebe* (A Poet's Love), written in 1840, the year of his marriage. The songs are based on sixteen love poems by Heinrich Heine.

Clara and Robert Schumann jointly wrote a song cycle in the year they were married based on verses by the poet Friedrich Ruckert. The cycle contained twelve songs, nine by Robert and three by Clara. "If You Love for Beauty's Sake" was among those published in the cycle. It is also a strophic song with four stanzas.

Clara and Robert Schumann. Courtesy Lebrecht Music and Arts Photo Library/Alamy.

LISTENING GUIDE 12.4

"IN THE LOVELY MONTH OF MAY," from *Dichterliebe*, op. 48, no. 1,
Robert Schumann, composed 1840

Dashboard

**HEAR STREAMING AUDIO
ON DASHBOARD**

What to Listen For

- Listen for the strophic form of the work. Both stanzas of poetry are set to the same music.
- Listen for the manner in which the piano sets the mood of the song and plays an important role in the middle and end of the song.
- Listen for the unresolved and incomplete sound of the final measures of the voice and piano parts.

TIMING	STROPHE	TEXT	TRANSLATION	WHAT TO LISTEN FOR
0:00	Piano intro			The piano introduction is a soft ascending line played in a lyrical fashion. It sets a mood of melancholy.
0:16	1	Im wunderschönen Monat Mai,	In the wonderful lovely month of May,	The voice enters softly and gently. It gains in intensity and volume as the last two lines of the verse are sung. The voice ascends on the words "rise up love."
0:22		Als alle Knospen sprangen,	As all the buds were bursting open,	
0:29		Da ist in meinem Herzen	then in my heart	
0:35		Die Liebe aufgegangen.	did burst forth love.	
0:41	Piano interlude			The interlude is similar in character and mood to the introduction.
0:52	2	Im wunderschönen Monat Mai,	In the wonderful lovely month of May	The first melody repeats. The end of the verse is less intense this time.
0:59		Als alle Vögel sangen,	As all the birds were singing	
1:06		Da hab' ich ihr gestanden	then I confessed to her	
1:12		Mein Schnen und Verlangen.	my longing and desire.	
1:18	Piano postlude			The piano material from the introduction returns in the same style. Both the final line of the vocal part and the piano postlude leave the song with an unresolved character, as do the words. Both end sounding as if there should be more.

If You Liked That, Try This

Liederkreis, op. 24, Schumann
Frauenliebe und -leben, Schumann
Mörike-Lieder, by Hugo Wolf

YouTube video: search on keywords
Horowitz and Fischer-Diskau play Schumann Dichterliebe, Op. 48 (1/3)

Remember to add to your personal playlist any of these samples that you like.

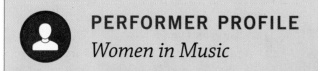

PERFORMER PROFILE
Women in Music

Why are so few women mentioned in this text as composers or performers?

You may have noticed that throughout the text there are more male musicians studied than female. The exception to this is any section in which music of the 20th century is examined. This is not because women musicians did not exist prior to the 20th century. In many cases they were amateur musicians, not women who made their livelihood making music. In the Classical and Romantic eras a young woman of social standing would have been required to study music and learn to sing and/or play an instrument. Society expected her to perform in the home for her family and friends, not on the concert stage. The exception to this was in the world of opera where female performers were common from the Baroque era to the current day. Because of this, talented women performers and composers did not gain the notoriety of their male counterparts. Even well-known women like Clara Schumann subjugated their musical careers to those of their husbands. Mozart and Mendelssohn both had sisters who were very talented composers and performers. Yet their music is rarely heard. As you can see from the number of 20th-century women performers, composers, and conductors featured throughout the book, times have changed. A few important women of the past include the following special musicians.

- **Barbara Strozzi** (1619–1677) grew up in Venice the adopted daughter of poet Giulio Strozzi. She studied music with the opera composer Francesco Cavalli and is best-known for her cantatas. She also wrote madrigals and sacred motets.
- **Maria Anna (Nannerl) Mozart** (1751–1829) was the older sister of Wolfgang Amadeus Mozart. She was an excellent harpsichord and fortepiano player. As a child, Maria Anna traveled with her father and brother performing for the crowned heads of Europe. When she reached a marriageable age her father ended her professional career.
- **Fanny Mendelssohn** (1805–1847) wrote a great number of works, some two hundred songs, over one hundred works for piano, as well as pieces for chorus and chamber ensembles. Most of her works were heard in the salons of her family and friends.
- **Augusta Holmès** (1847–1903) was born in Paris and was a student of composer César Franck. She wrote operas, choral works, cantatas, and program music for orchestra. Her best-known work, *Ode Triomphale*, was written for the 1889 celebration of the French Revolution.
- **Pauline Viardot-Garcia** (1821–1910) studied piano with Franz Liszt and composition with Anton Reicha and was a friend of Frederic Chopin and George Sand. In her professional career she was best-known as an opera singer but she was also a talented composer. She composed five "salon" operas, over fifty art songs, music for choir, and works for piano.

American composer Charles Ives. © Copyright Bettmann/Corbis/AP Images.

Charles Ives

In the 19th and 20th centuries art songs were written by most composers in Western art music. An important American composer of art song was Charles Ives (1894–1954). Though not recognized as such in his lifetime, Ives was one of the first great American composers. Ives was born in Danbury, Connecticut, and spent his adult life working in the insurance business. His father was a band director and Ives credited his compositional style to his father's love of experimenting with different sounds. Most of his music was written prior to 1921. Ives was an organist and spent his spare time composing. Despite the fact that the general public and many musicians didn't understand his musical innovations, by 1940 his music was heard and championed by a young group of American composers. In 1947 he won the Pulitzer Prize for his Third Symphony, written forty years earlier.

Ives's music is greatly influenced by folk traditions of America: revival hymns, music of town bands, dance music, Protestant church music of the day, and nationalistic music. Much of his music includes quotations of American folk songs or popular songs set in distortion and is known for its use of **polyrhythms**, **polytonality**, and **tone clusters**: things played intentionally out of tune or at the "wrong" time, having the ensemble play in two different keys at the same time. Despite the modernism of the tonality in Ives's works, they evoke nostalgic memories for listeners. Ives wrote four symphonies and other works for orchestra that he called "orchestral sets," a good deal of programmatic chamber music, organ music and music for the church, and over two hundred solo songs. The titles of his pieces are often descriptive or programmatic: *Three Places in New England: Concord, Mass. 1840–60*, *The Unanswered Question*, "The Things Our Fathers Loved." Ives's songs are some of the most often performed art songs today. In 1922 Ives published a collection of art songs entitled simply *114 Songs*. These works set for voice and piano demonstrate a wide range of complexity and include ballads, patriotic songs, protest songs, hymns, and romantic songs.

Polyrhythms: Rhythmic patterns that combine two or more individual rhythms to create a composite rhythm.

Polytonality: Use of two or more tonal centers or keys simultaneously.

Tone clusters: A group of adjacent notes in a scale, usually more than three notes.

Dashboard

CULTURAL CONNECTION: NATIVE AMERICAN SONGS

LISTENING GUIDE 12.5

"THE THINGS OUR FATHERS LOVED," from *114 Songs*, no. 43,
Charles Ives, composed 1917

Dashboard
**HEAR STREAMING AUDIO
ON DASHBOARD**

What to Listen For

- Listen for how Ives uses quotations from famous melodies of his time as the melodic basis of the song.

"Dixie," quoted fragment

"My Old Kentucky Home," quoted fragment

"Nettleton," quoted fragment

"The Battle Cry of Freedom," quoted fragment

"In the Sweet Bye and Bye," quoted fragment

- Listen for how the song ending sounds incomplete, as if there should be another chord (in this case a C major chord) following the last sound in order to resolve the work's tensions.
- Listen for how Ives changes the tempo and dynamics of the song midway through to create tension that moves toward the words "Now! Hear the songs!" in the text.
- Listen for how Ives's intentional insertion of "wrong" notes creates unusual harmonies that accompany the traditional songs.

TIMING	TEXT	SONG QUOTATION	WHAT TO LISTEN FOR
0:00	I think there must be a place	"Dixie"	"Wrong" notes in the harmonies.
0:09	in the soul all made of tunes, of tunes of long ago,	"My Old Kentucky Home"	The traditional song fragment.
0:25	I hear the organ on the Main Street corner,	"On the Banks of the Wabash"	The traditional song fragment.
0:32	Aunt Sarah humming Gospels; Summer evenings,	"Nettleton"	The traditional song fragment.
0:53	The village cornet band playing in the square, the town's Red, White and Blue all Red, White and Blue	"The Battle Cry of Freedom"	Ives's use of tempo and dynamic change creates tension.
1:05	Now! Hear the songs!	"In the Sweet Bye and Bye"	The traditional song fragment.
1:10	I know not what are the words		
1:15	But they sing in my soul		
1:29	Of the things our Fathers loved.		The last chord leaves the work sounding incomplete because the harmonies are not released of their tension. This contributes to the nostalgic nature of the work.

If You Liked That, Try This

"The Greatest Man," from *114 Songs*, no. 19, Ives
"Songs My Mother Taught Me," from *114 Songs*, no. 108, Ives
"The Circus Band," Ives

YouTube videos: search on keywords
Charles Ives songs
Hugo Wolf songs

Remember to add to your personal playlist any of these samples that you like.

The Singers' Contest at Wartburg Castle, by Moritz von Schwind. Courtesy Lebrecht Music and Arts Photo Library/Alamy.

The art song remains an important form of music. Other composers of this form in the Romantic era included Schumann's pupil Johannes Brahms, Hugo Wolf, Richard Strauss, and Gustav Mahler. During the early 20th century, Ives wrote over two hundred songs and French composers Claude Debussy and Gabriel Fauré wrote songs still regularly performed today in recital halls. Throughout the 20th century composers such as Leonard Bernstein, Samuel Barber, and Benjamin Britten continued to make use of the art song and song cycle as a form of vocal expression.

✓ **Build Your Own Playlist:** The works studied in the chapter Listening Guides serve as examples of different styles of songs from different eras. Now, build your own song playlist from those works listed in each IF YOU LIKED THAT, TRY THIS list or from other songs you find. Share your playlist with others by posting it to your class discussion board or Dashboard.

✓ **Audio Review:** Go to Dashboard to listen to Professor Bailey discuss vocal music for the recital hall and salon.

✓ **How Am I Doing?** Go to Dashboard to test your understanding of this material by taking the chapter quiz.

KEY TERMS

Art song	Polyrhythms	Strophic
Ballett	Polytonality	Tone clusters
Lied (plural Lieder)	Song cycle	Through-composed
Madrigal	Strophe	Word painting

Solo Keyboard Music

LEARNING OBJECTIVES

- **Name important forms and composers of solo works for organ.**

- **Recognize by listening examples musical forms used for piano music.**

- **Name important composers of the piano sonata and character piece for piano.**

- **Recognize by listening examples the differences in sound production between the piano, organ, and harpsichord.**

Key Concepts: character piece, chorale prelude, fugue, prelude, solo piano sonata, toccata

Opening image: Concert pianist Krystian Zimerman. Courtesy Getty Images.

Where It's Playing

Much of the music of this chapter was written for private study and performance in homes, and that is one of the places where it can still be heard today. Many homes have either a piano or an organ and members of the family learn to play all types of music on these instruments for their own pleasure. The advent of the electronic organ and the synthesizer, as well as the creation of the upright piano (a piano that has a vertical soundboard) have made keyboard playing even more common today than in the 19th century.

At a keyboard recital watching the performer is almost as interesting as hearing the music. The coordination of hands and feet, the changing of organ stops, the manipulation of pedals, and the horizontal movement required to play such a large keyboard all make a keyboard recital visually interesting.

Keyboard instruments may appear to be rigid, static instruments less capable of expressive nuances than wind or string instruments. However, this is not the case. An interesting exercise at a keyboard recital, especially a piano recital, is to note how the player shapes the work by accents and dynamics. The force with which the pianist strikes the keys helps determine this. At a piano recital also take note of the pianist's feet. The piano has pedals, which are used to soften and sustain notes.

When attending an organ recital, watch how the organist changes the timbre of the instrument. How often does this occur, and when? Controlling dynamics and timbre on the organ is largely a question of adding or subtracting pipes (accomplished by changing "stops"). Listen to and watch how the musical phrases transfer from hand to hand, and to feet with the organ. Are the hands and feet in conversation, complementary, or are they in contrary motion? What skills would it take to play music in which both hands and both feet require complete independence?

Dashboard

ATTEND AND REPORT

Each of the forms discussed in this chapter is now also heard in recital halls as regular parts of keyboard recitals. Most keyboard recitals consist of a mixture of piano sonatas and character pieces, works that were originally written for the salon. Many recital halls or concert halls, especially those at colleges and universities, have pipe organs built into the hall. It is also at a college or university where you will most often hear a harpsichord in live performance. Finally, a good deal of keyboard music is still heard in places of worship. This is especially true of organ music because so much of it was originally written for the church. And, many of the movements from piano sonatas or the character pieces for piano serve well as contemplative music for interludes in church services.

Music for the King of Instruments

The organ is sometimes called the king of instruments because of its ability to sound like other instruments, and its impressive power. Many of the world's greatest organs were built for and are located in churches and cathedrals, and recitals of organ music often take place there. Organs in recital and concert halls were usually constructed with the performance hall's acoustics in mind.

What types and forms of music are written for the organ?

Organ music performed at recitals is in a wide variety of styles, ranging from music of the Middle Ages to contemporary music. Often the selections are determined at least in part by the capabilities of the specific organ. Some organs were constructed for loud, bombastic works and others for light, soft polyphony. The organist manipulates the timbre of the organ by opening stops that allow air to pass through various pipes. These stops are within reach of the organ's keyboard so that the organist can quickly change the sound during a piece of music.

A large concert hall that has an organ usually uses the instrument either as a solo instrument to play a concerto or as an added instrument to the orchestra. Some composers wrote organ parts into their symphonic works to add to the power and timbre of the full orchestra.

In the recital hall and church recital the organist often plays works that might have first been heard in church services, usually as interludes in the service or at its beginning or end. Bach's **fugues** and those of other Baroque composers such as Handel are favorite performance pieces at organ recitals. These works are usually paired with a shorter work, called a **prelude**, to create the performance piece "prelude and fugue." The prelude often sounds less rigidly structured than the fugue and has an improvisatory character. It is based upon a single melodic or rhythmic motif that is embellished, sometimes freely, by the organist. It is usually homophonic and makes a good contrast to the polyphonic fugue that will follow it.

Another short form of organ literature is the **toccata**. This virtuosic piece has a free form. One of the most famous is the Toccata and Fugue in D minor by J. S. Bach. It was used much like the prelude as a contrasting style to the fugue and as an opportunity for the organist to display improvisatory skills.

Protestant congregations traditionally sing four-part hymns, or chorales, together as part of the regular service. Beginning in the Baroque era, organists created the **chorale prelude** to act as a sort of introduction to the hymn/chorale. As a congregation became more familiar with a hymn, they depended less on the chorale prelude. This allowed the organist to use the chorale prelude to display his virtuosic technique and improvising ability. In the chorale prelude the

Pipe organ. Courtesy haak78/Shutterstock.

Fugue: A polyphonic piece of music built on a single theme set in imitation.

Prelude: A work, often of a free or improvisatory nature, used as a companion work to a longer and more complex piece of music.

Toccata: A free-form instrumental work in one movement, usually highly technical.

Chorale prelude: A work, usually for organ, used to introduce a hymn to be sung by a congregation. The chorale prelude is essentially a variation or embellishment of the hymn melody.

J. S. Bach with his family. Courtesy Mary Evans Picture Library/Alamy.

hymn tune is embellished with scales, trills, and other ornaments. Over time it became a highly virtuosic and improvisational form of organ music of the Baroque era, and composers wrote hundreds of them. Bach alone wrote over 140 chorales and chorale variations for performance in Lutheran church services.

Chorale preludes take two primary forms. In one the hymn is stated and the melody is then embellished and varied with each successive statement, usually ending with a final clear statement. The other primary form of chorale prelude is the gap form, in which a small portion of the hymn tune is played, followed by a section of embellishments and variations on that part of the hymn. This is followed by another short section of the hymn tune and embellished section, and then another, until all the hymn has been stated.

J. S. Bach wrote a great number of chorale preludes, including 162 that appeared in his *Little Organ Book*. Today these pieces are standard repertory on organ recitals.

Johann Sebastian Bach

Clavichord: A keyboard instrument used from the Middle Ages through the Classical era. Its sound is created by a metal blade, called a "tangent," striking metal strings.

Johann Sebastian Bach's keyboard music is among the best ever written. Bach's keyboard works were written for the organ, harpsichord, and **clavichord**, but today they are often played on the piano. His most important work for keyboard is *The Well-Tempered Clavier*, consisting of forty-eight preludes and fugues.

The fugue is one of the most important forms of music of the Baroque era, especially for the keyboard. A fugue is a polyphonic piece built on a single theme set in imitation. The melody, or subject, of a fugue is stated in each part of the score and is almost always announced by itself in a single line. (Most keyboard scores have three or four lines or parts that are played by the hands and feet of the performer.) It is then taken up by each line while another melody, or counter-line, is introduced. The combinations of lines, and their imitation and manipulation, create the texture of a fugue. Short developmental sections are called **episodes** in fugues.

Episode: A short developmental section of a fugue.

LISTENING GUIDE 13.1

FUGUE IN C MINOR, from *The Well-Tempered Clavier*, Book 1,
J. S. Bach, composed 1722

The Fugue in C minor is from the 1722 book of keyboard pieces by J. S. Bach. The book is a series of twenty-four paired preludes and fugues. Bach wrote a second such book between 1738 and 1742. This fugue is rather short by Bach's standards and is in a minor key. The subject of the fugue is presented eight times with the final presentation set in a major key. The three most important compositional ideas in any fugue are repetition, imitation, and sequence.

Dashboard

**HEAR STREAMING AUDIO
ON DASHBOARD**

What to Listen For

- Listen for how the work gradually gains in complexity of rhythm as voices are added and the subject is developed. This increasing complexity is characteristic of fugues.
- The fugue has three parts, also called voices. Listen for when each enters playing the primary melody, called the subject, and for when each voice enters imitating the subject.
- Note that from the beginning to the end, the fugue is one long, continuous outpouring of melodic material. Listen for the unbroken and steady pulse.
- Listen to the first five notes of the fugue. This rhythmic structure and melodic shape is used as the primary idea on which the fugue is spun out.

TIMING	FORM: FUGUE	WHAT TO LISTEN FOR
0:00	Subject 1	The subject is presented unaccompanied in the alto voice.
0:07	Subject 2	The subject is presented in the soprano voice accompanied by a countersubject in the alto. The alto countersubject begins with a fast descending scale and then changes to a steady eighth-note rhythm.
0:13	Bridge	For two measures Bach uses the rhythm and shape of the subject to create a bridge to the third statement of the subject.
0:20	Subject 3	The subject is presented in the bass voice with a counter-line in soprano.
0:27	Episode 1	Once all voices have presented the fugue subject at least one time, fugal episodes usually begin. In this case the three subject presentations are followed by an episode that develops fragments of the subject.
0:32	Subject 4	The subject is presented in a major key in the soprano line.
0:41	Episode 2	The second episode features fast ascending scales in soprano played over eighth note steady rhythm in alto and bass.
0:48	Subject 5	The subject is presented in a minor key again by alto.
0:55	Episode 3	Ascending fast scales first in the alto, and then in bass, accompany fragments of the subject.
1:06	Subject 6	The subject is presented in soprano with a counter-line in alto.
1:13	Episode 4	Episode four is the longest of the episodes. It begins with subject fragments accompanied by descending fast scales in the bass line. The second part of this episode is an ascending sequence of the subject rhythm in the soprano.
1:29	Subject 7	The subject is presented in the bass line with a counter-line in the soprano.
1:42	Subject 8	The subject is presented in soprano in a major key. This subject is set off by what is the only pause (a very brief one) in the forward driving rhythm and is accompanied by a sustained bass line in the last seconds of the fugue.

If You Liked That, Try This

A Musical Offering, BWV 1079, Bach
The Art of Fugue, BWV 1080, Bach
Goldberg Variations, BWV 988, Bach

YouTube videos: search on keywords
Bach, "Little" Fugue (G minor, BWV 578)
Bach—Goldberg Variations: Aria (Glenn Gould)

Remember to add to your personal playlist any of these samples that you like.

LISTENING GUIDE 13.2

"CHRIST LAY IN DEATH'S PRISON," Chorale Prelude, BWV 625,
J. S. Bach, composed 1715

Dashboard
**HEAR STREAMING AUDIO
ON DASHBOARD**

In this organ chorale prelude the melody is played in the high pipes. Under it is a complex mix of counter-lines in florid and imitative fashion. The congregation would probably have sung the chorale following a performance of this prelude.

What to Listen For

- Listen for the chorale tune in the high pipes.

- Listen for the complex and full texture of the prelude.

- Listen for the brief stops in the forward motion of the rhythm. These are the phrases of the chorale and would have been used as breathing points for the congregation when the chorale is sung with the organ.
- Listen for the triumphant ending.

TIMING	FORM: AAB	WHAT TO LISTEN FOR
0:00	A	The first section of the chorale is presented in a four measure phrase. The organist takes a brief break before repeating this phrase.
		Listen for the low notes—these are being played by the organist's feet on the pedalboard of the organ.
0:15	A	The first phrase is repeated.
		Listen for the interweaving of the four different parts in the chorale. The organist would probably play two parts with the right hand, one with the left, and one with the feet.
0:30	B	The second section of the work is played in one phrase that is twice the length of the A section.
0:55		Listen for the slowing in tempo in the final measure of the chorale. This makes the work have a more dramatic ending and would have signaled to the congregation that they should sing the chorale with the organ on the next playing of the melody.

If You Liked That, Try This

Little Organ Book, Bach

YouTube videos: search on keywords
Toccata & Fugue in d minor (BACH, J.S.)
J. S. Bach—Organ Chorale Prelude

Remember to add to your personal playlist any of these samples that you like.

Solo Music for the Piano

What do the different forms of solo piano music sound like?

The piano became the most popular instrument during the Romantic era partly because it was affordable enough to be purchased for the home. The piano itself was greatly improved in the Romantic era. It was capable of much larger dynamic and accent ranges than its Classical predecessor, making it a much more expressive instrument. No instrument other than the violin has as much literature written for it. The Romantic era also saw the rise of the piano virtuoso as a popular figure. These performers were the rock stars of their day and enjoyed great popularity throughout Europe and America.

Solo sonata: An instrumental form for solo instrument, often piano, one to three movements in length. It should not be confused with the musical form called sonata.

Ludwig van Beethoven. Courtesy GL Archive/Alamy.

Piano Sonata

The sonata format of the Baroque trio sonata (studied in Chapter 14, "Instrumental Chamber Music") developed in the Classical and Romantic period into an important style of piano music for the recital hall—the **solo sonata**. Like their Baroque counterparts, these pieces were written to be performed in private residences, often by amateurs. The works were often designed as teaching pieces and piano teachers still use them in this manner today. The piano sonata is also an important form used by pianists on recitals. Composers turned out a large number of these works, sometimes as one-movement, multi-section works and sometimes as multi-movement works (usually three movements) similar in structure to the concerto. The term should not be confused with the sonata form studied in the chapter on the symphony and used in symphonic works. While a sonata form may be used as one of the movements of a piano sonata, this is not always the case.

Haydn, Mozart, and Beethoven all wrote influential piano sonatas during the Classical era. Beethoven's use of this form represents the height of its development. He wrote thirty-two piano sonatas of varying difficulty. His best-known is the so-called "Moonlight Sonata," written in 1801 and dedicated to Countess Giulietta Guicciardi, a young pupil of Beethoven's with whom he was enamored.

LISTENING GUIDE 13.3

SONATA NO. 14 IN C-SHARP MINOR FOR PIANO, op. 27, no. 2 ("Moonlight"), mvt. 1, Adagio sostenuto,
Ludwig van Beethoven, composed 1801

Dashboard

**HEAR STREAMING AUDIO
ON DASHBOARD**

The sonata is in three movements: Adagio sostenuto, Allegretto, and Presto agitato. Beethoven alters the usual tempo of the order of movements of the piano sonata. The first movement is an adagio rather than a fast tempo, as would be more common. The movement is in an ABA form that resembles a true sonata form. The B section is developmental of the A section but not to the point to where it can be called a true development section. This type of "mini-sonata" is sometimes called a sonatina. The work is considered to be a nocturne (night piece) in style meaning that it has a lyrical melody and clear harmonic structure.

The work was dubbed the "Moonlight Sonata" in 1832 by poet Ludwig Rellstab because it reminded him of moonlight on water. Beethoven never referred to it by this name. It appears Beethoven's intent was not one of moonlit inspiration but rather a sad and solemn processional.

What to Listen For

- Listen for the almost hypnotic character of the accompanimental rhythm.
- Listen for the declamatory theme A presented in the style of a processional.

TIMING	FORM: ABA	WHAT TO LISTEN FOR
0:00	Introduction	A short introduction of broken chords played in the low register of the piano sets up both the dark mood of the work and the gentle rocking sensation. This accompaniment helps make this sonata distinctive and immediately recognizable.
0:28	A	The theme is presented in the right hand in a combination of dotted and long notes. It sounds processional-like, and is accompanied by the rocking, broken chords.
0:56		The first part of the theme is repeated on a lower pitch and is expanded. In this expansion Beethoven heightens the expression by moving back and forth in half steps.
1:23		The second part of the theme is introduced.
2:06		The first part of the theme returns on a higher pitch.
2:30	B	This section lacks true melodic material. It consists of the rocking broken chords with a very brief three-note line. The section sounds like a dialogue between this three-note figure and the repeated arpeggio line.
3:47	A	The theme returns at the original pitch.
4:36		The second part of the theme returns.
5:26		The movement closes with the theme presented in low notes for the first time.

If You Liked That, Try This

Sonata no. 16 in C major for Piano, K. 545, Mozart
Sonata no. 21 in C major for Piano, op. 53, "Waldstein," Beethoven
Claire de lune, Claude Debussy

YouTube video: search on keyword
Debussy, Clair de lune (piano music)

Remember to add to your personal playlist any of these samples that you like.

The piano sonata continued to be used as an expressive means by composers of the Romantic era and into the 20th century. Claude Debussy wrote piano sonatas that are equal in fame to those of Beethoven. His impressionistic works *Clair de lune*, *Reflections in the Water*, and *The Sunken Cathedral* are well-established members of the piano recital repertory.

The form is still used today by composers of keyboard music, and the piano sonata is a standard form at solo piano recitals.

Character Piece

Character piece: A miniature piece for piano usually conveying one intense emotion. The titles of these works (e.g., nocturne, polonaise, etude, waltz, and scherzo) often indicate the style.

During the Romantic era composers developed miniature pieces for piano called **character pieces**. These works, like art song, were short—usually under five minutes. And, like art song they usually conveyed one intense emotion per piece. They were written at all difficulty levels, making them popular with amateurs and virtuosi alike. The titles often indicated their styles. *Nocturne,*

PERFORMER PROFILE
Pianist Lang Lang

Pianist Lang Lang. Courtesy Jin yi bj—Imaginechina/AP Images.

His name means "brilliant man" in Chinese. He was born in Shenyang, China, in 1982 and had a different childhood than most. Concert pianist Lang Lang says of his early life, "When I was nine, in fifth grade, I moved to Beijing to go to the Central Conservatory of Music. I woke up every day at five o'clock a.m. to practice piano for an hour. Then I went to school until three o'clock p.m., came home, practiced piano some more, and then did homework in the evening. I practiced piano five hours a day! But I still managed to have fun. We had ten-minute breaks between our classes at school, and that's when we would play games, tell jokes, and have fun. We watched cartoons, like *Tom and Jerry*. We also went to the park, played soccer, and ping pong. When I was two, I was watching a *Tom and Jerry* cartoon. I thought it was so funny to see this cat and mouse chasing each other to this song, Hungarian Rhapsody Number Two. I got very inspired by the music, so I tried to play it on the piano . . . and it turned out I could play it!"

Today, Lang Lang is one of the finest and busiest concert pianists in the world. He has performed as a soloist with most major orchestras and at a White House state dinner, made numerous recordings, and founded his own music school called the Lang Lang International Music Foundation.

Dashboard

EXPLORE

polonaise, etude, waltz, and *scherzo* were all titles given to piano character pieces of the Romantic era.

A **nocturne,** or night piece, usually has a lyrical melody and is homophonic. Melodies of nocturnes often create a melancholy or reflective work.

The **polonaise** is a Polish dance. These piano pieces usually have quick tempos and thick textures.

The piano **etude** is literally a study piece for piano. The pieces usually address one specific finger technique. Despite the fact that etudes are designed for technical practice, Romantic era composers made them musical works full of expression.

The **waltz** for piano is also a stylized dance. They often contain rubato that makes them inappropriate for dancing and are varied in tempo and style.

The **scherzo** was discussed in Chapter 7, "The Symphony." It is a fast work that is dance-like in form but not intended to be danced to.

Nocturne: In the 19th century a short one-movement piece for solo piano, intended to be evocative of nighttime.

Polonaise: A slow Polish dance in triple meter.

Etude: "Study" in French; a musical work intended to help the performer practice a particular technical skill.

Waltz: A folk or ballroom dance in triple meter.

Scherzo: A brief form in three parts usually in triple meter.

PERFORMANCE PRACTICE
Sound Production on the Piano

How is a sound produced on a piano?

Pianos, harpsichords, and organs all require regular maintenance in order to sound good. Especially important is that they be "tuned." On a piano this means that the strings inside the piano must be tightened to a degree of tension that produces a specific frequency. To produce a sound on the piano the player depresses a black or white key on the keyboard. This causes a hammer inside the piano to fly up and strike a string, or group of strings. Except in the lowest register of the piano each note is produced by three strings vibrating when they are struck by a single hammer. Each pitch in the scale has three strings assigned to it. This means that in order for the piano to sound good, or what we call "in tune,"

Piano strings and hammers. Courtesy Fotosearch/Fotosearch.

these three strings must all produce exactly the same frequency. And, each note must sound a specific distance from another note. All this means that people who tune pianos have two problems to deal with: first, they must get all three strings of each note vibrating the same frequency, and second, they must make the distance (interval) between notes fit the tuning system of the Western scale. There are eighty-eight notes on a piano and over two hundred strings. This is no easy task! It takes a professional to manage this, someone who has been trained in the science of temperament and who has a critical ear. The piano tuner must also adjust the pedals and other mechanisms to keep the hammers in working order.

Dashboard

EXPLORE

Frédéric Chopin. Courtesy North Wind Picture Archives/Alamy.

Frédéric Chopin

One of the greatest writers of the character piece for piano was Frédéric Chopin (1810–1849). Chopin was born in Poland but spent much of his adult life in Paris, where he was greatly influenced by great writers and painters of the day such as Honoré de Balzac, Victor Hugo, George Sand (Aurore Dudevant), and Eugène Delacroix. Chopin was a piano virtuoso himself but disliked playing in public. Instead, he found fame through composing. His works are some of the most important ever written for the piano. The use of rubato in his works allows the pianist to heighten the expression and tension in each piece. Most of Chopin's pieces were written for and first heard in private salons. Today, they fit wonderfully in the recital hall where their nuance and beauty can be heard even at the softest of dynamics.

LISTENING GUIDE 13.4

NOCTURNE IN E-FLAT, op. 9, no. 2,
Frédéric Chopin, composed 1831

This nocturne is one of Chopin's most popular works and was written when he was about twenty years old. Typical of this style it begins with a lyrical melody in a slow tempo. The work contains three melodies that create a melancholy feel in the piece.

The piece is one of three nocturnes published in 1833 in a set as opus 9. The set is dedicated to Marie Moke-Pleyel, a pianist in Paris who was married to the pianist, music publisher, and piano maker Camille Pleyel.

Dashboard

**HEAR STREAMING AUDIO
ON DASHBOARD**

What to Listen For

- Listen for how Chopin uses rubato and dynamics to heighten the expression of the piece.
- Listen for the increasing ornamentation of the melodies as they are repeated. This technique lends to the expression of the work.
- Listen for the small changes in tempo used in the themes. This rubato tempo makes the work more expressive.

• Listen for the reflective and expressive qualities of the work's three melodies.

TIMING	FORM: NOCTURNE	LISTEN FOR
0:00	A	The primary melody is an expressive and lyrical line. It has wide leaps between the notes, which contribute to the expressive quality. The accompaniment played in the left hand makes the work sound like a waltz. Note how the soft dynamic and gentle presentation creates a sweet-sounding opening.
0:26	A	The melody repeats with some ornamentation.
0:54	B	A second melody is introduced that at first sounds like it will move forward in tempo but is actually played with more rubato and expression than the first melody.
1:20	A	The first melody returns with further embellishment.
1:47	B	The second theme returns.
2:15	A	Theme A returns with new ornamentation.
2:42	C	A third theme is introduced at the end of the work. It contains even more opportunity for expression than themes A and B because of the repeated note figures and the wide leaps.
3:10	C	The third theme repeats with ornamentation. It becomes much more agitated than the other two themes. The work ends softly and gently.

If You Liked That, Try This

Polonaise in A major, op. 40, no. 1, Chopin
Carnaval, op. 9, Robert Schumann
Etude in C minor, op. 10, no. 12, Chopin
Waltz in D-flat, op. 64, no. 1, "Minute Waltz," Chopin

YouTube videos: search on keywords
Chopin Nocturne Op.9 NO.2 (Arthur Rubinstein)
Chopin Prelude in E minor Op. 28 No. 4

Remember to add to your personal playlist any of these samples that you like.

Franz Liszt

Many other great composers of the Romantic era composed character pieces for the piano. Among the finest works are those by Robert and Clara Schumann, Franz Schubert, and Franz Liszt (1811–1886). Liszt was the greatest piano virtuoso of his day and a friend of Chopin. He was a great showman and was the first true superstar performer. Born in Hungary, Liszt studied in Vienna and lived much of his life in Paris. He is best known today as a composer, especially of virtuosic piano pieces that at first only he could play. He toured Europe from 1839 to 1847, then gave up performing to become the court composer at Weimar, Germany. There he

Caricature of composer and pianist Franz Liszt. Courtesy INTERFOTO/Friedrich/Mary Evans.

composed many orchestral works and helped develop new program music for the orchestra. Late in his life Liszt traveled to Rome and took religious orders.

During this period he wrote mainly sacred works, primarily oratorios and masses. His piano pieces are virtuosic showpieces, making use of extreme dynamic changes, wide leaps in the melodic lines, and fast scalar passages. Most are incredibly virtuosic and considered at the time to be unplayable by anybody but him. His study pieces, called *Transcendental Etudes*, illustrate the incredible difficulty and passion of much of his piano music.

LISTENING GUIDE 13.5

TRANSCENDENTAL ETUDES, no. 10 in F minor, Allegro agitato molto,
Franz Liszt, composed 1851 (third version)

Dashboard
**HEAR STREAMING AUDIO
ON DASHBOARD**

This etude is the tenth of a set of twelve pieces by Liszt. It is titled "Allegro agitato molto." This etude is from the third version of these works. Liszt originally wrote them in 1826, revised them in 1839, and made them even more difficult in 1851. The final version is dedicated to his teacher Carl Czerny, a piano pedagogue whose works are still studied today. The title of the work indicates that the etude takes technique that transcends the ordinary to play it.

The work is in an ABA form that might be considered to be a sonatina since the B section is developmental material, but brief.

What to Listen For

- Listen for how Liszt changes the character of the work from an agitated and furious flurry to a more melodic style. He does this through dynamic ranges and melodic style.
- Listen for the use of the entire range of the piano. Liszt separates the right and left hands into regions of the piano (at least aurally). This helps give the impression that more than one person is playing the piece.
- Listen for the melodies set in octaves. This takes a large hand and strong technique to be able to play.

TIMING	FORM: ABA CODA	WHAT TO LISTEN FOR
0:00	A Theme 1	The opening section is an immediate virtuosic display of fast running notes and descending chords. It seems more like an improvisatory outburst than an actual theme. The section rises and falls in dynamics as the notes do. It closes with an agitated flurry of notes leading to a high line that sounds much more melodic in character and leads into the style of the second theme.
0:32	Theme 2	Theme 2 is much more melodic than theme 1. It is played in octaves high in the right hand and is dramatic. The theme is played with accents at a loud dynamic. It is accompanied by fast notes in the left hand.
1:07	Theme 3	This section continues with another flurry of notes covering the range of the piano. A third theme is introduced in low notes and sounds like a solemn march. Like Theme 2, it is played in octaves loudly with heavy accents and is accompanied by seemingly unrelated fast notes in the right hand.
1:35	B	The B section is a short developmental section of the first theme from section A. Liszt presents a wild flurry of agitated passages that move up and down the full range of the piano. He uses rubato, fast notes, and changing dynamics to create a dramatic section.
2:00	A	The first theme returns.
2:12		The second theme returns in a softer, more restrained version at first. The theme climaxes after a gradual buildup and is followed by an accented melody played in octaves in the high register of the piano. This is followed by another rhapsodic section of fast scales sweeping up and down the piano.
3:56		The solemn march returns.

If You Liked That, Try This

Liebesträume, S.541, Liszt
Consolation no. 3 in D-flat Major, S.172, Liszt
Totentanz, S.126, Liszt

YouTube video: search on keywords
Berezovsky—Liszt—Transcendental Etude No 5, Feux Follets

Remember to add to your personal playlist any of these samples that you like.

✓ **Build Your Own Playlist:** The works studied in the chapter Listening Guides serve as examples of different styles of keyboard music from different eras. Now, build your own playlist from those works listed in each IF YOU LIKED THAT, TRY THIS list or from other keyboard works you find. Share your playlist with others by posting it to your class discussion board or Dashboard.

✓ **Audio Review:** Go to Dashboard to listen to Professor Bailey discuss solo keyboard music.

✓ **How Am I Doing?** Go to Dashboard to test your understanding of this material by taking the chapter quiz.

Dashboard

KEY TERMS

Character piece	Fugue	Solo sonata
Chorale prelude	Nocturne	Toccata
Clavichord	Polonaise	Waltz
Episode	Prelude	
Etude	Scherzo	

Instrumental Chamber Music

LEARNING OBJECTIVES

- Explain the instrument membership of the string quartet.
- Compare the sonata form to the sonata as studied in this chapter.
- Summarize the use of instrumental chamber music.
- Name important composers of instrumental chamber music.
- Recognize by listening examples the string quartet and brass quintet.

Key Concepts: divertimento, harmonie band, serenade, string quartet, trio sonata

Where It's Playing

Chamber music: Music written for two to twelve players intended to be played in an intimate setting like a salon or small chamber.

The music of this chapter is most often heard in the recital hall as part of a formal concert. However, very little of it was written for such a venue. Most of the instrumental **chamber music** written prior to the last century was written for informal settings. It was a sort of useful music employed as background music to dinners or for after-dinner entertainment. Some instrumental chamber music was written for outdoor performance. Just like vocal chamber music and keyboard music, much instrumental chamber music was written for the salon concert or for home learning and enjoyment. Another important place where this music was heard in the past was on the street. **Harmonie bands** and some small string ensembles were the public MP3 players of the Classical era. Composers arranged popular opera and symphonic melodies for instrumental chamber ensembles, which performed them in city squares and street corners.

Harmonie band: A wind ensemble usually made up of eight players, popular in the Classical era.

It is interesting when attending a recital of chamber music to observe the interaction between the performers. Watch for which player gives cues to start and end the work. How do the players communicate rhythm and pulse without a conductor? Pay attention to which instrument is playing the melodic line and how the other instruments support or compete with that line. Above all, the players should appear to be having a musical conversation, and that conversation should involve the audience as well.

At a chamber music concert in a recital hall it is also possible to listen to the individual tone qualities of the players. This is not as possible when you attend a large orchestra concert. Listen for which instrument or player has the tone quality that you like the best.

Dashboard

ATTEND AND REPORT

Today this music continues to be used in a utilitarian manner serving as music that is heard prior to, during, and after events as a sort of live soundtrack. We hear it still in city squares, street corners, and train stations. It is used at important events in our lives such as weddings, receptions, and funerals. Like vocal chamber music, the recital has become the formal home of the string quartet and small wind band. College and university music programs produce many concerts of these types of ensembles each year, and the repertory is important in the study and preparation of music majors.

Instrumental chamber music takes a number of forms and styles and was written in all the historical periods discussed in this book. The term generally refers to any music written for two to twelve instruments and designed for intimate performance settings like the private home or recital hall.

Originally, chamber music was lighter in character than the symphonic music on which it was modeled. However, over the past two hundred years it has taken on the same scope of emotional expression of the larger symphonic forms. In many cases chamber music was originally written for amateur performance. Like the madrigal, much instrumental chamber music was intended as entertainment by a group of friends or family members. The titles of much chamber music include references to the number of musicians it is written for, such as "duo," "trio," and "quartet." Unlike the symphonic forms, chamber music is usually not conducted. Instead the ensemble controls its own rhythmic pulse and musical interpretation.

Performing chamber music challenges and delights most instrumentalists, as it requires them to act as soloists (only one instrument plays each part) and also to blend their sound into the ensemble.

String Quartet—Four Soloists Who Blend

Is a string quartet a group or a type of music?

The string quartet is one of the most popular forms of chamber music with both audience and composers. String quartet refers to both an ensemble and a musical form. The ensemble is a group of four string players—almost always two violins, one viola, and one cello. The form is a multi-movement work much like a symphony in structure, size, and scope. String quartets usually have four movements, often in structure similar to the symphonic form of fast, slow, dance-like, and fast. The movements are often structured like those of the Classical era symphony: sonata form, song form or variation form, minuet or scherzo and trio, and rondo or sonata.

Dashboard

SHARE

The string quartet became popular in the Classical era and is still composed today. It is perhaps the most important and widely used form of instrumental chamber music. The string quartet was initially intended for the salon. Today it is performed in the recital hall and often serves as dinner music or background music at special events such as weddings or receptions.

The most important composers of the string quartet were Haydn, Mozart, and Beethoven. Franz Schubert, the great song composer, also contributed to the development of the form. Since their time, composers have continued to use the form but few use it as extensively or expressively.

LISTENING GUIDE 14.1

STRING QUARTET NO. 3 IN C MAJOR, op. 76 ("Emperor"), mvt. 2, Poco adagio cantabile, and mvt. 3, Minuet and Trio,
Franz Joseph Haydn, composed 1797

Dashboard

**HEAR STREAMING AUDIO
ON DASHBOARD**

This string quartet is called the "Emperor" because it uses a theme Haydn wrote in 1796 in honor of Austrian Emperor Franz II. The theme, which is the primary melody of movement 2, was written at the request of

Austrian government ministers to serve as a national anthem for Austria.
It is also a popular Protestant hymn in those countries.

___

What to Listen For

- Listen for how equal in importance the four instruments of the quartet are. This is different from the violin-dominated symphony of the time.
- Listen for how hymn-like the second movement theme sounds. This is in contrast to the martial sounding national anthem of the United States.

MOVEMENT 2

TIMING	FORM: THEME AND VARIATION	WHAT TO LISTEN FOR
0:00	Theme 1	The melody is a strong-sounding tune, easy to remember and sing—appropriate for a national anthem. The melody is structured in three sections, with the first and last sections repeated. The theme is played by one violin with the other three instruments accompanying.
1:27	Variation 1	Variation 1 is set for the two violins. The theme is played by one violin while the other embellishes above it with scales and faster notes.
2:48	Variation 2	Variation 2 features the cello playing the theme. The two violins and viola play counterpoint lines.
4:12	Variation 3	In variation 3 the viola carries the theme, beginning alone. The other members gradually add playing counterpoint.
5:36	Variation 4	The theme is set once again in violin. The other instruments play a varied accompaniment that includes both chordal and polyphonic lines.

MOVEMENT 3, Minuet and Trio

The third movement is in the standard form for Classical-era string quartets and symphonies—minuet and trio. Both sections contain two themes. This movement has a light, dance-like quality. The violin carries the theme throughout much of the movement.

TIMING	FORM: MINUET AND TRIO	WHAT TO LISTEN FOR
0:00	Minuet Theme A	Theme A is played by the violin, with other quartet members accompanying.
0:22		Theme A is repeated.
0:44	Minuet Theme B	Theme B begins similarly in character and rhythm to theme A, and contains imitative entrances of the instruments.
0:57	Theme A	Theme A returns and is expanded upon.
1:23	Theme B	Theme B repeats.
1:36	Theme A	The extension of theme A repeats.
2:04	Trio Theme C	The term trio comes from the fact that the second or contrasting section of this dance form was originally played by a trio of instruments, creating a contrast in timbre as well as melody. Theme C is presented in violin. This theme is in a minor key.
2:40	Theme D	Theme D is played in a major key.
2:59	Theme C	Theme C returns in an extended fashion.
3:25	Theme D	Theme D is repeated.
3:55	Minuet	The Minuet is repeated without internal repeats.

If You Liked That, Try This

String Quartets nos. 1–6, op. 18, Ludwig van Beethoven
Strings Quartets, opp. 128, 130, 131, 133, Beethoven
String Quintet in C major, D. 956, Franz Schubert
String Quintet in G minor, K. 516, Mozart

YouTube video: search on keywords
Beethoven: String Quartets [EuroArts]

Remember to add to your personal playlist any of these samples that you like.

PERFORMANCE PRACTICE

How do chamber musicians communicate with each other during a performance?

When you attend a recital of an instrumental chamber ensemble or watch one of the videos recommended in this chapter you will notice there is usually not a conductor leading the ensemble. How do the musicians start together or keep the same tempo without a conductor? At rehearsals of a chamber ensemble who decides when to stop and work on a musical passage? Without a conductor who decides how fast or slow the music goes? And, without a conductor who picks the music? In a large orchestra or band, musicians give up much of their individuality and freedom of expression to be part of a larger whole. Chamber musicians don't have one person choosing the music, making the musical decisions, or leading their performance and this is one of the things that make chamber music fun to play. To answer all the questions posed here visit the homepages, or find them on YouTube, of two professional chamber music ensembles, eighth blackbird and the Canadian Brass Quintet and watch videos of these groups performing. As you watch the ensembles pay attention to the players' feet and head movements. Watch the string players' bows. See how the players' body language and movement help them start, stop, and maintain tempo.

Chamber sonata: A work for a chamber ensemble of three or more players in either a single-movement or three-movement form.

Sonata da chiesa: A chamber sonata intended for performance in the church and usually more serious in character than the dance-like sonata da camera.

Sonata da camera: A dance-like chamber sonata which was intended for performance in the court.

Trio sonata: A Baroque era sonata written in three lines, but played by four players.

Continuo: The instrument that plays the bass line in a trio sonata.

Sonatas of a Different Form

How does the sonata form of the Classical era differ from sonatas in chamber music?

A sonata consists of either one movement with multiple sections (usually three contrasting) or several movements of contrasting tempos and styles. The sonata originated in Italy during the 17th century and was performed in homes, courts, and churches. **Chamber sonatas** are sonatas written for a small group of musicians. As pointed out earlier, the number of musicians is often indicated in the title. The earliest sonatas for chamber music were written in the Baroque era for one to eight instruments. A **sonata da chiesa** was written for performance in a church and was usually more serious than the dance-like **sonata da camera**, which was intended for the court.

The most popular sonata in the Baroque era was the **trio sonata**, so called because there were three lines of music in the score. A trio sonata actually requires four players to play: usually two high melodic instruments (such as flute or violin), a harpsichord, and a **continuo** instrument (today usually a cello or bassoon) that plays the bass line.

Most composers of the Baroque era wrote sonatas, including Domenico Scarlatti (1685–1757), Vivaldi, and perhaps the most important such writer, Arcangelo Corelli (1653–1713). Corelli was Italian and composed and taught in Rome. He was a violinist and is credited with laying the foundations of modern violin technique.

LISTENING GUIDE 14.2

TRIO SONATA IN B-FLAT, op. 4, no. 9,
Arcangelo Corelli, composed 1689

Dashboard

**HEAR STREAMING AUDIO
ON DASHBOARD**

Stylized dance: Music written in dance forms intended for listening rather than dancing.

The Baroque trio sonata was usually a four-movement work and was played by four (not three) players. Often some, if not all, of the movements were **stylized dance** movements and in the same key. The movements usually progress in a slow-fast-slow-fast order and are often two pairs of dances. Corelli's trio sonatas are considered to be the best examples of this form from the Baroque era. Despite his reputation as the founder of modern violin playing, Corelli's violin parts in his trio sonatas are modest and lyrical in style rather than virtuosic. The two violin parts are usually equal in difficulty level and melodic interest. The dances are commonly in two-part form with each of the parts being repeated.

What to Listen For

- Listen for the simplicity of the melodic material, especially that part which is treated in an imitative fashion.
- Listen for the dominance of the violins as melodic instruments. The continuo part is played by cello and harpsichord and is strictly accompanimental.
- Listen for how the violinists alter and ornament the melodic material on the repeat sections. This was a common practice in the Baroque era.

Prelude
The Prelude is in two parts, both of which are repeated. The movement features the two violins playing not so much themes as imitative broken chords outlining the harmony.

The second section contains some scalar material as well.

TIMING	FORM: PRELUDE	WHAT TO LISTEN FOR
0:00	Part 1	The two violins imitate one another on broken chords.
0:35	Part 1	Part 1 repeats with some embellishment.
1:10	Part 2	The imitative material continues beginning on a different pitch.
1:51	Part 2	Part 2 repeats with embellishment.

Corrente

The corrente is a quick dance with three beats per bar. Like many second movements in trio sonatas, this one is fugal in style. The movement is in two parts that are each repeated.

TIMING	FORM: CORRENTE	WHAT TO LISTEN FOR
0:00	Part 1	Violin 1 introduces the melody. Two measures later violin 2 enters with the theme. The two violins seem to chase one another.
0:18	Part 1	Part 1 repeats with ornamentation.
0:37	Part 2	The imitative quality continues with the second violin entering one measure behind violin 1 this time. The key shifts to minor.
1:02	Part 2	Part 2 repeats with ornamentation.

Grave

The grave is a slow movement in G minor, the related key to B flat. Though no longer imitative, the violins continue to sound like they are chasing one another. The melodic line is for the most part a descending scale. The movement is short and through-composed. The work begins at a moderate volume and, as the melodic line descends in pitch the volume decreases to a soft ending.

Gavotte

Movement four is also in two sections that repeat. In section 1 the violins continue the imitative chase.

TIMING	FORM: GAVOTTE	WHAT TO LISTEN FOR
0:00	Part 1	Listen for the imitative melody in the two violins followed by unison rhythms. Listen for the sudden changes in dynamics from loud to soft. These so-called "terrace dynamics" were common in the Baroque era.
0:28	Part 1	Part 1 repeats
0:56	Part 2	Part 2 begins with the violins playing different lines; violin 1 plays a rapid eighth note line while violin 2 plays a slower syncopated line. In the second half of part 2 Corelli brings back the melody from part 1, this time at a fast tempo.
1:25	Part 2	Part 2 repeats. The movement closes with the two violins playing imitative fast notes.

If You Liked That, Try This

Trio Sonata no. 4 in D minor, TWV 42:d4, George Phillip Telemann
Trio Sonata in B-flat major, op. 5, no. 5, RV 76, Antonio Vivaldi
Trio Sonata in E-flat major, op. 8, no. 6, Giuseppe Tartini

YouTube video: search on keywords
Vivaldi—Trio Sonata in D Minor "La Folia" RV63

Remember to add to your personal playlist any of these samples that you like.

The sonata as a chamber music form has been important in each musical era since the Baroque period. Though eclipsed in popularity by the string quartet in the Classical era, it was revived in the form of the **duo sonata** in the Romantic period. In this form it also became important in the 20th century, especially in pieces written as teaching pieces for music conservatory students and in the repertories of wind instruments.

Duo sonata: A sonata written for one instrument and piano.

In the Romantic era composers began to write works for solo players that could be used to display their own compositional abilities and the technical abilities of the player in both the salon and recital hall. These Romantic era duo sonatas are written for a piano and one other instrument. As in the art song, the piano of the duo sonata is an equal partner to the solo instrument. No mere accompanist, the pianist of a duo sonata must possess the technical and expressive skills of the soloist for the work to be successful. This musical partnership is especially evident in the works for violin and piano and wind instruments and piano.

LISTENING GUIDE 14.3

SONATA IN E-FLAT FOR CLARINET AND PIANO, op. 120, no. 2, Allegro,
Johannes Brahms, composed 1894

Dashboard

HEAR STREAMING AUDIO ON DASHBOARD

This work, along with no. 1 in F minor, was written in 1894 and dedicated to clarinetist Richard Mühlfeld, the finest clarinetist of his time. It is the last piece of chamber music that Brahms wrote. The sonata is in three movements: Allegro amabile, Allegro appassionato, Andante con moto, allegro. The work was first performed on September 19, 1894, in the home of the sister of the Duke of Meiningen at Berchtesgaden with Richard Mühlfeld on clarinet and Brahms as pianist. This movement is in a sonata form.

What to Listen For

- Listen for the conversation between the clarinet and the piano. The piano's role changes throughout the piece from accompanist to partner to soloist.
- Listen for the fluid and lyrical style of the melody in the clarinet. These long, smooth lines are typical of Brahms's works.

- Listen for the wide leaps in the melodic lines. Brahms uses this technique to make the melody sound expressive.

- Listen for the changes in intensity in the work. As is typical of the Romantic sonata, the mood shifts over the course of the movement. Brahms uses changes of tempo and dynamics to accomplish this.

TIMING	FORM: SONATA	WHAT TO LISTEN FOR
0:00	Exposition A	The A theme begins without introduction in the clarinet. Brahms uses wide leaps to make the melody expressive.
1:06	B	The second thematic area begins with another wide leap, but this melody is more relaxed sounding than the opening. The piano line seems to answer the clarinet in this section, whereas it accompanied the clarinet line in the first.
1:23		The clarinet and piano trade the themes back and forth.

1:46		The work becomes much more agitated as piano and clarinet play faster lines at increasing dynamic levels and tempo.
2:19		The clarinet plays wide leaps in a short transition section and the tempo slows.
2:30	Development	Clarinet and piano trade altered versions of theme A.
2:54		Piano and clarinet play varied versions of theme B.
3:44		The section becomes more fragmented and tense as the clarinet and piano converse with triplet broken chords.
4:39		The development section closes with clarinet playing lyrical ascending two-note figures while the piano plays descending scales in block chords.
4:57	Recapitulation	The A theme returns in its original form.
5:47		The B theme returns.
7:12		The A material as stated at the beginning of the development section returns but this time it leads to a short coda section.
7:51	Coda	The movement ends in a peaceful and tranquil fashion.

If You Liked That, Try This

Les Nations, François Couperin
Duo Sonata in A major, D.574, Franz Schubert

YouTube video: search on keywords
Isaac Stern, Eugen Istomin, Leonard Rose play Brahms trio NO.2 op. 87

Remember to add to your personal playlist any of these samples that you like.

Chamber Music—No Strings Attached

What kind of chamber music is written for wind instruments?

In the Middle Ages and Renaissance wind instruments were considered the equal of the voice and a vast repertoire of music was written for chamber wind ensembles of four or five players. With the development of opera and string instruments during the Baroque era, wind instruments lost favor with composers.

A revival of sorts occurred in the Classical era. As wind instrument making advanced, composers returned to them as chamber music possibilities. During the Classical era a huge number of light entertainments called **divertimentos**, **serenades**, and **partitas** were written for wind ensembles of four to twelve players. Much of this music was meant for outdoor performance or as background music to events.

One of Mozart's greatest masterpieces was written for a wind ensemble, the so-called "Gran Partita." While it is much more virtuosic than most wind pieces of the day, it displays the care with which composers composed such pieces. The work is in seven movements and is written for a slightly larger ensemble than the typical wind ensemble of the day (usually consisting of eight players and called

Divertimentos, serenades, and partitas: Names given rather interchangeably to works written for light entertainment purposes.

Basset horn: An instrument similar in shape, size, and sound to the modern day alto clarinet. Used sparingly in the Classical era.

harmonie bands). In addition to the standard two oboes, two clarinets, two horns, and two bassoons of the harmonie band, Mozart added two **basset horns** (instruments that sound like low clarinets), two additional horns, and a string bass. The piece is one of the most influential of all wind works.

A great deal of such music exists from the Classical era. These pieces are usually written for the standard harmonie band instrumentation of the day. This octet also served as the basic wind section of the Classical era orchestra.

LISTENING GUIDE 14.4

SERENADE IN B-FLAT FOR WINDS, K. 361 ("Gran Partita"), mvt. 3, Adagio,
Wolfgang Amadeus Mozart, composed ca. 1782

Dashboard

HEAR STREAMING AUDIO ON DASHBOARD

Mozart did not title this work "Gran Partita." He used the word serenade in his numbered title. Along with the date of composition and purpose it is unknown who attached "Gran Partita" to this music. The work is not like other serenades of the time; it is much more serious and of much greater musical value. Several other subsequent wind band works have been influenced by this particular movement, including pieces by Antonín Dvořák, Richard Strauss, and Charles Gounod. This movement is often heard in background music to film and television usually in moments in which a character experiences or describes personal bliss. The movement is featured in the film *Amadeus* as rival composer Antonio Salieri describes the genius of Mozart.

What to Listen For

- Listen for how Mozart interweaves the clarinets and oboes to create the melody.
- Listen for the entrance of the second melody, which is in a minor key.
- Listen for the style of the accompaniment, what has been described as a "squeezebox" sound. The bassoons and horns play nothing in the movement except accompanimental material.

TIMING	FORM: ABA' CODA	WHAT TO LISTEN FOR
0:00	Introduction	A short introduction that outlines the primary chord and key of the work begins the work. All instruments play the introduction except for the solo oboe.
0:26	A	Theme A is presented in solo oboe and continued in solo clarinet. The theme begins on a high note and descends in scalar fashion.
2:26	B	The B section begins at the shift to a minor key. It is similar in character and shape to the first theme and is essentially a development of A theme material.
3:42	A'	Introduction material and theme A return.
5:49	Coda	A brief coda brings the movement to a gentle close.

If You Liked That, Try This

Serenade in C minor for Winds, K. 388, Mozart
Serenade in D minor for Winds, op. 44, Antonín Dvořák
Serenade in E-flat major for Winds, op. 7, Richard Strauss

YouTube videos: search on keywords
3rd Movement Mozart Serenade 'Gran Partita'
Salieri describing the music of Mozart

Remember to add to your personal playlist any of these samples that you like.

In the 20th century wind ensemble music production exploded. The most popular chamber wind ensembles are the brass quintet and the woodwind quintet. The brass quintet is made up of two trumpets, one horn, one trombone, and one tuba. The woodwind quintet contains one flute, one oboe, one clarinet, one bassoon, and one horn. Both ensembles are used throughout a wind musician's training and are among the most popular groups in today's music world. Music for these ensembles covers the gamut of possibilities from serious, sublime works to humorous and fun pieces. As in the Classical era, many of today's greatest composers write music for wind groups.

Dashboard

EXPLORE

A brass quintet consists of two trumpets, horn, trombone, and tuba or bass trombone. Courtesy Getty Images.

LISTENING GUIDE 14.5

QUINTET FOR BRASS, óp. 73, mvt. 3, Con brio,
Malcolm Arnold, composed 1961

The quintet is written for two trumpets, one horn, one trombone, and one tuba, the standard brass quintet. It is a virtuosic showpiece in three movements and is one of the standard pieces in the brass quintet repertory. Malcolm Arnold wrote the piece for the New York Brass Quintet. Arnold was a trumpet player and prolific composer. He wrote orchestral music, chamber music, and ballets, and won an Academy Award in 1957 for his film score to the movie *The Bridge on the River Kwai*.

What to Listen For

- Listen to how Arnold uses all the brass instruments in a melodic and accompanimental fashion. This shifting of roles is typical of brass ensemble music. Arnold uses the horn most often for the lyrical lines and the trumpets in fanfare figures.
- Listen for the interplay between the instruments, at times almost a conversation or duel between the two trumpets.

TIMING	FORM: SECTIONAL	WHAT TO LISTEN FOR
0:00	A	Theme A is presented immediately by trumpet 1 in a fanfare fashion followed by a brief pause.
0:12	A	Theme A is briefly treated in an imitative style as an introduction to the actual first statement of theme A.
0:17	A	Full statement of theme A. The melody is in the trumpet with all others playing short rhythmic figures as accompaniment.
0:23	B	Theme B is less a melody than a rhythm. All members of the group play a unison syncopated and slurred rhythmic motif.
0:34	B	Theme B is repeated with added slides in the trombone.
0:51	A	Theme A returns played by horn. It begins like before but this time, rather than playing a full version of theme A on the third start of the figure, the horn launches into a new theme.
1:05	C	Theme C is a lyrical theme played in the high register of the horn.
1:30	A	The A theme returns briefly played by the trombone and then treated in an imitative style.
1:40	Development	A development section follows using theme A material. Trumpets battle back and forth on a muted fast-note counter-line.
2:08		The low instruments play the fanfare fragment of theme A in imitative fashion.

2:20	A	Theme A returns in its original form.
2:45	Coda	A short coda is announced by a rip to a high note in the horn.
2:52		A running battle of the fanfare fragment of theme A between the trumpets ensues and continues to the end of the work.

If You Liked That, Try This

Quintet no. 3 in D-flat major for Brass, op. 7, Victor Ewald
Canzon Bergamasca, Samuel Scheidt
Canzon duodecimi toni, Giovanni Gabrieli

YouTube videos: search keywords
Canadian Brass Band—Just a Closer Walk (Gillis)
ABQ Juilliard School 7 October 2008

Remember to add to your personal playlist any of these samples that you like.

Contemporary Mixed Chamber Music

What kind of chamber music do modern composers write?
In the 20th century composers began to write music for groups without trying to fit their ideas into a prearranged format or instrumentation. Much of this modern chamber music is written for a combination of wind, string, and percussion instruments. It is characterized by a mixing of classical, popular, jazz, and world music genres. Many works for these "mixed chamber ensembles" use strong and repetitive rhythms mixed with non-Western harmonies and scales to produce an exotic and exciting sound. The music is often influenced by minimalism, tonal, and not written in any set form. It also usually requires a high level of artistry and technical ability on the part of the players, who are asked to employ extended techniques. Twenty-first century composers such as Jennifer Higdon, Steven Mackey, David Gordon, Charles Coleman, and Shafer Mahoney write such "mixed" chamber music for professional and collegiate ensembles. Such music is usually written for performance in the recital hall and draws upon the intimacy of the performance space. Groups such as Bang on a Can, Alarm Will Sound, the Absolute Ensemble, and eighth blackbird are dedicated to this new type of mixed instrument chamber music. The performers are experienced in world musics, jazz, and classical idioms, and use this performance knowledge to create hybrid works that are globally attractive.

Musicians play for tips on the streets of many major cities.
Courtesy Cristina Fumi Photography/Alamy.

LISTENING GUIDE 14.6

Dashboard

**HEAR STREAMING AUDIO
ON DASHBOARD**

ZAKA,
Jennifer Higdon, composed 2003

Jennifer Higdon is a Pulitzer Prize–winning composer. Her inspiration for this work is her definition of the word *zaka*, meaning "almost simultaneously and with great speed to zap, sock, race, turn, drop, sprint." The piece is in one movement about fifteen minutes long and is scored for flute, clarinet, violin, cello, piano, and percussion. *Zaka* has a primitivistic rhythmic sound to it. The rhythms are repetitive, insistent, and very accented. In this way it is similar in style to the music of 20th century composer Igor Stravinsky (studied in Chapter 17). The sections alternate between driving rhythmic sections and slow, lyrical sections. The piece is filled with unusual and contemporary performance techniques for the players. For example, the pianist plays on the strings inside the piano, the clarinetist disassembles the clarinet and plays rhythmic hand pops with it, the flutist uses special tonguing, the violinist, cellist, and pianist use crochet needles to create sounds, and the percussionist uses a bass bow to create sounds on percussion instruments. Eighth blackbird used this piece as the opening work on its Grammy award–winning album entitled *Strange Imaginary Animals*. Due to the length of this work we will sample only the first section (about two minutes in length).

What to Listen For

- Listen for the rhythmic drive of the work, often presented as a repeated figure.
- Listen for how the string instruments and piano are used to sound like percussion instruments.
- Listen for the contemporary techniques in strings and woodwinds that create moaning, stabbing, and sawing sounds. All the instruments use nontraditional techniques from the beginning.
- Listen for sounds from the acoustic instruments that seem to come from electronic instruments.

TIMING	FORM: SECTIONAL	WHAT TO LISTEN FOR
0:00	Section 1	The work begins with a percussive piano playing a low-note ostinato. The pianist plays the keyboard while also manipulating the strings inside the piano with the other hand.
0:06		The violin, cello, and flute enter with fast, rhythmic outbursts capped with violin whooshes and flute punctuated notes. Clarinet plays a rhythm created by removing part of the instrument and playing hand pops with it.

0:37	The cello and violin play a lyrical melody as the piano continues the ostinato. The woodwinds restate similar lines from the opening measures.
1:02	The woodwinds and strings create moaning effects while the pianist runs a finger-nail across the high strings inside the piano.
1:29	The clarinet enters with a running note melody that is answered by the flute.
1:44	The first large section ends with full ensemble over loud percussive piano. This section's repetitive, driving, and accented rhythm is primitivistic in style. The section builds to a climax followed by solo piano which introduces section 2.

If You Liked That, Try This

Absolution, Charles Coleman
Serial Blues, Matthew Herskowitz
Dog Breath Variations, Frank Zappa
Dance Machine, Shafer Mahoney

YouTube videos: search on keywords
This is Absolute Ensemble (Absolute Zawinul / Bach / Arabian Night / Tango)
Eighth Blackbird Strange Imaginary Animals

Remember to add to your personal playlist any of these samples that you like.

PERFORMER PROFILE
Modern Chamber Ensembles

Instrumental chamber music ensembles have become increasingly popular with musicians and audiences alike since the 1990s. In addition to the huge number of professional string quartets, brass quintets, and woodwind quintets, a new type of chamber ensemble has developed that plays a mix of classical, jazz, and world musics. These ensembles have a flexible instrumentation, adding players as called for by each piece of music they play. The work studied in Listening Guide 14.6 is an example of music for this new mixed chamber ensemble. Several of these groups have attained critical and commercial success including the San Francisco Contemporary Music Players, Alarm Will Sound, Bang on a Can, and the International Contemporary Ensemble. Two of the most successful are the Absolute Ensemble and eighth blackbird.

(continued)

eighth blackbird performing. Courtesy Getty Images.

Both are Grammy-winning ensembles whose members are classically trained musicians who are equally at home playing Bach, jazz, and ethnic music. Research the homepages of these two ensembles, watch the videos posted on their sites, sample their recordings, and learn about the backgrounds of the groups and individual players. Is this music what you think of when you think of "classical music"? Note that these players, in addition to recording, spend most of their time preparing for and presenting live concerts in recital halls. Share your ideas and opinions about this type of chamber music on your class discussion board or the textbook Dashboard.

✓ **Build Your Own Playlist:** The works studied in the chapter Listening Guides serve as examples of different styles of chamber music from different eras. Now, build your own chamber music playlist from those works listed in each IF YOU LIKED THAT, TRY THIS list. Share your playlist with others by posting it to your class discussion board or Dashboard.

✓ **Audio Review:** Go to Dashboard to listen to Professor Bailey discuss instrumental chamber music.

✓ **How Am I Doing?** Go to Dashboard to test your understanding of this material by taking the chapter quiz.

Dashboard

KEY TERMS

Basset horn	Divertimentos, serenades, and partitas	Sonata da camera
Chamber music		Sonata da chiesa
Chamber sonata	Duo sonata	Stylized dance
Continuo	Harmonie band	Trio sonata

Music of the Stage and Screen

The chapters in Unit 5 examine music that is heard in opera houses, musical theaters, and movie theaters. In the first three chapters of this unit you will listen to music designed as music dramas. Opera, operetta, musicals, and ballet are all forms created as ways of telling a story combining the visual and the aural. Some of this music, opera and ballet, began in the Baroque era. Other musics of this unit, such as the musical and film music, are 20th-century creations. Together this music represents 500 years of combining instrumental and vocal music with dance and acting to create expressive forms of storytelling.

Each of the forms studied in these chapters requires an instrumental accompaniment and because of this we hear this music performed in the concert hall in suite format as well as on the stage or screen in full-length dramatic productions. But the original intent of this music was that it be performed in a theater, and that is where you can most easily hear it today.

A good deal of the music of this unit has made its way into popular culture being used in ways beyond its intent. Songs from operas and musicals appear in advertisements, television shows, films, and often become hit songs on the popular music charts. Ballet and opera music is reused in everything from Disney movies to Olympic opening ceremonies. When asked, most Americans do not think they know opera or ballet music—but they are usually wrong. It is an unusual day in the United States when the general public does not encounter some music from an opera or ballet in a setting often very different from the original.

The music of the final chapter is different from all of the other music studied in the text—it is not written for live performance. Instead, it is written to be recorded in a studio for performance alongside a film in a movie theater. This means that the film composer can use both live musicians and electronic sounds to create the film score. And, in the recording process the composer and producer can cause

Opening image: The Metropolitan Opera performs in Lincoln Center, New York City. Courtesy Mike Liu/Shutterstock.

different sounds of the score to be heard from different speakers in the movie the-ater. Film scores can contain acoustic music and sound effects, and both the elec-tronic and live-musician sounds can be manipulated by recording techniques to create sounds not heard in the live world.

Much of the music of films is similar to the symphonic music that you heard in Unit 3. In fact, many of today's best film music composers are also classical music composers who write symphonies, string quartets, chamber music, and so on. Symphonic composers like Aaron Copland, Sergei Prokofiev, Philip Glass, and John Corigliano have all scored films in addition to writing art music for the concert hall. Film music is also often performed in live concert settings. Given the popularity of film soundtracks many orchestras include suites of film music on their concerts.

The Opera House and Musical Theater

The opera house and musical theater are similar to the concert hall in most ways. Both have large stages, good-size houses, backstage areas, and lobbies. However, halls that are constructed for opera, musical theater, and ballet usually have very different backstage areas and acoustics.

The backstage area of an opera house or musical theater requires large wings and fly space. The wings are on either side of the stage and run the full depth of the stage, sometimes deeper. They cannot be seen from the house. They are used for temporary staging of actors, dancers, and scenery/sets. The fly space is the space above the stage and must be high enough to allow for scenery to completely disap-pear into it and on which to mount many stage lights. This is accomplished with an intricate rigging system of ropes, cables, and pulleys. Many theaters have trap spaces beneath the stage as well, where actors can rise from or descend to during the performance. The finest and most modern theaters have onstage carousels that turn easily and quickly to change the set and scenery.

Directly in front of the stage in an opera house or musical theater is the or-chestra pit, where the orchestra sits and plays, for the most part unseen by the audience. The conductor stands in the pit with his back to the audience facing the stage so he can conduct the orchestra in the pit as well as the singers and dancers on stage. In most halls the pit is on a hydraulic lift so that the pit floor can be raised to be level with the stage. This rarely happens in an opera or musical, but is useful because it makes the stage floor space larger for other types of performances.

Unlike the concert hall, the backdrop in an opera house or musical theater is not a curtain or hard walls but is scenery specially constructed for each opera or musical. This scenery is constructed in a scene shop and moved to the hall for in-stallation immediately prior to the start of rehearsals.

Lighting is a very important part of any opera, musical, or ballet, and interacts with the music, dancing, acting, scenery, sets, and costumes in special ways. In the concert hall lighting is designed primarily so that performers can see their music and the audience can see the performers. In an opera house or musical theater lighting is used to enhance the drama and music and is an integral part of the performance.

A backstage crew member paints a piece of opera scenery. Courtesy Pxel/Alamy.

It takes a small army of workers, in addition to the musicians, to produce operas, ballets, or musicals. Over the years specialists have become important in the areas of wigs, costumes, makeup, lighting, set design, and sound amplification. Most shows require designers in all of these areas plus master craftsmen such as carpenters, electricians, tailors, and painters who construct the designs. There are also stage crew workers to move scenery, manipulate the lighting equipment, pull the curtain, raise and lower the pit, assist actors in costume changes, and cue the entrances of the actors. In most houses there is a prompter who assists an actor who has forgotten some of his lines. All of these people are under the command of the stage director and music director once the show is ready to be performed.

What to Expect at the Opera House or Musical Theater

Since many operas are not sung in English, most American opera houses project translations of the songs so audience members can read them during the opera. This projection may appear above the stage, on a side wall, or on seatbacks (much like the small screens that fit into the backs of airline seats). Most musicals are written in English and no projection is required.

Opera and musicals last about three hours with one or two intermissions. Ballets are commonly shorter than operas and often have two intermissions.

As in the concert hall, the best and most expensive seats are generally in the front rows of a balcony and midway up in the center of the first floor (referred to as the orchestra). Audience members may need opera glasses (small binoculars) to clearly see the actors' or dancers' faces and costumes.

Audience members usually receive a program that contains a synopsis of the work. Reading through this synopsis prior to the start of the evening, especially for opera and ballet, makes it much easier to identify characters and understand their motives and actions, and thus makes the performance much more enjoyable and understandable.

Attending an opera or a musical is much like attending a play. The difference is that some or all of the dialogue is sung. Looking at opera in this manner helps demystify the event for many first-time attendees.

What to Listen for at an Opera, Ballet, Musical, or Film

Attending an opera, musical, or ballet is a different experience than going to see a movie. However, the music is used in similar ways.

- At an opera or musical it is most important to listen to the songs, called arias, because the message of the show can be understood by threading these songs together. These songs are also most often the most beautiful music of the work.
- At an opera or musical it is also interesting to listen for the interaction between the orchestra and the vocalists. In most musicals the orchestra is simply accompanimental in purpose but in many operas the orchestral music is an integral part of the drama. As you will see, this is especially true in the music of Richard Wagner and in opera of the 20th century.

Of course, at the ballet there is no speaking or singing. The drama is created by the music and the dance. In this setting the music is extremely important in setting the mood for the action on stage.

- Listen for how the composer uses dynamics, accents, and orchestral timbre to enhance the ballet drama. Compare the sounds that you hear with the dance movements. Note how the actions seem to match the style of the music.

When we attend a film we often do not notice the music. But, we certainly would notice if it wasn't there. It is unusual when a film doesn't have background music throughout much of the action.

- When the film begins, listen for how the music sets the mood for the opening scene. Pay attention to when the director has allowed the music to be prominent and when he or she uses it softly in the background of a scene.
- Note whether or not there is one melody that seems to be most important throughout the film, or perhaps there is even a special song written to serve as the theme song of the entire movie.
- When considering music for the stage and screen listen for how the music is used to enhance the drama; this is its primary purpose.

Opera and Operetta

LEARNING OBJECTIVES

- **Recognize recitative and aria by listening.**

- **Explain how opera developed as a narrative form.**

- **Summarize the differences between opera seria, opera buffa, verismo, and music drama.**

- **Describe the features of Grand Opera.**

- **Name important composers of opera.**

- **Explain the differences between opera and operetta.**

Key Concepts: aria, leitmotif, music drama, opera buffa, opera seria, operetta, recitative, verismo

Where It's Playing

When fully staged, opera is heard in a theater that has an orchestra pit, extensive fly and wing space, and a large house. Songs from operas are also staple repertory for voice recitals in recital halls and private salons. They work well in these settings because the intimacy of these places helps heighten the emotional intensity of operatic music. But if asked on the street, the average person might say that they don't listen to opera or that they have never heard it. Yet, music from operas is heard in recordings, movies, and cartoons. For example, opera was an important part of the popular films *Pretty Woman*, *Apocalypse Now*, and *The Fifth Element*. It has been used in *Bugs Bunny* cartoons and *The Simpsons*, and it has been featured at the opening and closing ceremonies of the Olympic Games. In reality most people have heard and enjoyed opera in the popular culture that they experience every day. Like most of the music discussed in this book opera is much more a part of American life than people commonly think. And, like music generally, opera is easily understood and enjoyed when heard in a familiar context.

Opera contains some of the most expressive music ever written. It is a combination of aural and visual stimulation that touches the hearts and souls of those who understand and enjoy it. Opera lovers listen to opera for the beautiful melodies—so much so that they are even happy to hear them sung in languages that they don't understand. These melodies are musically the most important part of opera, and no opera is famous or in the standard repertory without at least one special song.

To gain an appreciation for opera melodies listen for how they fit into the drama of the work, because an opera would be unsatisfying without the drama, scenery, and story. Often you will find that the composer uses a song for the character to express how she is feeling about the action surrounding her. Listen for when melodies are used in this way, or when they are used in a conversational manner between two characters.

Listen for how the orchestral music interacts with the drama and singing on the stage. When does the music serve solely as an accompaniment and when is it used as another character in the opera?

Dashboard

RESEARCH

Florentine Noblemen Develop Baroque Opera

How and where did opera develop as a narrative form?

Opera began in Florence, Italy, in the last part of the 16th century. A group of artists and noblemen called the Florentine Camerata wished to create a dramatic presentation style replicating the tragedies of ancient Greece. They had only writings from ancient times on which to base their ideas. What they came up with was a sort of rhythmic sing-speech that followed the natural inflections of rhythm and pitch of speech. In this vocal style, called **recitative**, a solo singer was accompanied with simple chords. The recitative delivered the text of the action.

Composers soon realized that recitative alone created a rather dry, emotionless work. The addition of solo songs, called **arias**, allowed the plot and action to pause while the singer reflected on the emotion of the moment. Arias are melodic in nature and have become the most important musical aspects of opera.

As opera developed, composers added other types of music including the ensemble number and the chorus, in which several characters or groups express emotions. The orchestra gradually became more important to the overall drama, and instrumental-only pieces like the overture were added to enhance the play. Generally, the overture and instrumental interludes set the mood and introduce important melodies of the opera. The recitative moves the plot along and arias, choruses, and ensemble arias express emotions of characters or reflect upon and explain the action. We call these early works **opera seria** because of their serious plots, often taken from history or mythology.

The earliest opera of which we are aware was written in 1600 for the wedding ceremony of King Henry IV of France and Marie de' Medici, a Florentine noblewoman of one of the most powerful Renaissance Italian families. (Many early operas were written for ceremonial reasons.) Titled *Euridice*, it was written by Jacopo Peri and retells the Greek myth of Orpheus descending into Hades to retrieve his wife, Eurydice.

Opera first became available to the general public in Venice in 1637, marking the true beginning of public performances. Opera also marked the beginning of the virtuosic star solo singer and of the orchestra as an important instrumental ensemble. Three of the greatest early composers of opera are Claudio Monteverdi, George Frideric Handel, and Henry Purcell.

Claudio Monteverdi

The first great composer of opera was the madrigalist Claudio Monteverdi. His early masterpiece of Baroque opera, *Orfeo*, was written in 1607 and, like Peri's first work, retells the Orpheus myth. It was a large production (for the time) and included the first large orchestra, about forty players. Monteverdi included instrumental interludes and an overture, recitative, arias, choruses, and ensemble pieces, which became the standard musical numbers for an opera.

Recitative: A sort-of free rhythmical sung-speech. Used to progress the drama forward much like dialogue in a play.

Aria: A solo song with accompaniment used in opera to convey the thoughts and/or emotions of characters. It usually has a full orchestral accompaniment.

Opera seria: Earliest form of opera on serious subjects.

Dashboard

EXPLORE

LISTENING GUIDE 15.1

"TU SE' MORTA," from *Orfeo*,
Claudio Monteverdi, composed 1607

This section of the opera depicts Orpheus's decision to leave Earth and to follow his wife Eurydice into Hades to try to reclaim her. The music represents his feelings about leaving Earth. It is set in a recitative style.

Dashboard

HEAR STREAMING AUDIO ON DASHBOARD

What to Listen For

- Listen for the declaiming style of the singer. This lack of steady rhythm and phrase lengths that follow speech, rather than remaining regular, are characteristics of recitative.
- Listen for the simple and nonrhythmic style of the accompaniment. The original accompaniment was organ and lute. The instruments often play a broken chord to introduce the vocal line and then play a sustained sound under the recitative.
- Listen for word painting, especially on words that correspond to very high or very low notes. Monteverdi sets the words "stele" (stars) and "sole" (sun) to high pitches and "morte" (death) to low. He uses an ascending scale to represent the words "farewell heaven, farewell sun" as Orpheus gains strength and resolve to leave Earth.
- Listen for the quality of the voice and direction of the melodic line. Monteverdi uses both to express the passion that Orpheus feels about leaving Earth.

"Tu se' morta"

TIMING	TEXT	TRANSLATION	WHAT TO LISTEN FOR
0:00			Organ/lute begin to set mood of the recitative.
0:06	Tu se' morta, mia vita ed io respiro	You are dead, my life, but I breathe.	Note how much of the rhythm is chant-like in character and how passionate the singer is.
0:39	Tu se' da me partita. Per mai più non tornare, ed io rimango	You have left me And yet I remain.	
1:04	No, che se i versi alcuna cosa ponno	No, if my verses have power	
1:13	N'andrò sicuro a' più, profundi abissi	I will go to the deep abyss.	"Go to the deep" in the text is set to a descending melodic line.
1:24	E' internerito il cor del re de l'ombre	And, melting the heart of the King of Hades.	

1:37	Mecco trarotti a riverder le stelle,	I will bring you back to me to see the stars again.	"Stelle" is set to a high note and flourish.
1:50	o se cio negherammi empio destino,	Or, if pitiless fate denies me,	
1:59	Rimarro teco in compagnia di morte.	I will remain with you in death.	Monteverdi sets the word "death" on a low pitch.
2:19	Addio terra, addio cielo, e sole, addio.	Farewell earth, farewell sky, and sun, farewell.	He uses a high note on the word "sun."

If You Liked That, Try This

"Seneca's Death," from *The Coronation of Poppea*, Monteverdi
Prologue from *Euridice*, Jacobo Peri

YouTube videos: search on keywords
Peri, L'Euridice, Prologo "La Tragedia" e Coro "Se de' boschi"
Monteverdi—L'Orfeo—Savall

Remember to add to your personal playlist any of these samples that you like.

George Frideric Handel

As stated in Chapter 10, Handel is recognized today along with J. S. Bach as one of the two most important composers of the Baroque era. His operas are those most often heard today from this period. Like most early operas, his works were opera seria. Early in his life Handel wrote a few operas in Germany and Italy, but his best-known operas (about forty) were written in London. One of the best from this period is *Julius Caesar*, written in 1724. The work is a loose historical account of Caesar's reign and relationship with Cleopatra. In it Handel displays the important characteristics of opera seria, including the vocal showpiece aria. Many arias of the time were written with the sole purpose of allowing a star singer to display his or her virtuosity and breath control. Arias are filled with scales, high notes, and cadenzas that singers can use to show off their vocal talents.

LISTENING GUIDE 15.2

"LA GIUSTIZIA," from *Julius Caesar*,
G. F. Handel, composed 1724

The opera deals with Roman times during and after the reign of Julius Caesar. In this aria Sextus, the son of the Roman Pompey, vows to avenge his father's murder.

Dashboard
HEAR STREAMING AUDIO ON DASHBOARD

What to Listen For

- Listen for the use of word painting in this aria. Handel highlights words that convey the general message of the aria. For example, he uses fast scales and trills on words like justice, vendetta, traitor, and punish.
- Listen for the singer's cadenza near the end of the repeat of the A section. This does not appear during the first statement of the A section.
- Listen for how the orchestra accompaniment is more simple and sparse in the B section than in the A sections.
- Listen for the difference in the melody in the repeat of the A section. The singer embellishes and ornaments the melody on the da capo A section.

TIMING	FORM: ABA	TEXT	TRANSLATION	WHAT TO LISTEN FOR
0:00	A			The orchestra plays a short introduction that uses theme A.
0:15	Stanza 1	La giustizia ha già sull' arco Pronto strale alla vendetta Per punire un traditor	Justice now in its bow has primed the arrow of vengeance To punish a traitor.	
0:47	Stanza 1 repeats Stanza 1 repeats			Stanza 1 repeats twice with a dramatic pause near the end.
1:26	Ritornello			The orchestra introduction returns.
1:41	B Stanza 2	Quanto è tarda la saetta Tanto più crudele aspetta La sua pena un empio cor.	The later the arrow is shot The more cruel the pain suffered By an evil heart.	During this section fewer orchestral instruments play and the accompaniment is simpler.
2:07	A			Repeat of A section Vocalist embellishes the melody on the repeat of the A section.
3:21				Virtuosic cadenza is added at the pause on the repeat.

If You Liked That, Try This

"Lascia ch'io pianga," from *Rinaldo*, Handel
"Ah, mio cor," from *Alcina*, Handel

> **YouTube video: search on keywords**
> Farinelli—Venti turbini—Lascia ch'io pianga

Remember to add to your personal playlist any of these samples that you like.

Henry Purcell

Henry Purcell (1659–1695) was the most influential English composer of his day. He wrote in most forms of his time in both secular and sacred genres. Purcell wrote a large amount of incidental music to accompany plays and though he wrote only one true opera, *Dido and Aeneas* in 1689, it is considered a masterwork. Because of the political mores of the time, he wrote a number of works that are much like operas, called **masques,** in which the dialogue is spoken and which also include arias and instrumental interludes. These were popular during certain periods in English history when plays and operas were forbidden by the state, but a play with accompanying music could be advertised as a concert, and therefore performed.

Masques: Form of English opera in which there is also spoken dialogue.

English composer Henry Purcell. Courtesy World History Archive/Alamy.

Opera performance at the royal theater in Turin, Italy, circa 1740. Courtesy Gianni Dagli Orti/The Art Archive at Art Resource, NY.

Classical-Era Opera Adds Comedy

What are the differences between opera seria and opera buffa?

Opera in the Classical era was both serious and comic. It was the most widely heard type of art music by the general public in this time period. With the Age of Enlightenment came an interest in expressing the issues of daily life and the comic opera, called **opera buffa**, was born. Opera buffa had the trappings and form of opera seria, but the plots were generally light, full of mistaken identities, and often poked fun at the nobility and government. They usually revolved around some humorous and often amorous situation. Unlike opera seria, opera buffa is usually sung in the language of the country in which it is composed. Opera buffa often has exciting act-ending ensemble scenes that musically serve as wrap-ups to the acts and most have happy endings. In many cases the primary arias became the popular tunes of the day. As opera buffa progressed, it began to replace recitative with spoken dialogue. Opera seria continued throughout the Classical age, but buffa was the more popular and influential form.

By the Classical era opera was so popular with the public that most composers tried their hands at writing in this genre. Haydn was a prolific composer of both opera seria and opera buffa, but his works are rarely performed today, perhaps because they were written specifically to satisfy the taste of one person—his major patron, Prince Esterházy. Mozart's operas were not only favorites of the opera-loving Viennese public (including the emperor of the Austro-Hungarian Empire) but are also some of the most often performed operas of any era today. They represent the culmination of the opera buffa in their combination of the clarity and symmetry of the Classical melodic style with well-organized plots and exceptional wit.

Wolfgang Amadeus Mozart

Mozart wrote both opera seria and buffa, and his opera buffa are still popular today. He often worked with a librettist named Lorenzo da Ponte (1749–1838), and they collaborated on three of the greatest operas: *Don Giovanni, Cosi fan tutte,* and *The Marriage of Figaro.* Figaro is the classic opera buffa. It contains attractive and light arias, exciting ensemble pieces, confused identities, and humorous and amorous situations. It also went further in satire than its predecessors, not just poking fun at the ruling class but allowing the servants to openly outwit their masters. At the time it was a controversial work, but when it was produced at the Imperial Court Theater in Vienna in 1786 it was an immediate and huge success.

Mozart wrote his finest German opera, *The Magic Flute,* in 1791. Its fantastical plot, spoken dialogue, and memorable melodies make it one of his most loved works. *Don Giovanni,* composed in 1787, is classified as opera buffa but it also has serious subjects and events. Its mix of seria and buffa made it influential and showed that dark comedy could be popular in opera. The story is that of the Spanish lover Don Juan. The buffa aspects of the opera center on his many conquests, but his immoral acts serve as the serious side of the plot. When he kills the father of one of his lovers, he goes too far. The ghost of the father returns to convince him to change his ways. When Don Giovanni refuses, the ghost (called the "Commandant" in the opera) takes him back to hell with him.

Opera buffa: Comic opera, developed in the Classical era.

LISTENING GUIDE 15.3

"LÀ CI DAREM LA MANO," from *Don Giovanni*,
Wolfgang Amadeus Mozart, composed 1787

In this aria the peasant girl Zerlina is brought to Don Giovanni's villa under the promise of marriage, but his intention is only to seduce her. The aria, a flirtatious duet between the two, is one of the most famous melodies that Mozart wrote.

Dashboard

HEAR STREAMING AUDIO ON DASHBOARD

What to Listen For

- Listen for the seductive quality of the opening melody as sung by Don Giovanni. The simplicity and elegance of the tune makes it both singable and memorable—important aspects for popular song.
- Note that Zerlina's first statement is slightly longer than Don Giovanni's. Mozart used this device to help show her hesitancy.
- Note that as Don Giovanni gets more insistent in the second A section, the music gets faster and the voices go back and forth more quickly and overlap. This helps Mozart create more tension and urgency in the music.

TIMING	FORM: AABA CODA	TEXT	TRANSLATION	LISTEN FOR
0:00	A	Là ci darem la mano	There you will give me your hand	Giovanni's seductive, yet confident statement of the tune.
		Là mi dirai di sì.	There you will tell me yes.	
		Vedi, non è lontano	You see, it is not far	
		Partiam, ben mio da qui.	Let's go there my love.	
0:19		Vorrie e non vorrei	I'd like to, yet I don't want to	Zerlina's somewhat hesitant answer using the same melody.
		Mi trema un poco il cor.	My heart trembles a little.	
		Felice è ver, sarei,	It's true that I would be happy	
		Ma può burlarmi ancor.	But he may be tricking me.	
0:45	B	Vieni, mio bel diletto.	Come, my dearly beloved.	In a new melodic section the two sing to one another as Giovanni becomes more insistent.
0:50		Mi fa pietà Masetto.	I'm sorry for Masetto.	
0:56		Lo cangierò tua sorte.	I will change your life.	
1:00		Presto, non son più forte.	Soon I won't be able to resist.	
1:10		Vieni, Vieni.	Come! Come!	

1:14	A	Là ci darem la mano	There you will give me your hand.	Giovanni and Zerlina sing verse two of the original tune as a duet, first as a conversation and then as each one's thoughts.
1:19		Vorrie, e non vorrei.	I'd like to yet I don't want to.	
1:25		Là mi dirai di sì.	There you will tell me yes.	
1:29		Mi trema un poco il cor.	My heart trembles a little.	
1:34		Partiam, ben mio da qui.	Let's go there my love.	
1:36		Ma può burlarmi ancor.	But he may be tricking me.	
1:40		Vieni, mio bel diletto. Mi fa pietà Masetto.	Come, my dearly beloved. I'm sorry for Masetto.	
1:46		Lo cangierò tua sorte. Presto, non son più forte.	I will change your life. Soon I won't be able to resist.	
1:59		Andiam Andiam Andiam	Let us go, let us go, Let us go.	
2:10	Coda	Andiam, andiam mio bene A ristorar le pene D'un innocente amor!	Let us go, let us go my beloved. To soothe the pangs Of an innocent love.	The coda presents a new melody that the two sing together. It is a lilting dance-like tune that carries them off together.

If You Liked That, Try This

"Der Hölle Rache kocht in meinem Herzen," from *The Magic Flute*, K. 620, Mozart
"Non più andrai" from *The Marriage of Figaro*, K. 492, Mozart
"Martern aller Arten" from *The Abduction from the Seraglio*, K. 384, Mozart

YouTube video: search on keyword
Bryn Terfel—Le Nozze di Figaro—non più andrai
Susanna, or via, sortite—Mozart: LND Figaro, ROH 2006

Remember to add to your personal playlist any of these samples that you like.

Romantic-Era Opera Becomes Grand

What about Romantic era opera makes it "grand"?
The Romantic era was the golden age of opera. Throughout the 19th century everything about opera became bigger: the sets and scenery became more beautiful and exotic, the casts and orchestras became larger, lighting first became important,

and the works themselves were longer and more grandiose. The settings of many operas were often far off and exotic or make-believe, mythical places. Realism and realistic plots gave way to imaginative and fantastic stories.

During the 19th century opera, like many other forms of music, took on a nationalistic style. Popular throughout Europe, opera was a little different in each country. In the early part of the Romantic era four composers dominated and influenced the genre: Gioacchino Rossini (1792–1868), Gaetano Donizetti (1797–1848), Vincenzo Bellini (1801–1835), and Carl Maria von Weber (1786–1826). Rossini, Donizetti, and Bellini all created comic opera in a style called **bel canto**, literally "beautiful song." The arias were showpieces, written to display the talents of opera stars, especially women. Rossini's opera *The Barber of Seville* is still one of the most-performed operas today. Carl Maria von Weber was German and most of his works were based on German folklore and the supernatural. He placed more importance on the orchestra's playing music to help the storyline move forward, and his work *Der Freischütz* (*The Free Shooter*, or *The Marksman*) is among the most influential operas in German.

In France a style of opera called **grand opera** became popular. Its huge and spectacular sets, large choruses, complex dance scenes, fantastic costumes, and plots with nationalistic historical themes (often used for propaganda) made this form popular with the general public. Few grand operas are performed today.

The leading composers of opera in the Romantic era were Richard Wagner (1813–1883), Giuseppi Verdi (1813–1901), and Giacomo Puccini (1858–1924). Puccini composed a type of opera called **verismo**. Verismo abandons the fantastic or mythical plots of the late 19th century and focuses on realistic settings and realistic people struggling with real-life problems. His works are melodic in nature and the melodies are memorable. Verdi is still among the most popular of all opera composers and his operas stand as the high point of Romantic passion and dramatic effect. Wagner developed the idea of composing what he called **music dramas**, works in which the music, poetry, philosophy, acting, scenery, and drama are all of equal importance. He referred to this type of opera as *Gesamtkunstwerk*, or total work of art.

Bel canto: A form of opera from the Romantic era featuring beautiful arias.

Grand opera: A form of opera from the Romantic era that uses lavish sets, costumes, and props. Casts and orchestras are also usually large and the operas are often lengthy.

Verismo: Style of opera in which the plots are realistic.

Music dramas: Term to describe particularly Wagner's operas in which the music is nonstop throughout the opera.

Gesamtkunstwerk: Meaning total work of art, Wagner used the term to describe unification of all works of art in the theatre.

Giuseppi Verdi

Giuseppi Verdi was born in northern Italy in 1813 and began his musical career first as an organist and then as a municipal director of music. He wrote his first opera in 1839 and, with the help of an influential patron, it was produced at La Scala in Milan, the most influential opera house in Italy. Partly because of the untimely deaths in 1840 of his wife and two of his children, he did not write another successful opera until 1842. However, his opera *Nabucco*, produced at La Scala in 1842, made him a national hero. The work's theme of the oppression of Jews struck a chord with many Italian patriots who were striving to create a unified Italy free of Austrian influence. Verdi wrote six operas that are among the best-loved and most-performed today: *Rigoletto*, *Il trovatore*, *La traviata*, *Aida* (written to celebrate the opening of the Suez Canal), *Othello*, and *Falstaff*. These six make up a good portion of the repertory of many modern opera companies.

Most of his operas have serious plots and end unhappily, the notable exception being *Falstaff*, a comic opera. The orchestral music is always supportive of the

Opera composer Giuseppe Verdi.
Courtesy Chronicle/Alamy.

voice. Verdi's operas abandon the old recitative style of minimal accompaniment and replace it with a declaiming style fully supported by the orchestra. They also move faster and are more melodramatic than earlier operas. The difference between recitative and aria was less pronounced in his operas. His operas are filled with beautiful, singable arias descended from the bel canto style.

LISTENING GUIDE 15.4

"LA DONNA È MOBILE," from *Rigoletto*,
Giuseppe Verdi, composed 1851

**HEAR STREAMING AUDIO
ON DASHBOARD**

Rigoletto, one of Verdi's greatest works, is based on Victor Hugo's 1832 play *Le roi s'amuse* in which he depicts alleged romantic conquests of Francis I of France. At the insistence of censors Verdi set the work in Mantua with the main characters being a Duke, his jester Rigoletto, and Rigoletto's daugher, Gilda.

What to Listen For

- Listen for the orchestra's ritornello, which ties the aria together, and to the quartet that follows and introduces the main melody of the aria.
- Listen for how singable and memorable the aria is. This is one of the most popular arias in all of opera.
- Note that the melodic line is four statements of the same rhythm. The lilting quality of the theme is created by the three short, repeated notes followed by an upward smooth skip to a higher note.

TIMING	FORM: AA	TEXT	TRANSLATION	WHAT LISTEN FOR
0:00	Intro			The aria begins with the orchestra ritornello as an introduction. The waltz-like setting gives a lilting feel.
0:12	A	La donna è mobile Qual piuma al vento Muta d'accento E di pensiero.	Woman is flighty Like a feather in the wind, She changes her words And her mind.	The main theme of the melody is stated by the primary character of the opera, the Duke. The melody is in three phrases, with the first and last having the same text.

0:22		Sempre un amabile Leggiadro viso, In pianto o in riso È menzognero.	Always a sweet And pretty face, Weeping or laughing She is lying.	
0:33		La donna è mobile Qual piuma al vento Muta d'accento E di pensiero.	Woman is flighty Like a feather in the wind, She changes her words And her mind.	
1:00	Ritornello			The material from the introduction returns.
1:12	A	È sempre misero Chi a lei s'affida, Chi le confida Mal cauto il core.	He is always miserable Who trusts her, Who confides recklessly His heart to her.	The melody repeats with new words. This verse ends with a brief cadenza-like section for the vocalist ending on a very high and dramatic note.
1:22		Pur mai non sentesi Felice appieno Chi su quei seno Non liba amore.	And yet one who never drinks love on that bosom Never feels Entirely happy.	
1:32		La donna è mobile Qual piuma al vento Muta d'accento E di pensiero.	Woman is flighty Like a feather in the wind, She changes her words And her mind.	Listen for how Verdi allows the singer to "show off" on the words "accento" and "E di" by holding out the notes.
2:02	Ritornello			The orchestra ritornello returns and is used both to end this aria and to provide a transition into the quartet that follows.

If You Liked That, Try This

"Caro nome," from *Rigoletto*, Verdi
"Stride la Vampa," from *Il trovatore*, Verdi
"Pace pace mio Dio" from *La Forza de Destino*, Verdi

YouTube videos: search on keywords
LA TRAVIATA—Drinking Song
Luciano Pavarotti—La Donna è Mobile (Rigoletto)

Remember to add to your personal playlist any of these samples that you like.

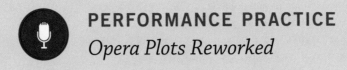

PERFORMANCE PRACTICE
Opera Plots Reworked

How do opera plots relate to today's music?

The plots of operas often seem convoluted and complicated to the novice opera-goer. But, they are usually based upon a myth, folk tale, popular story, or universal theme of human experience. During the 20th century other forms of musical theater began to rework and reuse plots from operas. Two popular examples are the musicals *Miss Saigon*, based on the same themes as Puccini's *Madame Butterfly*, and *Rent* which tells the same tale as Puccini's *La bohème*. Both *Miss Saigon* and *Rent* were popular Broadway musicals. A film example of plot borrowing is the 1990 film *Pretty Woman* starring Richard Gere and Julia Roberts. The movie's plot is essentially that of the opera that they attend in the film, Verdi's *La traviata*. The blockbuster three-part film series *The Lord of the Rings* is similar to the story of Wagner's four-part music drama *The Ring of the Nibelung*.

The story of *Miss Saigon* and *Madame Butterfly* is of the love and devotion of a young Asian woman for an American soldier. In the case of *Madame Butterfly* the story is set in Japan in the mid-1800s, when Commodore Perry and the American fleet opened Japan to trade with the Western world. In *Miss Saigon* the tale is reset in 1970s Saigon just as the United States military is about to withdraw from Vietnam. Both the opera and the musical deal with the difficulties of love between two different races and cultures of people. Further, both focus on the sacrifices mothers are willing to make for the lives of their children.

Rent and *La bohème* are stories of young artists living in desperate circumstances struggling to gain success in their respective fields. *Rent* takes place in present-day New York City and *La bohème* is set in the mid-1800s Latin Quarter of Paris. These works focus on the doomed love story of two of the characters, the struggle to survive with little or no money in both societies, and what people are able to endure for the sake of their art.

The success of these operas, musicals, and films shows that opera plots are no more confusing than those of other dramatic media. To hear how one such story is told in two different media compare Youtube videos of "Con onor muore" from *Madame Butterfly* with "I'd Give My Life for You" from *Miss Saigon*. Both touch the same themes and emotions but use different styles of music to accomplish their goal.

Richard Wagner

Richard Wagner was a dynamic figure in the history of German music who influenced most composers of the late 19th and early 20th centuries. He was born in Leipzig, Germany, in 1813 and, though he had little formal music education, worked as a young man directing a chorus in an opera house. Never a great performer himself, Wagner began composing early and was influenced by the works of Beethoven. His first successful opera, *Rienzi*, was produced in Dresden in 1842. Because of its success he was appointed conductor of the Dresden opera house, where he worked for six years. There he wrote three of his most popular operas, *The Flying Dutchman*, *Tannhauser*, and *Lohengrin*, all based upon folk legend. In 1848 Dresden erupted in a revolution in which Wagner participated. He was forced to flee Germany and took up residence in Zurich and Lucerne, Switzerland. Here, at first, he composed little and spent most of his time working on and publishing new theories of composition. Wagner's plots are often philosophical in nature and feature retellings of Germanic medieval myths and legends.

Wagner also pioneered the use of **leitmotif** in opera, particular melodies or rhythms identified with a specific character, a symbol, or a thing. The use of the leitmotif allows the composer to express what a character is thinking or feeling without having to have it sung or stated. Wagner used the device in his orchestral accompaniments allowing the orchestra to aid in plot development. This usage elevated the purpose of the orchestra from being merely an accompaniment to the voice. Leitmotif is prevalent today in movie scores.

Composer of German music dramas Richard Wagner.
Courtesy North Wind Picture Archives/Alamy.

Unlike other operas, Wagner's music dramas are not sectional or broken up by applause or into recitative and aria. The music flows together in one long stream of endless melody and follows the inflections of the German language. Wagner's use of the orchestra to contribute to the drama was unprecedented. The orchestra in Wagner's music dramas is not merely an accompaniment to the vocalists, but an equal partner in the unfolding of the storyline.

Wagner's music at this time went mostly unheard. He spent much of his time working on a massive four-opera cycle called *The Ring*. He also composed two works that are popular today, *Tristan und Isolde* and *Die Meistersinger*. In 1864 the young King Ludwig of Bavaria decided to fund Wagner's work. Ludwig was a fanatical follower of Wagner's music and he made the Munich opera house available to Wagner. Thanks to Ludwig, Wagner's massive music dramas were finally produced.

Wagner soon began work on a special theater designed to produce only his operas, paid for by Ludwig and a collection of Wagner clubs that had sprung up across Germany. This theater, Bayreuth, still produces only Wagner works. Soon Wagner became the unofficial voice of German nationalism as the German public responded to the subjects of his music dramas. His huge ego led him to declare himself "the most German of beings." His supporters followed and supported him in a maniacal fashion and he often took advantage of them personally and financially.

In 1876 Wagner finally presented *The Ring* as a cycle at Bayreuth. The premiere was a worldwide event covered by newspapers across the globe.

Leitmotif: In opera the idea of a particular melody, rhythm, or other musical element particularly associated with a character, idea, or prop in the opera such that the mere playing of the musical element evokes that character, idea, or thing in the mind of the listener.

Although Wagner is generally thought of only as a composer of opera, the manner in which he used the orchestra and the importance he placed on instrumental music, especially brass, have made him a favorite with lovers of orchestral music. Most of the overtures to his operas are part of the regular repertoire of professional symphony orchestras today. It is difficult to overstate the importance of Wagner to musicians who came after him. His works used an expanded tonality and sounded dissonant in their time.

LISTENING GUIDE 15.5

"RIDE OF THE VALKYRIES," from *The Valkyrie,*
Richard Wagner, composed 1856

This excerpt from the opera begins with perhaps the most famous bit of music that Wagner wrote, the "Ride" motif. It is presented in the introduction of the third act and announces the nine women warriors, Valkyries, returning to Valhalla. They meet on mountain peaks calling to each other and bearing wounded warriors. English translation by Stewart Robb.

Dashboard
**HEAR STREAMING AUDIO
ON DASHBOARD**

What to Listen For

- Listen for how the orchestral material sets two moods or scenes. The swirling runs of the strings and woodwinds at the opening help us imagine the wind in a wild place. The "Ride" fanfare theme matches the heroism of the warriors.

- Note the cry-like motifs of the warriors as they call to one another. Wagner set these calls beginning on a high note that descends on a dotted rhythm to an octave below.

- Listen for how the ride and wind motifs continue throughout the section, reminding us of the locale and mood of the scene.
- Note that the language is German. Wagner felt that opera should be sung in the language of the country where it was written.

TIMING	FORM	TEXT	TRANSLATION	WHAT TO LISTEN FOR
0:00	Prelude			Orchestra plays swirling fast scales in strings and woodwinds to imitate the wind.
0:22				The Ride motif appears first in horn, then trumpet, and finally in full orchestra. The curtain rises on the third act as the motif is played in full orchestra.
1:18		Hojotoho Hojotoho Heiaha Heiaha Helmwige, Hier, Hieher mit dem Ross.	Hojotoho Hojotoho Heiaha Heiaha Helmwige, here. Hie here with your horse.	The warriors call to one another.
1:44				The Ride motif returns in brass with swirling strings and winds. Listen for the calls of the Valkyries as they enter the gathering.
2:22	Main section	*Ortlinde* Zu Ortlinde's Stute stell'deinen Hengst Mit meiner Grauen gas't gern dein Brauner	Your stallion should be by Ortlinde's mare My gray is glad to graze with your brownie.	The warriors musically converse with one another. This style of music is typical of the music dramas of Wagner. The section is neither aria nor recitative but a mixture of the two. The Ride motif continues as an accompaniment. This scene is set in four sections interrupted by orchestral interludes. Three of these interruptions are statements of the Ride motif.
2:28		*Waltraute* Wer hängt dir im Sattel?	Who hangs from your saddle?	
2:31		*Helmwige* Sintolt, der Hegeling.	Sintolt the Hegeling.	
2:33		*Schwertleite* Führ deinen Brauenen fort von der Grauen Orlindes Märes trägt Wittig, den Irming.	Lead off your brownie far from my gray one. Ortlinde's mare now bears Wittig the Irming.	
2:38		*Gerhilde* Als Feinde nur sah ich Sintold und Wittig.	As foemen I saw just Sintolt and Wittig.	

(continued)

TIMING	FORM	TEXT	TRANSLATION	WHAT TO LISTEN FOR
2:42		*Ortlinde* Heiaha. Die Stute stösst mir der Hengst.	Heiaha. Your horse is butting my mare.	
2:47		*Gerhilde* Ha ha ha ha ha ha ha ha Der Recken Zwist entzweit noch die Rosse.	The warriors' strife makes foes of the horses.	Gerhilde laughs on a descending scale.
2:53		*Helmwige* Ruhig, Braunner. Brich unicht den Frieden.	Quiet Brownie. Peaceful does it.	
2:56		*Waltraute* Hoioho. Hoioho. Siegrune, hier Wo säumst du so lang?	Hoyoho, Hoyoho, Siegrune here. Why were you so long?	
3:03	Orch			The Ride motif returns.
3:10		*Siegrune* Arbeit gab's. Sind die and'ren schon da?	Work to do. Are the others all here?	
3:22		*Schwertleite, Waltraute* Hojotoho, Hojotoho, Heiaha. *Gerhilde* Heiaha		
3:29		*Grimgerde, Rossweisse* Hojotoho, Hojotoho, Heiaha *Waltraute* Grimgerd' und Rosswiesse. *Gerhilde* Sie Reiten zu zwei	They ride as a pair.	
3:41	Orch			The Ride motif returns.
3:58		*Helmwige, Ortlinde, Siegrune* Gegrüsst, irh Reisige, Rossweiss' und Grimgerde	Greetings, riders, Rossweiss, and Grimgerde	
4:05		*Rossweisse, Grimgerd* Hojotoho, Hojotoho, Heiaha.		

4:12	*The other riders* Hojotoho, Hojotoho, Heiaha.		The section climaxes on a heroic setting of Hojotoho, Hojotoho, Heiaha and a descending line in the orchestra leads to the final section.
4:52	*Gerhilde* In' Wald mit den Rossen zu Rast und Weid'!	Your steeds to the forest for feed and rest.	
4:59	*Ortlinde* Führet die Mähren fern von einander. Bis unsrer Helden Hass sich gelegt.	Tether the mares away from each other Until our heroes' hate is allayed.	
5:06	Ha ha ha ha ha ha ha ha.		Valkyries laugh on a descending scale.
5:10	*Helmwige* Der Helden Grimm büsste schon die Graue.	The gray has paid for wrath of the heroes.	
5:16	Ha ha ha ha ha ha ha ha.		Valkyries laugh again on a descending scale set in sequence.
5:24	*Rossweisse, Grimgerde* Hojotoho. Hojotoho		
5:27	*The other Valkyries* Wilkommen. Wilkommen	Welcome. Welcome.	
5:35			The act continues to a new scene in the drama without break.

If You Liked That, Try This

"Johohoe! Traft ihr das Schiff," from *The Flying Dutchman*, Wagner

"Mild und leise," from *Tristan und Isolde*, Wagner

"Morgenlich Leuchtend" (Prize song), from *Die Meistersinger von Nürnberg*, Wagner

YouTube videos: search on keywords
Wagner—Siegfried—Siegfried forges Notung (1)
Wagner—Die Walküre: "The Ride of the Valkyries" (Boulez)

Remember to add to your personal playlist any of these samples that you like.

Italian opera composer Giacomo Puccini. Courtesy GL Archive/Alamy.

Giacomo Puccini

The last great opera composer of the 19th century was Giacomo Puccini. Born in Lucca, Italy, in 1858, he wrote some of the best-loved operas of the late 19th and early 20th centuries. Puccini studied music at the Milan conservatory and had early success with an opera called *Manon Lescaut* in 1893. In 1896 he wrote *La bohème*, which made him internationally famous and rich. He followed this success with *Tosca* and *Madame Butterfly*. By the early 1900s opera had become important in America and in 1910 the Metropolitan Opera in New York premiered Puccini's *The Girl of the Golden West*, set in the Old West of the United States. His final work, *Turandot*, was left unfinished at his death but contains one of the most famous arias of all opera "Nessun dorma."

LISTENING GUIDE 15.6

"NESSUN DORMA," from *Turandot*,
Giacomo Puccini, composed 1924

This aria appears in the final act of *Turandot* and is sung by Calaf, the unknown prince. Turandot is the princess who lures princes by offering them a challenge of answering three questions. If he answers correctly, she will marry him; if not, she beheads him. Calaf answers the questions correctly, but instead of marrying her, he offers a challenge to the haughty Princess Turandot: guess his name by dawn. If she does, she can kill him; if she doesn't, she has to marry him. This game is an attempt to break her cold heart and cause her to marry him for love rather than duty. The title "None shall sleep" comes from her command that no one in her kingdom should sleep that night until Calaf's name is discovered. If her subjects fail her, she will kill them all. The aria is written for tenor and was the signature work for opera great Luciano Pavarotti. The aria is in two phrases and the second phrase is the more recognized section.

Dashboard
**HEAR STREAMING AUDIO
ON DASHBOARD**

What to Listen For

- Listen for the offstage chorus of women who sing, "No one will know his name and we, alas, must all die." When Calaf hears this, he becomes confident that he will win and sings the dramatic ending of the aria, "Vincerò"—"I shall win."
- Listen for the dramatic ending phrase "Vincerò." expressing Calaf's confidence.
- Listen for the return of the beginning of the aria. In the repeat Puccini condenses the first few measures of the melody as if Calaf is in a hurry to win.

TIMING	FORM	TEXT	TRANSLATION	WHAT TO LISTEN FOR
0:00	A	*Calaf* Nessun dorma, nessun dorma	None shall sleep, none shall sleep.	The aria opens with a simple one measure introductory broken chord in the orchestra.
0:20		Tu pure, o Principessa. Nelia tua fredda stanza Guardi le stelle che tremano d'amore e di speranza.	Even you, Princess. In your cold bedroom Watch the stars that tremble with love and hope.	
0:52	B	Ma il mio mistero è chiuso in me,	But my secret lies hidden within me	
		Il nome mio nessun saprà.	No one will know my name.	
1:16		No, no sulla tua bocca lo dirò	None, I will reveal it only on your lips	
		Quando la luce splenderà.	When daylight shines.	
	A'	*Calaf*		
1:35		Ed il mio bacio scioglierà il silenzio che ti fa mia.	and my kiss will break the silence that makes you mine.	
		Women's chorus		
1:55		Il nome suo nessun saprà E noi dovrem, ahimè. Morir, morir.	No one will know his name. And, alas, we all will have to die, die.	
		Calaf		
2:10		Dileua, o notte! Tramontate, stelle! Tramontate, stelle!	Depart night! Set stars! Set stars.	
2:36		All'alba vincerò. Vincerò! Vincerò!	At dawn I shall win! I shall win, I shall win!	
2:47	Coda			The orchestra plays a powerful and triumphant ending to the aria.

If You Liked That, Try This

"O soave fanciulla," from *La bohème*, Puccini
"O mio babbino caro," from *Gianni Schicchi*, Puccini
"Vissi d'arte," from *Tosca*, Puccini

YouTube videos: search on keywords
Nessun Dorma—Placido Domingo
Nessun Dorma (Pavarotti, NY 1980)

Remember to add to your personal playlist any of these samples that you like.

One of the greatest operatic tenors of all time, Luciano Pavarotti. Courtesy Associated Press.

Reprise: In opera the return of a melody, rhythm, or entire aria from earlier in the opera.

Puccini continued the 19th century concept of melding recitative and aria and added the concept of a **reprise** of an idea through music in different acts. Two of his works, *Madame Butterfly* and *La bohème*, have been reworked as the popular 20th century musicals *Miss Saigon* and *Rent*.

LISTENING GUIDE 15.7

"UN BEL DÌ," from *Madame Butterfly*,
Giacomo Puccini, composed 1904

Dashboard
HEAR STREAMING AUDIO ON DASHBOARD

Puccini drew the subject of this opera from David Belasco's play of the same name. The work is an example of verismo opera but also contains some aspects of exoticism making use of both Japanese and American music. The story is set in Nagasaki, Japan, in the mid 1800s around the time that trade with Japan was opened to the world through negotiations of the American naval fleet and Commodore Matthew Perry. It is the story of a young geisha, Cio-Cio-San (known as "Butterfly"), and the American naval officer Pinkerton. Butterfly renounces her profession and religion and agrees to the arranged marriage to Pinkerton despite having never met him. Soon after marrying her Pinkerton departs Japan for several years. Meanwhile Butterfly bears their son and patiently awaits his return. In the aria "Un bel dì" (One beautiful day) Butterfly rebukes her maid Suzuki for doubting that Pinkerton will ever return and describes how beautiful their reunion will be. Pinkerton does return three years after his marriage to Butterfly but with an American wife in tow. He has learned that he and Butterfly have a son, and has come to claim the child and take him to America. When told of Pinkerton's plans and other wife, Butterfly accepts the situation, says farewell to her son, and commits suicide.

What to Listen For

"Un bel dì" is some of the most memorable music ever written for opera. Listen for how Puccini sets the two primary ideas of the aria effectively. The opening is a dreamlike melody consisting of high notes sung smoothly and softly without accent or strong inflection. The melody is accompanied by solo violin, which adds to the dreamy effect.

- Listen for how Puccini changes the accompaniment and style of the aria in the final section. Here, Butterfly declares strongly that "I will wait for him." Puccini brings the orchestra to a full dynamic climax to accompany Butterfly's strong and accented declamation of faith in Pinkerton's return.

"Un bel dì"

TIMING	TEXT	TRANSLATION	WHAT TO LISTEN FOR
0:00	Un bel dì, vedremo levarsi un fil di fumo sull' estremo confin del mare.	One fine day we will see a thread of smoke rising at the distant edge of the sea.	The melody is soft, high, and dreamlike. It is accompanied by high violin with simple rhythm.
0:36	E poi la nave appare poi la nave bianca entra nel porto. romba il suo saluto.	And then the ship appears then the white ship enters the harbor. The ship's cannon rumbling its salute.	A bass drum is used to symbolize the cannon.
0:58	Vedi? E venuto! Io non gli scendo incontro. Io no.	You See? He has come! I don't go down to meet him. Not I.	The melodic line descends to match text.
1:19	Mi metto lá sul cieglio del colle e aspetto gran tempo e non mi pesa, la lunga attesa.	I go to the edge of the hill and wait, wait a long time, but the long long wait doesn't bother me.	
1:45	E uscito dall folla cittadina un uomo, un picciol punto s'avvia per la collina.	And emerging from the crowded city a man, a tiny speck. starts towards the hill.	The melodic line ascends to match the text.
2:16	Chi sará? Chi sará? E come sará giunto che dirá? Che dirá?	Who is it? Who? And when he arrives what will he say? What will he say?	The rhythm remains undefined and somewhat chant-like as she describes the scene.
2:25	Chiamerá Butterfly dalla lontana. Io senza dar risposta me ne starò narcosta un po' per celia	He'll call "Butterfly" from the distance. I, without answering, will stay hidden partly to tease him	
2:48	e un po' per non morire al primo incontro ed egli alquanto in pena chiamerá- piccina mogliettina olezzo di verbena,	and partly that I do not die at our first meeting. and he, a little worried, calls "little wife, verbena blossom,"	On the word "die" the rhythm becomes regular and the melody more dramatic.
3:25	i nomi che mi dava al suo venire tutto questo avverrá, te lo prometto	the names he called me when he first arrived here. All this will happen, I promise you.	The orchestra and voice line become more intense and louder as she assures herself that this will all happen.
3:55	Tienti la tua paura, io con sicura fede l'aspetto.	Keep your fear to yourself, with perfect faith, I wait for him.	

If You Liked That, Try This

"Recondita armonia," from *Tosca*, Puccini
"Musetta's Waltz," from *La bohème*, Puccini
"Ch'ella mì creda libero," from *La fanciulla del West*, Puccini

YouTube videos: search on keywords
My Choice 200—Puccini: Vissi d'Arte—Kiri Te Kanawa
Luciano Pavarotti—Recondita Armonia (Concert)

Remember to add to your personal playlist any of these samples that you like.

Modern Opera Continues Romantic Traditions

Opera continues to be an important art form, both for live performance and composition, today. American composers Philip Glass and John Adams have made significant contributions to the repertory. Glass's work *Einstein on the Beach* (1976) was the first of a trilogy of operas based on men whose ideas changed the world. *Satyagraha* (1980) based on the early life of Mahatma Gandhi and *Akhnaten* (1983) centered on the life of the Egyptian pharaoh complete the trilogy. He produced a second opera trilogy in the mid-1990s based on the writings and films of Jean Cocteau. This trilogy included *Orpheé* (1993), *La belle et la bête* (1994), and *Les Enfants Terribles* (1996). Adams's 1987 work *Nixon in China*, the 1991 opera *Death of Klinghoffer*, and his 2005 work *Dr. Atomic* continue in the verismo style in 20th century musical language and setting.

Dashboard

CULTURAL CONNECTION:
KABUKI

PERFORMER PROFILE
Beverly Sills

Are most opera singers European?

In her day, opera divas weren't American—they were European, or at least trained in Europe. They certainly weren't child stars who grew up singing Rinso White soap ads on the radio! But, soprano Beverly Sills was a different kind of opera singer. She was fun, and she was from Brooklyn, New York, not Milan or Paris. America heard her sing on the great operatic stages of the 1950s, '60s, and '70s and in their homes on their favorite television shows. She was so much fun that they called her "Bubbles." At three years old she was singing on the radio. At seven she sang in a movie, and at nine she was a regular on one of America's favorite radio shows "Major Bowes' Capitol Family Hour." She went on to star in the great opera houses of the world, including La

American soprano Beverly Sills performing at the Metropolitan Opera, New York City. © Wally McNamee/CORBIS.

Scala in Milan, London's Covent Garden, the New York City Opera, and the Metropolitan Opera. By the time she retired from the operatic stage in 1980 she was one of the world's leading opera stars and America's favorite classical musician.

Beverly Sills (1929–2007) was a soprano known for lending her comic abilities to the opera stage. Her breakthrough role came in 1966 when she appeared as Cleopatra in Handel's little-known (at the time) opera *Julius Caesar*. By 1971 her career was in full swing and *Time* magazine put her on their cover labeling her "America's Queen of Opera." She

(continued)

performed in London, Milan, La Scala, and Vienna but spent most of her time performing for the New York City Opera and the Metropolitan Opera. After her retirement in 1980 she became director of the New York City Opera, later chair of Lincoln Center, and finally chair of the Metropolitan Opera. Sills helped popularize opera in America through her numerous appearances on television shows such as *The Tonight Show with Johnny Carson*, *The View*, *The Dick Cavett Show*, *Merv Griffin*, and *The Muppet Show*. She even hosted her own NBC Saturday morning show *Lifestyles with Beverly Sills* for which she won an Emmy. Sills was the first American soprano to gain international superstardom in the world of opera. To hear Beverly Sills sing, visit her website and choose one of the videos.

Operetta

How does operetta differ from opera?

Operetta: A form of light and comic opera developed in the late 19th century that includes dancing and speech.

Operetta is a form of comic opera that was developed in the late 19th and early 20th centuries. It is similar in form, size, and scope to opera but has some important differences. First, the dialogue of an operetta is spoken, not sung. Second, the plots are lighter in character than operas, always have happy endings, and often are amusing and far-fetched farces.

Operetta settings are often in some imaginary tiny country of Eastern Europe and involve the mixing, sometimes socially inappropriately, of aristocrats and commoners. Furthermore, the music of operettas is simpler in harmony and orchestration than that of operas. An operetta is filled with high-spirited dances and melodies that rival popular tunes in universality and popularity. The composers of these works were well-known composers who chose to apply their considerable talents to this genre. The three most popular were Johann Strauss Jr. (1825–1899), Franz Lehár (1870–1948), and Arthur Sullivan (1842–1900).

LISTENING GUIDE 15.8

"I AM THE VERY MODEL OF A MODERN MAJOR-GENERAL," from
The Pirates of Penzance,
W. S. Gilbert and Arthur Sullivan, composed 1879

Dashboard
**HEAR STREAMING AUDIO
ON DASHBOARD**

The Pirates of Penzance, or The Slave of Duty premiered in New York City on December 31, 1879. It opened in London in April 1880 though an official premiere of sorts had been given on December 30, 1879, in order to establish copyrights in England. Like most operettas by Gilbert and Sullivan the plot of the piece is complicated. In fact, the twists and turns of the plot are one of the endearing qualities of these operettas. The pirates are a tender-hearted bunch of "orphans" who raid off the Cornish coast of

England. One pirate, Frederic, was indentured by mistake to the pirates by Ruth, his nurse. When told to apprentice him as a pilot she heard pirate, and at the beginning of the opera he is just completing his apprentice-ship. Unlikely as it seems, Frederic has never seen a woman's face other than Ruth's. Frederic encounters the daughters of Major-General Stanley when they happen into his cove on a picnic and he soon chooses one daughter, Mabel, as his bride. The other pirates arrive and each claims a bride of their own from among the sisters. Enter the Major-General, who announces to the pirates that he too is an orphan, and his daughters are immediately returned to him by the pirates. The Major-General is a member of the *nouveau-riche* and has claimed as his ancestors the former, now-buried residents of his newly purchased castle. Once it is found that the Major-General is not an orphan the Pirate King mounts an attack on the castle. The pirates overcome local constabulary (here poking fun at the police) but give up when the police invoke the name of Queen Victoria. Ruth discloses that the pirates are all actually English peers who have gone wrong. In the end the pirates promise to return to their rightful places in the House of Lords taking with them as their wives the daughters of the Major-General.

This aria is a patter aria (very fast rhythms with complicated text almost rap-like) sung by the Major-General upon his appearance at the picnic. It is a satirical song making fun of the educated British officer of the day. The Major-General describes his education, of which none seems to pertain to being an officer in the army. The authors even poke fun at themselves by mentioning the success of a previous operetta *H.M.S. Pinafore*.

What to Listen For

- Listen for the speed and clarity with which the singer must deliver the lines. Each syllable of the words corresponds to a note in the rhythm of the song. As part of the comedy of the piece the singer is expected to get faster and faster with each verse.
- Listen for the pauses that are taken in the second section of each verse. In the operetta the Major-General pauses supposedly to think up a line that will rhyme with the line he has just sung.

TIMING	FORM	TEXT	WHAT TO LISTEN FOR
0:00	Introduction		Orchestral introduction
0:13	Verse 1	*Major-General* I am the very model of a modern Major-General, I've information vegetable, animal, and mineral, I know the kings of England, and I quote the fights historical From Marathon to Waterloo, in order categorical;	Note the speed with which the words are delivered.
0:23		I'm very well acquainted, too, with matters mathematical, I understand equations, both the simple and quadratical, About binomial theorem I'm teeming with a lot o' news,	
0:31		With many cheerful facts about the square of the hypotenuse.	Major-General pauses to think up a rhyme to "lot o' news."
0:35		*Chorus response* With many cheerful facts about the square of the hypotenuse. With many cheerful facts about the square of the hypotenuse. With many cheerful facts about the square of the hypotenuse.	The cast members respond in typical operatic fashion repeating the final words of the Major-General.
0:42	Orchestral Interlude		
0:44		*Major-General* I'm very good at integral and differential calculus; I know the scientific names of beings animalculous: In short, in matters vegetable, animal, and mineral, I am the very model of a modern Major-General.	Listen for the repetitiveness of the melodic line, which for most of the aria simply alternates between two notes.
0:54		*Chorus response* He is the very model of a modern Major-General. He is the very model of a modern Major-General. He is the very model of a modern Major-General.	Listen for the nature of the melodic line, which simply goes up and down by steps in the scale.

0:58	Orchestral Introduction		
1:00	Verse 2	*Major-General* I know our mythic history, King Arthur's and Sir Caradoc's; I answer hard acrostics, I've a pretty taste for paradox, I quote in elegiacs all the crimes of Heliogabalus,	Note that the Major-General delivers almost all of this dialogue in one breath. This, along with the speed of the words, is one of the challenging aspects of this patter aria.
1:11		In conics I can floor peculiarities parabolous; I can tell undoubted Raphaels from Gerard Dows and Zoffanies,	
1:19		I know the croaking chorus from *The Frogs* of Aristophanes! Then I can hum a fugue of which I've heard the music's din afore, And whistle all the airs from that infernal nonsense *Pinafore*.	Major-General pauses in search of a rhyme for "din afore." *H.M.S. Pinafore* was a very successful operetta by Gilbert & Sullivan that preceded *The Pirates of Penzance*.
1:25		*Chorus response* And whistle all the airs from that infernal nonsense *Pinafore*. And whistle all the airs from that infernal nonsense *Pinafore*. And whistle all the airs from that infernal nonsense *Pinafore*.	
1:32	Orchestral interlude		
1:34		*Major-General* Then I can write a washing bill in Baby-lonic cuneiform, And tell you ev'ry detail of Caractacus's uniform: In short, in matters vegetable, animal, and mineral, I am the very model of a modern Major-General.	Note that the Major-General lists obscure talents, none of which would be helpful to a military strategist.
1:44		*Chorus response* In short, in matters vegetable, animal, and mineral, He is the very model of a modern Major-General.	
1:48	Orchestral introduction		

(continued)

TIMING	FORM	TEXT	WHAT TO LISTEN FOR
	Verse 3	*Major-General*	
1:51		In fact, when I know what is meant by "mamelon" and "ravelin,"	Verse 3 is sung much slower and with numerous pauses.
		When I can tell at sight a Mauser rifle from a javelin,	This verse lists actual abilities that would be needed by a Major-General.
		When such affairs as sorties and surprises I'm more wary at,	
2:07		And when I know precisely what is meant by "commissariat"	
		When I have learnt what progress has been made in modern gunnery,	
2:17		When I know more of tactics than a novice in a nunnery—	
		In short, when I've a smattering of elemental strategy—	Major-General pauses to create a rhyme to "strategy." A "gee" is a horse.
		You'll say a better Major-General has never sat a-gee.	
2:24		*Chorus response* You'll say a better Major-General has never sat a-gee You'll say a better Major-General has never sat a-gee. You'll say a better Major-General has never sat a-gee.	
2:31	Orchestral interlude		
2:33		*Major-General* For my military knowledge, though I'm plucky and adventury, Has only been brought down to the beginning of the century; But still, in matters vegetable, animal, and mineral, I am the very model of a modern Major-General.	This final verse is usually taken even faster than the first two.
2:42		*Chorus response* But still, in matters vegetable, animal, and mineral, He is the very model of a modern Major-General.	
2:47	Orchestral ending		The orchestra rushes to the end. An encore verse is often inserted after applause and taken even faster, as fast as the Major-General can perform it.

If You Liked That, Try This

"Three Little Maids from School," from *The Mikado*, Gilbert and Sullivan
"Mein Herr Marquis," from *Die Fledermaus*, Strauss
"A Wandering Minstrel I," from *The Mikado*, Sullivan
"Women, Women," from *The Merry Widow*, Lehár

YouTube videos: search on keywords
"Three Little Maids From School Are We"
I Am The Very Model Of A Modern Major-General (George Rose)

Remember to add to your personal playlist any of these samples that you like.

✓ **Build Your Own Playlist:** The works studied in the chapter Listening Guides serve as examples of different styles of operas from different eras. Now build your own opera playlist from those works listed in each IF YOU LIKED THAT, TRY THIS list or from other works you find. Share your playlist with others by posting it to your class discussion board or the textbook Dashboard.

✓ **Audio Review:** Go to Dashboard to listen to Professor Bailey discuss music of the stage and screen.

✓ **How Am I Doing?** Go to Dashboard to test your understanding of this material by taking the chapter quiz.

Dashboard

KEY TERMS

Aria	Masques	Operetta
Bel canto	Music dramas	Recitative
Gesamtkunstwerk	Opera buffa	Reprise
Grand opera	Opera seria	Verismo
Leitmotif		

Musical Theater

LEARNING OBJECTIVES

- Summarize the precursors of the Broadway musical.

- Compare characteristics of musical theater with those of opera and operetta.

- Name important composer/lyricist teams of musical theater.

- Recognize by listening example the verse, bridge, and chorus of a musical song.

Key Concepts: book musical, bridge, chorus, French revue, minstrel show, refrain, vaudeville

Opening image: *Les Miserables* is one of the most successful musicals of the past thirty years.
Courtesy KEITH MAYHEW/Alamy.

Where It's Playing

Musicals are performed on many different types of stages. Shows that we call Broadway musicals are performed in theaters much like those used for opera. These theaters have an orchestra pit, wing and fly space, and a large house. Musicals are sometimes referred to as "Broadway" musicals because in the early days of musical theater many of the theaters where they were performed were on, or near, that street in New York City. The theater district of New York still is centered on this area and the area around Times Square. In addition to New York, the other major musical theater capital is London. Most popular musicals have opened on stages in either London or New York City.

Musicals have become so popular that they are also performed in high schools and colleges across the United States in student productions. The theater and/or music departments of many colleges and universities offer degree programs in musical theater and produce several musicals each year. Musicals are also produced as part of dinner theater shows where patrons eat dinner and view a musical in the same venue. Further, most musicals that are successful in New York City tour the nation's other major cities to present the show. These touring shows, in recent years, have afforded many more people the opportunity to see live musical theater of professional quality than just those who can travel to New York or London. Musicals are popular on cruise ships and even as Las Vegas shows. In 2006 a special production of *The Phantom of the Opera* opened at the Venetian casino and hotel.

The most important part of a musical is the songs. Regardless of the style or era, the songs still carry the message. Listen for how the songs move the plot line forward. Like opera arias, these songs usually explain how a character is feeling about some action that has taken place or is about to take place. In each act of the musical (musicals are usually in two acts) the composer places a song at the climactic moment of the act. This planned musical climax usually ties together all the events of the act and either adds to the tension of the scene (as is the case at the end of the first act) or resolves the important issues of the show.

Many musicals contain a song called a "showstopper"—a song that is so interesting, enjoyable, and important to the plot that at its end the audience applause is so long that the show's progress is literally stopped. These songs can be big production numbers that involve lots of dancing and the entire cast, or focus simply on one character in an emotional song. It is these songs that have become the hit tunes of Broadway musicals over the decades. Each of the songs of this chapter's listening guides is such a number. Listen for these showstoppers when you attend a live performance of a musical.

In addition to the principal songs of the musical there are many other things worthy of your attention. For example, does the composer use the orchestra strictly as an accompaniment or in a more significant manner? Is there an overture to each act or does the action begin immediately with the curtain up? How important is dance in the musical, and who does the dancing? In many popular musicals it is the second set of leading actors who dance rather than the primary leads. The visual aspects of a musical are often as enjoyable as the music itself.

Precursors of the Musical

How did the modern musical develop?

The musical developed from a number of sources, the most important of which were the opera and operetta of the late 19th century. However, it also has roots in minstrelsy, vaudeville, and French revue. **Minstrelsy** was a type of entertainment that first developed in America around 1840. The first performers were African-Americans. A minstrel show usually was in three acts and consisted of jokes, songs, dancing, variety acts, and parodies of operettas of the time. Often the performers sat on stage in a half-circle and took turns stepping to center stage to entertain the crowd. By 1870 white performers had begun to participate in minstrel shows in "blackface," smearing burnt cork, greasepaint, or shoe polish on their faces. Several popular songs by American composer Stephen Foster were introduced to the public at minstrel shows, including "Camptown Races," "My Old Kentucky Home," "The Old Folks at Home," and "Jeannie with the Light Brown Hair."

Vaudeville was a type of variety show that usually included juggling, animal acts, dramatic readings, dance, and song. The name came from a small village in France, Val de Ville, where residents were known for putting on entertainments. Vaudeville emerged in America around 1870 in New York City. Over the next few decades touring companies were formed that appeared in most cities throughout the nation. The most important vaudeville venue was the Palace Theater in New York, owned by a man who insisted that all acts be "clean" and presentable as family entertainment. This theater helped change vaudeville into a more respectable form of entertainment than it had originally been and rather than just a series of unrelated acts including singers, dancers, jugglers, and burlesque artists, vaudeville became more focused on song, dance, and story and joke telling.

The **French revue** was also a variety type show and was very popular in Paris. It had no script and was often built around one star performer's special abilities. The revue consisted of comedy routines, dances, songs, and dramatic sketches. In America the most famous such entertainment was based in New York and was called the Ziegfeld Follies, which ran from 1907 to 1931.

Minstrelsy: Form of American light entertainment dating from the mid-1800s, usually including dancing, singing, joke-telling, and other forms of entertainment. Often associated with whites in "blackface" performing in imitation of African-American slaves.

Dashboard

EXPLORE

Vaudeville: A variety show that usually included juggling, animal acts, dramatic readings, dance, and song.

French revue: A variety type show without script built around one star performer's abilities. The revue consisted of comedy routines, dances, songs, and dramatic sketches. The Ziegfeld Follies were the most famous American revues.

Humorist Will Rogers was one of the most popular vaudeville performers. Courtesy Getty Images.

By around 1910 shows began to be produced in New York that were more story-driven. These shows usually had lighthearted and sometimes silly plot lines and there was a good deal of focus on elaborate costumes and sets. The script was usually just a framework for presenting a series of songs, and many American popular songs now considered standards were premiered in these shows. Composers such as Irving Berlin (1888–1989), George Gershwin (1898–1937), Cole Porter (1893–1964), and Jerome Kern (1885–1945) were important writers of these early musical comedies, common until about 1940.

Variety Shows Add Plots

How does the modern musical differ from early variety shows and revues?
The modern musical was born in 1927 when Jerome Kern wrote the musical *Showboat*. It is considered the first modern musical because it attempted to meld a serious plot line with music to create a dramatic effect. The musical examines serious subjects such as racial prejudice and mixed-race marriage in the songs and plot. Kern's use of the operatic concept of leitmotif in this musical influenced most Broadway musicals of the second half of the 20th century. The musical is set on and around a showboat traveling the Mississippi River, stopping in many ports to present shows. The story depicts the lives of the entertainers and workers on the showboat. "Ol' Man River" is the most famous and the most important song of the musical. The text of the song relates the hardships of African-Americans and is used by Kern to comment on the story's events set against the passage of time and the human condition. In this sense it functions as a leitmotif representing both the river and the passing of time. This song, and the musical as a whole, proved that musicals could treat difficult subjects, have mixed or unhappy endings, and still be popular with the public.

Paul Robeson sang "Ol' Man River" in the 1936 film *Showboat*. Courtesy Moviestore collection Ltd/Alamy.

LISTENING GUIDE 16.1

"OL' MAN RIVER," from *Showboat*,
Jerome Kern and Oscar Hammerstein II, composed 1927

"Ol' Man River" is used in *Showboat* as a sort-of anchor song, which portrays many of the ideas and emotions of the musical. The song is sung by the character Joe, an African-American dockworker who travels with the showboat. The song is in a standard musical song form of verse, chorus, (AABA).

Dashboard

**HEAR STREAMING AUDIO
ON DASHBOARD**

What to Listen For

- Listen for the register of the voice. The work is sung by a bass voice. It is unusual in musicals for important songs to be written for this register. Most male lead songs are written for the baritone or tenor range.
- Listen for the rhythmic structures. The repetitive rhythms evoke the constancy of the river.
- Listen for the form of the song, which follows the standard musical form: Verse, Chorus, AABA.

"Ol' Man River"

TIMING	FORM	TEXT	WHAT TO LISTEN FOR
0:00	Intro		Orchestral introduction.
0:36	Verse	Dere's an ol' man called de Mississippi . . .	The music is presented with a less than steady rhythmic beat. The verse introduces the two main ideas: the constancy of the river and the struggles of the people.
1:13	Chorus-A	Ol' man river, Dat ol' man river . . .	The main melody of the song is presented. Note the repetitive rhythm of the melody that again matches the idea of the constancy of the river and time.
1:40	Chorus-A	He don't plant taters, He don't plant cotton . . .	The melody is repeated with new text recontrasting the constancy of the river with the shortness of human life.
2:07	Release-B	You an'me, we sweat an' strain, Body all achin' an' racked wid pain . . .	New music moves faster in a more agitated fashion as if hurrying along like the river. The lyrics tell of how life mixes difficulty of work with a bit of fun.
2:31	Chorus-A	But I keep laughin' instead of cryin' I must keep fightin' . . .	The melody returns. The text becomes more hopeful and focuses on the ability of the human spirit to bear and overcome hardship leaving the listener inspired by Joe's resiliency rather than depressed by his lot in life.

If You Liked That, Try This

"Long Ago (And Far Away)," from *Cover Girl*, Jerome Kern and Ira Gershwin

"The Way You Look Tonight," from *Swing Time*, Jerome Kern and Dorothy Fields

"The Last Time I Saw Paris," from *Lady Be Good*, Jerome Kern and Oscar Hammerstein II

YouTube video: search on keywords
Paul Robeson—Ol' Man River (Showboat—1936) J. Kern O. Hammerstein II

Remember to add to your personal playlist any of these samples that you like.

Book musical: Modern style of Broadway musical in which song, dance, and stage play interact to produce a well-connected story line.

Verse: Introductory section of a Broadway song preceding the chorus. The verse is often not in a strict rhythm and is recitative-like.

Chorus: Also called the refrain, this section is the main melody of the song.

Bridge: Sometimes called the release, the bridge is the middle section of a song.

Book Musicals

From approximately 1940 through 1965 American composers created what has become the standard repertory of musicals that are performed annually by high school, community, university, and professional companies today. The first of these standard works was the 1943 Rodgers and Hammerstein musical *Oklahoma!* This is considered the first **book musical** in which songs and dance were created to serve the text and to move the story forward, rather than interrupting it. Richard Rodgers and Oscar Hammerstein created many of the musicals in today's standard repertory, including *Carousel, South Pacific, The King and I,* and *The Sound of Music.* Other musicals of this era include *My Fair Lady, Fiddler on the Roof, Guys and Dolls, Hello Dolly, Man of La Mancha, The Music Man,* and *West Side Story.*

Composers and lyricists Alan Jay Lerner and Frederick Loewe, and Leonard Bernstein and Stephen Sondheim all followed in the path of Rodgers and Hammerstein. Most of these works have an upbeat and inspiring plot line with memorable songs that often became popular hit songs. They usually include two couples with some love interest as a story basis. The first couple sings most of the primary songs and carries the serious message of the show. The second couple is comedic in nature, lighthearted, and often performs dance numbers. The songs of a musical follow a standard format of **verse**, **chorus** or **refrain**, and **bridge** or release. The verse introduces the song and is a bit like recitative in that the accompaniment is usually sparse and the rhythm is free. The chorus is the main melody of the song and the part that is most memorable. It is usually sung three times with different words each time and delivers the important message. The bridge is a middle part of a song that usually is in a contrasting or reflective mood and tempo.

LISTENING GUIDE 16.2

"PEOPLE WILL SAY WE'RE IN LOVE," from *Oklahoma*,
Richard Rodgers and Oscar Hammerstein II, composed 1943

The song is a love duet between the main characters. It is sung twice by
Laurey and Curly, first as a flirtatious warning to one another and later in
the musical as a celebration of their engagement. The form of this song is altered from the standard form and is Verse, Chorus (AB), Verse, Chorus (AB)

Dashboard

**HEAR STREAMING AUDIO
ON DASHBOARD**

What to Listen For

- Listen for the inner structure of the chorus.
- Listen to the lyrics, which are a list of "don'ts." Rodgers created a melody
  that uses a repetitive phrase three times with a final phrase that answers
  the don'ts.

"People Will Say We're in Love"

TIMING	FORM	TEXT	WHAT TO LISTEN FOR
0:05 0:11 0:18	Verse	Laurey—Why do they think up stories . . . Curly—Why do the neighbors . . . Laurey—I know a way to prove . . .	Laurey sings a warning to Curly about not making people think they are a couple. In some versions this is a musical conversation between Laurey and Curly.
0:36	Chorus—A	Don't throw bouquets at me . . .	Laurey sings the main melody of the song in which she lists things that Curly should not do. The list is actually a list of things they have already done together or things she would like him to do.
1:28	Bridge—B	Don't start collecting things . . .	Laurey continues with her list in a new section of the song. Note that while she is telling him not to be demonstrative, she still calls him "Sweetheart."
2:03	Verse 2	Some people claim that you are to blame as much as I . . .	Curly answers with his own warning to Laurey.
2:34	Chorus—A	Don't praise my charm too much . . .	Curly sings the main melody with his list of things that Laurey should not do. Like Laurey's list it is a list of things he desires.
3:30	Bridge—B	Don't dance all night with me . . .	Laurey and Curly agree that they are in love and that the items on their lists are things they should do for one another.

If You Liked That, Try This

"You'll Never Walk Alone," from *Carousel*, Rodgers and Hammerstein

"I'm Gonna' Wash That Man Right Outa My Hair," from *South Pacific*, Rodgers and Hammerstein

"Getting to Know You," from *The King and I*, Rodgers and Hammerstein

"My Favorite Things," from *The Sound of Music*, Rodgers and Hammerstein

YouTube videos: search on keywords
OKLAHOMA "People Will Say We're In Love" with lyrics
Carousel—1956—If I loved you duet
South Pacific—A Wonderful Guy (Sing-along)
The Music Man "Ya Got Trouble"

Remember to add to your personal playlist any of these samples that you like.

A dance scene from the Rodgers and Hammerstein musical *Oklahoma!* Courtesy Geraint Lewis/Alamy.

Another important musical, Lerner and Loewe's *My Fair Lady*, was based on the George Bernard Shaw play *Pygmalion*. The story centers on the relationship between a poor London girl (Eliza Doolittle) who sells flowers for a living and an aristocratic man (Henry Higgins) who is a linguist. As a challenge he agrees to teach her to lose her Cockney accent and speak like an English lady.

LISTENING GUIDE 16.3

"I COULD HAVE DANCED ALL NIGHT," from *My Fair Lady*,
Frederick Loewe and Alan Jay Lerner, composed 1956

Dashboard

HEAR STREAMING AUDIO ON DASHBOARD

As the final test of her transformation, Eliza will be presented at the Embassy Ball. In this song, "I Could Have Danced All Night," Eliza realizes that she is beginning to have feelings for her tutor.

What to Listen For

- Listen for the form of the song. The chorus is sung three times with different words each time. The bridge is very short and is presented in sung-speech by another character.
- Listen for how the orchestra is used throughout the song. It is accompanimental but also usually doubles the melody line and presents countermelodies.
- Listen for the countermelodies in the second chorus presented by the other women.
- Listen for how the song climaxes at the very end. This is typical of this type of solo song in a musical.

"I Could Have Danced All Night"

TIMING	FORM	TEXT	WHAT TO LISTEN FOR
0:00	Intro		A very brief descending scale in the orchestra introduces the song.
0:02	Verse	*Eliza*—Bed! Bed! I couldn't go to bed! . . .	The verse is stated. Notice that the rhythmic structure is like recitative in an opera. Though this verse has a more regular rhythm than much recitative, it is still delivered in a declamatory style.
0:18	Chorus—A	I could have danced all night! . . .	The main melody is presented. The melody is doubled in cello, and woodwinds (flutes) present counter-lines that move when the melody sustains. In this first chorus Eliza states how she feels about the excitement of the evening and begins to recognize her feelings.
1:10	Bridge—B	*Servant 1*—It's after three now . . .	The voices of housemaids enter with a rhythmical line that is a bit like the verse in that it is recitative-like.

(continued)

TIMING	FORM	TEXT	WHAT TO LISTEN FOR
1:17	Chorus—A	*Eliza*—I could have danced all night! . . .	Eliza restates the song's main melody and the characters from the bridge offer a rhythmical counter-line.
2:12	Bridge—B	*Mrs. Pearce*—I understand, dear . . .	Using the same rhythmical motif as in the first bridge, Mrs. Pearce presents new lyrics in an attempt to calm Eliza and get her to go to bed.
2:25	Chorus—A	*Eliza*—I could have danced all night . . .	Eliza states the principal message of the song once more.

If You Liked That, Try This

"There But for You Go I," from *Brigadoon*, Lerner and Loewe
"If Ever I Would Leave You," from *Camelot*, Lerner and Loewe
"Wand'rin Star," from *Paint Your Wagon*, Lerner and Loewe

YouTube videos: search on keywords
Clint Eastwood-I Talk To The Trees
Go home with bonnie Jean
My Fair Lady-Horse race scene

Remember to add to your personal playlist any of these samples that you like.

Many Broadway musicals, including *My Fair Lady*, were reworked into Hollywood film versions. Along with cast recordings, these films have made the works available to a much larger audience. Another such musical was Leonard Bernstein's *West Side Story*, a modern version of Shakespeare's *Romeo and Juliet* with rival gangs in place of rival families. The gangs compete for turf in New York City while Tony (Romeo) and Maria (Juliet) fall in love.

West Side Story was a groundbreaking musical that dealt with very serious subjects. It proved that a successful musical could contain street language, sexually-charged dance styles, and a tragic ending. Because it represented two cultures, the music was more varied than in previous musicals. It incorporated operatic styles such as the ensemble finale, music that sounded like jazz of the day, and traditional slapstick routines. The choreography included energetic dances that expressed the violence and frustration of the gang members, as well as ballet-like numbers for the innocent Maria.

The Jets perform "Cool" from Bernstein's *West Side Story*. Courtesy Associated Press.

"Tonight" is the climactic number in Act 1 in which the characters express several emotions and moods. The two warring gangs have just agreed to a fight between each gang's best man, and Tony, the friend of one, and Maria, the sister of the other, have just pledged their love for one another.

LISTENING GUIDE 16.4

"TONIGHT," from *West Side Story*,
Leonard Bernstein and Stephen Sondheim, composed 1957

"Tonight" is an ensemble number, meaning that a group of characters sing it. Bernstein creates intricate counterpoint and overlapping melodies and text to create this showstopping song. Members of the ensemble present their individual visions of what tonight will bring for each of them.

Dashboard

**HEAR STREAMING AUDIO
ON DASHBOARD**

What to Listen For

- Listen for the lyrical soaring quality of the song as first Tony and then Maria sing it.
- Listen for the accented figures in the accompaniment as the gangs sing their challenges.
- Listen for the more seductive quality of the melody as it is sung by Anita, the girlfriend of the Sharks' leader.
- Listen for the complex interweaving of the gang song and the lyrical "Tonight" as the ensemble piece builds to a climax. This is characteristic of an ensemble finale in which several points of view are expressed at the same time.

"Tonight" ensemble

TIMING	FORM	TEXT	WHAT TO LISTEN FOR
0:00	Intro		The orchestra plays a brief rhythmic introduction that sets up the idea of two warring groups by its alternating high and low register motifs.
0:07	Verse	*Jets*—The Jets are gonna have their day, Tonight.	
0:12		*Sharks*—The Sharks are gonna have their way, Tonight.	
0:16		*Jets*—The Puerto Ricans grumble . . .	
0:24	Verse	*Sharks*—We're gonna hand 'em a surprise, Tonight	
0:29		*Jets*—We're gonna cut 'em down to size, Tonight	
0:34		*Sharks*—We said OK, no rumpus no tricks . . .	
0:44		*All*—We're gonna rock it tonight . . .	Both gangs sing together to end the opening section of the song.
0:56		*Riff and Jets*—Well, they began it!	
0:58		*Bernardo and Sharks*—Well, they began it!	
0:59		*All*—And we're the ones to . . .	

(continued)

TIMING	FORM	TEXT	WHAT TO LISTEN FOR
1:07	Verse	*Anita*—Anita's gonna get her kicks . . .	The gang melody is repeated by Anita, who sings in a seductive style of her dreams for tonight.
1:25	Chorus-A	*Tony*—Tonight, tonight . . .	Tony sings the lyrical *Tonight* love song.
2:23		*Jets*—I'm counting on you to be there Tonight . . .	
2:40	Chorus-A	*Maria*—Tonight, tonight . . . *Riff*—So can I count on you boy? *Tony*—All right *Riff*—We're gonna have us a ball *Tony*—All right *Riff*—Womb to tomb! *Tony*—Sperm to worm! *Riff*—I'll see you there about eight *Tony*—Tonight . . .	The ensemble aspect of the song grows as Riff, Tony, and Maria sing simultaneously.
2:53		*Bernardo*—We're gonna rock it tonight	
	Chorus	*Bernardo*—We're gonna jazz it tonight . . . *Anita*—Tonight . . . *Riff*—They began it . . .	All begin singing at once, reprising what they've sung before.
3:06		*Maria*—Tonight there will be . . . *Tony and Maria*—Today, the minutes seem like hours . . .	As Tony and Maria sing the B section together the gangs continue their interjections. The ensemble builds to a climactic finish with all expressing their expectations of what tonight will bring.
3:29		*All*—Tonight!	

If You Liked That, Try This

"Maria," from *West Side Story*, Bernstein and Sondheim
"If I Were a Rich Man," from *Fiddler on the Roof*, Sheldon Harnick and Jerry Bock
"The Impossible Dream," from *Man of La Mancha*, Mitch Leigh and Joe Darion

YouTube videos: search on keywords
Sunrise Sunset
West Side Story-Tonight (Ensemble)

Remember to add to your personal playlist any of these samples that you like.

PERFORMER PROFILE
Ethel Merman

By today's standards Ethel Merman (1908–1984) was an unlikely Broadway star. Her voice was brassy with a nasal quality, she was gawkish, not very attractive, and arrogant. Even her first name seemed to be old fashioned and staid. But by the end of her career she was considered the "Queen of Musicals." Ethel Merman was a Broadway performer who could always be depended on to pack the house with theatergoers. From the 1930s into the 1960s she appeared in hit after hit and introduced some of the best-loved Broadway songs including, "There's No Business Like Show Business," "I Got Rhythm," "You're the Top," "Anything You Can Do," and "Everything's Coming Up Roses." Merman worked with some of the greatest writers of Broadway musicals including Jule Styne, George Gershwin, and Stephen Sondheim. Her greatest successes came in the Broadway hits *Annie Get Your Gun*, *Call Me Madam*, *Anything Goes*, and *Gypsy*.

Perhaps Merman's greatest influences on the musical were her style of singing and her acting ability. She had a very powerful voice, one that needed no amplification. Yet it also had a quality to it that was completely different from that of opera sopranos. Her voice was piercing, almost strident to today's ears. At the same time it possessed a purity of intonation and tone. She was famous for her breath control and ability to hold notes for long periods of time. This combination of power, breath control, and nasal tone quality created a voice that became the model for the musical comedy. Her ability to "belt" out a Broadway song using her powerful voice was unmatched in her time.

Ethel Merman was also a skilled actor. At a time when many musicals demanded nothing more than a little dancing ability and a sweet voice, Merman's approach to her roles added depth to her characters. As musicals changed from silly farces with bare plot lines to works that dealt with the important social issues of the day, acting became more important. Throughout her career Merman's acting ability was praised and won her a Golden Globe in 1953.

The leading women of today's Broadway shows may not look like Ethel Merman or have her brassiness of personality. But like her they are "triple threats"—able to dance, sing, and act at very high levels. And, recent Broadway leading ladies such as Kristin Chenoweth, Megan Hilty, Idina Menzel, Audra McDonald, and Sutton Foster all have the ability to bring in audiences to hear them belt out Broadway's greatest songs.

Elena Roger as Eva Peron in *Evita*. Courtesy Associated Press.

Rock, Electronics, Opera, and *Cats*

What have contemporary composers added to musicals to keep the audience interested?

Around 1970 a new generation of composers, including Stephen Sondheim (b. 1930), Andrew Lloyd Webber (b. 1948), and Claude Michel-Schonberg (b. 1944), used traditional training and their experiences growing up surrounded by American pop culture to create a new style of musical that melded the worlds of opera, musical, and popular music. Many of the works, such as *Evita, Jesus Christ Superstar, Company,* and *A Little Night Music* were social and political commentaries or histories and popular, serious compositions. Two of these works, *Evita* and *Jesus Christ Superstar,* might be better described as operas because they have no spoken dialogue.

Perhaps the most successful and influential writer of musicals since 1980 is Andrew Lloyd Webber. His rock musical *Jesus Christ Superstar* (1971) and opera/musical *Evita* (1978) established him as a serious composer in this genre, and his works *Cats* (1981) and *Phantom of the Opera* (1986) were record-breaking successes both on the London stage and on Broadway. These works, as well as *Miss Saigon* and the Disney musicals all incorporate a good deal of modern technology both in the pit and on stage to make the musical's action more dramatic and realistic.

Evita began life as an album project, not a musical. In 1976 Lloyd Webber and lyricist Tim Rice produced an album of songs about Eva Peron, wife of the one-time president of Argentina, Juan Peron. The success of the album caused them to rework the material into a musical that premiered in London in 1978 and on Broadway in 1979. In 1996 it was made into a film starring Madonna as Evita. The story relates the events of Peron's rise to power alongside Eva's rise as first an actress and then the politically influential first lady of Argentina.

LISTENING GUIDE 16.5

"DON'T CRY FOR ME ARGENTINA," from *Evita*,
Andrew Lloyd Webber and Tim Rice, composed 1976

This song is used in the musical as Evita recounts her rise to power and deals with her terminal illness. She delivers the song to a crowd of supporters from a balcony in what is the iconic scene of the show. The form of the song is unusual in that the verse continues to alternate with the chorus and ends the song on a chant-like soft phrase.

Dashboard
HEAR STREAMING AUDIO ON DASHBOARD

What to Listen For

- Listen for the form of the song, which is not typical of Broadway musicals. The traditional roles of the verse and chorus are switched as the verse is sung four times and the chorus only three.
- Listen for the contrast in style between the verse and the chorus. The verse is recitative-like and the chorus is in a tango style. The tango is a dance of Argentina.
- Listen for how the orchestra plays the climactic final chorus without words from the soprano.

"Don't Cry for Me Argentina"

TIMING	FORM	TEXT	WHAT TO LISTEN FOR
0:00	Introduction		The orchestra plays the verse as an introduction.
0:54	Verse	It won't be easy You'll think it strange . . .	The soprano sings verse 1 in a recitative-like style, making use of a rhythmic figure on repeated pitches. In this section Evita reflects on how she once was when the public first knew her.
1:31		I had to let it happen . . .	Verse is repeated with new words and a slightly varied rhythmic structure. Evita continues explaining how things changed for her over the past years as she became more in the public eye.
2:10	Chorus	Don't cry for me Argentina . . .	The chorus is presented in a tango rhythm. This melodic line (the most famous of the musical) also has a recitative aspect with the use of repeated pitches.
2:34	Verse	And as for fortune and as for fame . . .	Verse is repeated in a much more flowing rhythm than in the opening. Evita states that she never wanted fame and fortune but they were necessary for her to achieve the country's goals.
3:11	Chorus	Don't cry for me Argentina	The chorus is repeated in abbreviated form with the orchestra playing a major role.
3:42	Chorus	Don't cry for me Argentina . . .	The chorus is restated in its original form
4:06	Verse	Have I said too much . . .	Evita states a final recitative that begins like verse 1.
4:31	Chorus		The orchestra states a grandiose version of the chorus without the vocalist.

If You Liked That, Try This

"All I Ask of You," from *The Phantom of the Opera*, Lloyd Webber, Hart, and Stilgoe

"I Don't Know How to Love Him," from *Jesus Christ Superstar*, Lloyd Webber and Rice

"High Flying, Adored," from *Evita*, Lloyd Webber and Rice

"Memory," from *Cats*, Lloyd Webber and Nunn

"I Can Do That," from *A Chorus Line*, Marvin Hamlisch and Edward Kleban

YouTube videos: search on keywords
musical cats [Memory]
Madonna—Evita—05 Buenos Aires (1996)
I Don't Know How To Love Him

Remember to add to your personal playlist any of these samples that you like.

PERFORMANCE PRACTICE
Tryouts

Where do most musicals premiere?

Not all musicals begin their runs on the stages of London's West End or Broadway in New York City. There is a thriving theater scene "off Broadway" as well. These off-Broadway shows usually have small budgets, lack star performers, and are experimental in design or style of music—but that doesn't make them any less interesting or influential to the larger world of musical theater. Some of these shows become so popular that they attract financial backing and move to theaters on Broadway. For example, *The Fantasticks* first appeared at the Sullivan Street Playhouse in Greenwich Village in 1960 and ran there continuously until 2006 when it moved to the Snapple Theater in the New York Theater district. The 1990s hit *Rent* opened off-Broadway at the New York Theater Workshop and became a Tony Award– and Pulitzer Prize–winning musical "on Broadway" in 1996.

In the early days of the modern musical all shows opened somewhere outside of New York City. These out-of-town tryouts usually resulted in the addition of finishing touches or last-minute rewrites, and sometimes resulted in cancellation of the New York run. The groundbreaking 1943 musical *Oklahoma!* had its out-of-town tryout at the Schubert Theater

Dashboard
ATTEND AND REPORT

in New Haven, Connecticut. It was not very successful until the authors retitled the show (its original title was *Away We Go*) and added the show-stopping title number "Oklahoma." The popular Stephen Sondheim musical *Into the Woods* opened its tryout run in 1986 *way*-off-Broadway at the Old Globe Theater in San Diego, California! Given the cost of mounting a production in the theater districts of London or New York these out-of-town tryout productions have proven important tools in the testing and honing process of musical theater.

The last two decades of the 20th century saw increased public interest in the musical. Many older musicals were revived on Broadway to great success and several new works were premiered that quickly became standards of the repertory. Still other new works were based upon older operas or plays. Two such successful works were *Miss Saigon*, based on the same plot line as Puccini's opera *Madame Butterfly*, and *Rent*, which used the same plot material as the opera *La bohème*. Elton John and Tim Rice also reworked the opera *Aida* into a successful musical of the same name.

Miss Saigon was written by Claude Michel-Schönberg, who also wrote the hit musical *Les Miserables*. *Miss Saigon*, which opened in London in 1989 and on Broadway in 1992, is set in South Vietnam and tells the story of an American soldier's tragic love affair with a Vietnamese girl just before the American withdrawal in April 1975. Chris, an American sergeant meets and falls in love with Kim, a Vietnamese bar girl. Chris' attempts to get her out of Vietnam when he leaves fail, and she is left behind, pregnant with his child as North Vietnam takes

A scene from Disney's Broadway musical *The Lion King*. Courtesy PR NEWSWIRE.

over Saigon. Chris marries and begins a new life in America while Kim struggles to survive with their son in Communist Vietnam. Eventually Chris learns that they have a son and returns to Vietnam with his American wife to try to help them. Kim realizes that her son's best chance of having a good life is for him to return to America with his father without her. She commits suicide and her son leaves for America with Chris.

Another contemporary composer of Broadway musicals is Stephen Schwartz (b. 1948). Schwartz wrote the early 1970s hit musicals *Godspell* and *Pippin* and worked on the Disney musical film projects *Pocahontas* and *The Hunchback of Notre Dame*, for which he won Academy awards. His musical *Wicked* (2004) focuses on Glinda and Elphaba, two young witches who later become the Good Witch of the North and the Wicked Witch of the West, respectively, in *The Wizard of Oz*. The musical, which tells their stories before Dorothy arrives in Oz, is based on a novel by Gregory Maguire, *Wicked: The Life and Times of the Wicked Witch of the West*.

A number of other recent successful Broadway musicals began as films. The Disney children's movies *Beauty and the Beast* and *The Lion King* were both successfully reworked to be presented on the stage, as were the movies *Hairspray*, *The Full Monty*, *The Producers*, and *Young Frankenstein*.

LISTENING GUIDE 16.6

"YOU CAN'T STOP THE BEAT," from *Hairspray*,
Marc Shaiman and Scott Wittman, composed 2002

Hairspray began life as a 1988 film and was brought to Broadway by composer Marc Shaiman and lyricist Scott Wittman in 2002. The musical's mix of rhythm and blues with 1960s pop music made it a hit. The musical is set in Baltimore, Maryland, in the '60s around a local TV dance show and is based on the real *Buddy Deane Show* of that era. The musical deals with serious themes of racial integration, prejudice, and obesity alongside teenage problems of growing up.

Dashboard

HEAR STREAMING AUDIO ON DASHBOARD

What to Listen For

- Listen for how each character tells his or her personal story.
- Listen to the words, which express the dreams and hopes of each of the characters.
- Listen for the driving, repetitive beat as it contributes to and reinforces the idea of unstoppable.
- Listen for the altered form of this song compared to the other musicals in the chapter. Instead of the standard Verse/Chorus format the melody is presented in a simple AB two-part structure. Within the larger AB structure each of those sections also has a two-part inner form.

TIMING	FORM	TEXT	WHAT TO LISTEN FOR
0:00	Intro		A combination of a rock band and studio orchestra play an exciting introduction that sets up the driving rhythm of the song.
	A	*Tracy and Link*	
0:10	a	You can't stop an avalanche As it races down the hill . . .	Note the repetitive chant-like rhythm of the section common in verses.
0:28	b	Cause the world keeps spinnin' . . . Round and round . . .	
	B	Ever since this old world began	The driving rhythms and fast melody con-
0:39		A woman found out if she shook it . . .	tinue in the second section of the melody.
0:50		The motion of the ocean . . .	In the B section the second part of the melody is a repeat of the first part.
1:09	A	*Penny and Seaweed*	
1:12	a	You can't stop a river As it rushes to the sea . . .	This verse deals with the show's main theme of racial integration.
1:30	b	Cause the world keeps spinning . . . Round and round . . .	
1:42	B	Ever since we first saw the light A man and woman liked to shake it . . . The motion of the ocean . . .	
2:09	A	*Edna (Tracy's mother)*	
2:15	a	You can't stop my happiness Cause I like the way I am . . .	This verse deals with the show's idea of ac-ceptance of who you are regardless of what
2:32	b	Cause the world keeps spinning Round and round . . .	you look like.
2:44	B	Ever since this old world began A woman found out if she shook it . . . The motion of the ocean . . .	
3:11	A	*Maybell*	
3:17	a	You can't stop today As it comes speeding down the track.	Maybell's verse continues the theme of racial integration and its inevitability in
3:34	b	Cause the world keeps spinning . . . Round and round . . .	America.
3:46	B	Ever since we first saw the light A man and woman liked to shake it . . . The motion of the ocean . . .	
4:08	Interlude/Bridge		During the interlude section the groups of teenagers (white and African-American) come together to dance together for the first time on live TV.
4:25	B	Ever since we first saw the sun . . . The motion of the ocean . . .	
4:48	Coda	*Entire company* You can't stop the beat . . .	

If You Liked That, Try This

"I Want to Be a Producer," from *The Producers*, Mel Brooks and Thomas
    Meehan
"I Can Hear the Bells," from *Hairspray*, Marc Shaiman and Scott Wittman
"Electricity," from *Billy Elliott*, Elton John and Lee Hall

YouTube videos: search on keywords
Springtime for Hitler
Defying Gravity Tony Awards
"You're Just In Love" Kristin Chenoweth and Nathan Lane
Blast!—Malaguena
The Little Mermaid on Broadway—Under the Sea

Remember to add to your personal playlist any of these samples that you like.

**Kristin Chenoweth and Idina
Menzel perform in *Wicked*.** Courtesy
Associated Press.

The plots and settings of musicals have become very diverse. Some musicals are dance-inspired, such as the popular *A Chorus Line* (1975), *Stomp* (1994), *Bring In da' Noise, Bring In da' Funk* (1995), and *Contact* (2000). Jukebox musicals like *Mamma Mia* have showcased the songs of specific pop groups. *Blast* (2000) even brings the marching band genre to the Broadway stage. This diversification has greatly increased the popularity of the musical and made it more accessible to a larger audience.

Dashboard

EXPLORE

✓ **Build Your Own Playlist:** The works studied in the chapter Listening Guides serve as examples of different styles of musicals from different eras. Now, build your own playlist from those works listed in each IF YOU LIKED THAT, TRY THIS list or from other works you find. Share your playlist with others by posting it to your class discussion board or the textbook Dashboard.

✓ **Audio Review:** Go to Dashboard to listen to Professor Bailey discuss musical theater.

✓ **How Am I Doing?** Go to Dashboard to test your understanding of this material by taking the chapter quiz.

Dashboard

KEY TERMS

Book musical	French revue	Vaudeville
Bridge	Minstrelsy	Verse
Chorus		

Ballet Music

LEARNING OBJECTIVES

- Explain the development of ballet in the Romantic and Modern eras.
- Explain the relationship of the ballet suite to ballet.
- Name important composers of ballet music.

Key Concepts: ballet suite, choreography, ostinato, primitivism

Opening image: Members of the American Ballet Theatre. Courtesy Associated Press).

317

Where It's Playing

Ballet music is written to be performed by an orchestra as accompaniment to a dance performance. In almost all cases this means it was first performed in a theater much like those used for opera or musicals. **Ballets** require large stages for the dances, wide wing space from which the dancers can enter the stage, and fly space for scenery. In most ballets there are few items on the stage to create the scene. Instead, so-called "drops" with scenes painted on them are raised and lowered ("flown" in and out) from the overhead fly space. Ballet theaters, like those used for opera, also require an orchestra pit so that the orchestra is out of the sight line of the audience. In cities that boast both an opera company and a ballet troupe most often these organizations share the same performance venue.

When listening to ballet music at a dance performance, remember that it is accompanimental in nature. Try to focus on how the dance moves relate to the music. Pay attention to how the dance begins; for example, how does the dancer know when to start? Note how the conductor works with the dancers to coordinate the music with the dance. In some ballets you will hear melodies associated with different characters. Listen for how this technique moves the story forward.

Ballet music is also commonly heard today in the concert hall played by a symphony orchestra as part of a concert. Composers of the great ballets extracted the most popular music of the ballet and shaped it into a **ballet suite**. These suites are much shorter than the full-length ballet and feature only the best music from the ballet. Like opera, ballet is very expensive to produce and most companies in the United States give just a few ballet performances each year. For most people it is much more common to hear a ballet suite performed as part of an orchestra concert than to hear the full ballet. Over time the suites to ballets such as *The Rite of Spring*, *Romeo and Juliet*, *Swan Lake*, and *Sleeping Beauty* have become part of the standard concert repertory of orchestras.

In the concert hall, ballet music is usually presented as a ballet suite and as such becomes a sort of program music. In many cases the concert program will contain a scenario or program note telling the story of the ballet for you to follow. As you listen to the music imagine the types of moves that you think are appropriate to match with the music. Try to match important points of the scenario or program with musical sections of the suite. For example, listen for the accents and loudest moments of the music. These might be accompanied by

Ballet: Form of artistic and classical dance originating in France in the Baroque era.

ATTEND AND REPORT

Ballet suite: A collection of the best music from a ballet combined into a work for performance in a concert setting.

jumps or leaps by a male dancer in the ballet version. Or, listen for the softest and most subtle musical moments. In the ballet these often accompany a tender moment between the ballerina and lead male dancer. It is this matching of sound with movement that makes the music of the ballet interesting.

Development of Ballet

How and where did ballet become an important art form?

Ballet as an art form originated in 17th century France, where court ballets consisted of dance scenes united by a very minimal plot thread. These ballets were danced by courtiers and kings and came to their zenith in the court of Louis XIV. Dance was such an important part of his court that he created a special ballet school and professional company of dancers in 1661. Many steps and customs of modern ballet originated at this school, including the turnout, in which the dancer turns the inside of his or her foot towards the audience. Louis was an avid ballet dancer himself and gained his nickname the "Sun King" from a ballet role that he danced.

Ballet first became popular with the general public through opera during the Classical era. Many early operas used ballets during interludes between acts so scenery and costumes could be changed. In the 18th century ballet became an important art form in its own right separate from opera and reached its zenith in 19th century Russia. The Russian school of ballet still influences today's dancers.

The most important ballets were written in the Romantic era and at the beginning of the 20th century. The plots of many ballets of this time period are fairy tale–like. In most cases dances were created to fit with an existing piece of music. In a few cases, however, the music was written after the dance was choreographed. Much music written for the ballet is now commonly performed in suites in the concert hall.

The earliest ballet music still in the standard repertory is *Giselle* by Adolphe Adam, a French composer who lived from 1803–1856. Written in 1841, the work makes use of musical leitmotif with the characters of the dance. A version still performed today was choreographed by a great Russian choreographer, Marius Petipa, who worked at the Imperial ballet school in St. Petersburg. Another early ballet in the standard repertory is *Coppélia*, written by Léo Delibes (1836–1891) in 1870. Like his teacher, Adam, Delibes was French. The music for this work is heard often in a concert suite today.

King Louis XIV of France as Apollo from the ballet *La nuit.*
Courtesy Bibliotheque Nationale de France (BnF) © RMN-Grand Palais/ Art Resource, NY.

Pyotr Il'yich Tchaikovsky

The most important ballets of the Romantic era were written by Pyotr Il'yich Tchaikovsky and his most famous include *Swan Lake, Romeo and Juliet, Sleeping Beauty,* and *The Nutcracker.* Tchaikovsky was the first Russian composer to gain international fame. *The Nutcracker* contains some of the most famous of all ballet music. In America it is heard primarily at Christmas time because the work takes place on Christmas Eve. It is based on a story by E. T. A. Hoffman. Act I takes place at a Christmas party in the home of two children, Clara (sometimes called Marie) and Fritz. Clara receives a Nutcracker soldier as a Christmas present from an eccentric inventor who is a close friend of her parents. She falls asleep and has a fantastic dream involving a great battle between her dolls (including the Nutcracker) and mice, all of which are human-sized. In Act II she travels with the Prince (who was the Nutcracker in Act I) to the land of sweets (called Comfiturembourg) where the Sugarplum Fairy rules. Here she views a series of dances representing sweets and foods from different lands.

Russian composer Pyotr Il'yich Tchaikovsky. © Maxim Anisimov. Courtesy iStock.

LISTENING GUIDE 17.1

"MARCH" and "DANCE OF THE REED PIPES," from *The Nutcracker*, *Pyotr Il'yich Tchaikovsky, composed 1892*

The Nutcracker was first performed in St. Petersburg, Russia in December 1892. The basis of the work is a fairy tale by E. T. A. Hoffman from 1816 called "The Nutcracker and the Mouse King." Alexandre Dumas altered the story into a version aimed at children, and the ballet master of the Imperial Ballet of Russia, Marius Petipa commissioned Tchaikovsky to set it to music. The ballet suite contains eight pieces from the ballet; a shortened overture, the "March," "Dance of the Sugarplum Fairy," "Trepak," "Arabian Dance," "Chinese Dance," "Dance of the Reed Pipes," and "Waltz of the Flowers."

Dashboard

HEAR STREAMING AUDIO ON DASHBOARD

What to Listen For

* Listen for how Tchaikovsky uses the instruments to create bright tone colors. Each dance is set in a different mood. Listen for how Tchaikovsky uses instrumentation to help create moods.
* Listen for the melodies, which are some of the most recognizable in Western music.

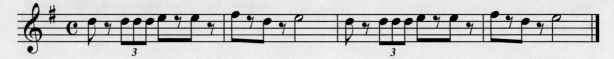

"March"

TIMINGS	FORM	WHAT TO LISTEN FOR
0:00	A	The brass section begins the march with a theme that resembles a fanfare.
0:06		The strings answer in a descending melody that sounds like a "hopping" or "skipping" tune.

TIMINGS	FORM	WHAT TO LISTEN FOR
0:13		The brass and strings repeat their opening sections.
0:19		
0:26	B	The brass and strings play a section similar to the opening but varied.
0:38	A	The brass and strings return to the opening material.
0:50		As before, the section repeats.
1:03	C	Woodwinds play fast, short notes in a descending scale.
1:16	A	The march theme returns accompanied by sweeping strings.
1:23		The strings answer the brass just as at the beginning.
1:29		The section repeats.
1:42	B	The brass and strings play a section similar to the opening but varied.
1:54	A	The brass and strings return to the opening material.
2:07		As before, the section repeats.

"Dance of the Reed Pipes"

TIMING	FORM	WHAT TO LISTEN FOR
0:00	A	Three flutes play theme A after a short introduction by the strings.

TIMING	FORM	WHAT TO LISTEN FOR
0:16		The section repeats.
0:29		English horn plays a lyrical melody while flutes continue short, fast notes.
0:41		The flute theme returns and repeats.
1:06	B	Trumpets play a melody of repeated short notes. The melody is in a minor key and sounds somewhat ominous.

TIMING	FORM	WHAT TO LISTEN FOR
1:19		Strings restate the trumpet melody.
1:36	A	Flutes state theme A and strings join them.
1:49		The section repeats.

If You Liked That, Try This

Swan Lake, Tchaikovsky
Sleeping Beauty, Tchaikovsky
Giselle, Adolphe Adam

YouTube videos: search on keywords
Swan Lake Ballet, Scene
Sleeping beauty Pas de deux
The History of The Nutcracker Ballet
Dance of the Reed pipes from The Nutcracker (Mariinsky)
18-Swan Lake

Remember to add to your personal playlist any of these samples that you like.

Tchaikovsky's ballet *The Nutcracker* is a holiday favorite in the United States. Courtesy Igor Bulgarin/ Shutterstock.

Modern Ballet

What were the important ballet developments of the Modern era?

Early 20th century ballet was dominated by a Russian impresario, a ballet company, and a composer. The impresario was Sergei Diaghilev (1872–1929), whose Ballet Russe moved to Paris just prior to World War I due to political turmoil in Russia. Diaghilev commissioned composer Igor Stravinsky to write three great ballets for his company: *The Firebird, Petrushka,* and *The Rite of Spring.*

Primitivsm

Igor Stravinsky's ballet *The Rite of Spring* illustrates one of the earliest styles of music of the 20th century, **primitivism**. In this style repetitive and powerful rhythms drive the work. Percussive sounds and hard accents dominate the music. Primitivism was used not only by Stravinsky in music but also by Picasso in painting. His work *Les Demoiselles d'Avignon* was an example of this style.

Primitivism: A style of music in which rhythm is the most important element using strong accents and ostinato patterns.

Igor Stravinsky

Igor Stravinsky (1882–1971) was born near St. Petersburg, Russia, and grew up in a musical family—his father was a singer in the Imperial Opera. He is considered to be one of the two most influential composers of the 20th century, along with expressionist Arnold Schoenberg. During his lifetime he composed in most of the important new compositional styles of the 20th century and was the leading composer in two: neoclassicism and primitivism. Stravinsky was also one of the earliest classical composers to use jazz style in his music.

Russian composer Igor Stravinsky. © Copyright Bettmann/Corbis/AP Images.

Because of the Russian Revolution Stravinsky spent the first part of his career in France and the latter part in the United States. Early in his career he collaborated with the great ballet impresario Sergei Diaghilev. Diaghilev commissioned Stravinsky to write three fantastic ballets for the Russian Ballet (based in Paris): *The Firebird* (1910), *Petrushka* (1911), and *The Rite of Spring* (1913). The music of each has found its way into the concert repertory of the orchestra. Stravinsky's style changed throughout his career. His early works are considered primitivistic, the works from his mid-career are labeled neoclassical, and late in his career he turned to expressionism. He is considered a master of orchestration, using instruments in combinations that created new tone colors, and made timbre an important musical element in his works. Rhythm was the other important musical element in Stravinsky's music, especially in his primitivistic music and his works influenced by jazz.

A scene from Stravinsky's *The Rite of Spring* danced by the Bolshoi Theater of Moscow, Russia. Courtesy Associated Press.

Dashboard

EXPLORE

The Rite of Spring is a primitivistic work that had a great influence on the music of the 20th century. At its premiere the audience rioted, reacting to the violent and harsh sounds of the orchestra and the provocative dancing. The piece was originally titled *The Great Sacrifice* and Stravinsky claims to have conceived of it in a vision. Stravinsky said of the work, "I saw in imagination a solemn pagan rite: wise elders, seated in a circle, watching a young girl dance herself to death. They were sacrificing her to propitiate the god of spring." The work is in two parts: part I, "Introduction, Omens of Spring—Dance of the Youths and Maidens" and "Ritual of Abduction," and part II: "Sacrificial Dance." It is written for a large orchestra and is one of the earliest pieces to make use of an extensive percussion section.

LISTENING GUIDE 17.2

THE RITE OF SPRING,
Igor Stravinsky, composed 1913

This work is one of the most controversial and important pieces of music of the 20th century. The use of primativistic rhythms and polytonal harmonies made it sound different from anything of its time. Stravinsky used pentatonicism (emphasis on only five notes of the scale) to evoke a folk-like sound in the work. The work is through-composed with little repetition of ideas, save the opening bassoon solo.

Dashboard

**HEAR STREAMING AUDIO
ON DASHBOARD**

What to Listen For

- Rhythm is the most important aspect of the work. Listen for driving, punctuated, irregular rhythms. These rhythms are the main factor contributing to the violent sound of the piece.
- Listen for the large number of different tone colors produced by the oversized orchestra. Use of the bassoon, English horn, and muted trumpet all help to create a harsh tone.

Extreme dynamics are used throughout the section to create animalistic calls and accents. The melodies are folk-like, using some compositional devices of Russian folk song.

TIMING	FORM	WHAT TO LISTEN FOR
0:00	Introduction	Theme A is presented in very high bassoon.

TIMING	FORM	WHAT TO LISTEN FOR
0:21		Fragments of the theme are repeated in other woodwind instruments including clarinet and English horn. The theme is a part of a Russian folk song. Stravinsky uses woodwinds to create changing tone colors. The theme is intended to portray the "awakening of nature."
0:45		Oboe introduces a new fanfare theme.
2:31		Near the end of the section a high clarinet cry is heard that is taken over by muted trumpet.
3:03		Theme A returns at the end of the section.
3:23		The section ends with low clarinet and string pizzicatos.
0:00	"Omens of Spring— Dance of the Youths and Maidens"	Strings play a repeated harsh and dissonant chord 32 times, punctuated and percussive. The section has examples of offbeat strong accents and the resulting rhythm is primitivistic in nature.
0:19		Strings continue with melodic interjections from other instruments such as the high trumpet and piccolo.
0:39		Strings repeat the punctuated chords. Several instruments interject melodic motifs.
0:49		Theme B appears in bassoon accompanied by the string primitive chords. The theme also has offbeat accents and is folk-like.

TIMING	FORM	WHAT TO LISTEN FOR
1:08		Theme B repeats with fragments played by trombone and woodwinds.
1:19		Section ends with a sudden stop in the driving pulse. Timpani enters and low winds play sustained notes.
1:25		A new steady rhythm begins with loud string ripping notes. This introduces Theme C.
1:43		Theme C is presented in horn and is also a folk-like melodic fragment.

TIMING	FORM	WHAT TO LISTEN FOR
1:55		Fragment is answered in oboe and trumpet.
2:04		A lyrical melody from earlier in the movement is heard in flute while strings continue a machine-like rhythmic accompaniment.
2:20		Trumpets present Theme D and add it to the texture that continues from the thematic section of C.

TIMING	FORM	WHAT TO LISTEN FOR
2:37		A sudden change of texture occurs with repetitive rhythms and harsh accents. Melodic fragments are interjected by various instruments and the section builds in dynamics and intensity toward the "Ritual of Abduction" section. The rhythmic structure has a scurrying sound.

(continued)

TIMING	FORM	WHAT TO LISTEN FOR
0:00	"Ritual of Abduction"	The section begins with sustained loud brass chords and strong notes from timpani and bass drum.
0:15		Horn calls are followed by a high trumpet line.
		The section is marked by short and fast rhythms with interjections from many instruments creating a cacophony of crescendo. Horn calls and woodwind screeches fill the section. Percussion continues to interrupt the wind lines.
0:46		Horn calls end the section.
0:59		A trumpet call begins the final section of part 1.
1:07		Strings create a whirling sound punctuated by loud strikes on timpani.
1:17		Full orchestra and percussion play loud percussive chords.
1:21		The section ends with extended trills in the violins and flute.

If You Liked That, Try This

The Firebird, Stravinsky
Petrushka, Stravinsky

YouTube videos: search on keywords
Rite of Spring. THE RIOTOUS PREMIERE! (from the film "Riot at the Rite" part-2)
The Rite of Spring Part 1
Fantasia 1940—The Rite of Spring—Part 2: Evolution
Stravinsky: Petrushka, Scene I—The Shrovetide Fair

Remember to add to your personal playlist any of these samples that you like.

PERFORMANCE PRACTICE
Matching the Music with the Dance

Which comes first, the music or the dance?

Just like opera it takes a team of artists to create a ballet, including a composer, a choreographer, a costume designer, set designer, music director, and director. It is the director's vision of the piece that guides the work of the other artists. Sometimes the director is also the choreographer—the person who designs the dance movements. To begin, it is usually the director who creates what is called a "scenario," a very brief description of the place, time, mood, and story of the ballet. This scenario can often be expressed in just a few sentences and is not as complicated as a plot line. In fact, it often can be expressed as a single idea. In *The Rite of Spring* that idea might simply be as Stravinsky put it "the mystery and great surge of creative power of Spring." The choreographer and composer work closely together both making many minor and sometimes a few major alterations to their own work and visions as they consider the ideas of the other. The composer and choreographer work together on timings of certain passages, where the placement of accents in the music might be most advantageous to the dance, or how long certain sections of the music should be. These decisions are guided by the director's vision, and the scenario. In the end, it is the director who makes the final artistic decisions about both the music and the choreography. In this way, ballet music is very differently composed in most cases from other orchestral music. It must be composed within more restrictive boundaries and this takes a special compositional talent. Composers such as Stravinsky, Tchaikovsky, and Sergei Prokofiev excelled at molding their musical ideas to fit scenarios, timings, and the physical demands of the dance. A modern pair of collaborators in the United States was composer Aaron Copland and choreographer Martha Graham. Research their important collaboration *Appalachian Spring* to discover how this work was created. Which came first, the music or scenario? What was its original title? What does the final title mean? Report your findings to your course discussion board or the textbook Dashboard.

Aaron Copland

America's first world-recognized great composer of art music was Aaron Copland. Copland was born in Brooklyn, New York, and early in his career wrote music influenced by jazz and neoclassical styles. His most successful and popular works portrayed the American West, the American spirit, and the landscape of the United States. The titles of his works for ballet such as *Billy the Kid*, *Rodeo*, and the popular *Appalachian Spring* all sound American.

His film music for *Of Mice and Men*, *Our Town*, and *The Red Pony* extended this nationalistic spirit to the screen. From the 1930s he attempted to narrow the gap between the contemporary art music composer and the general listening audience that had developed during the first part of the 20th century. Copland said of this change in style, "It made no sense to ignore them (most concertgoers) and to continue writing as if they didn't exist. I felt it worth the effort to see if I couldn't say what I had to say in the simplest possible terms." This desire led to his best-loved work, *Appalachian Spring*.

Dashboard

EXPLORE

Appalachian Spring was originally written for a ballet in 1944. In 1945 Copland rearranged the score as an orchestral suite, which is how the work is most often heard today. *Appalachian Spring* uses only one American folk song, "Simple Gifts," a Shaker melody. It combines rhythmic enthusiasm with a clear tonal center and a singable melody. The piece represents a "pioneer celebration in spring around a newly built farmhouse in the Pennsylvania hills" in the early 1800s. The ballet has four primary characters: a bride and groom, a neighbor, and a preacher. The rhythms and melodic structures remind of us of American folk music used in barn dances and hymn tunes.

Copland's ballet *Rodeo* is the story of a cowgirl who loves the head wrangler, but he seems more interested in the rancher's daughter. The ballet is in five parts, four of which have been made into an orchestral suite. In part 1 the cowgirl attempts to attract the champion's attention by showing off her own skills as a cowhand. The final part, which we examine here, "Hoedown," is the climactic dance scene in which the couple finally come together.

American composer Aaron Copland. ©
Copyright Bettmann/Corbis/AP Images.

LISTENING GUIDE 17.3

"HOEDOWN," from *Rodeo*, **Scene 5,**
Aaron Copland, composed 1942

Rodeo, subtitled "The Courting at Burnt Ranch" was written in 1942 and choreographed by Agnes de Mille for the Ballet Russe de Monte Carlo. It was premiered at the Metropolitan Opera House in New York and was an immediate success. De Mille had already prepared much of the dance before Copland began to compose the music. The work is in five sections: "Buckaroo Holiday," "Ranch House Party," "Corral Nocturne," "Saturday Night Waltz," and "Hoedown." Copland prepared a ballet suite, which omitted the Ranch House Party section.

Dashboard

**HEAR STREAMING AUDIO
ON DASHBOARD**

What to Listen For

- Listen for tunes that sound like folk songs. Copland quotes three folk dance tunes: "Bonaparte's Retreat," "Miss McLeod's Reel," and "Gilderoy."
- Listen for how Copland uses the strings to evoke the feel of a folk fiddle tune.
- Listen for the syncopated and accented rhythms of the work, which make it sound American and provide choreography opportunities.
- Listen for the use of piano and woodblock, which evoke the Wild West.

"Hoedown"

TIMING	FORM	WHAT TO LISTEN FOR
0:00	A—Dance tune 1	The piece opens with full orchestra repeating the first few measures of the fiddle tune "Bonaparte's Retreat." This material is used throughout the movement as a unifying factor.
0:14		Dance tune 1 begins again.
0:19		The dance tune is interrupted by a reprise of material from the first movement of the suite, "Buckaroo's Holiday." This material, with its rhythmic structure, helps evoke the American West.
0:40		Dance tune 1 returns.
0:48		Strings play a variant from the fiddle tune "Gilderoy." A second important rhythmic motif is introduced in the horns and trumpets.
0:56		Dance tune 1 returns.
1:04		Strings and oboes play a variant of "Gilderoy." A variant of the horn rhythmic motif is played in the horn section.
1:12		Full orchestra plays the horn rhythmic motif while strings and upper woodwinds continue "Gilderoy" quote.
1:20		Dance tune 1 returns.
1:40	B	The middle section begins with the fiddle tune "Miss McLeod's Reel" stated in the trumpet.
1:47		Parts of the reel are played first by oboe and then violin.
1:54		Trumpet plays the reel melody again.
2:03		A variant of the horn rhythmic motif from section A is played.
2:25	A'	The final section returns to a statement of the "Rodeo" theme from the first movement, just as it was presented in the first A section of "Hoedown."
2:49		Dance tune 1 returns in clarinets and strings.
3:02		The horn rhythmic motif is played by brass while strings and upper woodwinds play "Gilderoy" variant.
3:10		Dance tune 1 returns.
3:25		The work ends with three short and accented pitches.

If You Liked That, Try This

Appalachian Spring, Copland
Romeo and Juliet, Sergei Prokofiev
Cinderella, Prokofiev

YouTube videos: search on keyword
Romeo & Juliet—Prokofiev
Prokofiev: Cinderella (Paris Opera Ballet)

Remember to add to your personal playlist any of these samples that you like.

The Russian composer Sergei Prokofiev is the last of the influential Russian ballet composers. His *Romeo and Juliet* from 1940 and *Cinderella* from 1945 are regularly performed on stage and in the concert hall as suites.

PERFORMER PROFILE
Ballerina Maria Tallchief

Ballerina Maria Tallchief. Courtesy Associated Press.

Maria Tallchief was born in 1925 on the Osage Indian Reservation in Oklahoma. Her father was a chief in the Osage tribe and a real estate executive. She began piano and ballet at age three and her mother wanted her to become a concert pianist. But, it soon became clear that her dancing abilities were unusual. By the time she was fifteen she was a professional dancer, and when she graduated from high school Maria joined a professional ballet company in New York. Maria Tallchief, a Native American, was to become America's first ballerina recognized on the international stage. She spent much of her professional career working with famed choreographer George Balanchine whom she also married. Under his tutelage she was the prima ballerina of the New York City Ballet throughout the 1950s. Working with Balanchine she danced his choreography of *The Rite of Spring* and originated the role of the Sugarplum Fairy in his version of Tchaikovsky's *The Nutcracker*. Tallchief was the first American ballerina to dance with the Paris Opera Ballet. Her signature role became *The Firebird*. Following her retirement from the stage she founded, along with her sister, the Chicago City Ballet. To see her perform, search YouTube for Maria Tallchief.

✓ **Build Your Own Playlist:** The works studied in the chapter Listening Guides serve as examples of different styles of ballet music from different eras. Now build your own playlist from those works listed in each IF YOU LIKED THAT, TRY THIS list or from other works you find. Share your playlist with others by posting it to your class discussion board or Dashboard.

✓ **Audio Review:** Go to Dashboard to listen to Professor Bailey discuss ballet music.

✓ **How Am I Doing?** Go to Dashboard to test your understanding of this material by taking the chapter quiz.

Dashboard

KEY TERMS

Ballet	Ballet suite	Primitivism

Film Music

LEARNING OBJECTIVES

- **Explain how silent films were not really silent.**

- **Explain the types of music used in film including original and source music.**

- **Name important film composers and directors of different film eras.**

- **Summarize the uses of music in film.**

Key Concepts: leitmotif, recording, silent movie music, source music, theme song, underscoring

Where It's Playing

It seems a bit obvious to say that film music is most often heard in a movie theater as a recorded portion of a film. But film music is also performed live in concert halls and is delivered digitally in many different situations in our daily lives. Film composers, just like ballet composers, create concert versions of their popular soundtracks. These suites of the best music from a film are often performed by symphony orchestras at so-called "pops concerts" during which the orchestra plays popular and less serious music. Such concerts consist of light music that the orchestra and the public generally believe is not art music.

The best film music becomes iconic in our culture and represents specific ideas, moods, or values. It conjures up images of heroes, deeds, events, and reminds us of feelings and emotions we associate with events in our own lives. As such, film music is heard in other media such as advertising, television, sporting events, and so on to set a mood or to associate a product with a particular emotion. This use of film music works only once a particular melody or rhythm of the music takes on a meaning that is universal within a culture. Much like the best of symphonic music or opera, film music is present throughout our lives as a sort of background to daily events.

When you attend a movie take note of how the music enhances the action and drama. As it begins, listen to how the music helps create a mood or contributes to the action. How does it influence how you feel about a character or a scene? Pay attention to the placement of the speakers in the theater. Do certain sounds come from certain speakers? Why would a recording be structured in this way? Try to identify the leitmotifs that are associated with the main characters. Listen for the mix of musical styles and how they relate to characters, emotions, or action. How much music is familiar to you already and how much has been written for the film?

Dashboard

ATTEND AND REPORT

How can a film about space be related to "The Blue Danube Waltz" written almost one hundred years before? Or, to a German tone poem written in 1896? In 1968 film director Stanley Kubrick, while working on his iconic film *2001: A Space Odyssey*, used a so-called "temp track" of music to accompany scenes of the movie. The temp track was supposed to be just that, a temporary background of music that matched the mood of scenes as the director visualized them while composer Alex North finished the real music for the movie. In the end Kubrick liked the effect of the temp track so much that North's score was never used. Today it is hard to imagine the film without Richard Strauss's *Also sprach Zarathustra* as its main theme music.

Music is such an integral part of film that before we watch the first scene, the music has already set the mood. The film industry has always recognized the power of music and used it to suggest characters and ideas, to create an atmosphere, suggest a time period, and to advance the story. However, music does not always mirror the action on the screen. Some composers use music that runs counter to the action to heighten the emotion. For example, in the film *Pulp Fiction* violent scenes play out against casual and lighthearted music.

Film music can be original to the movie or existing music. Most films today contain both types. Many films feature a composition that serves as the film's theme music. Often this piece of music becomes a popular song. For example, playing the first few notes of the theme music for the James Bond films evokes images of spies and intrigue. Over the decades film music has contributed greatly to American popular culture.

When creating music for film, a composer usually watches the movie and then works with the director and producer to decide where music should be added. The goal is to create music that evokes a certain emotional response in the viewer. The composer must decide whether to insert existing music or write new compositions for various scenes. Most films require at least one part of the score to be an original piece that can be associated with the movie. The composer and director also decide where music should be subordinate to the dialogue and action (called the **underscoring**), and where it should be more prominent. Sometimes the music will be used in place of dialogue or action to advance the story. Much film music is so subtle in its composition and placement that it goes unnoticed at the first viewing. However, if the audience saw the same scene again without music, the scene would likely have a different effect.

Underscoring: Music in a film played under the action and/or dialogue.

Music to Accompany Silent Films

Were silent films really silent?

The early film period extended from around the turn of the last century through World War II. The first half of that period is often called the Silent era, but movies have never really been silent—they have always been accompanied by music. A showing of a series of short films in Paris in 1895 by Auguste Lumiere used a live pianist to play popular songs along with the films. In 1908 a Paris company hired the classical composer Camille Saint-Saëns to write music to be played live to accompany the showing of *The Assassination of the Duke of Guise*. With this the concept of commissioning special music for an individual film was born. These two methods of providing music to accompany films dominated the Silent era.

By 1912 the demand for music to accompany movies was so great that the publishing company of Carl Fischer created a list of suggested film music. The list suggested specific sections of famous compositions that could be used for such moments as a hero's entrance, a villain lurking, a storm or mob scene, and so on. This music, primarily classical, was rearranged to fit the timings of the films. At first it was played by a single pianist or organist, but eventually large theaters employed orchestras and conductors. The music director of these theater orchestras would preview the film, choose the appropriate music, and then arrange and

Dashboard

EXPLORE

rehearse it before the movie opened. This meant that theaters could use different music to accompany the same film.

One of the first great films for which original music was written was the D. W. Griffith classic *The Birth of a Nation*. Joseph Breil composed the music for this 1915 silent movie, which contained both original music and adapted classics.

Music for "Talkies"

What was music like for early motion pictures with synchronized sound?
In 1927 the first motion picture with sound, including both music and speech, was released—*The Jazz Singer*, starring Al Jolson. It took several years for technology to advance sufficiently that music could be well synchronized with drama, but in 1933 *King Kong* was released with a full musical score, written by Max Steiner.

Max Steiner

Film composer Max Steiner (1888–1971) had an excellent European music pedigree, having studied piano with Brahms and composition with Mahler. Austrian composer Johann Strauss was his godfather, and his grandfather was the manager of the most important Austrian theater, the Theater an der Wien. Steiner became the first important composer of film scores, including *Gone with the Wind* and *Casablanca*, and worked primarily in the Warner Brothers studio. *Gone with the Wind* was a 1936 novel by Margaret Mitchell that won her the Pulitzer Prize. In 1939 it was made into a major motion picture starring Clark Gable and Vivian Leigh. The book and movie tell the story of a wealthy Georgia family before, during, and after the American Civil War.

Composer Max Steiner. Courtesy Redferns

The plantation house "Tara" from the film *Gone with the Wind*. Courtesy Hemis/Alamy.

LISTENING GUIDE 18.1

"TARA'S THEME," from *Gone with the Wind*,
Max Steiner, composed 1939

"Tara's Theme" is associated with not just the magnificent house of the same name, but the Southern spirit that endured the hardships of the war. This excerpt is some of the earliest film music to enter the American popular culture in an iconic manner.

Dashboard
**HEAR STREAMING AUDIO
ON DASHBOARD**

What to Listen For

- Listen for the wide interval leap that makes up the primary idea of the theme. This large interval is used as an expressive device.
- Listen for how the composer uses the same melodic idea throughout the piece. There is no secondary theme. Instead, the melodic motif is developed. This monothematic approach helps cement the theme in the mind of the listener and attach it to the mood the director wishes to evoke.
- Note how the theme is sometimes used heroically and sometimes nostalgically or sadly, depending upon the orchestration, dynamics, and tempo.

"Tara's Theme"

TIMING	FORM	WHAT TO LISTEN FOR
0:00 0:14	Introduction	The orchestra plays music that builds in intensity and volume. A portion of the primary melodic motif is stated in trumpet as an introduction to the theme. Brass introduce the main theme.
0:33	Theme	The theme is presented in the strings and answered in the winds.
0:50	Theme	The theme is restated in full orchestra while brass play a counter-line.
1:08	Development	The interval of the theme is fragmented and developed in an imitative fashion while the rhythmic gesture remains intact.
1:28	Theme	The theme is restated in the brass instruments.
1:48	Development 2	A second, longer developmental section is stated. The end of the section builds to the climactic return of the theme.
2:30	Theme	The theme is restated as a climax of the piece in full orchestra with horn counter-line.
2:48	Theme	Theme is stated a final time with less rhythmic drive. It fades to the end with a statement by the trumpet.

If You Liked That, Try This

Theme from *A Summer Place*, Max Steiner
Soundtrack to *King Kong*, Max Steiner
Soundtrack to *The Sea Hawk*, Erich Korngold

YouTube videos: search on keywords
Max Steiner—Greatest Hits
Erich Korngold—The Sea Hawk 1/2
Gone With the Wind (1939)—MainTitle (Tara's Theme)

Remember to add to your personal playlist any of these samples that you like.

Most early films that included a good deal of music were musicals. Early filmmakers believed that the music had to come from the film itself and used it primarily when a scene called for it. By the mid-1930s, however, musical scores were unique to each film and were used to establish the overall mood. In this time the expressive quality of music was exploited.

The 1930s are often referred to as the "Golden Age of Film." The music of this era was big and lush, and romantic in character. It was used to express emotions and to build momentum or tension. Filmmakers also used music to communicate things like profanity, sex, or violence that couldn't be seen or spoken because of censorship rules, or that they felt could be better expressed by music than words.

Though not from this early era, one of the best examples of this use of music is in the shower murder scene early in the 1960 thriller *Psycho*. *Psycho* is an Alfred

Hitchcock thriller released in 1960. The movie involves a psychotic motel owner, Norman Bates, and a secretary, Marion, who makes the mistake of staying at the Bates Motel for the evening. Bates stabs her to death while she showers, in the most famous scene from the film. The music was written by Bernard Hermann, who wrote the music for several of Hitchcock's thrillers. He also wrote the music for Orson Welles's radio sensation *War of the Worlds* and his movie *Citizen Kane*. His most famous music is from his collaborations with Hitchcock.

LISTENING GUIDE 18.2

"THE MURDER," from *Psycho*,
Bernard Hermann, composed 1960

Dashboard
**HEAR STREAMING AUDIO
ON DASHBOARD**

The musical segment for the shower scene in *Psycho* is called "The Murder" and it contains some of the most iconic music ever used in film. The knife stabs are accompanied by screeching high strings, an unusual, yet very effective choice. Hermann said that he wished to match the black-and-white film with a single tone color.

The music is in four major sections. The first contains the stabbing chords from the shower theme at a low pitch. The second is slow and contrasts the extreme high register of the violin with low bass sounds. This moves directly into the music used during the stabbing. The third section begins with strings trills and dynamic swells that sound bee-like. Following this the low strings begin a meandering scalar line. As the violins break off into the high register again, the low strings present a line made up of three wide leaps. Pizzicato notes in the bass follow while the high strings ascend in long notes. Solo violin plays a theme of wide leaps. The stabbing screams of the violins return at the beginning of the final section. More bee-like sounds from the violins sound over a bass line. Cello plays a solo lyrical line and is joined in imitation by upper strings. Sustained strings continue in extremes of ranges and the bass line leads the string ensemble to a climax on loud chords at the end of the work.

What to Listen For

- Listen for the sound effects created by acoustic instruments; the screeching violins, the fast notes that create the bee swarming sounds.
- Listen for the use of high and low register instruments to match the action.

"The Murder"

TIMING	SCENE	WHAT TO LISTEN FOR
0:00	The scene begins with no music playing. All we hear is the shower.	
0:01 0:09 0:13	The killer pulls aside the shower curtain and brings the knife down.	The screeching string notes begin in high strings. The screeches extend to lower strings. The string screeches return to high strings and extend lower again.
0:25	The dying Marion slips down the side of the shower.	The music changes to the low register of the strings and alternates between the high and low string instruments.
0:44	Marion grabs the shower curtain and falls forward, dead.	Long pitches in low strings are used to accompany blood running down the drain.

If You Liked That, Try This

Music from *Twisted Nerve*, Hermann
"Silent Noon," from *The Devil and Daniel Webster*, Hermann
Music from *Taxi Driver*, Hermann

Remember to add to your personal playlist any of these samples that you like.

Post–World War II Film Music

How was music used in films in the second half of the 20th century?

After World War II several of the world's great art music composers wrote music for movies, including Malcolm Arnold, Benjamin Britten, Aaron Copland, Gustav Holst, Sergei Prokofiev, and Ralph Vaughan Williams. From about 1945 through the 1960s films used a good deal more **source music** than in previous films or since. Source music is music that needs to be in the film because of the scene. For example, characters walk into a dance hall or bar, a character turns on a radio or plays a recording, or cast members sing.

Source music: Music that is required to be in the film because of the scene.

By the 1960s there began a revival of sorts in the use of music in films. Once again music was used throughout the film as an underscore and most of it was originally written for the films. Movie theme songs often became popular tunes of this period. For example, the song "Moon River" became the theme song for the 1961 movie *Breakfast at Tiffany's*. Important composers of this era included Elmer Bernstein, Jerry Goldsmith, and Henry Mancini. These composers were capable of writing music of different styles that included sounds from all over the world and spanned both classical and popular genres. By the 1970s composers like John Williams had revived the use of the operatic technique of leitmotif as an important compositional element in film.

Audrey Hepburn in *Breakfast at Tiffany's* singing the hit song "Moon River." Courtesy AF Archive/Alamy.

Contemporary Film Composers Work Closely with Directors

How do modern directors and composers work together on film music?

John Williams

John Williams is the most successful and best-known film music composer of our time. Some of his music has become iconic in American popular culture. His music for the *Star Wars* movies, *Indiana Jones* films, *Jaws*, *The Cowboys*, and other films is so recognizable and meaningful that we hear it every day as a soundtrack to the activities of our daily lives.

Williams was born in 1932 in New York and studied at the Juilliard School. He worked as a jazz pianist for studio recording sessions where he met film composer Henry Mancini. Following his study at Juilliard he moved to Los Angeles where he became an orchestrator, arranger, and eventually composer for film studios and television shows. Williams won his first of five Academy Awards for his score adaptation for the music of *Fiddler on the Roof* in 1971. His most important association in the film industry has been with director Steven Spielberg. The

Composer John Williams with film directors Martin Scorsese (left) and Steven Spielberg (right). Courtesy Associated Press.

two first worked together on a 1974 film called *The Sugarland Express* but it is their work together on films such as *Jaws*, *E.T.*, *Close Encounters of the Third Kind*, the *Indiana Jones* series, *Jurassic Park*, and *Schindler's List* that is best known. The list of blockbuster films for which Williams provided the music is too long to list here but it covers more than a forty-year period in filmmaking.

John Williams also composed some of the best known music for television and the Olympics. His fanfare written for the 1984 Summer Olympics in Los Angeles has become the unofficial theme song of the Olympic Games. His music is used for the opening of *NBC Nightly News*, *The Today Show*, *Meet the Press*, and *Great Performances*. He has written a number of classical styled concertos and concert works for orchestra. From 1980 until 1993 Williams also served as conductor of the Boston Pops Orchestra, one of the most important and popular professional orchestras in the United States. To learn more about John Williams's music visit his homepage. Note the list of television shows and films for which he has written the music. Many of your favorite movies will be on this list.

LISTENING GUIDE 18.3

"PRINCESS LEIA'S THEME" from *Star Wars*,
John Williams, composed 1977

Dashboard
**HEAR STREAMING AUDIO
ON DASHBOARD**

In "Princess Leia's Theme" Williams creates a melody that is gentle and na-ïve but can change into a theme evoking love, passion, and heroism. It appears in Episodes IV, V, and VI when the princess is onscreen or important to the action. It also is used as part of the love theme of Han Solo and Leia in Episode V. Williams uses it at times when the princess is vulnerable or in trouble, and in Episode III it appears at her birth.

What to Listen For

- Listen for the wide interval that opens the theme and creates an expressive and lyrical melodic motif.

- Listen for Williams's choice of instruments. He uses horn first, then high woodwinds, and finally strings. The horn is traditionally a heroic sounding instrument and lends this quality to the theme. The high woodwinds evoke the openness of space and the strings provide a lush quality to the theme when Williams wants it to sound passionate.

"Princess Leia's Theme"

TIMING	FORM	WHAT TO LISTEN FOR
0:00 0:09	Introduction	The orchestra plays a soft, nonrhythmical introduction. High woodwinds help set the ethereal mood.
0:15	Theme	Leia's theme is presented in horn. It is a lyrical theme that uses a repeated rhythmic motif. The opening wide leap interval helps the melody sound expressive.
1:30		Theme is repeated by the flute and high woodwinds. The pure, high tone of the flute sounds electronic and fits with the setting in space.
2:26		Theme is stated by the strings with a soaring horn counter-line.
3:01		Theme is stated by the full orchestra with a stronger and more rhythmical counter-line in horn and percussion. This statement of the melody is the climax of the excerpt.
3:49	Coda	The ending section of the excerpt gradually gets softer with a solo violin.

If You Liked That, Try This

Theme from *Jaws*, Williams
Theme from *E.T.*, Williams
Soundtrack from *Harry Potter and the Sorcerer's Stone*, Williams
Theme from *The Pink Panther*, Henry Mancini
Music from *Patton*, Jerry Goldsmith

YouTube videos: search on keywords
The Magnificent Seven—Elmer Bernstein
The Great Escape (1963)—The Great Escape March
John Williams scoring ET

Remember to add to your personal playlist any of these samples that you like.

Since the 1970s film music has made use of both musicians and electronic music. The music of recent films usually consists of a soundtrack that underscores the drama and a feature song that often becomes a popular song. The style of music from the past three decades is eclectic, but for the most part it can be described as neoromantic and lush, with sweeping rhythmic gestures and memorable melodies. There is also a much wider use of music that was not originally written for the film. Many films use older pop songs and classical music side by side.

In addition to John Williams some of the most successful composers of film music include Danny Elfman, Hans Zimmer, James Horner, Philip Glass, and John Corigliano. Elfman and Zimmer are both popular musicians who turned to film composing. They both make wide use of technology in their scores. Elfman is responsible for the music for *Batman*, *Men in Black*, and *Spider Man*, and works closely with director Tim Burton. Zimmer has written music for *The Lion King*, *Gladiator*, and the *Pirates of the Caribbean* movies.

The score to the first of the three *Pirates of the Caribbean* movies was a group project. It is very similar to Hans Zimmer's music in the film *Gladiator*. Composers Klaus Badelt and Hans Zimmer had worked together on projects in Zimmer's studio "Media Ventures." The score is credited to Badelt but Zimmer was a major contributor and a number of other Hollywood composers were called upon to provide music for the film since the music was needed in a very short period of time.

LISTENING GUIDE 18.4

Music from *PIRATES OF THE CARIBBEAN,*
Klaus Badelt, composed 2003

The movie is an adventure film inspired by a ride at Disneyland of the same name. The story revolves around three primary characters, Captain Jack Sparrow, Will Turner, and Elizabeth Swann. Elizabeth is kidnapped by Sparrow's former shipmates, who sail on the Black Pearl under a terrible curse and believe that only Elizabeth's blood can release them from their curse. Will, who is in love with Elizabeth, enlists the aid of Sparrow to rescue her. The music for the movie is as adventure-filled as the film itself. The main title music conjures up images of a ship afloat on a wild sea. The driving rhythm of this music represents the ship at sea and the courage of the adventurer.

Dashboard

HEAR STREAMING AUDIO ON DASHBOARD

What to Listen For

- Listen for the driving rhythms of the piece. These ostinato patterns help create the sense of the ship on the waves.
- Listen for the cymbal crashes. The repetitive crashes give the impression of waves crashing or sea spray splashing.

"He's a Pirate"

TIMING	FORM	WHAT TO LISTEN FOR
0:00	Introduction	Low strings create an ostinato rhythm.
0:05 0:18	Theme A	Strings play a rhythmic theme that has a high energy level. A is repeated in higher strings with more cymbal crashes.
0:45	Theme B	Heroic theme is stated in horns. Accompaniment is another ostinato pattern. This theme is used also in another section, "Will and Elizabeth."
1:00	Theme C	Theme C is structured on theme A and is an elaboration or second part of that material. The percussive ostinato is stronger. This theme is also used in another section, "The Black Pearl."

If You Liked That, Try This

Theme from *Batman*, Danny Elfman
Soundtrack to *Avatar*, James Horner
Soundtrack to *Titanic*, James Horner
Music from *The Red Violin*, John Corigliano

YouTube videos: search on keywords
Danny Elfman—Greatest Hits
Titanic- Hymn to the sea
The Red Violin (Very sad violin music)
Tour in Hans Zimmer Studio
Indiana Jones 4—John Williams interview PART 1/2
Geoff Zanelli DISTURBIA Film Score Composer Interview
Philip Glass Discussion at Popcorn Taxi
HANS ZIMMER PIRATES OF THE CARIBBEAN ORCHESTRA SOUNDTRACK
   HANS ZIMMER
Michael Kamen on composing Robin Hood score

Remember to add to your personal playlist any of these samples that you like.

PERFORMER PROFILE
Hans Zimmer

Hans Zimmer (b. 1957) is a German-born film composer. His musical background is in rock having been a member of a New Wave band called the Buggles whose 1979 music video "Video Killed the Radio Star" helped popularize MTV. Zimmer began his film work in London where he pioneered the mixing of electronic and live music for film scores. Upon moving to Hollywood his first Academy Award–nominated film was the 1988 Tom Cruise/Dustin Hoffman hit *Rainman*. Zimmer won an Oscar in 1994 for the score to *The Lion King*. Zimmer has written the music for such blockbusters as *Crimson Tide*, *Pearl Harbor*, *The Last Samarai*, *Gladiator*, *The Dark Knight*, *Sherlock Holmes*, *Blackhawk Down*, *Inception*, some of the *Pirates of the Caribbean* films, and many others. In all he has scored over one hundred films and in addition to the Academy Award he has won two Golden Globe Awards and four Grammy Awards.

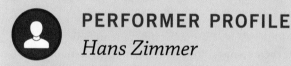

Dashboard

EXPLORE

(continued)

In London, Zimmer worked with and was influenced by mentor Stanley Meyers. Meyers, a well-established film composer in his own right, guided Zimmer's talents and helped launch his career. In Hollywood Zimmer set up a composition studio called Remote Control Productions where he composes and also mentors and guides younger composers. The studio has had such success as a breeding ground for young talent that one of his protégés, Klaus Bedalt, was assigned the task of completing the score to the first *Pirates of the Caribbean* movies because Zimmer was too busy. This mentoring of the next generation of film composers and his contributions in the electronic film music field are perhaps his strongest legacy.

Film composer Hans Zimmer with his Academy Award for the score to *The Lion King*. Courtesy Associated Press.

John Corigliano and Philip Glass are important contemporary film composers who have brought their compositional craft from the traditional classical world to film scoring. Corigliano combines Asian musics with sounds from the Baroque and Romantic eras in his Academy Award winning score to *The Red Violin*. Glass incorporates minimalism in his film music, including music for *The Matrix*.

PERFORMANCE PRACTICE
Recording Film Music

How do musicians match the music with the action?

Recording the music for a feature film is an interesting mix of live musicians, electronics, and raw film footage. Composers bring their finished film scores to a special recording studio that has the capability of running a motion picture in the studio. As the conductor (often the composer) leads the orchestra he/she also watches the soundless film to keep the music on pace with the action. The conductor matches the musical climaxes, rhythms, and melodies with specific timings, which appear on the screen alongside the film. Since live musicians are used, there are sometimes errors that require re-recording of the same material. The recording is done in small segments that are spliced together along with the film to create the final version. The editor balances the musical sounds with the dialogue and the other sound effects to create the underscore.

Composer Michael Kamen (1948–2003) wrote music for some of the most popular films since the 1980s. His work includes music for *Robin Hood*, *Prince of Thieves*; *Mr. Holland's Opus*; *The Three Musketeers*; *Highlander*; *License to Kill*; the *Lethal Weapon* series of movies; the *Die Hard* series; and the HBO series *Band of Brothers*. He also wrote or arranged music for such diverse groups as Pink Floyd, the Canadian Brass, Queen, Eric Clapton, Aerosmith, Sting, Herbie Hancock, the San Francisco Symphony Orchestra, the Eurythmics, and Metallica. In 1991 his song from *Robin Hood*, "Everything I Do, I Do It for You" as sung by Bryan Adams was a number one hit. But his artistic home was in film scoring. Visit the textbook website section Helpful Resources for Chapter 18 for a link to a video in which composer Michael Kamen talks about how he created music for a film and how he matched the music to the action.

✓ **Build Your Own Playlist:** The works studied in the chapter Listening Guides serve as examples of different styles of film music from different eras. Now build your own playlist from those works listed in each IF YOU LIKED THAT, TRY THIS list or from other works you find. Share your playlist with others by posting it to your class discussion board or Dashboard.

✓ **Audio Review:** Go to Dashboard to listen to Professor Bailey discuss film music.

✓ **How Am I Doing?** Go to Dashboard to test your understanding of this material by taking the chapter quiz.

Dashboard

KEY TERMS

Source music   Underscoring

GLOSSARY

A cappella: In music a term meaning unaccompanied voice. Literally, the term means "for the chapel."

Aria: A solo song with accompaniment used in opera to convey the thoughts and/or emotions of characters. It usually has a full orchestral accompaniment.

Ars Nova: Literally "new art," commonly referred to as the years ca. 1300–1450 during which time music was in transition from the style of the Middle Ages to that of the Renaissance.

Atonal: A piece of music that is not centered around one individual pitch or key.

Avant garde: Modernistic and often unusual art, including music.

Ballet: Form of artistic and classical dance originating in France in the Baroque era.

Ballet suites: Concert versions of some of the best music extracted from a ballet.

Ballett: A form similar to the madrigal but more dancelike in character and almost always homophonic with the melody in the highest voice. Characterized by "fa-la-la" refrains.

Band: A large ensemble of woodwind, brass, and percussion instruments. The ensemble has been in use since the Middle Ages but gained wide use and acceptance in the 20th century.

Basset horn: An instrument similar in shape, size, and sound to the modern-day alto clarinet.

Bebop: A high energy style of jazz begun around the time of World War II that emphasizes improvisation on a chord progression rather than based on a melody.

Bel canto: A form of opera from the Romantic era featuring beautiful arias.

Book musical: Modern style of Broadway musical in which song, dance, and stage play interact to produce a well-connected storyline.

Bridge: Sometimes called the release, the bridge is the middle section of a song.

Cadence: A repetitive rhythmic pattern on a percussion instrument that is easily recognizable.

Cadenza: A brief interlude in a concerto in which the soloist plays alone. Cadenzas are often improvised.

Call: A brief melody, usually played on a bugle, to communicate a military order to troops.

Call and response: Performance style in which one performer states a musical idea (the call) and other performer(s) repeat it or answer in a similar fashion (the response).

Cantata: A vocal work in several movements with instrumental accompaniment, most popular in the Baroque era and used widely in Lutheran church services.

Canzona: A short imitative work for instruments developed in the late Renaissance and early Baroque periods.

Chaconne: A form based on continuous variations on the harmonic progression of a work.

Chamber music: Music written for two to twelve players intended to be played in an intimate setting like a salon or small chamber.

Chamber sonata: A work for a chamber ensemble of three or more players in either a single-movement or three-movement form.

Chanson: A solo song originating in France as a love song.

Chant: A monophonic melody usually set with religious text.

Character piece: A miniature piece for piano usually conveying one intense emotion. The titles of these works (e.g., nocturne, polonaise, etude, waltz, and scherzo) often indicate the style.

Chorale prelude: A work, usually for organ, used to introduce a hymn to be sung by a congregation. The chorale prelude is essentially a variation or embellishment of the hymn melody.

Chorus: Also called the refrain this section is the main melody of the song.

Chromatic harmony: Harmonic structure in which all twelve pitches of the chromatic scale are used rather than simply the primary eight of a major or minor scale.

Church modes: A system of organizing the seven tones of a scale in varying sequences of half and whole steps.

Clavichord: A keyboard instrument used from the Middle Ages through the Classical era. Its sound is created by a metal blade, called a "tangent," striking metal strings.

Concert overture: A one-movement work usually in sonata form for orchestra. The form became important in the Romantic era.

Concertino: A group of soloists featured in a concerto.

Concertmaster: The leader of the violin section and orchestra.

Concerto: A showpiece written for a single instrument accompanied by an ensemble, usually orchestra or band. The concerto is often in three movements.

Concerto grosso: A multi-movement (usually three) work for orchestra in which a small unit from within the orchestra plays contrasting sections with the full orchestra.

Consort: A set or group of the same instrument made in varying sizes.

Continuo: The instrument that plays the bass line in a trio sonata.

Cool jazz: A form of jazz similar in intent to bebop but with a much less frenetic energy and pace. Most wind players of this style played with a particular kind of relaxed tone quality from which the name cool was derived.

Cornetto: A wind instrument usually of wood and often covered with leather and having up to six tone holes.

Dance suite: An instrumental form dating from the Renaissance era. The dance suite consisted of short, contrasting style dances often in pairs and was written for instruments.

Declaiming: The setting of words of a song to the natural rhythms of speech.

Development: The section of a multi-sectional musical form in which the primary melodic material is altered and varied.

Disjunct: Indication that a melody has a wide range and contains wide leaps between notes, rather than being scalar in nature.

Dissonances: Musical sounds that sound to our ears as not being at rest, as if they need to be followed by another more restful sound.

Divertimento, serenade, and partita: Names given rather interchangeably to works written for light entertainment purposes.

Dixieland: Also called New Orleans jazz this style is characterized by collective improvisation and driving rhythmic style.

Drone: A long and usually low note that accompanies a melody.

Duo sonata: A sonata written for one instrument and piano.

Duple meter: A repetitive pattern of beats grouped in twos with one strong and one weak beat in each pattern.

Etude: "Study" in French; a musical work intended to help the performer practice a particular technical skill.

Exotic music: Music that evokes the atmosphere and culture of a particular country. This style differs from so-called nationalistic music in that it is often written by a composer about a country other than his or her home country.

Exposition: The opening section of a sonata form in which the primary melodies of the work are presented.

Expressionism: A style of music of the mid-20th century characterized by hyper-expression, abandonment of tonal centers, extreme ranges used in melodic structures, forceful accents, and abrupt dynamic changes.

Formalism: Any style of music that rigidly follows set rules or composition.

Forte: Italian musical term meaning loud.

Free jazz: A style of jazz developed in the 1960s which focuses almost entirely on free improvisation. The players perform without set rules or guidelines of rhythm or melody.

French overture: An orchestral work in two parts. The first section is slow and stately and the second section is fast and lively.

French revue: A variety type show without script built around one star performer's abilities. The revue consisted of comedy routines, dances, songs, and dramatic sketches. The Ziegfeld Follies were the most famous American revues.

Front: To lead the band.

Fugue: A polyphonic piece of music created by imitation of a theme by all parts individually.

Fusion: A style of jazz which combines rock and jazz elements.

Galliard: A fast dance originating in France in triple meter. It, like the saltarello, contains a jump step that ends in a pose. The galliard is often paired with the pavane.

Gamelan: An Indonesian ensemble of percussion instruments, flutes, bowed instruments, and sometimes vocalists. The term refers to the collective ensemble.

Gregorian chant: Specifically chant for the Catholic Church liturgy named for Pope Gregory I.

Harmonie band: A wind band popular in the Classical era, usually made up of eight players.

Harpsichord: A keyboard instrument particularly important in the Renaissance and Baroque eras, from which sound is produced by a plucked string as the player depresses a key.

Hocket: A compositional device in which one voice rhythmically and melodically imitates the other in alternation. Often described as a musical hiccup.

Homophonic: Music that moves generally rhythmically in unison and has multiple parts sounding simultaneously without imitation.

Homorhythmic: Unison rhythmic movement of multiple parts or lines.

Idée fixe: A primary idea of a work, literary or musical, which repeats throughout the work.

Impresario: A presenter and promoter of public concerts.

Impressionism: An artistic movement beginning in visual art of the late 19th century that spread to music which turns away from the traditional major/minor tonal system and regular rhythms of Western art music.

Improvisation: The spontaneous creation of music or the elaboration of existing music.

Incidental music: Music written to accompany a play or drama, usually for orchestra in the Romantic era.

Isorhythm: The compositional technique of using the same rhythmic pattern with different melodies.

Italian opera overture: A musical prelude to an opera played by the orchestra usually introducing the primary themes of the opera.

Klangfarbenmelodie: A system of composition in which each pitch of a melody has a distinct tone color.

Leitmotif: In opera the idea of a particular melody, rhythm, or other musical element particularly associated with a character, idea, or prop in the opera such that the mere playing of the musical element evokes that character, idea, or thing in the mind of the listener.

Lied: German term for song. *Lieder* is the plural form.

Lute: A string instrument of the Middle Ages and Renaissance similar in sound to our modern-day mandolin or guitar.

Madrigal: A chamber piece for small vocal ensemble, usually four to six voices. Stemming from the Renaissance period the madrigal is a mix of polyphonic and homophonic styles.

March: A short, multi-sectional work that combines memorable melodies with a regular and steady beat pattern.

Masques: Form of English opera in which there is also spoken dialogue.

Mass: The liturgy of the Catholic Church.

Melismatic: A melody, or most often chant that has more than one pitch per syllable of text.

Minimalism: Music based upon the repetition of melodic, harmonic, and/or rhythmic motifs with little or no variation.

Minstrelsy: Form of American light entertainment dating from the mid-1800s, usually including dancing, singing, joke-telling, and other forms of entertainment. Often associated with whites in "blackface" performing in imitation of slaves.

Minuet and trio: Originally a dance form, the minuet and trio is a three-part form often used as the third movement of a symphony.

Monophonic: A piece of music with a single part or voice.

Motet: A polyphonic work with at least three distinct parts or melodic lines, one of which is usually a chant.

Motif: A musical idea.

Music dramas: Term to describe particularly Wagner's operas in which the music is nonstop throughout the opera.

Musical interactivity: Musical style which combines human and electronic sounds.

Musique concrete: A style of music of the early 20th century which used recorded sounds of nature manipulated electronically.

Neoclassicism: A style of music of the Modern era which seeks to return to the symmetry and simplicity of style of the Classical era.

Neoromanticism: Music of the 20th century in which composers returned to the formal and tonal structures of music of the Romantic era.

Nocturne: In the 19th century a short one-movement piece for solo piano, intended to be evocative of nighttime.

Opera: A large-scale drama set to music using costumes, scenery, music, and acting. Dating from the late Renaissance era this form became the most important large-scale vocal form.

Opera buffa: Comic opera, developed in the Classical era.

Opera seria: Earliest form of opera on serious subjects.

Operetta: A form of light and comic opera developed in the late 19th century that includes dancing and speech.

Oratorio: A sacred work designed for the concert hall using choir, soloists, and orchestra.

Orchestra: A large ensemble of string, woodwind, brass, and percussion instruments in which the strings are the most important section. The ensemble has been in use since the Baroque era.

Orchestral suite: A large-scale work for orchestra consisting usually of a set of contrasting dances in movements. The suite was used in the Baroque era and is considered a predecessor of the Classical era symphony.

Ordinary: Parts of the Mass that remain the same each day.

Organum: Music used in Catholic liturgy that combines a chant and at least one other melody simultaneously.

Passion: A large-scale work for chorus, orchestra, and soloists depicting the final days of Jesus Christ and based upon biblical text. The passion is similar in style to the oratorio.

Patronage system: A system of financial relationships between nobleman and musician used through the Classical era in which musicians were high-level servants of nobles.

Pavane: A slow dance in duple meter often used as a processional, thought to have originated in France.

Pentatonic scale: A five-note scale.

Pipe: Any number of wind instruments from the Middle Ages that involve an air column passing through pipes with tone holes cut to create different pitches.

Pizzicato: Technique of plucking a string on a string instrument rather than using a bow to produce the sound.

Polonaise: A slow Polish dance in triple meter.

Polychoral motets: Motets dating from late Renaissance in Venice employing more than one ensemble. These ensembles, some vocal and some instrumental, were placed at different locations within the church and made use of echo and natural reverberation of the space.

Polyphonic: A work with at least two parts or voices.

Polyrhythm: Simultaneous playing of more than one rhythm.

Polytonality: More than one tonality or key center played simultaneously.

Prelude: A work, often of a free or improvisatory nature, used as a companion work to a longer and more complex piece of music.

Primitivism: Use of percussion and repetitive rhythms to evoke images of primitive cultures and peoples.

Program music: Instrumental music that is suggestive of a mood, story, poem, or phrase.

Program symphony: Multi-movement work similar to tone poems and symphonic poems in intent. Each movement or section of the symphony contains its own program.

Proper: Parts of the Mass that change appropriate to the time of the liturgical year.

Pure music: Also called absolute music. Music that has no allegorical or pictorial meaning.

Ragtime: An early-20th-century popular form of piano music played in saloons, dance halls, and brothels.

Rebec: A three-string instrument bowed much like the violin and used mostly in the Middle Ages.

Recapitulation: The section of a multi-sectional musical form in which the primary melodic material returns.

Recitative: Used in opera as a sort-of free rhythmical sung-speech. It is used to progress the drama forward much like dialogue in a play. It usually has a simple accompaniment without a steady rhythmic pulse.

Recorder: A wind instrument usually of wood with open tone holes in the body that create different pitches.

Reprise: In opera the return of a melody heard earlier in the work, usually a shorter version of the melody, often with new text.

Requiem Mass: A Mass for the dead.

Rhythm and blues: A type of popular music that combines the styles of gospel, jazz, and blues.

Ritornello: Meaning a recurring theme or passage in a work, often the main theme of a multi-theme piece.

Rondo: A form consisting of contrasting melodies with one of the melodies used as a unifying return theme. Each time a new melody is presented and completed, the original rondo theme returns. Perhaps best illustrated by the letters ABACADA, where A represents the original melody.

Sacred: Having to do with religious beliefs.

Saltarello: An Italian dance in triple meter. The dance is characterized by a jumping step.

Scherzo: A three-part form used in Romantic era symphonies as the third movement, replacing the Classical minuet and trio. The work is usually faster and more agitated in style than its predecessor.

Secular: Having to do with the nonspiritual world.

Sequence: A melodic and/or rhythmic idea that is repeated beginning on different pitch levels.

Serialism: A compositional technique of the mid-20th century led by composer Arnold Schoenberg that treats all twelve pitches of the Western scale equally. The technique is a highly organized style of writing music.

Shawm: A reed instrument similar in sound to today's oboe, used primarily in the Middle Ages and Renaissance.

Shout chorus: A section of a jazz piece of music in which all members of the band play the melody in unison.

Sinfonia: A multi-part form of instrumental music for orchestra.

Solo concerto: A concerto designed to display the virtuosity of one player.

Solo sonata: An instrumental form for solo instrument, often piano, one or three movements in length.

Sonata da chiesa: A chamber sonata intended for performance in the church and usually more serious in character than the dance-like sonata da camera which was intended for the chamber.

Sonata form: A short work for orchestra usually used as the first and/or last movements of a symphony. The sonata form is a three-part form based upon the development and expansion of melodic ideas.

Song cycle: A set of songs that are connected in some manner, usually by the text.

Source music: Music that is required to be in the film because of the scene.

Sprechstimme: A vocal delivery that is a sort of mixture of singing and speaking.

Staccato: Indication to play notes separated from one another or short.

String quartet: The term is both an ensemble of four string instruments and a musical form. When used as a form it usually indicates a multi-movement work similar in size and scope to the symphony.

Strophic: A form which uses the same music for each stanza of the song.

Stylized dance: Music written in dance forms intended for listening rather than dancing.

Subscription concert: A prepaid ticketed event usually sponsored by an impresario or the composer/performer himself and open to anyone with the price of admission.

Swing: A style of jazz most popular from the late 1920s through the 1940s as dance music. The name comes from the practice of altering the notated rhythmic patterns so that the music "swings."

Syllabic: A melody that has one note for each syllable.

Symphonic poem: A long piece of program music for orchestra in which the music depicts a story, scene, or mood.

Symphony: A large-scale work usually for full orchestra dating to the Classical era and still in use today. Often divided into at least four contrasting movements. The term is derived from Greek and means "to sound together."

Syncopated rhythms: Rhythmic patterns in which the emphasis or accent is placed on divisions of the strong and weak beats.

Synthesizer: An electronic instrument that is used to record, manipulate, and play sounds.

Tafelmusick: Music written specifically to be performed as entertainment during mealtime.

Terraced dynamics: Sudden changes in volume.

Theme and variations: A form of music in which one melody is presented and followed by embellishments, enhancements, or developments.

Through-composed: A form that uses different music for each stanza of the song.

Toccata: A free-form instrumental work in one movement, usually highly technical.

Tonal centre: The most important pitch of a scale or musical work on which the work is based.

Tonality: Structure of a musical melody or work around a particular note, scale, or key center.

Tone: See **Pitch**.

Tone clusters: A group of neighbor pitches played simultaneously.

Tone color: The particular quality of a musical sound, also called timbre.

Tone poem: A late-Romantic era term for symphonic poem.

Traditional canon: A set of masterworks from all eras regularly performed.

Trio sonata: A Baroque instrumental form for two solo instruments and continuo. The continuo part was played by two instruments, usually a cello and a harpsichord. Trio refers to the fact that there are three individual parts.

Triple meter: A repetitive pattern of beats grouped in threes with one strong and two weak beats in each pattern.

Two-step: A popular dance in duple meter, named for the fact that the dancer takes two steps in the same direction.

Vaudeville: A variety show that usually included juggling, animal acts, dramatic readings, dance, and song.

Verismo: Style of opera in which the plots are realistic.

Verse: Introductory section of a Broadway song preceding the chorus. The verse is often not in a strict rhythm and is recitative-like.

Vibrato: An audible pulsation on a particular tone not intended to produce a rhythm but instead to give color to the tone by slightly altering the intonation of the note higher and lower.

Virtuoso performer: A musician highly skilled in a particular specialty area who performs in public.

Walking bass: A bass line that moves on each beat in a scalar fashion at the tempo of the work.

Waltz: A folk or ballroom dance in triple meter.

Whole-tone scale: A seven-note scale consisting entirely of alternating whole steps.

Word painting: A compositional device in which a particular sound is created to evoke an idea or represent a specific word in a song.

INDEX